9-24
45.00

HOTEL FRONT OFFICE MANAGEMENT

HOTEL FRONT OFFICE MANAGEMENT

THIRD EDITION

James A. Bardi, Ed.D., CHA

The Pennsylvania State University

John Wiley & Sons, Inc.

For general information on our other products and services or for technical support, please contact our Customer Care Department within the United States at (800) 762-2974, outside the United States at (317) 572-3993 or fax (317) 572-4002.

Wiley also publishes its books in a variety of electronic formats. Some content that appears in print may not be available in electronic books.

Library of Congress Cataloging-in-Publication Data:

Bardi, James A.
    Hotel front office management/ James A. Bardi.—3rd ed.
        p. cm
    ISBN 0-471-01396-X (cloth : alk. paper)
    1. Hotel Management. I. Title
    TX911.3.M27 B35 2003
    647.94'068—dc21

                                                            2002024087

Printed in the United States of America

10 9 8 7 6 5 4 3 2 1

To Linda

Your love and encouragement made this book possible.

and

Maria, Ryan, and David

The joy of sharing this book with you makes it all worthwhile.

Contents

Preface

The third edition of *Hotel Front Office Management* continues to address the demands of the hotel industry in the new millennium. Educators who are preparing professionals for roles as front office managers and general managers in hotels are required to meet the challenges of operations, technology, training, empowerment, and international applications. This edition continues to encourage students to take an active role in applying these concepts to the exciting world of hotel operations.

The emphasis on management continues to play a central role in this third edition. The structure presented in this text will assist students as they prepare for positions as entry-level managers. The logical presentation of chapters in order of operations—overview of lodging hospitality, tour of the front office, review of the guest cycle, and analysis of guest services—will allow students to gain insight into a front office manager's role in the hotel.

The "Front Office Essentials" chapter from the second edition has been deleted because a majority of hotels employ a property management system as opposed to a manual front office operation. Those portions of the chapter that referred to a property management system are included in the new Chapter 4, "Property Management Systems."

The third edition contains updated pedagogical features, including an "Opening Dilemma," which presents students with a mini–case study problem to solve with the help of material presented in the chapter; a "Solution to Opening Dilemma" is included at the end of each chapter. "Hospitality Profiles"—commentaries from hotel front office managers, general managers, and other department managers in hotels—add an extra human relations element to the text. "International Highlights"—articles of interest that accentuate the international workforce and international career opportunities for graduates—provide a forum for professors and students to discuss this aspect of hotel management. "Frontline Realities" includes unexpected yet very predictable situations. Students are asked to discuss those situations and develop methods for handling them. More "Case Studies" have been added to each chapter, allowing students to apply theory. A glossary of terms has been included, summarizing terms introduced in each chapter (which appear in **boldface** in the text).

The author is very pleased to have the opportunity for instructors and students to use instructional software with this text. Dr. Sheryl Fried Kline of Purdue University and William Sullivan of Widener University and University of Delaware have prepared an excellent new book and CD-ROM package, *Hotel Front Office Simulation: A Workbook and Software Package* (New York: John Wiley & Sons, © 2003) (ISBN 0-471-20331-9). This simulation has been reflected in chapters dealing with reservations, registrations, customer service, posting, and the night audit. This combination of the third edition of *Hotel Front Office Management* and Kline and Sullivan's software simulation will allow hospitality professors to offer their students an optimal learning opportunity.

A completely revised instructor's manual is available for the third edition for qualified adopters of the book. Please contact your Wiley sales representative for details.

Will you like the third edition of *Hotel Front Office Management*? I think you will, and I would appreciate hearing your comments (jxb21@psu.edu).

My very best to the future professionals of the hotel industry.

Acknowledgments

The author wishes to acknowledge the following professors who provided insightful reviews of individual chapters of this and previous editions. Without your concern and thoughtful commentary, this effort for our students would not have been possible: Thomas Jones, University of Nevada at Las Vegas; Robert McMullin, East Stroudsburg State University; and James Reid, New York City Technical College.

I would like to express my appreciation to the following hospitality professionals who provided commentary for the Hospitality Profiles included in this third edition: Dulcie Baker, director of sales, Tide Water Inn, Easton, Maryland; Kevin Corprew, director of rooms operation, Marriott, Overland Park, Kansas; Michael DeCaire, food and beverage manager, Houston Hilton, Houston, Texas; Doug Gehret, director of rooms, Waldorf=Astoria, New York City; Charles Gellad, general manager, Homewood Suites, Alexandria, Virginia; Greg Goforth, general manager, Best Western Merry Manor, South Portland, Maine; James Heale, controller, Sheraton Reading Hotel, Wyomissing, Pennsylvania; Lee Johnson, director of corporate sales, Pier 5 Hotel and Brookshire Suites, Inner Harbor, Baltimore, Maryland; John Juliano, director of safety and security, Royal Sonesta Hotel, Cambridge, Massachusetts; Eric Long, general manager, Waldorf=Astoria, New York, New York; Joseph Longo, general manager, The Jefferson Hotel, Richmond, Virginia; Patrick Mene, vice president of quality, The Ritz-Carlton Hotel Company, L.L.C.; Thomas Norman, C.H.A., general manager, Holiday Inn Grenada, Grenada, Mississippi; Randy Randall, general manager, Eldorado Hotel, Santa Fe, New Mexico; Todd Sheehan, managing partner, Lincoln Plaza Hotel & Conference Center, Reading, Pennsylvania; and Mike Schofield, general manager, Holiday Inn Express, Salem, Oregon.

One additional acknowledgment is offered to Dr. Trish Welch of Southern Illinois University, who was instrumental in the first edition of *Hotel Front Office Management*. Her words of support to Van Nostrand Reinhold for the initial prospectus and sample chapter are still greatly appreciated.

Introduction to Hotel Management

OPENING DILEMMA

A hospitality career fair is scheduled at the end of the week at your college or

university. Your recent review of this chapter has enticed you to explore the

career opportunities in limited-service and full-service hotels. Your instructor

has asked you to prepare a list of possible questions to ask the recruiter. What

would you include in that list?

CHAPTER FOCUS POINTS

- Historical overview of the hotel industry
- Hotel classification system
- Trends that foster growth and employment in the hotel industry
- Career development

The mere mention of the word *hotel* conjures up exciting images: a busy lobby filled with international dignitaries, celebrities, community leaders, attendees of conventions and large receptions, businesspersons, and family vacationers. The excitement that you feel in a hotel lobby is something you will have forever in your career. Savor it and enjoy it. It is the beginning of understanding the concept of providing hospitality to guests. As you begin to grasp the principles of a well-operated hotel, you will discover the important role the front office plays in keeping this excitement intact.

The **front office** is the nerve center of a hotel property. Communication and accounting are two of the most important functions of a front desk operation. Effective communications—with guests, employees, and other departments of the hotel—are paramount in projecting a hospitable image. Answering guest inquiries about hotel services and other guests, marketing and sales department requests for information on guest room availability, and housekeeping department inquiries concerning guest reservations are but a few of the routine tasks performed almost constantly by a hotel front desk in its role as communications hub. Accounting procedures, involving charges to registered and nonregistered hotel guest accounts, are also very important in the hospitality field. Itemized charges are necessary to show a breakdown of charges if a guest questions a bill.

Services for which fees are charged are available 24 hours a day in a hotel property. Moreover, because guests may want to settle their accounts at any time of the day, accounts must be current and accurate at all times. Keeping this data organized is a top priority of good front office management.

Founders of the Hotel Industry

A history of the founders of the hotel industry provides an opportunity to reflect upon our heritage. Learning about the founding giants such as Statler, Hilton, Marriott, Wilson, and Schultz, to name a few, allows a student of the hotel industry to discover the interesting lineage of hoteliers. The insights afforded by the efforts of these innovators who carved out the modern hotel industry may help future professionals with their own career planning.

E. M. Statler

To begin to understand the history of the modern hotel industry, let's look at some of the forerunners in the industry who were entrepreneurs motivated by wealth and fame on a grand scale.[1] Ellsworth M. Statler (1863–1928) developed the chain of hotels that were known as Statlers. He built and operated a hotel in Buffalo, New York, at the Pan-American Exposition of 1901. Among his hotels were ones located in Boston, Cleveland, Detroit, New York City, and St. Louis. In 1954, he sold the Statler chain of hotels to Conrad Hilton.[2]

> Statler devised a scheme to open an incredible two-story, rectangular wood structure that would contain 2,084 rooms and accommodate 5,000 guests. It was to be a temporary structure, covered with a thin layer of plaster to make it appear substantial, although simple to tear down after the fair closed.[3]

Conrad Hilton

Conrad Hilton (1887–1979) became a successful hotelier after World War I, when he purchased several properties in Texas during its oil boom. In 1919, he bought the Mobley Hotel in Cisco, Texas. In 1925, he built the Hilton Hotel in Dallas, Texas.[4] His acquisitions during and after World War II included the 3,000-room Stevens Hotel (now the Chicago Hilton) and the Palmer House in Chicago and the Plaza and Waldorf=Astoria in New York City. In 1946, he formed the Hilton Hotels Corporation, and in 1948, he formed the Hilton International Company, which came to number more than 125 hotels.[5] With the purchase of the Statler chain in 1954, Hilton created the first major chain of modern American hotels, that is, a group of hotels all of which follow standard operating procedures such as marketing, reservations, quality of service, food and beverage operations, housekeeping, and accounting. Hilton Hotels have expanded their entrepreneurship to include Hilton Garden Inns, Doubletree, Embassy Suites, Hampton Inns, Harrison Conference Centers, Homewood Suites by Hilton, Red Lion Hotels and Inns, and Conrad International.

Cesar Ritz

Cesar Ritz was a hotelier at the Grand National Hotel in Lucerne, Switzerland. Because of his management abilities, "the hotel became one of the most popular in Europe and Cesar Ritz became one of the most respected hoteliers in Europe."[6]

William Waldorf Astor and John Jacob Astor IV

In 1893, William Waldorf Astor launched the 13-story Waldorf Hotel at Fifth Avenue near Thirty-fourth Street in New York City. The Waldorf was the embodiment of Astor's vision of a New York hostelry that would appeal to his wealthy friends by combining the opulence of a European mansion with the warmth and homey qualities of a private residence.

Four years later, the Waldorf was joined by the 17-story Astoria Hotel, erected on an adjacent site by William Waldorf Astor's cousin, John Jacob Astor IV. The cousins built a corridor that connected the two hotels, which became known by a single hyphenated name, the Waldorf-Astoria.

In 1929, after decades of hosting distinguished visitors from around the world, the Waldorf-Astoria closed its doors to make room for the Empire State Building.

The 2,200-room, 42-floor Waldorf=Astoria Hotel was rebuilt on its current site at Park and Lexington avenues between Forty-ninth and Fiftieth streets. Upon the hotel's opening, President Herbert Hoover delivered a message of congratulations. It is interesting to note that President Hoover became a permanent resident of the Waldorf Towers, the luxurious "hotel within a hotel" that occupies the twenty-eighth through the forty-second floors. The hotel was purchased in 1949 by Conrad N. Hilton, who then purchased the land it stood on in 1977. In 1988, the hotel underwent a $150 million restoration. It was designated a New York City landmark in January 1993.[7]

Kemmons Wilson

Kemmons Wilson started the Holiday Inn chain in the early 1950s, opening his first Holiday Inn in Memphis, Tennessee. He wanted to build a chain of hotels for the traveling family and later expanded his marketing plan to include business travelers. His accomplishments in real estate development coupled with his hotel management skills proved to be a very successful combination for Wilson.

Wilson blazed a formidable path, innovating all along the way with amenities and high-rise architecture, including a highly successful round building concept featuring highly functional pie-shaped rooms. Wilson also introduced the unique in-house Holidex central-reservation system that set the standard for the industry for both the volume of business it produced and the important byproduct data it generated (allowing it, for example, to determine feasibility for new locations with cunning accuracy).[8]

J. W. Marriott and J. W. Marriott Jr.

J. W. Marriott (1900–1985) founded his hotel empire in 1957 with the Twin Bridges Marriott Motor Hotel in Virginia (Washington, D.C., area). Marriott Hotels and Resorts had grown to include Courtyard by Marriott and American Resorts Group at the time of J. W. Marriott's death in 1985, at which time J. W. Marriott Jr. acquired Howard Johnson Company; he sold the hotels to Prime Motor Inns and kept 350 restaurants and 68 turnpike units. In 1987, Marriott completed expansion of its Worldwide Reservation Center in Omaha, Nebraska, making it the largest single-site reservations operation in U.S. hotel history. Also in 1987, Marriott acquired the Residence Inn Company, an all-suite hotel chain targeted toward extended-stay travelers. With the introduction of limited-service hotels—hotels built with guest room accommodations and limited food service and meeting space—Marriott entered the economy lodging segment, opening the first Fairfield Inn in Atlanta, Georgia, in 1987.[9]

Ernest Henderson and Robert Moore

Ernest Henderson and Robert Moore started the Sheraton chain in 1937, when they acquired their first hotel—the Stonehaven—in Springfield, Massachusetts. Within two years, they purchased three hotels in Boston and, before long, expanded their holdings to include properties from Maine to Florida. At the end of its first decade, Sheraton was the first hotel chain to be listed on the New York Stock Exchange. In 1968, Sheraton was acquired by ITT Corporation as a wholly owned subsidiary, and ambitious development plans were put into place to create a truly global network of properties. In the 1980s, under the leadership of John Kapioltas, Sheraton's chairman, president, and chief executive officer, the company received international recognition as an industry innovator.[10] The Sheraton chain is currently owned by Starwood Hotels & Resorts Worldwide.

Ray Schultz

In the early 1980s, Ray Schultz founded the Hampton Inn hotels, which was a company in the Holiday Inn Corporation. This type of hotel was tagged as limited-service, meeting the needs of cost-conscious business travelers and pleasure travelers alike. His pioneering efforts in developing a product and service for these market segments have proved to be a remarkable contribution to the history of the hotel industry.

Historical Developments

The history of the hotel industry is also filled with notable concepts that shaped the products and services offered.

The atrium concept design, limited-service hotels, and technology were notable innovations. Management concepts such as marketing and total quality management (TQM) offered managers a new way to do business in hotels. The major U.S. economic reorganization in the late 1980s shaped the way hotels could become profitable. Also, in the 1990s, a new term appeared that changed the financial structuring and operation of hotels—*real estate investment trusts* (REITs).

Also, the terrorist events of September 11, 2001, will have an impact on how hotels market their products and services and deliver hospitality.

Atrium Concept

The hotel industry has had many notable developments over the past years. The **atrium concept,** a design in which guest rooms overlook the lobby from the first floor to the roof, was first used in the 1960s by Hyatt Hotels.

The dramatic approach to hotel style [was] exemplified by the Hyatt Regency in Atlanta. Designed by architect John Portman, with a striking and impressive atrium soaring up its 21 stories, the hotel literally changed the course of upscale hotel design. As a result hotels became more than a place to rest one's head. They became hubs for excitement, fun, relaxation and entertainment.[11]

Limited-Service Hotels

The movement of hotel construction from the downtown, center-city area to the suburbs in the 1950s coincided with the development of the U.S. highway system. The **limited-service** concept—hotels built with guest room accommodations and limited food service and meeting space—became prominent in the early 1980s, when many of the major chains adopted this concept for business travelers and travelers on a limited budget.

Technological Advances

Technology has played a major role in developing the products and services offered to guests. Recent adaptations of reservations systems, property management systems, and in-room guest checkout are only the successors of major advances in technology. Notable "firsts" in the adaptation of technology to the hotel industry can be reviewed in Figure 1-1. It is interesting to note how many of the developments we call technology were adapted in recent times.

Figure 1-1. *Introduction of technological advances to the hotel industry.*

1846	Central heating
1859	Elevator
1881	Electric lights
1907	In-room telephone
1927	In-room radio
1940	Air-conditioning
1950	Electric elevator
1958	Free television
1964	Holiday Inn reservation system with centralized computer
1965	Message lights on telephone Initial front office computer systems introduced followed by room status capability
1970s	Electric cash register POS (point of sale) systems and keyless locks Color television standard
1973	Free in-room movies (Sheraton)
1980s	Property management systems In-room guest checkout
1983	In-room personal computers Call accounting systems
1990s	On Command Video (on-demand movies) LodgeNet Entertainment (interactive video games) Interactive guest room shopping, interactive visitor's guide, fax delivery on TV, interactive guide to hotel's facilities and activities, reservations from the guest room for other hotels within the same organization, and interactive weather reports Internet reservations Introduction of legislation that monitored hotel ownership through real estate investment trusts (REITs)

Sources: American Hotel and Motel Association; Madelin Schneider, "20th Anniversary," *Hotels & Restaurants International* 20, no. 8 (August 1986): 40 (copyright *Hotels* magazine, a division of Reed USA); Larry Chervenak, "Top 10 Tech Trends: 1975–1995," *Hotel & Motel Management* 210, no. 14 (August 14, 1995): 45.

Marketing Emphasis

An emphasis on marketing to guest niches was the theme in the 1970s era. This technique surveyed potential guest markets and built systems around guests' needs.

The larger hotel-management and franchise companies also were discovering the advantages of forging strong reservations and marketing systems. For a guest, this meant that by calling a single phone number, he or she could be assured of a reservation and feel confident of the quality of accommodations expected.[12]

Total Quality Management

Total quality management (TQM), a management technique that helps managers to look at processes used to create products and services with a critical eye on improving those processes, is being practiced in many hotels today. This emphasis on analysis of the delivery of services and products with decision making at the front lines has created a trend in the 1990s. This concept will be discussed in more detail in chapter 11.

Major Reorganization 1987–1988

The economic period of 1987–1988 saw a major reorganization of the hotel industry.

1986 Congress unravelled what it had stitched together in 1981. The revised Tax Act made it clear that passive losses on real estate were no longer deductible. Hotels that were previously economically viable suddenly were not. At this time, there were plenty of Japanese who seemed intent on buying up, at astronomical prices, any piece of U.S. property with a hotel or golf course on it. As a result, the value of American hotel properties continued to increase. Between 1990 and 1995, the recession began and ended, and the full impact of the 1986 law and overbuilding were experienced. Some investors who had built properties in the early 1980s found their properties sales or replacement value had fallen to 50 percent or less of original cost. Some owners simply abandoned their properties to their mortgage holders— which in many cases turned out to be Uncle Sam, because of the simultaneous S&L debacle.[13]

Hotel Investment

Real estate investment trusts (REITs) have provided an investment opportunity for hoteliers. In the spring 2000 *Virginia Hospitality and Leisure Executive Report,* P. Anthony Brown of Arthur Andersen writes the following about the U.S. Tax Relief Extension Act of 1999. It is important to note that this information is useful as you plan your career direction.

The most significant provision, however, is creation of a new type of corporation—a "Taxable REIT Subsidiary" (effective January 1, 2001)—which will allow REITs to create new incremental income streams. With new growth opportunities, shareholders should be rewarded with higher stock prices since companies with increased growth rates typically trade in the market at higher earnings multiples.

Under the terms of the 1999 legislation, Taxable REIT Subsidiaries can provide non-customary services to tenants through their subsidiaries. This legislation should enable REITs to provide better customer service, create stronger customer loyalty and sell new, non-customary services to tenants. In addition these new subsidiaries can lease lodging facilities from REITs. However, the lodging facilities must be managed by an independent contractor that is actively engaged in the trade or business of operating lodging facilities for any person other than the REIT.

With these changes, hotel REITs will be able to reorganize their structure in order to retain more of the income generated by their hotels. For example, FelCor Lodging Trust Inc., a hotel REIT based in Irving, Texas, currently leases its hotels to two tenants: 1) a company owned by its executives and directors; and 2) Bristol Hotels and Resorts, a publicly traded company. With the new legislation, FelCor will be able to form a new Taxable REIT Subsidiary and transfer the leases of its hotels to this new subsidiary. Accordingly, the net income of the existing lessee would be transferred to the new Taxable REIT Subsidiary. However, a management company (not owned by FelCor) must manage the hotels and must be actively engaged in the trade or business of operating lodging facilities for any person other than the REIT.[14]

September 11, 2001

The tragic terrorist events of September 11, 2001, will have a lasting effect on how a hotel markets its products and services and delivers hospitality. The immediate impact of the terrorist attacks has resulted in a decreased number of people willing to fly and, thus, a decrease in a need for renting hotel rooms. Hoteliers (as well as restaurateurs, tourist attractions, government agencies, and the like) and the federal, regional, and state tourism associations have banded together to address the issue of fear as it relates to travel and tourism.

Hoteliers have to review their marketing plans and determine how the corporate traveler can be attracted back into their properties. The corporate guest who was always viewed as a huge market can no longer be taken for granted. Corporate executives, travel planners, and traffic managers have to be greeted personally by hotel staff to ask for their business and inquire about when to expect business as usual. While the efforts of attracting and maintaining corporate travelers are assessed, new methods to attract other markets, such as local and nearby residents, have to be developed. These efforts take the form of special packages emphasizing local history and culture, businesses, sporting events, and natural attractions and are combined with the products and services of an individual hotel. Is this an easy challenge? Indeed it is not; yet it is one that future hoteliers will have to grasp with eagerness and enthusiasm in order to succeed.

The delivery of hospitality in hotels has also come under review. For example, hoteliers are reviewing security plans to include the frontline employee who has to take immediate action based upon observations at the front desk, in the dining room and recreational areas, and on guest and public floors. The frontline employee who sees uncommon activities has to know the importance of reporting concerns to supervisors. Special training on what to look for with regard to guest interactions in public areas and on guest floors will assist the frontline person in becoming proactive.

Hoteliers must also be concerned with how to support hospitality as part of being responsible citizens in their communities. Hotel general managers should develop emergency plans to allow for offering immediate public space to medical personnel and disaster victims. Short-term concerns such as feeding disaster victims and emergency personnel and long-term commitments such as housing for displaced members of the community are just some of the issues faced by the hotel industry.

These issues of marketing and delivering hospitality as well as other issues will emerge as we prepare to respond to the events of September 11, 2001.

Overview of the Hotel Industry

A working knowledge of the classifications used in the hotel industry is important to understanding its organization. The various types of properties, their market orientation and location, sales indicators, occupancy and revenues as they relate to levels of service, and various types of business affiliations are all means of classifying hotel properties. Figure 1-2 will serve as a reference point throughout this discussion.

Types of Lodging Facilities

Classification of hotel facilities is not based on rigid criteria. The definitions can change, depending on market forces, legal criteria, location, function, and, in some cases, personal preference, but the definitions that follow are generally accepted and are the ones intended for these classifications throughout this text.

Hotels

A hotel usually offers guests a full range of accommodations and services, which may include reservations, suites, public dining and banquet facilities, lounge and entertainment areas, room service, cable television, personal computers, meeting rooms, specialty shops, personal services valet, laundry, hair care, swimming pool and other recreational activities, gaming/casino operations, ground transportation to and from an airport, and concierge services. The size of the property can range from 20 to more than 2,000 rooms.

Figure 1-2. *Hotel industry overview.*

I. Types of hotel properties
  a. Hotels
  b. Motels
  c. All-suites
  d. Limited-service hotels
  e. Extended-stay hotels

II. Market orientation/location
  a. Residential
    i. Center-city
      1. Hotels
      2. All-suites
      3. Limited-service
      4. Extended-stay
    ii. Suburban
      1. All-suites
      2. Limited-service
      3. Extended-stay
  b. Commercial
    i. Center-city
      1. Hotels
      2. All-suites
      3. Limited-service
      4. Extended-stay
    ii. Suburban
      1. Hotels
      2. Motels
      3. All-suites
      4. Limited-service
      5. Extended-stay

Hotels are found in center-city, suburban, and airport locations. Guest stays can be overnight or long-term, as much as several weeks in length. These properties sometimes specialize in catering to particular interests, such as conventions or gambling. Casino hotels usually take a secondary role to the casino operation, where the emphasis is on profitable gaming operations.

Motels

Motels offer guests a limited range of services, which may include reservations, vending machines, swimming pools, and cable television. The size of these properties averages from 10 to 50 units. Motels are usually in suburban highway and airport locations. Guests

iii. Airport
    1. Hotels
    2. Motels
    3. All-suites
    4. Limited-service
iv. Highway
    1. Motels
    2. All-suites
    3. Limited-service
    4. Extended-stay

III. Sales indicators
  a. Occupancy
  b. Average daily rate (ADR)
  c. Yield percentage
  d. Revenue per available room (RevPAR)

IV. Levels of service
  a. Full-service
  b. All-suites
  c. Limited-service
  d. Extended-stay

V. Affiliation
  a. Chain
    i. Franchise
    ii. Company-owned
    iii. Referral
    iv. Management contract
  b. Independent

typically stay overnight or a few days. Motels may be located near a freestanding restaurant.

All-Suites

The all-suites concept, a new addition to the hotel industry, developed in the 1980s as a separate marketing concept, offers guests a wide range of services, which may include reservations, living room and separate bedroom, kitchenette, optional public dining room and room service, cable television, videocassette players and recorders, specialty shops, personal services valet and laundry, swimming pool, and ground transportation to and

Joseph Longo is the general manager of The Jefferson Hotel, a 265-room historic property in Richmond, Virginia. As one of only 17 hotels in North America to receive both the Mobil Five Star and AAA Five Diamond ratings, The Jefferson Hotel offers guests the highest level of products and services available, with a strong commitment to warm, genuine, and gracious service.

Mr. Longo obtained a B.S. degree in both business administration and communication from Saint John's University in New York. While in college, he worked at the front desk at The Saint Regis Hotel in New York City and began his professional career at the Sheraton-Carlton Hotel in Washington, D.C., as the rooms division manager. He then became general manager of The River Inn hotel in Washington, D.C., and from there the regional director of operations for the Potomac Hotel Group. Prior to becoming general manager of The Jefferson Hotel, Mr. Longo was regional director of operations for Field Hotel Association in Valley Forge, Pennsylvania.

The sales and marketing effort for this independently owned property requires aggressive sales and public relations strategies. Focus is placed not only on the guest rooms but also on the 26,000 square feet of function space and the two restaurants, one an AAA Five Diamond Award winner.

Mr. Longo encourages students who are pursuing a hospitality management career to remember that, as innkeepers, your hotel is like your home, where all of your guests are made to feel welcome. This involves providing all guests with the basics of hospitality: a comfortable room, exceptional food, and a friendly staff to serve them. He adds that hospitality is a diverse business, offering a unique work experience each day.

---

from an airport. The size of the operation can range from 50 to more than 100 units. This type of property is usually found in center-city, suburban, and airport locations. The length of guest stay can be overnight, several days, or long-term. Although this type of hotel may seem new, many downtown, center-city hotels have offered this type of accommodation with in-room kitchenette and sitting rooms since the early 1900s. Now with **mass marketing**—advertising products and services through mass communications such as television, radio, and the Internet—this type of hotel is considered new.

Limited-Service Hotels

Limited-service hotels appeared on the hotel scene in the mid-1980s. Hampton Inn and Marriott were among the first organizations to offer limited-service properties.

The concept of limited service was developed for a specific segment of the market—business and cost-conscious travelers. The range of accommodations and services may include reservations, minimal public dining and meeting facilities, cable television, personal computers, personal services (valet and laundry), and ground transportation to and from an airport. The size of the property can range from 100 to more than 200 rooms. Limited-service hotels are found in center-city, suburban, and airport locations. They are usually located near restaurants for guest convenience. Guest stays can be overnight or long-term. These properties sometimes specialize in catering to the business traveler and offer special business technology centers.

Extended-Stay Hotels

In "Survey Results of the Extended Stay Lodging Industry," The Highland Group of Atlanta, Georgia, reports the following information, about this newest hotel product on the market which includes the 31 extended-stay brands as well as some independent hotels.

Extended-stay hotel room supply in the United States increased more than 50 percent in 1997 over 1996. There will be more economy-price than upscale extended-stay rooms before the end of 1998. This is a significant reversal from prior years and indicates a change in the way extended-stay lodging is used by American travelers. Projected extended-stay hotel supply will be more than half a million rooms through 2002. At this level, extended-stay hotel rooms will represent some 12 percent of total lodging inventory.

Assuming supply growth projections are fully realized through 2002, this represents a significant change from the current price distribution of extended-stay hotels and marks a change in the way Americans use extended-stay lodging. Use of extended-stay lodging will have expanded from the corporate expense-account

HOSPITALITY PROFILE

Charles Gellad is the general manager of the Homewood Suites in Alexandria, Virginia. He began his career at the Hampton Inn in Alexandria, Virginia, as a front desk clerk and progressed to guest services manager there. Then he took a position as sales manager at the Hampton Inn in Fairfax, Virginia, and then as director of sales at the Hampton Inn in Alexandria, Virginia. He was on board as director of sales prior to the opening of the Homewood Suites in Alexandria, Virginia.

Mr. Gellad said his market for guests includes those persons who are going to be in town for an extended period of time because of government contracts, special projects, training, or relocation in the military or in the private sector. Relocation is the common characteristic with this market.

His extended-stay hotel offers a breakfast in the morning and a manager's reception (light foods and beverages); a fitness center and an indoor whirlpool; a coin-operated laundry; an executive center that is equipped with a fax machine, personal computer, copying machine, and other office amenities; a convenience store called a "Suite Shop"; free parking; and free local, credit-card, and collect calls.

Mr. Gellad's entry-level experience has provided him with many opportunities to learn how to deal with different personalities. He says that when you become a supervisor of people, those people want to be treated as individuals, but you have to do so by being fair in interpreting the polices to everyone. He also extends his hope that you will develop a balance between work and a personal life. This business can be very time consuming, but you have to take time to develop a life outside the hotel.

Mike Schofield, general manager of the Holiday Inn Express in Salem, Oregon, feels that the crux of the hotel business focuses on friendliness, service, and extension of courtesy to the guest. He also stresses that a manager has to impress the importance of extending courtesy to employees.

Most of the guests at the Holiday Inn Express are transient leisure travelers, although some are business travelers. Those guests are looking for cleanliness, a good and convenient location, and amenities such as a continental breakfast, a pool and a spa, and a business center. About 60 percent of those guests arrive at the Holiday Inn Express because of brand recognition, another 25 percent to 35 percent use the reservation system, and a final 5 percent stay at Mr. Schofield's hotel because of his property's local marketing efforts.

Mr. Schofield attended Cypress College in Cypress, California. He started in the hotel business in 1985 at the Riverside Inn in Grants Pass, Oregon, doing accounting and taxes and then serving as general manager. He continued his career as general manager with Sea Venture Resort in Pismo Beach, California; as general manager at The Inn at Otter Crest near Newport, Oregon; and as general manager of Super 8 Motel in Grants Pass, Oregon.

market to encompass most demographic segments. Corporations are taking advantage of the availability of these facilities for training, relocation and temporary assignments at all levels.[15]

At Hilton's Homewood Suites, the following room amenities are included: king-size bed or two double beds in the bedroom and foldout sofa in the living room; two remote-controlled color televisions; fully equipped kitchen with a microwave, refrigerator with ice maker, coffeemaker, twin-burner stove, and kitchen utensils; a spacious, well-lit dining area; and ceiling fans and iron and ironing board. Additional hotel services include a business center, an exercise room, and a pool. This hotel concept also structures its room rates to attract the long-term guest.

Market Orientation

Market orientation in the hotel industry is categorized into two segments: (1) **residential hotels,** which provide guest accommodations for the long term; and (2) **commercial hotels,** which provide short-term accommodations for traveling guests.

Residential properties include hotels, all-suites, limited-service, and extended-stay properties. Services may include (but are not limited to) public dining, recreational facilities, social activities, and personal services. These hotels are usually located in center-city and suburban areas where other activities (shopping, arts and entertainment, business services, public transportation) are available to round out the living experience.

Commercial properties service the transient guest, whose stay is short in duration.

Services include (but are not limited to) computerized reservation systems, public dining, banquet service, lounge and entertainment areas, personal services, and shuttle transportation to airports. They may be located almost anywhere.

It is essential to note the very gray areas in using these two types of categories. A commercial lodging establishment may have a certain percentage of permanent residents. Likewise, a residential hotel may have nightly rentals available. Owners and general managers need to exhibit a great deal of flexibility in meeting the needs of the available markets.

Sales Indicators

Sales indicators, including hotel occupancy and average daily rate, are another means for describing hotels. This information is necessary for business investors to estimate the profitability of a hotel.

There are four factors that measure a hotel's degree of financial success: occupancy percentage, average daily rate, yield percentage, and **revenue per available room (RevPAR). Occupancy percentage** is the number of rooms sold divided by the number of rooms available. **Average daily rate (ADR)** is the total room revenue divided by the number of rooms sold. **Yield percentage,** the effectiveness of a hotel at selling its rooms at the highest rate available to the most profitable guest, reveals a facility's success in selling its room inventory on a daily basis. RevPAR is used to indicate the ability of each guest room to produce a profit. Once the daily sales opportunity has presented itself, it cannot be repeated (excluding the opportunity to sell a room at a half-day rate).

Occupancy

Occupancy percentages measure the effectiveness of the marketing and sales department as well as the front office in its external and internal marketing efforts. Occupancy percentage is also used by investors to determine the **potential gross income,** which is the amount of sales a hotel might obtain at a given level of occupancy, average daily rate, and anticipated yield. However, it is also important not to assume that occupancy is standard each night. Variations occur on a daily basis and by season.

Average Daily Rate

The average daily rate (sometimes referred to as average room rate) is also used in projecting **room revenues**—the amount of room sales received—for a hotel. However, this figure also affects guests' expectations of their hotel experience. Guests expect higher room rates to correlate with higher levels of service: the hotel with a rate of $150 per night is expected to offer more services than a hotel in the same geographic area with a rate of $55 per night. These expectations have been extensively capitalized upon by major hotel chains, by developing different properties to meet the expectations of various segments of the hotel market, as discussed earlier in the chapter.

Yield Percentage

Yield percentage measures a hotel manager's efforts in achieving maximum occupancy at the highest room rate possible. Since this term will be discussed more fully in Chapter 6, it is sufficient to note that this concept is relatively new in the hotel industry. Prior to the 1990s, hotel managers relied on occupancy and average daily rate as indicators of meeting financial goals. Yield percentage forces managers to think in more active terms.

RevPAR (Revenue per Available Room)

RevPAR is determined by dividing room revenue received for a specific day by the number of rooms available in the hotel for that day. The formulas for determining RevPAR are as follows:

$$\frac{\text{room revenue}}{\text{number of available rooms}}$$

or

$$\text{hotel occupancy} \times \text{average daily rate}$$

For example, RevPAR for a hotel that has $10,000 in room revenue for the night of September 15 with 200 rooms available would equal $50 ($10,000 ÷ 200 = $50).

This same hotel on September 15 with 200 rooms, room revenue of $10,000, 125 rooms sold, an average daily rate of $80 ($10,000 ÷ 125 = $80), and hotel occupancy of 62.5 percent (125 rooms sold ÷ 200 rooms available × 100 = 62.5 percent) would still produce the same RevPAR (.625 × $80 = $50).

RevPAR is used in hotels to determine the amount of dollars each hotel room produces for the overall financial success of the hotel. The profit from the sale of a hotel room is much greater than that from a similar food and beverage sale. However, the food and beverage aspect of the hotel industry is essential in attracting some categories of guests who want conference services. Chapter 6, "Yield Management," discusses the importance of considering the potential income from room and food and beverage sales.

Consider the following article, "January RevPAR Grows Nearly Ten Percent at Suburban Lodge Company-Owned Hotels," which was published on-line. It shows Suburban Lodges of America's use of RevPAR to inform its shareholders. (Suburban Lodges of America owns, franchises, and manages Suburban Lodge hotels, the nation's largest chain of economy extended-stay hotels, and franchises GuestHouse International hotels, the midmarket nightly-stay hotel chain with the franchisee-friendly franchise agreement.)

ATLANTA—(BUSINESS WIRE)—Feb. 8, 2001—Suburban Lodges of America, Inc. (NASDAQ: SLAM) announced today that weekly revenue per available room ("RevPAR") for Company-owned Suburban Lodge hotels increased 9.7%, to $145.07, for the month of January 2001 in comparison to RevPAR of $132.26 in January 2000. The increase in current year RevPAR was attributable primarily to a 9.0% increase in the hotels' average occupancy rate, to 73.8% from 67.7% in January 2000, combined with a small increase in average weekly rate ("AWR") to $197.68 from $196.75 in January 2000. The Company believes that its January 2000 RevPAR and occupancy rates were negatively impacted by reduced travel resulting from Y2K-related concerns.

In commenting on the release of this information, Chief Financial Officer Chuck Criscillis stated, "Like many other companies, we are looking for ways to better communicate our progress with our shareholders. Reporting our hotels' operating data on a monthly basis is one way to accomplish this. By releasing these numbers, we are not intimating that similar RevPAR increases will be achieved for the balance of the year. While we are anticipating RevPAR growth for the balance of 2001, we don't view the January growth rate as sustainable because of the weakness in January 2000 occupancy rates. Nonetheless, our January 2001 statistics provide strong evidence that our strategy of focusing on occupancy more than on room rates can yield meaningful revenue growth."

The matters discussed in the foregoing paragraphs of this news release include forward-looking statements that involve risks and uncertainties that could cause results to differ from anticipated results, including, but not limited to, general economic conditions, weather patterns, individuals' plans for business and personal travel, and other risks indicated in the Company's filings with the Securities and Exchange Commission.[16]

This article addresses the importance of using RevPAR to present a fuller financial picture that is based on factors that impact room sales, such as economic conditions, weather patterns, and business and personal travel.

Levels of Service

The four commonly used **market segments**—identifiable groups of customers with similar needs for products and services—are full service, all-suites, limited service, and extended stay. There is a great deal of overlap among these divisions, and much confusion, some of which occurs because leaders in the hotel industry do not agree on terminology. Some industry leaders avoid the "budget" tag because of its connotations of cheapness and poor quality. Others welcome the label because it appeals to those travelers who are looking for basic accommodations at very inexpensive rates. Nevertheless, the following definitions provide some idea of what is offered at each level of service.

Full service is a level that provides a wide range of conveniences for the guest. These services include, but are not limited to, reservations, on-premise dining, banquet and meeting facilities, and recreational facilities. Examples of a full-service hotel include Marriott Hotels and Resorts, Renaissance Hotels, and Holiday Inns.

As discussed earlier, **all-suites** indicates a level of service for a guest who will desire a more at-home atmosphere. Services include separate sleeping and living areas or working areas, kitchenette facilities, wet bars, and other amenities at the midprice level. This concept appeals to the business traveler as well as to families. Marriott Suites and Embassy Suite Hotels are examples of all-suite hotels. It is interesting to note that this concept is also employed in older center-city commercial hotels, in which adjoining rooms alongside the bedroom and bath have been remodeled into living rooms and kitchenettes to create suites.

Limited service emphasizes basic room accommodations, guest amenities, and minimal public areas. A continental breakfast and/or an evening cocktail is often included in the price of the room. The guest has the opportunity to trade the public meeting room for free in-room movies, the dining room for free local phone calls. Hampton Inns and Ramada Limited are examples of limited-service hotels.

Extended stay is a level of service that offers a "home away from home" atmosphere for business executives, visitors, and families who are planning to visit an area for an extended period of time. A fully equipped kitchenette allows international guests to prepare foods that provide comfort in a new environment. Also, the spacious bedrooms and living areas provide work and recreational areas. Light breakfast and evening meals are also included. An example of this level of service is Hilton's Homewood Suites hotels.

HOSPITALITY PROFILE

Greg Goforth is the general manager of the Best Western Merry Manor in South Portland, Maine. The Merry Manor is a full-service hotel with 151 guest rooms, 6 meeting rooms, and a restaurant. Guest amenities include a year-round outdoor heated pool, an 18-foot indoor hot tub with a therapeutic waterfall, and a kiddie pool. Mr. Goforth has a degree in hotel and restaurant management from the University of New Hampshire. He says that guests are looking for the basic comforts of home—clean, comfortable, well-equipped rooms with everything in working order. He has noticed a trend toward added amenities in the rooms. Irons, ironing boards, and hair dryers are now considered necessities, and having breakfast available is a must. Business-friendly rooms with a large desk, in-room fax machines, and easy and fast Internet access are also a necessity for attracting a corporate clientele.

Mr. Goforth indicates that the occupancy in the Portland market has remained fairly consistent. Growth in occupancy has barely kept up with the constant increase in supply. The average daily rate has been rising faster than inflation; however, increased guest demands and increased payroll expenses have added to the challenge of making a profit. The greatest challenge for hospitality in the next few years will be attracting and retaining qualified help.

Business Affiliations

Business affiliations, which indicate either chain or independent ownership of hotels, also categorize the hotel industry. These classifications are the most easily recognizable by consumers with regard to such features as brand name, structural appearance, and ambience. Long-lasting marketing effects develop a brand loyalty and acceptance that are most important in long-term profitability for a hotel.

Chain Affiliation

When asked to name several **chain** operations (a group of hotels that follow standard operating procedures such as marketing, reservations, quality of service, food and beverage operations, housekeeping, and accounting), most people would probably mention Holiday Inn, Marriott, Sheraton, Days Inn, Hyatt, Hilton, or Econo Lodge. Students should stay up to date regarding developments in the industry, such as acquisitions, restructuring, and other changes in these organizations. This information, which will be important to know when making career decisions, can be obtained from trade journals such as *Hotels* (published by Cahners, Des Plaines, Illinois), whose annual July issue includes a listing of hotel chains, addresses, and number of rooms; the *Wall Street Journal;* and other newspapers, magazines, and Web sites.

Chain affiliations, which include hotels that purchase operational and marketing services from a corporation, are further divided into franchisee, referral, company-owned properties, and management contract companies. Franchise corporations offer support to the franchisee, who is the owner of the land and building, in the form of reservation systems, advertising, operations management, and management development. In return for these services, the franchisee pays fees for items such as initial start-up, rental of signs and other equipment, use of the corporation's reservation referral system, and national advertising, among others.[17]

Anyone wishing to enter the hotel business by investing personal funds wants to be sure a profit will be realized. Perhaps because of a lack of experience in operating a hotel or motel or a lack of business acumen, a poor credit rating, or limited knowledge of real estate development, this type of entrepreneur may need to seek the guidance of others. He or she can receive direction from a corporation, such as Days Inn, Sheraton, or Hilton, concerning land, building, and management development.

Referral Property

Sometimes a hotel organization will choose to become a **referral property,** a hotel operating as an independent that wishes to be associated with a certain chain. Since the property has been physically developed, the entrepreneur may only want assistance with management, marketing and advertising, and/or reservation referral. Likewise, the fees are based on services required. The chain's quality assurance standards must, however, also be met by the referral property.

Company-Owned Property

A **company-owned property,** a hotel that is owned and operated by a chain organization, allows the hotel company developer to act as an independent entrepreneur. The hotel company developer operates the hotel property in competition with all other properties in the area. It uses its own expertise in site selection, property development, marketing and advertising, and operations management. The hotel company developer recruits talented professions into the organization to manage such properties. It uses the chain's reservation system. The hotel company developer may set a limit on the number of franchises so that a majority of the properties remain company-owned.

Management Contract Property

A **management contract property,** a hotel that is operated by a consulting company that provides operational and marketing expertise and a professional staff, is similar to a referral property. There are several management contract organizations that develop business relationships with existing hotels and operate the hotels as their own. Their business relationship requires financial accountability and profitability. Management contract companies may choose to operate each hotel as a member of a franchise or as an independent.

Independent Properties

An **independent hotel** is one that is not associated with a franchise. It provides a greater sense of warmth and individuality than does a property that is associated with a chain. Independent hotels have particular characteristics, which include an owner who functions as a manager, room rates similar to chain properties, rooms decorated in different styles, and inviting dining rooms. These hotels may be residential or commercial, with locations in the center city, suburbia, along the highway, or near an airport. The number of rooms can range from 50 to 1,000. They may offer full services to the guest, including suites, dining room, room service, banquets, gift shop, beauty shop, athletic facilities, swimming pool, theaters, valet services, concierge, and airport shuttle service. Some older independent hotels have refurbished their suites to capture their share of the all-suites market.

With all of these advantages, why aren't all lodging properties independent? The answer lies with the U.S. economy. The development of large chains and of smaller properties often brings tax advantages and improved profits to investors. Millions of dollars in capital are required to develop a 2,000-room full-service property. Business, financial, and managerial expertise is more readily available in a company in which there is a pool of skilled experts. Large corporations can also offset financial losses in certain fiscal years or from certain properties against financial gains of other companies or properties in their diversified portfolios.

The independent entrepreneur operates his or her business without the advantages of consultation and assistance. This person may have worked for a large chain or gained a great deal of operations and development experience in the industry. He or she may also purchase a hotel property to balance an investment portfolio. As with any financial investment, the entrepreneur will seek a professional to manage and operate the establishment. The person chosen for this job must manage all aspects of the business—room, food and beverage, housekeeping, security, maintenance, parking, controller's office, and marketing and sales. All business decisions on expenditures must be coordinated with a profit-and-loss statement and a balance sheet. Every sale of a guest room, every guest purchase of food and beverage, occurs because the management of that property has been able to market and manage the property effectively. The challenge of managing an independent property can be overwhelming. It can, however, also offer enormous satisfaction and financial independence.

Trends That Foster Growth

Future professionals in the hotel industry must be able to analyze who their customers will be and why they will have customers. Marketing classes teach how to determine the buyers of a particular product—who the potential guests of a particular hotel property are. Such courses show how to evaluate **demographic data** (size, density, distribution, vital statistics of a population, broken down into, for example, age, sex, martial status, and occupation categories) and **psychographic data** (emotional and motivational forces that affect a service or product) for potential markets.

The second question—why there will be customers—is an important one. Students will explore this question many times during their career in the lodging industry. A manager must plan for profitable results. This plan must take into account the reasons why customers purchase a product—what trends will increase or decrease the need for hotel facilities? Such factors include the growth of leisure time, the development of the "me/pleasure" concept, the increase in discretionary income, the trend toward smaller families, the changes in business travel, and the expansion of the travel experience. Other economics and political trends—such as public liability, insurance costs, overbuilding, the value of the U.S. dollar overseas, gasoline prices, safety from random danger while traveling, and legislation—affect commerce; labor and the airline industry also have an impact on current sales as well as growth in the lodging industry.

Leisure Time

The trend toward increased leisure time—in the form of three-day weekends, paid vacations and personal days, a workweek of 40 hours or less, and early retirement—has set the stage for the growth of the lodging industry. As more people have available leisure time to explore new geographical areas, try new hobbies, sample different culinary trends, participate in sporting events, and just relax, the customer base of the hotel industry expands.

Workers are spending fewer years in the labor force as the concept of early retirement becomes more popular. And as the population segment known as the baby boom ages, the number of retirees is projected to soar. Many of these people will take on a second career, but part-time jobs will likely be more common. With the two prime ingredients for using hotel facilities—time and money—readily at hand, these people will be a primary market for the hotel industry.

Me/Pleasure Concept

The idea of deserving recreation away from the job to restore mental acuity and improve attitude had evolved over the years. The work ethic of the eighteenth and nineteenth centuries strongly influenced the way Americans play, as recreation and leisure were considered privileges reserved for the wealthy. Today, most workers enjoy vacations and experience the feeling of getting away from it all. This trend toward self-gratification will continue into the twenty-first century. The idea that satisfying personal needs is a prerequisite to satisfying the needs of others has a good hold in American society.

The isolated nature of many jobs increases the need for respite. As more and more people find themselves spending more time communicating via computers and other machinery rather than face-to-face, social needs will continue to grow stronger. Workers need the away-from-job experience to balance their social and mental needs with their demands. Travel helps to satisfy these needs, and the hotel industry benefits as a result.

Discretionary Income

Discretionary income, the money remaining from wages after paying for necessities such as food, clothing, and shelter, is the most important of all the trends that support the growth of the hospitality industry. One of the main reasons for the increase in discretionary income of American families is the emergence of the two-income family. An almost double-income family unit had emerged over the years as more married women joined or stayed in the labor force. The strong growth in this segment of the labor force will undoubtedly continue. As more income becomes available to pay for the necessities of life, discretionary income for leisure time and corresponding goods and services also becomes available.

Discretionary income is not a constant. It is definitely affected by various economic factors: an economic downturn with increased unemployment reduces discretionary income, for example. And different economic conditions tend to favor different ways of spending discretionary income: for example, low interest rates, which make the purchase of high-ticket items (such as homes, cars, boats, and aircraft) more desirable, make less discretionary income available for short vacations or quick day trips. Students of the U.S. economy need only review the effects of a recession or the energy crisis of the 1970s to see how quickly discretionary income formerly directed to the hospitality industry can evaporate.

Family Size/Household Size

The current trend toward smaller families also indicates growth for the hospitality industry. The discretionary income available for a family with two children is greater than that for a family with five children when total incomes are equal. Household size—the number of persons in a home—has continued to decrease over the years. Like the trend toward smaller families, the increased number of small households indicates that more discretionary income is available. The costs associated with a one- or two-person household are less than those for a household of four or more people. Moreover, those who live in smaller households are more likely to dine out, travel, and participate in quality leisure-time activities.

Business Travel

Corporate business travel should not be taken for granted by hotel managers in today's world of high energy prices and speedy communication. Oil prices significantly affect business travel; as the cost of fuel oil rises, higher prices for air travel and other means of transportation result. A business is not always willing or able to budget more for travel. When travel costs increase, less travel is done and the necessity of any business travel is reviewed. Executives will no longer hop the next plane to clinch a deal if the same task can be accomplished via a phone call, a (**conference call**), in which three or more persons are linked by telephone (or **PictureTel** which is the use of telephone lines to send and receive video and audio impressions). Shorter trips (day trips or one-night stays) are another response to the increased cost of travel.

The volume created by business travel often represents the largest portion of the regular income of a hotel property. This prime market must be constantly reviewed for economic details that affect its viability.

Female Business Travel

Female business travelers are on the rise and represent an increasing segment of the corporate travel market. As previously discussed, their travel is also affected by energy prices and speedy communication. This particular market segment requires close attention to fulfilling special needs. Female travelers request particular amenities and demand close attention to safety. Marketing and sales managers need to develop products and services that will capture this growing market segment.

Travel as Experience

At one time, people traveled primarily out of necessity; business and family visits were the usual reasons for traveling. Today, people travel for many reasons, including education, culture, and personal development. Many people want to learn more about the society in which they live. They have studied American and/or world history and want to see the places that they have read about. Cultural pursuits—art, theater, music, opera, ballet, and museums—can attract a constant flow of people into an area. Sports and nature attract travelers who want to enjoy the great outdoors as well as those who prefer to watch their favorite teams. The push for lifelong learning has provided an incentive for many to take personal development/enrichment courses, whether to update professional skills or to increase knowledge of a particular hobby. **Ecotourists,** tourists who plan vacations to study the culture and environment of a particular area, want to enjoy nature in its unblemished and unsullied form.

Career Development

An introductory chapter in hotel management would not be complete without attention to career development. Those who are planning a career in the hotel industry need to review the fundamentals of career development, which revolve around five very important concepts: educational preparation, practical experience, membership in professional organizations, ports of entry, and growth areas for the industry.

Educational Preparation

As you enter the twenty-first century, the educational base you build now will serve you well. The classes you are taking in your major course of study—including management and supervision, cost control, human resources management, quantity food production, hotel management, purchasing, sanitation, layout and design, accounting, and marketing—will build a strong foundation for your continued development of technical skills. Courses outside your major—such as English, speech communication, computer training, arts, economics, psychology, sociology, nutrition, science, and math—will help develop the skills you need to cope in the professional world. The formal education you receive in your classroom study will be enhanced by extracurricular activities such as clubs, student government, sports, and other areas of special interest. These activities are a microcosm of the environment in which you will apply your technical, liberal arts, and science courses. Clubs associated with your major in particular allow you to apply theoretical concepts learned in class to a real-life business environment.

Your educational experience will open the door to your career. You must apply your skills and knowledge after graduation to be an effective, successful employee in the hotel industry. Use your degree as a starting point for an exciting career in hospitality.

The educational experience you are now obtaining must be nurtured beyond graduation day. There are many opportunities for **in-service education,** which include courses that update a professional's educational background for use in current practice; these are offered by such groups as professional organizations, sponsors of trade shows, community colleges and universities, technical schools, correspondence schools, trade journals, and other industry groups. These organizations offer the professional an opportunity to stay up to date in industry practices.

Just as professionals in other industries take classes to refresh their skills and learn new concepts and procedures, so must professionals in the hotel industry maintain awareness of industry advances. One particularly relevant area is computer training. Professionals who attended school before the early 1980s had little exposure to computers and the ever-changing technology in the computer industry; even recent graduates are not always aware of the most current trends and advances. The professional has the choice of overlooking this need or enrolling in computer applications courses to explore these concepts. The next choice is to determine whether these new procedures and equipment are applicable to his or her particular establishment.

Professional organizations—such as the **American Hotel & Lodging Association;**—the Hotel Sales and Marketing Association, International; and the National Restaurant Association—offer professionals continuing education opportunities through correspondence courses and seminars. The American Hotel & Lodging Association offers opportunities for hotel employees to earn certification as Certified Hotel Administrator (CHA) and Certified Rooms Division Executive (CRDE) as well as other certifications. Trade shows sponsored by these organizations promote the latest concepts in technology, products, and supplies, as well as providing miniseminars on how to use current technology in human resources management, food production, marketing, and general management. Community colleges and technical schools offer special-interest courses in management and skills application to keep you and your staff abreast of new areas and to review basic concepts. Attending these courses can provide new insight into particular operational problems.

Correspondence courses are another way to learn new skills and understand new areas. New technology in **distance learning**—learning that takes place via satellite broadcasts, cable, PictureTel, or on-line computer interaction—is offered by various colleges, universities, and professional groups to encourage members to remain current.

Trade journals are also extremely helpful in keeping professionals up to date on new management concepts, technical applications, marketing principles, equipment innovations, and the like. The isolation experienced by managers in out-of-the-way hotel establishments can be alleviated by reading trade journals. Such journals help all managers feel connected to the community of hotel industry professionals, perhaps providing insight into solving technical problems as well as boosting morale.

Education is a lifelong venture: it does not stop with the attainment of a degree from a university or community college. It is only the beginning of a commitment to nurturing your career.

Work Experience

The practical experience you obtain from entry-level hotel jobs—whether you are a desk clerk, waiter/waitress, host/hostess, maid/houseman/room attendant, bellhop, or groundsperson—will be invaluable to you as you begin to plan and develop your career in the hotel industry. It will give you an opportunity to learn what these people do and how departments interact, as well as expose you to the momentum of a hotel—the time frame of service available for the guest, management applications, and service concept applications, to name just a few.

Your work experience will enable you to evaluate theoretical concepts offered in the classroom. You will have a basis for comparing work experiences with other students. You will also develop your own beliefs and behaviors, which can be applied to other hotel properties throughout your career. At times, you will have to think on your feet in order to resolve a guest complaint, to evaluate equipment proposals, to reorganize work areas for efficiency, or to achieve cost-effective spending. It is this work experience that provides you with the proper foundation on which to base a successful career.

Professional Memberships

A professional trade organization is a group of people who have voluntarily pooled their efforts to achieve a set of goals. These goals may have a political nature, such as lobbying legislators or providing certification of achievement.

Professional trade organizations in the hospitality industry serve its members in many ways. First and foremost, they are a political voice for you in government. Through use of membership fees, these organizations are able to lobby local, state, and federal legislators to be sure the entrepreneur's views are recognized. These organizations also offer significant opportunities for continuing education by sponsoring seminars and trade shows. They offer group plans for insurance and other programs that can be very cost-efficient to the entrepreneur. Professional trade associations also allow you to interact with others in the industry on both a professional and a social level. Valuable advice and rewarding friendships often result.

Ports of Entry

A review of the organizational structure of a hotel shows that there are many departmental managers in a large organization. Which area is the best for you to enter to develop your career goals? Four of the ports of entry are marketing and sales, front office, food and beverage, and controller. It is impossible to say which is the best port of entry; all are avenues for career development.

The hotel industry demands a great deal from its professionals. All employees must have extensive knowledge of all areas of the facility, and they must understand the overall function of all departments. This understanding must be reflected in professional business plans. Employees must also have good communication skills and good interpersonal skills. The industry requires great flexibility in scheduling work responsibilities and personal life. It demands that the professional understand the entrepreneurial role of the corporate owners while operating within budgeted resources.

Students who enter the lodging industry will find that each area in which they work contributes to a good background for the ultimate position of general manager. When trying to decide where to begin, consider reviewing the job responsibilities of various department managers, to learn what types of tasks are required to complete each job and who is involved in doing so.

Try to work in as many areas as you can before you take the leap into a general manager position. The job will be a lot easier, and you will go a long way toward meeting the establishment's goals, if you are well prepared. You will make mistakes, no matter how much experience you have had; however, your success rate will be much higher if you have a varied background in many departments.

Researching Growth Areas in the Hospitality Industry

Areas that offer the most potential for growth need to be explored. Since such areas change frequently, it is not possible to list the most current trends in a textbook. However, some of the trends that support continued growth and strong business activity are regularly reported in such publications as *Trends in the Lodging Industry* by Pannell, Kerr, and Forster. They usually cover such issues as new hotel developments; hotels under consideration; activities of convention and visitors' bureaus; strength of local economies; development of business, recreation, and arts activities; and need for office space; as well as area hotel occupancy percentages and average room rates. This information is listed for selected cities both within the United States and at international sites.

The Internet is increasingly being used as a method for researching career opportunities in hospitality management. Various search engines will produce multiple listings of hospitality recruiters with key words such as "hotel manager," "front office manager," and "hotel careers." Also, professional hospitality organizations usually offer a job-posting service on their Web sites.

The Internet provides many opportunities for a new graduate to examine trends that are driving the industry and new technologies that will shape a career in hotel management. This information will assist a job applicant in exploring the employment possibilities and prospects in different geographic areas.

Your survey of career possibilities should include a review of a potential employer's economic performance on a balance sheet and other selected features of its profit-and-loss statement. This information is available on computerized business databases. Take

INTERNATIONAL HIGHLIGHTS

Students of hotel management should consider international employment opportunities. A recent listing of international hotel openings in *Hotel & Motel Management* included Global Hotel Development Group's efforts to construct six hotels in Poland in 2001. Jones Lang LaSalle Hotels offered research concerning a $700 million addition to the Indian hotel industry. "An additional 4,000 upscale and upper-upscale rooms are expected by 2004, and room supply will be driven by growth in Mumbai, Delhi, and Chennai."[18]

FRONTLINE REALITIES

Esther, front office manager of The Times Extended-Stay Hotel, received a phone call from the home office of The Times Hotel Management Company asking her to participate in a meeting to discuss the new trend in long-term visitors. The home office is thinking of renovating some of the rooms to reach the guest who wants to stay for 5 to 15 days. How would you prepare for this meeting?

the time to research the economic potential of the company you are considering. Your preinterview preparations should include reviewing the regional economic prospects and the company's economic performance. This preparation could set the stage for an investment that lasts many years, perhaps a lifetime.

Solution to Opening Dilemma

The effort you put into preparing for a visit to a career fair is essential for making this a learning and networking opportunity for you. Some typical questions you could use when visiting with a representative from a limited-service hotel include, "What are the typical management responsibilities of an assistant general manager in your organization? What types of visitors frequent your hotels during the week and on the weekend? What is the typical size of your hotels?" Questions you may want to consider for visiting with a representative from a full-service hotel could include, "What size staff is employed in your hotel? Do you have any convention hotels in your portfolio? What are the services that you typically include in a hotel in your organization?" These types of questions will open the lines of communication for you and help you present yourself as a future professional.

Chapter Recap

This chapter introduced the future professional to the hotel industry. It began with a historical review, including founders of the hotel industry—Statler, Hilton, Ritz, Astor, Waldorf, Wilson, J. W. Marriott and J. W. Marriott Jr., Henderson and Moore, and Schultz. It also discussed historical developments that have shaped the products and services offered to guests, management trends, and economic factors such as the atrium concept, marketing and operational emphasis, geographic relocation, the emergence of limited-service hotels, the major reorganization of 1987–1988, adoption of total quality management, and various technological advances in the hotel industry. It provided an overview of the hotel industry in terms of types of hotels; market orientation/location—residential, commercial, airport, and highway; sales indicators of occupancy, average daily rate, and RevPAR; levels of service—full-service, all-suites, limited-service, and extended-stay; and type of affiliation or nonaffiliation—franchise, referral, company-owned, management contract, or independent ownership. A review of trends that foster growth in the hotel industry was presented—leisure time, me/pleasure concept, discretionary income, family size, household size, business travel, female business traveler, and travel as an experience. Factors affecting a student's career development choice were discussed, including educational preparation, work experience, professional memberships, ports of entry in a hotel, and researching growth areas in the hospitality industry.

End of Chapter Questions

1. Name some of the hotels you have visited. What were some of the exciting things you noticed while you were a guest there?

2. With which departments of the hotel did you come into contact before, during, and after your visit at the property?

3. Investigate some of the properties in your area. In what year were they built? What kind of competition did they have? What services or facilities did they introduce to your community?

4. How do residential and commercial properties differ?

5. What are the four most common locations for hotel properties? What determines the end destination of the guest?

6. Define sales indicators. Give working examples of these concepts.

7. Define four levels of service. Relate them to room rates and guest expectations.

8. Name some of the types of properties developed by major chains to meet demands by market segments.

9. Differentiate between franchises and company-owned properties in a chain. What is the difference between franchises and referral groups?

10. What are the major differences between chain and independent properties?

11. Review a recent article in the *Wall Street Journal* that reports on growth in leisure time of the American worker, the me/pleasure concept, discretionary income, or travel habits of the business traveler.

12. List the local attractions in your area that may entice visitors. Do these attractions provide education, culture, or personal development? What makes them attractions?

13. Compare your career plans with the concepts presented in this chapter. Do you feel the steps presented here will be useful to you in your first job? In subsequent jobs?

14. Go to a current hospitality-related Web site such as www.hotel-online.com and research a trend in the hotel industry such as real estate investment trusts (REITs), extended-stay hotels, or RevPAR. How does that concept affect your future career plans?

15. Go to the Web site of the American Hotel & Lodging Association (www.ahla.com) and determine how this professional trade association (formerly known as the American Hotel & Motel Association) will be helpful to you in your future career.

CASE STUDY 101

Professor Catherine Vicente has allotted time in the HRI-201 Introduction to Front Office Management course for a field trip this semester. After the first few lectures, she wants to take her class to the hotel establishments in the vicinity of City College. The area is well known for its tourist attractions and is the headquarters of several major U.S. businesses. She appoints a group of students to assist her in setting up tours.

One of the students, Maria, is a resident of the area and suggests they visit the grand old St. Thomas Hotel in the downtown area. She would also like to see a hotel located at the Wide World Airport. Ryan, another student, has worked at a limited-service property in his hometown. He understands there is another hotel in that chain located on the outskirts of the city. David, who is applying for a job at a local hotel, wants to get information on all-suites hotels. Linda has heard there is a new extended-stay hotel in town and wants to know what makes that type of hotel different from a limited-service hotel.

The group has sifted through all the requests and decided to form five teams to visit these places. Each team will appoint one spokesperson for a panel discussion. The spokesperson will present a five-minute summary of what was learned from the visit.

What items do you think each spokesperson will include in his or her summary?

CASE STUDY 102

A recent survey in a suburban community has revealed that there will be an influx of new citizens into the area. Several computer industries will be relocating to this area, and they are expected to employ 25,000 persons at all levels of the organizations. Also, one of these computer companies will locate its corporate headquarters here, with an additional 500 executives arriving soon.

The local hotel association has contacted Professor Catherine Vicente of the HRI program at City College to assist them in determining the impact these new residents of the area will have on their hotels with regard to occupancy and use of facilities.

If you were Professor Vicente, what actions would you undertake? Justify your responses with regard to hotel operations and development. If you lived in this community, how would these developments affect your career in the hotel industry?

Notes

1. Madelin Schneider, "20th Anniversary," *Hotels & Restaurants International* 20, no. 8 (August 1986): 35–36.
2. 1993 Grolier Electronic Publishing.
3. Paul R. Dittmer and Gerald G. Griffin, *The Dimensions of the Hospitality Industry: An Introduction* (New York: John Wiley & Sons, 2002), 56.
4. 1993 Grolier Electronic Publishing.
5. 1993 Grolier Electronic Publishing.
6. Dittmer and Griffin, *Dimensions of the Hospitality Industry*, 41–43.
7. John Meyjes, Lou Hammond & Associates, 39 E. Fifty-first Street, New York, N.Y. 10022.
8. Ray Sawyer, "Pivotal Era Was Exciting," *Hotel & Motel Management* 210, no. 14 (August 14, 1995): 28
9. Marriott Corporate Relations, Marriott Drive, Department 977.01, Washington, D.C. 20058.
10. ITT Sheraton Corporation, Public Relations Department, 60 State Street, Boston, Mass. 02109.
11. Saul F. Leonard, "Laws of Supply, Demand Control Industry," *Hotel & Motel Management* 210 no. 14 (August 14, 1995): 74.
12. Ibid., 74, 80.
13. Ibid., 80.
14. P. Anthony Brown, "Hotel REITs—Legislation Heralds a New Era," *Virginia Hospitality and Leisure Executive Report* (spring 2000), as reported for Arthur Andersen at hotel-online.com: www.hotel-online.com/Neo/Trends/Andersen. (Copyright © 2000 Andersen.)
15. Highland Group, "Survey Results of the Extended Stay Lodging Industry," 1111 Rosedale Drive, Atlanta, Ga. 30306, as reported in www.hotel-online.com/Neo/News/PressReleases1998/ExtendedStaySurvey_March98.html.
16. Paul Criscillis Jr., "January RevPAR Grows Nearly Ten Percent at Suburban Lodge Company-Owned Hotels," Suburban Lodges of America (120 Interstate N. Parkway SE, Atlanta, Ga. 30339).
17. Tony Lima, "Chains vs. Independents," *Lodging Hospitality* 43, no. 8 (July 1987): 82.
18. "International News," *Hotel & Motel Management* 216, no. 2 (February 5, 2001), 6.

Key Words

all-suites
American Hotel & Lodging Association
atrium concept
average daily rate (ADR)
business affiliations
chain
chain affiliations
commercial hotels
company-owned property
conference call

demographic data
discretionary income
distance learning
ecotourists
extended stay
front office
full service
independent hotel
in-service education
limited service

management contract property
market segments
mass marketing
occupancy percentage
PictureTel
potential gross income
psychographic data
real estate investment trust (REIT)

referral property
residential hotels
revenue per available room (RevPAR)
room revenues
sales indicators
total quality management (TQM)
yield percentage

Hotel Organization and the Front Office Manager

OPENING DILEMMA

At a recent staff meeting, the general manager of The Times Hotel asked if

anyone wanted to address the group. The director of housekeeping indicated

that he was at a loss in trying to work with the front desk clerks. He had

repeatedly called the desk clerks last Tuesday to let them know that general

housecleaning would be performed on the seventh and eighth floors on Wednes-

day morning and that they should not assign rooms on those floors to guests on Tuesday

night. When the cleaning crew came to work on Wednesday morning, they were faced

with 14 occupied rooms on the seventh floor and 12 occupied rooms on the eighth floor.

This cost the hotel several hundred dollars because the cleaning crew was from an out-

sourced contract company, which charged the hotel a basic fee for failure to comply with

the contract. The front office manager retorted that a bus group called two weeks ago

and asked if any rooms were available because there was a mix-up in room rates at the

bus group's original hotel. The front office manager indicated that something must have

CHAPTER FOCUS POINTS

- Organization of lodging properties
- Organization of the front office department
- Staffing the front office
- Function of the front office manager

gone awry in the computer system. After all, this was a good opportunity to bring in 26

additional room nights.

Organization of Lodging Properties

The objective of most hospitality establishments is to produce a profit. To meet this goal, factors such as current economic conditions, marketing plans, competition, and staff size and ability are constantly reviewed.

The **general manager,** the person in charge of directing and leading the hotel staff in meeting its financial, environmental, and community responsibilities, develops and stylizes organization charts that fit his or her plan to meet the goals of the particular company. The **organization charts**—schematic drawings that list management positions in an organization—that are included in this chapter are offered only as instructional examples. An organization chart represents the span of control for the general manager. Not all hotels have every position listed in these organization charts. Persons pursuing a career in the hotel industry will be called upon many times throughout their career to develop or restructure an organization. The people who are part of these operational plans will have a direct influence on the type of structure you develop or regroup. The goals of the organization must be paramount in the decision-making process. However, there must be flexibility to make the plan work. This section points out the major organizational features of a lodging property and typical managerial duties of the people within the organization.

It is not uncommon for a general manager of a property to move people around in various departments of the hotel. This is done for many reasons. A **front office manager,** the person responsible for leading the front office staff in delivering hospitality, may express interest in the position of **controller,** the internal accountant for the hotel, or in a position in the marketing and sales department. The general manager realizes that a candidate must possess certain skills before being placed in any new position. To prepare someone for an opening in the controller's office, the general manager may assign some of the busywork of the controller's office to the front office manager. The front office manager might also spend some slack periods with the **director of marketing and sales**— the person who analyzes available markets, and sells these products and services at a profit—to become familiar with that department.

The general manager may also use the weekly staff meeting to explain the financial condition and marketing plans of the property. This tactic will reinforce the management team concept. By exposing interested employees to the responsibilities of other departments and by keeping the staff informed of the current situation of the property, the general manager is enabling staff members to meet their career goals within the organization.

Flexibility is the key to hospitality organization. On the operations level, familiarity with the staff's strengths and weaknesses is essential to meet the demands of a particular situation. When the property experiences an expected slow period, regrouping may be necessary to maintain full-time positions. The front office manager may have to assist the marketing and sales office in advertising or hosting tour directors for a specific weekend. The food and beverage director might have to spend some time in the controller's office completing reports and developing budgets with the controller. This interdepartmental cooperation provides the backdrop for a smooth-running organization. Such flexibility prevents departmental jealousies and territoriality from becoming roadblocks to communication.

Organization Charts

The major positions found in a large, full-service hotel or resort are presented in Figure 2-1. This lodging property features:

- 500+ rooms in a commercial property
- Center-city or suburban location
- (ADR) $110 **average daily rate**—number of rooms sold versus room income
- 70 **percent occupancy**—number of rooms sold versus number of rooms available
- 58 **percent yield**—number of rooms sold at average daily rate versus number of rooms available at **rack rate,** the highest room rate category offered by a hotel
- $18.5 million in revenues
- Full service
- Chain—company ownership
- **Corporate guests**—frequent guests who are employed by a company and receive a special room rate
- **Convention guests**—guests who attend a large convention and receive a special room rate
- Meeting and banquet rooms
- Dining rooms
- Lounge with entertainment
- Exercise facilities with indoor pool
- Gift shop
- Business office and retail rentals
- Attached parking garage
- **In-house laundry**—a hotel-operated department that launders guest linens
- **Referral reservation service**—a service offered by a management company of a chain of hotels to franchisee members

To function as a well-run lodging facility, this property requires the following department heads:

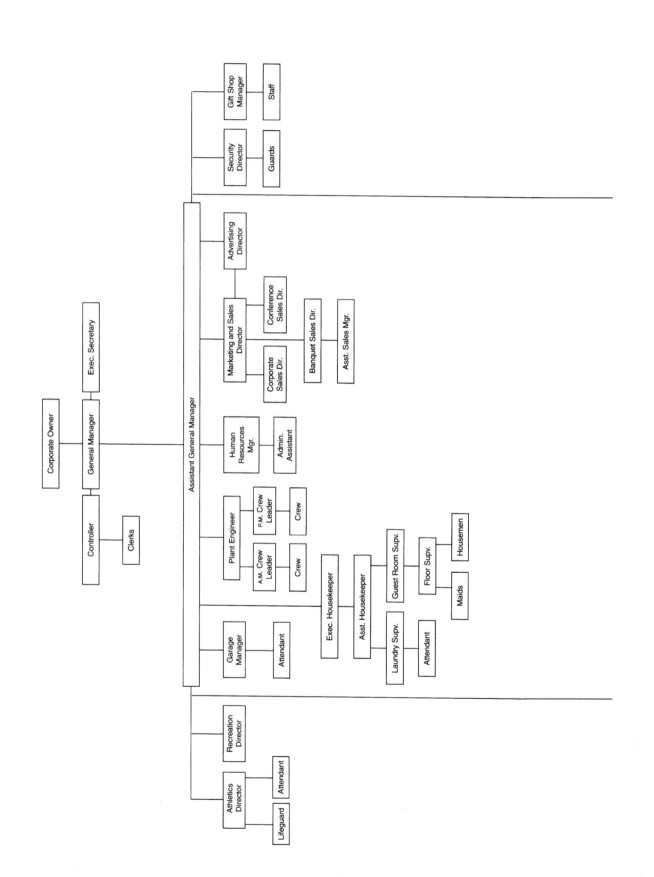

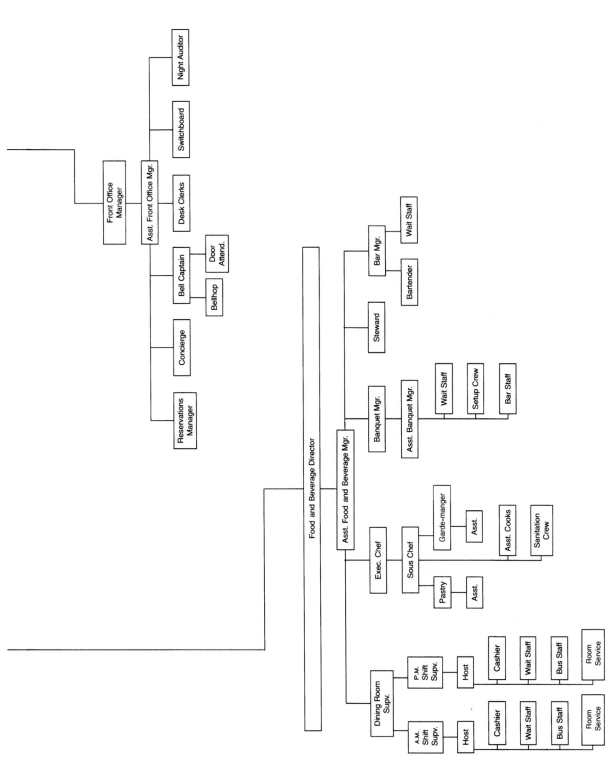

Figure 2-1. *The organization of a large, full-service hotel requires many positions to provide service to the guest.*

- General manager
- Assistant general manager
- Controller
- Plant engineer
- Executive housekeeper
- Human resources manager
- Recreation director
- Athletics director
- Marketing and sales director
- Gift shop manager
- Front office manager
- Food and beverage director
- Garage manager

The corporate owners have entrusted the financial success of this organization to the general manager, who must organize departments to provide optimum service to the guest. Each department is well organized and staffed to allow the supervisor time to plan and develop the major revenue-producing areas. The marketing and sales director, gift shop manager, front office manager, food and beverage director, and garage manager develop programs that increase sales and profits and improve cost-control methods. Those supervisors who do not head income-generating departments—controller, plant engineer, executive housekeeper, human resources manager, recreation director, and athletics director—provide services to the guest, principally behind the scenes.

For example, the controller develops clear and concise performance reports that reflect budget targets. The physical **plant engineer,** the person responsible for the operation and maintenance of the physical plant, establishes an effective preventive maintenance program. The **executive housekeeper,** the person responsible for the upkeep of the guest rooms and public areas of the lodging property as well as control of guest room inventory items, keeps on top of new trends in controlling costs and effective use of personnel. The **human resources manager,** the person who assists department managers in organizing personnel functions and developing employees, provides leadership in attracting new hires and maintaining a stable yet progressive approach to utilization of personnel. The **recreation director,** the person who is in charge of developing and organizing recreational activities for guests, and the **athletics director,** who is responsible for supervising physical exercise facilities for guests, provide direct hospitality services for the guest, helping to ensure a safe and interesting guest stay.

Figure 2-2 outlines the organization of a somewhat smaller lodging property. This hotel features:

- 200 rooms in a commercial property
- Suburban location
- 65 percent occupancy
- 53 percent yield

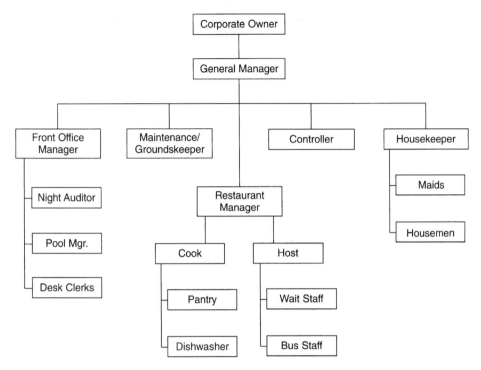

Figure 2-2. *Notice that several of the positions listed in the full-service hotel organization chart have been eliminated from this one for a medium-size lodging property.*

- $4.5 million in revenues
- $75 average daily rate
- Full service
- Chain—franchise
- Corporate guests
- Local-community guests
- Dining room
- Lounge
- Outdoor pool
- Referral reservation service

The department heads required include:

- General manager
- Maintenance/groundskeeper
- Front office manager
- Controller

- Restaurant manager
- Housekeeper

This managerial staff seems somewhat skeletal when compared to that of a large hotel or resort. This type of organization chart is possible because the level of service provided to guests has been reduced. At this property, the guest's stay is one to two nights, and a dining room and lounge are provided for convenience. Many of the department heads are **working supervisors,** which means they participate in the actual work performed while supervising. Laundry and other services are contracted out. The controller provides accounting services as well as human resources management. The maintenance/grounds-keeper oversees indoor and outdoor facilities. The front office manager and the clerks take care of reservations as well as registrations, posting, checkout, and the like. The restaurant manager works very closely with the cook and hostess in maintaining quality and cost control and guest services. The housekeeper inspects and cleans rooms and maintains linen and cleaning supply inventories as well as providing leadership for the housekeeping staff.

Figure 2-3 shows the organization chart of a typical limited-service property, much scaled down from that of a large hotel. The features of the property are:

- 150 rooms in a commercial property
- Highway location
- 60 percent occupancy
- 51 percent yield
- $2.2 million in revenues
- $65 average daily rate
- Limited service
- Chain—franchise
- In-house laundry
- Vacation travelers
- Business travelers
- Complimentary **continental breakfast**—juice, fruit, sweet roll, and/or cereal

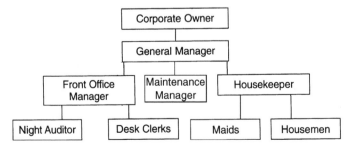

Figure 2-3. *The organization chart for a small, limited-service lodging property includes only minimal staffing. Several duties have been combined under various positions.*

- Referral reservation service
- **Business services and communications center**—guest services that include copying, computers, fax, and so forth

The department heads include:

- General manager
- Front office manager
- Housekeeper
- Maintenance manager

The general manager is a working supervisor in that he or she participates in the actual work performed while supervising at the front desk. The general manager at this type of property assists with marketing plans, reservations, maintenance, and groundskeeping, maintains financial records; and implements cost-control measures. The front office manager works regular shifts to provide coverage along with the night auditor and desk clerks. The housekeeper, also a working supervisor, assists the **room attendants,** employees who clean and maintain guest rooms and public areas.

The organization charts shown here have been developed by evaluating the needs of the guests. The organization of departments and the subsequent staffing are influenced by the labor pool available, economic conditions of the region, and the financial goals of the organization. Each organization chart varies depending on the factors influencing a particular lodging establishment. Flexibility is essential in providing service to the guest and leadership to the staff.

Typical Job Responsibilities of Department Managers

As you begin your career in the lodging industry, you will undoubtedly come in contact with the various department managers in a hotel. Some of the positions seem to be shrouded in mystery, while others are clear. The controller, for example, holds one of those positions that seems to be performed behind the scenes, and little is obvious as to his or her role. The security director seems to be everywhere in the hotel, but what does this person do, and for what is he or she responsible? The food and beverage director holds a very visible position that seems to encompass much. The general manager must see both the forest and the trees, overseeing all operations while staying on top of the small details. How can all of these positions be coordinated to provide hospitality to the guest and profit to the investors?

General Manager

Several years ago I invited a guest speaker to my class. This person was the general manager of a local inn in our community. He was very well prepared for the lecture and described the organization chart and staff he had developed. After he explained the work that goes on in the various departments and the responsibilities of the respective supervisors, a student asked, "What do you do as the general manager if all the work is being done by your staff?" This type of honest question has always made me terribly aware that the role of the general manager is not easy to understand. Indeed, detailing this managerial role could fill volumes, encompassing decades of experience. However, the legitimacy of the question still compels me to be specific in describing this very important job in the organization chart.

The leadership provided by the general manager is undoubtedly the most important quality a person brings to this position. He or she orchestrates the various department directors in meeting the financial goals of the organization through their employees. The general manager is required to use the full range of managerial skills—such as planning, decision making, organizing, staffing, controlling, directing, and communicating—to develop a competent staff. Performance is judged according to how effectively supervisors have been directed to meet the goals of the organization. Efficiency depends not on how well tasks are performed, but on how well employees are motivated and instructed to meet the goals and objectives of the plans the general manager and staff have formulated. Figure 2-4 presents a group of managers, supervisors, and frontline employees who carry out the goals of the general manager.

The plans developed by the general manager along with the department supervisors provide the vision the business needs to compete for the hospitality markets. The evaluation of candidates for positions based on a well-structured division of labor begins the process of meeting the goals and objectives of the planning stage. Who should be chosen to meet the demands of a leader of operations? What skills and strengths are necessary to get the job done? What business acumen must this person have? What vision does this person bring to the job? How will the new hire fit into the existing staff? These are just a few questions that a general manager must consider and act upon.

The **operational reports**—operational data on critical financial aspects of hotel operations—that a general manager must review can be overwhelming. However, the efficient general manager should know which key operating statistics reflect the profitability and efficiency of operations. Do the food cost percentage, labor cost percentage, alcohol beverage cost percentage, and sales item analysis provide enough information to indicate the success of the food and beverage department? Are the daily occupancy percentage, average daily room rate, and total sales for the day adequate to indicate a profitable hotel? Each general manager has developed key indicators that measure the financial success and operational success of various department directors. These concepts are flexible, depending on the goals the corporate ownership has established.

Communicating ideas and goals and providing feedback on performance are skills the general manager must develop. The general manager is a pivotal link in the communication process. Each department director takes the lead from communications received (or not received) from the general manager. Weekly staff meetings serve as a major vehicle for sharing communication. In addition, individual meetings with department directors enable the communication process to become more effective. At these one-on-one meet-

Figure 2-4. *The general manager of a hotel is responsible for orchestrating the efforts of managers and employees to produce a financially successful establishment. (Photo courtesy of Red Lion Hotels.)*

ings, the department director can transform organizational goals into operational functions.

The general manager offers supervisory training to his or her staff in practical terms. For example, the director of marketing and sales may have set a goal of increasing guest room sales by 10 percent for the next quarter. At an individual meeting with the general manager, the director of marketing and sales will agree to meet that goal over the next four months.

What does a general manager do? He or she provides leadership to meet organizational goals of profitability and service. It is acquired by studying theories of management and the behavior of other managers as well as actually practicing leadership and receiving constructive criticism from superiors on efforts expended. The role of general manager is a professional position. It is a career goal based on operations experience and education.

The role of the general manager, whether in a full-service or limited-service property, must encompass the concepts previously discussed. The general manager in a limited-service property may perform additional hands-on responsibilities, but he or she is required to provide leadership to the other members of the management team. The use of **total quality management (TQM)** concepts, which involve application of managerial concepts to understand operational processes and develop methods to improve those processes (described in Chapter 11), allows managers in full-service and limited-service properties to extend their role of leadership to frontline supervisors and employees. In full-service and limited-service properties, where profit margins are based on lean departmental budgets, total quality management is encouraged.

Assistant General Manager

The **assistant general manager** of a lodging property holds a major responsibility in developing and executing plans developed by the corporate owners, general manager, and other members of the management staff. The relationship between the general manager and the assistant general manager must be founded on trust, skill, and excellent communications. The assistant general manager works with department directors to meet their respective goals and objectives through efficient operations. Often he or she is the liaison between management and operations. The more the assistant general manager is informed of the reasons for management decisions, the better able he or she is to communicate plans to the operations supervisors. The assistant general manager is sometimes referred to as rooms division manager, who is responsible for the entire front office operations, which includes front desk, housekeeping, bell staff, concierge, and parking garage.

The assistant general manager often must oversee the beginning of a job and ensure that others complete it. This position also requires the completion and review of statistical reports, which the assistant general manager summarizes and shares with the general manager. The assistant general manager is "everywhere" on the property, checking on operations, providing feedback, and offering assistance as needed. This job requires a wide variety of previous operational skills, such as front office, food and beverage, marketing and sales, and accounting. Depending on the size of the operation and the personnel available, a large property may divide these responsibilities into rooms division manager and operations division manager.

Limited-service hotels usually do not have this type of position in their organization chart. The department managers report directly to the general manager to streamline guest services and operational budgets. Again, the general manager of a limited-service property may perform additional hands-on responsibilities, but he or she is required to provide direct leadership to the other members of the management team.

Food and Beverage Director

The **food and beverage director** is responsible for the efficient operation of the kitchen, dining rooms, banquet service, room service, and lounge. This includes managing a multitude of details with the supervisors of these outlets. Such details include food quality, sanitation, inventory, cost control, training, room setup, cash control, and guest service, to name a few. The food and beverage director keeps a keen eye on new trends in food and beverage merchandising, cost-control factors in food and beverage preparation, and kitchen utilities. The food and beverage director works closely with the assistant food and beverage director, a highly skilled executive chef, a dining room supervisor, a banquet manager, and a bar manager. This team's goal is to provide quality products and services on a 24-hour basis, every day of the year. Constant supervision of products, employees, and services is required to ensure a fair return on investment.

Although food and beverage are served for a continental breakfast or cocktail hour at a limited-service property, there is no food and beverage director position. The responsibility for serving food and beverages is an extension of the front office manager's duties. However, the same principles of sanitation, food purchasing and storage, marketing, standards of service, and so forth need to be followed to provide good service to the guest.

Physical Plant Engineer

The plant engineer is very important in the overall delivery of service to the guest. This person oversees a team of electricians; plumbers, heating, ventilating, and air-conditioning contractors; and general repairpeople to provide behind-the-scenes services to the guests and employees of the lodging property. With today's emphasis on preventive maintenance and energy savings, he or she must be able to develop a plan of action that will keep the lodging property well maintained, within budget targets. Knowledge of current advances in equipment and machinery is essential. This position requires a range of experience in general maintenance and a positive attitude about updating skills and management concepts through continuing education.

The plant engineer interacts with all the departments of the hotel. This person is part of the management team and can be relied on to provide sound advice about structural stability, equipment maintenance, and environmental control. He or she can be one of the most treasured assistants in the lodging business.

A role similar to that of the plant engineer in a limited-service property is that of **maintenance manager,** a staff member who maintains the heating and air-conditioning plant, produces guest room keys, helps housekeeping attendants as required, and assists with safety and security of personal comfort to the guest. The limited-service property emphasizes quality in guest service, which is delivered by an efficient staff.

Executive Housekeeper

The executive housekeeper is responsible for the upkeep of the guest rooms and public areas of the lodging property. This person truly must work through other people to get the job done. Each room attendant must be thoroughly trained in cleaning techniques. Each **floor inspector,** a person who supervises the housekeeping function on a floor of a hotel, and each housekeeping employee must be trained in standard inspection techniques. (Many hotels are moving away from the use of floor inspectors, however.) Speed and efficiency are paramount in performing the very important service of maintaining guest rooms and public areas.

Skill in supervising unskilled labor is essential. Survival-fluency in foreign languages is important to the executive housekeeper, who needs to communicate effectively with employees. Accurate scheduling of employees is also necessary to maintain control over labor costs. The executive housekeeper is also responsible for maintaining and controlling an endless inventory, which includes linens, soap, guest amenities, furniture, in-house marketing materials, live and artificial plants, and more. The executive housekeeper, like the plant engineer, must keep abreast of new ideas and techniques through trade journals and continuing education courses.

If the lodging property operates an in-house laundry, this is also supervised by the executive housekeeper. The equipment, cleaning materials, cost controls, and scheduling are handled in cooperation with the laundry supervisor.

The limited-service property depends on this member of the management team to supervise a staff that provides clean rooms and operates an in-house laundry. This hands-on supervisor works with the staff to provide the many behind-the-scenes guest services required. Because many limited-service properties are fairly small, the housekeeper travels the elevators of these high-rise buildings, stopping at each floor to provide employees with constant supervision and motivation.

Interdepartmental cooperation and communication with the front desk and maintenance department in full-service and limited-service hotels are vital for the executive housekeeper. The release of cleaned rooms for occupancy and the scheduling of periodic maintenance are only two functions demonstrating why interdepartmental cooperation is critical. In addition, the marketing and sales efforts in both types of hotels depend on the housekeeper to enforce cleanliness and appearance standards in the public areas so that guests are attracted to and impressed by the property.

Human Resources Manager

In a full-service lodging property, the luxury of employing a human resources manager is beneficial for everyone. This person is responsible for administering federal, state, and local employment laws as well as advertising for and screening job candidates and inter-

INTERNATIONAL HIGHLIGHTS

Managers in a hotel have a particular responsibility to prepare their employees to communicate with their guests. This is very important for international guests. Frontline employees can assist an international guest by adopting an attitude of "hospitality without question." This simple concept encompasses a frontline employee's maintaining a watchful eye for guests who appear confused, express difficulty in communicating in the local language, or seem hesitant about responding to inquiries. Training programs that include role-playing exercises that focus on visitors who can't communicate in the local language and employees who have to respond to their inquiries allow frontline employees to practice hospitality without question. This concept can be further advanced when a front office manager maintains an inventory of current employees who speak various international languages.

viewing, selecting, orienting, training, and evaluating employees. Each department director can rely on the human resources manager to provide leadership in the administration of complex personnel.

Staffing a food and beverage or housekeeping department involves many time-consuming tasks:

- Writing and placing classified ads
- Preinterviewing, interviewing, testing, and selecting candidates
- Orienting, training, and evaluating new employees

The preparation of job descriptions, while perceived by many in the hotel industry as a luxury, is mandatory if the employees are represented by a **collective bargaining unit**—that is, a labor union. The human resources manager can assist in preparing the job analysis and subsequent job description. This process helps him or her develop realistic job specifications.

The development of employees by providing a plan for the growth of each employee within a hotel takes a great deal of planning and evaluating. Each department director works under pressure to meet budget guidelines, quality-control levels, sales quotas, and other goals. The human resources manager can assist each director in making plans to motivate employees, to develop career projections for them, to provide realistic pay increases, and to establish employment policies that reflect positively on the employer.

Limited-service properties do not employ a human resources manager but elect to divide the responsibilities among department heads. Although emphasis remains on well-planned and -delivered human resources activities, the streamlined limited-service property relies on interdepartmental cooperation to accomplish its objectives.

Marketing and Sales Director

Notice that in the title of this position, "marketing" is emphasized. The person in this position plays an essential role in all departments of the hotel. An effective director of marketing and sales will not only want to attract external sales such as conventions, small business conferences, wedding receptions, and dining room and lounge business but will also provide direction for promoting in-house sales to the guests.

This is an exciting position that requires endless creativity. The director of marketing and sales is constantly evaluating new markets, reviewing the needs of the existing markets, watching new promotions by the competition, organizing sales blitzes, working with community and professional groups to maintain public relations, working with other department directors to establish product and service specifications and in-house promotional efforts, and following up on details, details, details. This is a high-energy position that not only provides financial vitality but also fosters the attainment of financial goals by all departments.

Some limited-service properties employ a full-time or half-time marketing and sales director. This position may also be shared by the general manager and front office manager. The previous discussion of duties (with the exception of soliciting food and beverage business) performed by the marketing and sales director in a full-service hotel is also a good indicator of what is required in a limited-service hotel. Competition for room sales to the corporate, group, and pleasure travel markets is enormous, and each hotel has to address this planning need.

Front Office Manager

Given the significance of the role of the front office manager in this text, it will be detailed more completely later on in this chapter. Some of the major responsibilities of the front office manager include reviewing the final draft of the **night audit,** a daily review of the financial accounting procedures at the front desk and other guest service areas during the previous 24-hour period and an analysis of operating results; operating and monitoring the reservation system; developing and operating an effective communication system with front office staff and other department directors; supervising daily registrations and checkouts; overseeing and developing employees; establishing in-house sales programs at the front desk; preparing budgets and cost-control systems; forecasting room sales; and maintaining business relationships with regular corporate and community leaders. The front office manager works with an assistant front office manager, a night auditor, a reservations manager, and a bell captain to tend to the details of running an efficient department.

These are just a few of the responsibilities of the front office manager. The front office is a pivotal point in communication among in-house sales, delivery of service to the guest, and financial operations. It requires an individual who can manage the many details of guest needs, employee supervision, interdepartmental communication, and transmittal of financial information. This exciting position enables the person to develop an overview of the lodging property with regard to finances and communication.

Controller

The controller is the internal accountant of a hotel. He or she is responsible for the actual and effective administration of financial data produced on a daily basis in the hotel. In the lodging property, daily financial status must be available to corporate owners, management, and guests. This requires a well-organized staff, not only to prepare oper-

---

FRONTLINE REALITIES

A future guest has called the hotel and wants to arrange a small dinner party for his guests on the first day of his visit. The marketing and sales office is closed for the day, and the banquet manager has left the property for a few hours. What would you suggest that the front desk clerk do to assist this future guest?

ating statistics but also to assist the general manager in determining the effectiveness of each department manager. Often the general manager relies on the controller to provide financial insight into the operations of the property. These include cash flow, discounts, evaluation of insurance costs, fringe-benefit cost analysis, investment opportunities, computer technology applications, banking procedures, and more.

This department processes **accounts payable**—amounts of money the hotel owes to vendors; **accounts receivable**—amounts of money owed to the hotel by guests; the **general ledger**—a collection of accounts that the controller uses to organize the financial activities of the hotel; **statement of cash flows**—a projection of income from various income-generating areas of the hotel; the **profit-and-loss statement**—a listing of revenues and expenses for a certain time period; and the **balance sheet**—a listing of the financial position of the hotel at a particular point in time. It is a busy department that provides financial information to all department directors.

The general manager of a limited-service property acts as the controller with the assistance of the night auditor. (In some properties, the night audit is performed during the day, and the night auditor is replaced with a lower-salaried front desk clerk for late-night coverage.) Also, the ownership of a limited-service property hotel may be a part of a larger financial portfolio of a business, which assists the general manager to perform the controller's responsibilities.

Director of Security

The **director of security** works with department directors to develop cost-control procedures that help ensure employee honesty and guest safety. This person supervises an ongoing training program in cooperation with department directors to instruct employees in fire, job, and environmental safety procedures. Fictional stories often depict the security director as someone who investigates crimes after the fact. On the contrary, this person's primary responsibility is to implement programs that make employees "security-minded," helping to prevent crime from occurring.

Unfortunately, the lodging industry has always been involved in lawsuits, which have multiplied in both number and cost in recent years. A substantial body of law provides regulations under which properties must operate. Preventive security precautions are the central theme of the security department today. The director of security's background is usually in police or detective work or in security or intelligence in the armed services. He or she has usually developed an understanding of the criminal mind and the practices of criminals. This person is constantly on the lookout for suspicious people and circumstances.

This necessary position in a limited-service property is shared by the front office manager and the general manager. Outsourcing of security services for on-site and parking-lot patrol is also used. The outsourcing of this vital guest service does not relieve the general manager of the need to develop and provide ongoing procedures to train employees to become security-minded.

Parking Garage Manager

The responsibility of ensuring a safe environment for guests' vehicles falls to the **parking garage manager,** the person responsible for supervising the work of garage attendants and maintaining security of guests and cars in the parking garage. Garage maintenance, in cooperation with the engineering and housekeeping departments, is another responsibility of this position. Often a hotel rents out parking spaces to local businesses and professional people. The accounting process associated with this service involves the accurate billing and recording of funds and subsequent deposits. This person also has to develop budgets and recruit and train employees. The garage manager often provides driver assistance to guests when their cars break down. Providing directional information to departing guests is also a frequent task of the garage manager. Even though these jobs may seem small in the overall operation of a lodging property, they build a strong foundation in providing service to the guest.

Organization of the Front Office Department

The organization chart in Figure 2-5 depicts a typical organization of staff for a front office manager. The staff includes desk clerk, cashier, reservations manager, concierge, night auditor, telephone operator, bell staff, room key clerk, and elevator operator. Not all of these positions are found in every lodging establishment. In some operations, the front desk clerk acts as desk clerk, cashier, telephone operator, and reservations clerk, as required by the volume of business. Many large, full-service hotels employ the complete staff as listed.

Staffing the front desk positions incurs a cost to the lodging establishment. The front office manager, in consultation with the general manager, usually prepares a personnel budget that is related to salary levels throughout the lodging establishment.

The responsibilities of the front office staff are quite varied. The position of the **desk clerk** can encompass many duties, which typically include verifying guest reservations, registering guests, assigning rooms, distributing keys, communicating with the housekeeping staff, answering telephones, providing information about and directions to local attractions, accepting cash and giving change, and acting as liaison between the lodging establishment and the guest as well as the community.

The position of **cashier** includes processing guest checkouts and guest legal tender and providing change for guests. This position is found in a number of lodging establishments, and it helps to make the front desk workload manageable when a **full house,** a hotel that has all its guest rooms occupied (sometimes referred to as 100 percent occupancy) is checking out. Given the possibility that a 400-guest convention could all check out in a short time period, this division of labor is a well-planned concept. Even with the best-planned systems—such as **express checkout,** whereby the guest uses computer technology in a guest room or a computer in the hotel lobby to check out; **prior approved credit,** the

Eric O. Long, general manager of the Waldorf=Astoria in New York City, has been employed with Hilton Corporation for 30 years. He served in various management positions, including the Hilton Short Hills, Chicago Hilton and Towers, Hilton Walt Disney Village, Fontainebleau Hilton Resort, and the Palmer House.

His well-thought-out career with Hilton has allowed him to develop a strong network of relationships and vital experience to prepare him for the position he holds today. Mr. Long indicates that there are four major areas of responsibility in his job—finance, marketing, customer service, and human resources management. Although he has persons assigned to work on the day-to-day administration of those departments, he feels he is ultimately responsible for the success of those departments. For example, he wants to ensure that a marketing and sales plan is current and operating. He also attends an 8:00 A.M. customer feedback meeting each day to review feedback on the previous day's efforts to provide quality service. He adds that he wants to ensure that the level of talent in the organization is nurtured through motivation, training, development, and so forth.

Early in Mr. Long's career, his mentor encouraged him to gain expertise in any three areas of the hotel and a solid working knowledge in all the other areas. He feels this has been an overriding factor in his career progression. He encourages future hoteliers who are entering the field "to take complete ownership and responsibility for your own career. Don't take promotions just for the sake of the promotion; be selective of the moves that you make. Each move should be weighed against the potential that it will have in growing your career."

use of a credit card to establish creditworthiness; or **bill-to-account,** an internal billing process—the lines at the cashier station can be long when a guest is in a hurry.

The **reservations manager** is a position that can be found in many of the larger lodging establishments. This person is responsible for taking incoming requests for rooms and noting special requests for service. The particulars of this position are endless, aimed at providing the guest with requested information and services as well as accurate confirmation of these items. The reservations manager is responsible for keeping an accurate room inventory by using a reservation module of a property management system. This person must communicate very effectively with the marketing and sales department. Peak as well as slow periods of sales must be addressed with adequate planning.

The **night auditor** balances the daily financial transactions. This person may also serve as desk clerk for the night shift (11:00 P.M. to 7:00 A.M.). He or she must have a good grasp of accounting principles and the ability to resolve financial discrepancies. This position requires experience as a desk clerk and good communications with the controller.

The **telephone operator** has a very important job in the lodging establishment. This person must be able to locate the registered guests and management staff at a moment's notice. He or she is also expected to be able to deal with crises such as life-threatening emergencies. With the introduction of **call accounting,** a computer technology application that tracks guest phone calls and posts billing charges to lodging establishments, the

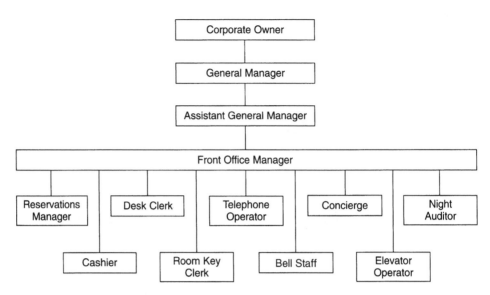

Figure 2-5. *This organization chart lists positions found in a front office.*

telephone operator's job has been simplified, as the tracking of telephone charges to reg-istered guests can now be done with ease. This person may also assist the desk clerk and cashier when necessary.

The **bell captain,** with the entourage of bellhops and door attendants, is a mainstay in the lodging establishment. The **bell staff** starts where the computerized property man-agement system stops. They are the people who lift and tote the baggage, familiarize the guest with his or her new surroundings, run errands, deliver supplies, and provide the guest with information on in-house marketing efforts and local attractions. These people also act as the hospitality link between the lodging establishment and the guest. They are an asset to a well-run lodging establishment.

The **key clerk** can be found in very large, full-service hotels that do not have electronic key systems. This clerk is responsible for issuing keys to registered guests and for related security measures. Often he or she will sort incoming mail for registered guests and the management staff. This position has become obsolete in most hotels.

The **elevator operator,** a person who manually operates the mechanical controls of the elevator, is almost an extinct species in the lodging establishment. This person has been replaced by self-operated elevators and escalators. Some of these people have been relo-cated to serve as **traffic managers,** who direct hotel guests to available elevators in the lobby. In large, full-service hotels, the traffic manager can be a welcome sight; often the confusion of check-ins and checkouts can be lessened when he or she is on duty.

The **concierge** (Figure 2-6) provides extensive information on entertainment, sports, amusements, transportation, tours, church services, and baby-sitting in the area. He or she must know the area intimately and must be able to meet the individual needs of each

Figure 2-6. *The concierge provides information on tourist attractions and entertainment in the area to hotel guests. (Photo courtesy of Lincoln Plaza Hotel & Conference Center, Reading, Pennsylvania.)*

guest. This person also obtains theater tickets and makes reservations in restaurants. In most cases, the concierge is stationed at a desk in the lobby of the lodging property.

The organization chart in Figure 2-7 portrays a much more simplified workforce than seen with a full-service property. The desk clerks perform multiple duties such as reservations and registrations, and they act as cashiers, telephone operators, and so forth. Whatever guest need is presented, the front desk clerk is called on to provide hospitality with efficiency and professionalism. In limited-service properties, the general manager may also assist, when needed, to process reservation requests, check guests in upon arrival, and check guests out upon departure.

The night auditor's role in a limited-service property is very different from that of his or her counterpart in a full-service hotel. Because there are usually no departmental transactions from restaurants, banquets, lounges, gift shops, or spas, the night auditor is mainly concerned with posting room and tax charges and preparing statistics for the hotel. With the utilization of computer technology, the completion of the night audit has been reduced to a minimum of time. As previously mentioned, this task may be performed early in the morning prior to guest checkouts.

Figure 2-7. *The front office staff in a limited-service hotel includes a minimal number of employees.*

Function of the Front Office Manager

A successful front office manager conveys the spirit of a particular lodging property to the customer. By applying management principles, he or she works through the front office staff to communicate feelings of warmth, caring, safety, and efficiency to each guest. The front office manager must train personnel in the technical aspects of the **property management system (PMS),** a hotel computer system that networks the software and hardware used in reservation and registration databases, point-of-sale systems, accounting systems, and other office software. He or she also must maintain the delicate balance between delivery of hospitality and service and promotion of the profit centers, and maintain the details of the communication system.

The front office manager has at his or her disposal the basic elements of effective management practice: employees, equipment, inventory (rooms to be sold), a budget, and sales opportunities. This manager is responsible for coordinating these basic elements to achieve the profit goals of the lodging property.

Front office employees must be trained properly to function within the guidelines and policies of the lodging establishment. The front office manager cannot assume that an employee knows how to do certain tasks. Every employee needs instructions and guidance in how to provide hospitality; front office employees' attitudes are of utmost importance to the industry. To ensure that the proper attitude prevails, the atmosphere in which employees work must motivate them to excel and nurture morale and teamwork.

The equipment available to the front office manager is varied. With the advent of computers, the property management system has provided the front office manager with an unlimited opportunity for managerial control. He or she can now easily track information such as zip codes of visitors, frequency of visits by corporate guests, and amount of revenue a particular conference generated and pass this information on to the marketing and sales department.

An unsold guest room is a sales opportunity lost forever. This is one of the major challenges of the front office manager. Cooperation between the marketing and sales department and the front office is necessary to develop profitable advertising and point-of-sale strategies. The subsequent training of front office personnel to seize every opportunity to sell vacant rooms helps to ensure that the financial goals of the lodging property are met.

Budgetary guidelines must be developed by the front office manager and the general manager, since the front office manager does have a large dollar volume under his or her control. The budgeting of money for payroll and supplies, the opportunity for daily sales, and accurate recording of guest charges require the front office manager to apply managerial skills.

The foremost concept that characterizes a front office manager is "team player." The front office manager does not labor alone to meet the profit goals of the lodging property. The general manager sets the goals, objectives, and standards for all departments to follow. The assistant manager offers the various department heads additional insight into meeting the operational needs of the establishment. The controller supplies valuable accounting information to the front office manager as feedback on current performance and meeting budgetary goals. The food and beverage manager, housekeeper, and plant engineer provide essential services to the guest. Without cooperation and communication among these departments and the front office, hospitality cannot be delivered. The director of marketing and sales develops programs to attract guests to the lodging property. These programs help the front office manager sell rooms. The human resources manager completes the team by providing the front office with competent personnel to accomplish the goals, objectives, and standards set by the general manager.

Job Analysis and Job Description

A **job analysis,** a detailed listing of the tasks performed in a front office manager's job, provides the basis for a sound job description. A **job description** is a listing of required duties to be performed by an employee in a particular position. Although almost nothing is "typical" in the lodging industry, certain daily tasks must be performed. A job analysis is useful in that it allows the person preparing the job description to determine certain daily procedures. These procedures, along with typical responsibilities and interdepartmental relationships involved in a job, form the basis for the job description. The future professional will find this management tool very helpful in preparing orientation and training programs for employees. It also helps the human resources department ensure that each new hire is given every opportunity to succeed, by laying a foundation for a job specification. The following is the job analysis of a typical front office manager:

7:00 A.M.   Meets with the night auditor to discuss the activities of the previous night. Notes any discrepancies in balancing the night audit.

7:30   Meets with the reservation clerk to note the incoming reservations for the day.

8:00 A.M.   Greets the first-shift desk clerks and passes along any information from the night auditor and reservation office. Assists desk clerks in guest check-out.

8:30   Meets with the housekeeper to identify any potential problem areas of which the front office staff should be aware. Meets with the plant engineer to identify any potential problem areas of which the front office staff should be aware.

9:00   Meets with the director of marketing and sales to discuss ideas for potential programs to increase sales. Discusses with the banquet manager details of groups that will be in-house for banquets and city ledger accounts that have left requests for billing disputes.

9:30   Checks with the chef to learn daily specials for the various restaurants. This information will be typed and distributed to the telephone operators.

9:45   Meets with the front office staff to discuss pertinent operational information for the day. Handles guest billing disputes.

11:00   Meets with the general manager to discuss the development of the next fiscal budget.

12:30 P.M.   Works on forecasting sheet for the coming week.

1:00   Has a lunch appointment with a corporate business client.

2:15   Works on **room blocking**—reserving rooms for guests who are holding reservations—for group reservations with the reservations clerk.

2:30   Works with the controller on budgetary targets for the next month. Receives feedback on budget targets from last month. Checks with the housekeeper on progress of room inspection and release.

2:45   Checks with the plant engineer on progress of plumbing repair for the eighteenth floor.

3:00   Greets the second-shift desk clerks and relays any operational information on reservations, room assignments, room inventory, and the like.

3:15   Assists the front desk clerks in checking in a tour group.

4:00   Interviews two people for front desk clerk positions.

4:45   Assists the front desk clerks in checking in guests.

5:15   Reviews trade journal article on empowerment of employees.

5:45   Telephones the night auditor and communicates current information pertinent to tonight's audit.

6:00 P.M.   Checks with the director of security for information concerning security coverage for the art exhibit in the ballroom.

6:30   Completes work order request forms for preventive maintenance on the front office posting machine.

6:45   Prepares "things to do" schedule for tomorrow.

This job analysis reveals that the front office manager has a busy schedule involving hands-on participation with the front office staff and communication with the various department heads in the lodging establishment. The front office manager must be able to project incomes and related expenses, to interview, and to interact with potential business clients.

Based on this job analysis, a job description for a front office manager would be easily prepared, as shown in Figure 2-8. The job description is an effective management tool because it details the basic tasks and responsibilities required of the front office manager. These guidelines allow the individual to apply management principles in the development of an effective front office department. They also challenge the person in the job to use prior experience and theoretical knowledge to accomplish the tasks at hand.

The Art of Supervising

The art of supervising employees encompasses volumes of text and years of experiences. Management experts have analyzed some of the complexities of supervising employees. Some of your other management courses will explain in detail the concept of management. This chapter covers a few concepts that will assist you in developing your own supervisory style.

The first step in developing a supervisory style is to examine a manager's position in the scheme of the management team. As the front office manager, you are assigned certain responsibilities along with certain authorities. These are areas for participation, growth, and limitation on the management team. Although this is a simplified overview of the management team, it does help to clarify managerial practice. At this time, a manager should review personal career goals with this organization. The ports of entry to the position of general manager (described in chapter 1) will help an aspiring general manager clarify goals. This information will help you to understand which of the various areas of the hotel will provide good exposure and experience. Once you have clarified your arena of participation and plan for growth, you can decide how best to lead a team to financial success and personal growth.

The first concept a new supervisor (whether 20 or 60 years of age) should address is employee motivation. What helps each employee perform at his or her best? The emphasis is on *each* employee; different incentives motivate different people. The better shift scheduling that motivates the second-shift desk clerk may have no effect on the part-time night auditor who is a **moonlighter,** a person who has a full-time job at another organization

Figure 2-8. *This job description is based on the job analysis of a front office manager.*

JOB DESCRIPTION

Title: *Front Office Manager*
Reports to: *General Manager*

Typical duties:
1. Reviews final draft of night audit.
2. Operates and monitors reservation system for guest room rentals.
3. Develops and operates an effective communication system with front office staff.
4. Supervises daily operation of front office—reservations, registrations, and checkouts.
5. Participates with all department heads in an effective communications system facilitating the provision of guest services.
6. Plans and participates in the delivery of marketing programs for the sale of rooms and other hotel products and services.
7. Interfaces with various department heads and controller regarding any billing disputes involving guests.
8. Develops final draft of budget for front office staff.
9. Prepares forecast of room sales for upcoming week, month, or other time period as required.
10. Maintains business relationships with various corporate community leaders.
11. Oversees the personnel management for the front office department.
12. Performs these and other duties as required.

Review cycle:

1 month   _____
              (date)

3 months   _____
              (date)

6 months   _____
              (date)

1 year   _____
              (date)

and a part-time job at a hotel, two days a week on your property. The young person who prefers the second shift (3:00–11:00 P.M.) because the schedule better fits his or her lifestyle will not be inspired by the possibility of working the first shift. Tuition reimbursement may motivate the recent graduate of an associate degree program who wants to continue toward a four-year degree. This same incentive will mean little to someone uninterested in higher education. The possibility of promotion to reservations clerk may not have the same motivating effect on a telephone operator who is a recently displaced worker concerned about a schedule that meets the needs of a young family as it does on a front desk clerk who has no dependents. There are other cases in which a supervisor cannot figure out what motivates a person. It is a manager's ultimate challenge to discover how to motivate each member of his or her staff. By using this knowledge, a manager can promote not just the best interests of the employee but also the best interests of the hotel.

Another supervisory responsibility is to achieve a balance among varying personalities in a group work setting. This is a constant and evolving situation. Very often, a new supervisor does not have time to assess each employee's relationship with others on the team, yet these dynamics are key to establishing a positive and effective "team" setting. The front office staff is jockeying for position with the new boss. This is common practice and a situation that needs to be addressed as part of the job. Once the new supervisor shows himself or herself capable and competent, the supervisor can move on to the day-to-day tasks. The staff needs this time to learn their new manager's reactions under stress. They also want to make sure that their supervisor will be their advocate with top management. All new supervisors will be tested in this way. You should not be discouraged by this challenge but embrace it as the first of many challenges to come.

After working out whatever personality clashes may exist among the employees, the manager must be objective about the strengths and weaknesses of the staff. Who is the unofficial leader of the group? Who is the agitator? Who is the complainer? Objective views of staff are probably shared by the rest of the team. Often, the staff members are quite aware of the shortcomings of their co-workers. They also know whom they can rely on to check out the full house and check in the convention three hours later. The unofficial leader of the group can assist the supervisor in conveying important ideas.

Some supervisors will respond negatively to such accommodation of the staff. Their response is based on the assumption that the supervisor has the first and last word in all that goes on in the front office. Of course, authority is important, but any supervisor who wants to maintain that authority and have objectives met by the staff must constantly rework his or her strategy.

Adequate personnel training (discussed in Chapter 12) makes the job of a supervisor much easier. When training is planned, executed, and followed up, the little annoyances of human error are minimized. As previously discussed, each job description lists the major duties of the employees, but the gray areas—handling complaints, delivering a positive image of the lodging property, selling other departments in the hotel, and covering for a new trainee—cannot be communicated in a job description. **On-the-job training,** employee training that takes place while producing a product or service, and videotape training are excellent methods for clarifying the gray areas of different tasks of a job. They serve not only to demonstrate skills but also to communicate the financial goals, the objectives of hospitality and service, and the idiosyncrasies of the lodging property and the people who work in it.

Employees will always have special scheduling needs as well as other job-related requests. Supervisors should try to accommodate their needs. The new hire who has made commitments four to six months prior to accepting a position at the front desk will appreciate and return a supervisor's consideration. The individual who wants to change shifts because of difficulties with another person on the job may just need advice on how to handle the other person. These individuals may make a good team, but they wear on each other's patience. A longtime employee might ask you how he or she can advance in the organization. You may not have an immediate response, but you can indicate that you will act on the request in the near future. Sometimes employees know that a good thing takes time to develop. Listen to their needs; their requests may answer your problems by fitting into the demands of the job. For example, a desk clerk who is in need of additional income may have requested overtime hours. Later on, an opportunity may arise for this employee to fill a vacancy caused by another employee's illness or vacation.

The responsibility of communications within the hotel usually rests with the front office. From the guests' perspective, this department is the most visible part of the lodging establishment. The various departments in the hotel realize that the transfer of information to guests is best done through the front office. When such communications fail to reach guests, it is often the front office that bears the brunt of their unhappiness at checkout time.

The more systematic the communication process can become, the better for all concerned. For example, messages that will affect the next shift of desk clerks can be recorded in the **message book,** a loose-leaf binder in which the front desk staff on various shifts can record important messages. This communication tool is vital to keeping all front office personnel informed of additions, changes, and deletions of information and activities that affect the operation of a front office. Additionally, **daily function sheets,** listing the planned events in the hotel, and their updates must be delivered to the front office on a routine basis. The daily function board or electronic bulletin board in guest rooms available on in-room television or in public areas is usually maintained by the front office. The guest who complains about the maintenance of a room must have the complaint passed along to the right person. The complaint is then reviewed by a member of the staff, front office manager, member of the housekeeping staff, housekeeper, member of the maintenance staff, and/or maintenance director to ensure it is resolved.

Inquiries about hotel services, reservations, **city ledger accounts**—a collection of accounts receivable of nonregistered guests who use the services of the hotel—accounts payable, scheduled events, and messages for registered guests constitute only some of the many requests for information. Desk clerks and telephone operators are expected to know the answers to these questions or know to whom they should be referred.

Some of this advice is based on my own experiences. One of the jobs I was responsible for as a front desk clerk included manning the switchboard. This job was truly stressful, involving accuracy at every contact. Finding the right department head to meet the request of an incoming caller or ensuring that a message is passed along to a guest are only some of the tasks required every minute a person is on the job. If a message is conveyed inaccurately or if an employee fails to complete the communication process, hospitality is not projected to the guest.

Ways of applying employee empowerment concepts will be explored in chapter 12. The contemporary front office manager needs extensive training and experience in this vital area to manage a workforce that can deliver hospitality on a daily basis. Ensuring that an employee can conduct business without constant approval from a supervisor is the goal of empowerment. The mastery of empowerment requires a supervisor to train employees and to practice much patience. Employees who have been accustomed to direct supervision on all matters will not readily adapt to a work environment that requires independent thinking to solve challenges.

Staffing the Front Office

The schedule for the front office staff is based on both budgetary targets and anticipation of guest check-ins and checkouts. An increase in the frequency of guest requests for information and various front office services may affect the schedule. The front office manager must also determine labor costs by reviewing salaries and hourly wages and respective rates. The resulting figures will show if the front office manager has adhered to the projected budget. Table 2-1 (page 65) shows how the costs for staffing are determined. Table 2-2 (page 68) compares these projected costs with the projected revenue generated by room rentals, which allows for a preevaluation of income and labor expenses.

Solution to Opening Dilemma

Communication in a hotel is paramount to efficiency, delivery of quality service, and profit making. In this particular case, the front office staff failed to place a room block in the computer system for the additional 26 rooms. Does this happen frequently in the hotel business? Unfortunately, it does. However, the delivery of quality service is dependent on the upkeep of a hotel's physical property, and this is an important operational procedure. The front office manager and the director of housekeeping have to cooperate in setting up times for taking guest rooms out of available inventory. The front office manager must be made aware of the costs involved in contracted services and work in partnership with the director of housekeeping.

Chapter Recap

This chapter outlined the organizational structure of various lodging properties and typical job responsibilities of department managers. Specific review of the role of the front office manager revealed many related concepts. Success in providing effective supervision begins with a review of the resources available to the front office manager, such as employees, equipment, room inventory, finances, and sales opportunities. After analyzing these resources, the front office manager can direct the department more effectively; the objectives of making a profit and delivering hospitality to the guest can be achieved more easily.

The functional role of the front office manager can be understood by preparing a job analysis and job description. This process allows the future professional to see the major responsibilities of the job and the various departmental relationships involved.

The many positions found on a front office staff have the common goal of providing hospitality to the guest. Training, empowerment, and flexibility are necessary to make the team work.

Forecasting, scheduling, developing a supervisory style, motivating personnel, balancing staff personalities, delegating tasks, training, and effectively communicating are only a few of the skills a good supervisor must master. It is a lifelong effort developed through continuing education and trial and error.

End of Chapter Questions

1. If you are employed in the hotel industry, sketch the organization chart of the property where you work. Have you seen this hierarchy change since you have been employed there? If so, what do you think caused this change?

2. Compare the organization of a full-service hotel and a limited-service hotel. How can a limited-service property operate with such a seemingly minimal staff?

3. If you are employed in the hotel industry, describe the tasks your general manager performs on a daily basis. Describe the tasks your department director performs on a daily basis. What relationship do both of these departments have to the overall success of the hotel?

4. How are the positions in a front office organized? Describe the positions found at a front office in a full-service hotel. Which positions are most crucial to providing guest service?

5. If you have ever worked in a front office in a lodging property, summarize what you think the front office manager does. If you have not worked in a front office of a hotel, you might want to visit with a front office manager and ask for insight into this position.

6. What are the resources available to the front office manager? Rank the importance of these resources in providing service to guests and supervising employees.

7. How does the front office manager relate to other members of the hotel management staff? Give examples.

8. Why should the job analysis be performed prior to preparing a job description? Do you think this procedure is necessary? Why or why not?

9. What are the three steps required in preparing a schedule?

10. How do you think your supervisor developed his or her supervisory style? What do you think will be the basis for developing your supervisory style?

11. What does "the art of supervision" mean to you? Reflect upon your answer and highlight which concepts are important to your future supervisory style.

12. Why does trying to understand individual motivations help in supervising?

13. What are some of the personality clashes you have noticed where you work? How did your supervisor handle them? Would you have handled them differently if you were the supervisor?

14. Generally speaking, what benefits can a well-trained front office person offer the front office manager?

15. Give some examples of how the front office is responsible for communication with other departments, with hotel guests, and with the public.

CASE STUDY 201

Ana Chavarria, front office manager, has been with The Times Hotel for several years. She recalls her first few months as a time of great stress. There was Milo Diaz, personnel manager, who was always calling her to post her schedules on time and authorize payroll forms. Thomas Brown, executive housekeeper, seemed a great friend off the premises of the hotel, but at work, he continually badgered the front desk clerks on guest check-in and checkout problems. Yoon-Whan Li, executive engineer, also had communication issues with Ana, such as the time when a desk clerk called Yoon-Whan at home to indicate that an elevator was stuck on the fourth floor when it was only manually stopped by a group of children. Eric Jones, food and beverage manager, continued to blame Ana's desk clerks because hotel guests were not frequenting the dining room and lounge, asking her, "When will the desk clerks ever learn to talk about those free coupons for the dining room and

lounge that they so stoically hand out?" Then there was Lorraine DeSantes, director of marketing and sales, who had just about all she could take from desk clerks who misplaced phone messages, directed hotel guests to restaurants across the street, and offered information on "a good restaurant right around the corner."

Ana has taken those comments to heart and feels she can justify her shortcomings and those of her staff. She knows the schedules are to be posted by Tuesday morning of each week, but several of her employees give her last-minute requests for days off. Her payroll forms are usually delayed because she wants to spend time with the guests who are registering or checking out. The front desk clerks have made some major errors in checking guests into room that are not ready, but she offers, "It must be that the computer system gives them the wrong information." The elevator issue wasn't the front desk clerk's fault. It was his third night on the job, and no one had thought to explain what constitutes an emergency call to the executive engineer. She wants her front desk clerks to distribute those food and beverage coupons, but they just don't get excited about it. And Lorraine DeSantes's messages are always given to her; "She just makes no attempt to look in her mailbox."

She also remembered when Margaret Chu, general manager of The Times Hotel, asked her to visit in her office. She let Ana know that her six-month probationary period would be over in one month and it was time to discuss Ana's progress before a decision could be made on whether to continue Ana in the role of front office manager. Ana was very uneasy

knowing that her colleagues had reported major errors on her behalf. However, Margaret Chu took an approach that was very different from that of other general managers with whom Ana had worked. Margaret asked her to prepare a list of strategies that she could use in working toward improvement in the following areas:

- Employee motivation
- Personnel training
- Effective scheduling of employees
- Communication
- Empowerment

Ms. Chu has asked you to assist Ana in developing strategies to use for improving her ability in the art of supervising employees. What would you suggest?

CASE STUDY 202

A local hotel developer has called you to assist her corporation in designing job descriptions for a new hotel. This is the corporation's first venture into the hotel business, so the developer wants you to be very explicit in writing the job descriptions. The description of the hotel is similar to the 500+-room full-service hotel as depicted in Figure 2-1.

Prepare job descriptions for the following management positions:

- General manager
- Front office manager
- Executive housekeeper
- Food and beverage director

Key Words

accounts payable
accounts receivable
assistant general manager
athletics director
average daily rate
balance sheet
bell captain
bell staff
bill-to-account

business services and communications
   center
call accounting
cashier
city ledger accounts
collective bargaining unit
concierge
continental breakfast
controller

Table 2-1. *Front Office Scheduling Process*

Step 1. Estimate Needs (Review Front Office Forecast First)

	10/1	10/2	10/3	10/4	10/5	10/6	10/7
Desk Clerks							
Night Auditors							
Cashiers							
Concierges							
Telephone Operators							
Bell Captain							
Bellhops							

Step 2. Develop Schedule

	10/1	10/2	10/3	10/4	10/5	10/6	10/7
Desk 1	7–3	7–3	7–3	7–3	X	X	7–3
Desk 2	9–5	X	9–2	10–6	X	7–3	9–Noon
Desk 3	3–11	3–11	3–11	3–11	3–11	X	X
Desk 4	X	X	X	3–7	7–3	3–11	3–11
Aud. 1	11–7	11–7	11–7	X	X	11–7	11–7
Aud. 2	X	X	X	11–7	11–7	X	X
Cash.	8–Noon	X	9–2	9–Noon	X	X	11–3
Concierge 1	Noon–8	Noon–8	Noon–8	Noon–5	Noon–5	X	X
Concierge 2	X	X	X	X	X	Noon–5	Noon–8
Tel. 1	7–3	X	X	7–3	7–3	7–3	7–3
Tel. 2	3–11	3–11	3–11	X	X	3–11	3–11
Tel. 3	X	7–3	7–3	3–11	3–11	X	X
Bell Capt.	7–3	7–3	7–3	7–3	X	7–3	X
Hop 1	9–5	X	X	10–6	7–3	3–11	7–3
Hop 2	3–11	X	3–11	3–11	3–11	X	3–11
Hop 3	X	3–11	8–2	X	X	X	11–5

Table 2-1. *(Continued)*

Step 3. Calculate Anticipated Payroll

10/1	10/2	10/3	10/4
Category: Desk Clerk = $1,300.00			
8 hrs. @ $ 9.50 = $ 76.00	8 hrs. @ $ 9.50 = $ 76.00	8 hrs. @ $ 9.50 = $ 76.00	8 hrs. @ $ 9.50 = $ 76.00
8 hrs. @ $11.00 = $ 88.00	8 hrs. @ $11.00 = $ 88.00	8 hrs. @ $11.00 = $ 88.00	8 hrs. @ $11.00 = $ 88.00
8 hrs. @ $ 8.00 = $ 64.00		5 hrs. @ $ 8.00 = $ 40.00	8 hrs. @ $ 8.00 = $ 64.00
			4 hrs. @ $ 8.00 = $ 32.00
$228.00	$164.00	$204.00	$260.00
Category: Night Auditor = $704.00			
8 hrs. @ $13.00 = $104.00	8 hrs. @ $13.00 = $104.00	8 hrs. @ $13.00 = $104.00	8 hrs. @ $11.50 = $ 92.00
$104.00	$104.00	$104.00	$ 92.00
Category: Cashier = $128.00			
4 hrs. @ $ 8.00 = $ 32.00	0 hrs. @ $ 0 = $ 0.00	5 hrs. @ $ 8.00 = $ 40.00	3 hrs. @ $ 8.00 = $ 24.00
$ 32.00	$ 0.00	$ 40.00	$ 24.00
Category: Concierge = $501.00			
8 hrs. @ $11.00 = $ 88.00	8 hrs. @ $11.00 = $ 88.00	8 hrs. @ $11.00 = $ 88.00	5 hrs. @ $11.00 = $ 55.00
$ 88.00	$ 88.00	$ 88.00	$ 55.00
Category: Telephone Operator = $920.00			
8 hrs. @ $ 8.00 = $ 64.00	8 hrs. @ $ 9.00 = $ 72.00	8 hrs. @ $ 7.50 = $ 60.00	8 hrs. @ $ 8.00 = $ 64.00
8 hrs. @ $ 9.00 = $ 72.00	8 hrs. @ $ 7.50 = $ 60.00	8 hrs. @ $ 9.00 = $ 72.00	8 hrs. @ $ 7.50 = $ 60.00
$136.00	$132.00	$132.00	$124.00
Category: Bell Staff = $720.00			
8 hrs. @ $ 7.00 = $ 56.00	8 hrs. @ $ 7.00 = $ 56.00	6 hrs. @ $ 7.00 = $ 42.00	8 hrs. @ $ 7.00 = $ 56.00
8 hrs. @ $ 7.50 = $ 60.00		8 hrs. @ $ 7.50 = $ 60.00	8 hrs. @ $ 7.50 = $ 60.00
$116.00	$ 56.00	$102.00	$116.00

Category: Salaries—Front Office = $1,757.00

Front Office Manager:	$807/wk.
Reservations Manager:	$575/wk.
Bell Captain:	$375/wk.

Table 2-1. *(Continued)*

10/5	10/6	10/7
8 hrs. @ $ 8.00 = $ 64.00	8 hrs. @ $ 8.00 = $ 64.00	8 hrs. @ $ 9.50 = $ 76.00
8 hrs. @ $11.00 = $ 88.00	8 hrs. @ $ 8.00 = $ 64.00	8 hrs. @ $ 8.00 = $ 64.00
		3 hrs. @ $ 8.00 = $ 24.00
$152.00	$128.00	$164.00
8 hrs. @ $11.50 = $ 92.00	8 hrs. @ $13.00 = $104.00	8 hrs. @ $13.00 = $104.00
$ 92.00	$104.00	$104.00
0 hrs. @ $ 0 = $ 0.00	0 hrs. @ $ 0 = $ 0.00	4 hrs. @ $ 8.00 = $ 32.00
$ 0.00	$ 0.00	$ 32.00
5 hrs. @ $11.00 = $ 55.00	5 hrs. @ $11.00 = $ 55.00	8 hrs. @ $ 9.00 = $ 72.00
$ 55.00	$ 55.00	$ 72.00
8 hrs. @ $ 8.00 = $ 64.00	8 hrs. @ $ 8.00 = $ 64.00	8 hrs. @ $ 8.00 = $ 64.00
8 hrs. @ $ 7.50 = $ 60.00	8 hrs. @ $ 9.00 = $ 72.00	8 hrs. @ $ 9.00 = $ 72.00
$124.00	$136.00	$136.00
8 hrs. @ $ 7.00 = $ 56.00	8 hrs. @ $ 7.00 = $ 56.00	8 hrs. @ $ 7.00 = $ 56.00
8 hrs. @ $ 7.50 = $ 60.00		8 hrs. @ $ 7.50 = $ 60.00
		6 hrs. @ $ 7.00 = $ 42.00
$116.00	$ 56.00	$158.00

Table 2-1. *(Continued)*

Step 4. Summary

Desk Clerks	$1,300.00
Night Auditors	704.00
Cashiers	128.00
Concierges	501.00
Telephone Operators	920.00
Bell Staff	720.00
Salaries	1,757.00
Subtotal	$6,030.00
Taxes/Fringe Benefits ×	.27
=	$1,628.10
+	6,030.00
Total Projected Payroll for Week	$7,658.10

Table 2-2. *Comparison of Projected Income from Weekly Room Sales and Projected Weekly Payroll*

	10/1	10/2	10/3	10/4	10/5	10/6	10/7
Yesterday's sales	135	97	144	147	197	210	213
Departures	−125	−10	−72	−75	−5	−15	−125
Stayovers	10	87	72	72	192	195	88
Arrivals	+72	+40	+50	+125	+10	+15	+35
Walk-ins	+20	+20	+30	+10	+10	+5	+50
No-shows	−5	−3	−5	−10	−2	−2	−3
Number sold	97	144	147	197	210	213	170

Total rooms sold (sum of number sold each day)	1,178
Income from rooms sold (at average daily rate of $75.00)	$88,350.00
Projected payroll budget (from weekly estimate, Table 2-1)	$7,658.10
Percentage of income required for payroll ([payroll × 100] ÷ income)	8.66%

convention guests
corporate guests
daily function sheet
desk clerk
director of marketing and sales
director of security
elevator operator
executive housekeeper
express checkout
floor inspector
food and beverage director
front office manager
full house
general ledger
general manager
human resources manager
in-house laundry
job analysis
job description
key clerk
maintenance manager
message book
moonlighter

night audit
night auditor
on-the-job training
operational reports
organization chart
parking garage manager
percent occupancy
percent yield
plant engineer
prior approved credit
profit-and-loss statement
property management system (PMS)
rack rate
recreation director
referral reservation service
reservations manager
room attendants
room blocking
telephone operator
total quality management (TQM)
traffic managers
working supervisors

Effective Interdepartmental Communications

OPENING DILEMMA

The leader of a workshop in one of the conference rooms is very anxious about

his program today. After noticing that the connection for the teleconference is

not working, he stops by the front desk and asks if the convention representative

could come to the conference room. The desk clerk on duty offers to locate the

convention representative and send her to the room. After the workshop leader

leaves the front desk area, the desk clerk remarks, "You would think we have

to be all things to all people all the time!"

Role of the Front Office in Interdepartmental Communications

The front office plays a pivotal role in delivering hospitality to guests. It sets the stage for a pleasant or an unpleasant visit. Guests, often in an unfamiliar setting and anxious to proceed with their business or vacation plans, are eager to learn the who, what, when, where, and how of their new environment. Requests for information often begin with the doorman, bellhop, switchboard operator, front desk clerk, cashier, or concierge, because these employees are the most visible to the guest and are perceived to be the most knowledgeable. These employees are believed to have their finger on the pulse of the organization and the community. Their responses to the guests' requests for information on public transportation, location of hotel facilities, special events in the community, and the like indicate how well the hotel has prepared the front office staff for this important role. Front office managers must take an active role in gathering information that will be of interest to guests. They must also be active in developing procedures for the front office to disburse this information.

The relationships the front office manager develops with the other department directors and their employees are vital to gathering information for guests. Developing positive personal relationships is part of the communication process, but it cannot be relied on to ensure that accurate and current information has been relayed. How does the front office manager encourage effective **interdepartmental communication** (communication between departments)? This chapter provides some background for you as you begin your professional career. It is also important to note that **intradepartmental communication** (communication inside a department) is applicable to this discussion.

Figure 3-1 shows the various departments in a hotel that interact with the front office. The front office is at the center of this diagram to illustrate the many interdepartmental lines of communication that exist. These lines are based on the direction each department has been given to provide hospitality in the form of clean rooms, properly operating equipment, safe environment, well-prepared food and beverages, efficient table service, professional organization and delivery of service for a scheduled function as well as accurate accounting of guest charges, and the like. These general objectives help department

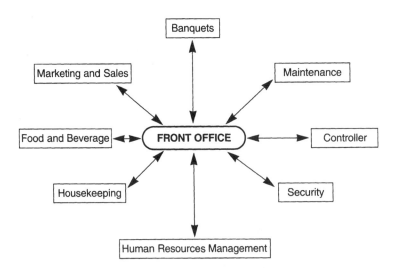

Figure 3-1. *The front office serves as a clearinghouse for communication activities.*

directors organize their operations and meet the overall goal of delivering professional hospitality. However, in reality, it requires constant effort to manage the details of employees, materials, procedures, and communication skills to produce acceptable products and services.

Front Office Interaction with Other Departments in the Hotel

The front office staff interacts with all departments of the hotel, including marketing and sales, housekeeping, food and beverage, banquet, controller, maintenance, security, and human resources. These departments view the front office as a communication liaison in providing guest services. Each of the departments has a unique communication link with the front office staff.

Marketing and Sales Department

The marketing and sales department relies on the front office to provide data on **guest histories,** details concerning each guest's visit. Some of the information gathered is based on zip code, frequency of visits, corporate affiliation, special needs, and reservations for sleeping rooms. It is also the front office's job to make a good first impression on the public, to relay messages, and to meet the requests of guests who are using the hotel for meetings, seminars, and banquets.

The guest history is a valuable resource for marketing and sales, which uses the guest registration information to target marketing campaigns, develop promotions, prepare mailing labels, and select appropriate advertising media. The front office staff must make every effort to keep this database current and accurate.

The process of completing the booking of a special function (such as a wedding reception, convention, or seminar) depends on the availability of sleeping rooms for guests. The marketing and sales executives may have to check the lists of available rooms three, six, or even twelve months in the future to be sure the hotel can accommodate the expected number of guests. A database of available rooms is maintained in the property management system by the front office.

The first guest contact with the marketing and sales department is usually through the hotel's switchboard. A competent switchboard operator who is friendly and knowledgeable about hotel operations and personnel will make a good first impression, conveying to the prospective client that this hotel is competent. When the guest finally arrives for the function, the first contact with the hotel is usually through the front office staff. The front office manager who makes the effort to determine which banquet supervisor is in charge and communicates that information to the desk clerk on duty demonstrates to the public that this hotel is dedicated to providing hospitality.

Messages for the marketing and sales department must be relayed completely, accurately, and quickly. The switchboard operator is a vital link in the communication between the prospective client and a salesperson in the marketing and sales department. The front office manager should instruct all new personnel in the front office about the staff in the marketing and sales department and what each person's job entails (this applies to all departments in the hotel, not just marketing and sales, as explained in Chapter 12). Front office employees should know how to pronounce the names of all marketing and sales employees. To help front office staff become familiar with all these people, managers should show new employees pictures of the department directors and supervisors.

Requests for service at meetings, seminars, banquets, and the like are often made at the front office. The **banquet manager,** a person who is responsible for fulfilling the details of service for a banquet or special event, or **sales associate,** a person who books the guest's requirements for banquets and other special events, might be busy with another function. If a guest needs an extension cord or an electrical outlet malfunctions, the front desk staff must be ready to meet the guest's needs. The front office manager should establish standard operating procedures for the front office employees to contact maintenance, housekeeping, marketing and sales, or the food and beverage department to meet other common requests. Knowing how to find a small tool kit, adapters, adhesive materials, extra table covers, or window cleaner will help the guest and will save the time involved in tracking down the salesperson in charge.

Housekeeping Department

Housekeeping and the front office communicate with each other about **housekeeping room status,** the report on the availability of the rooms for immediate guest occupancy. Housekeeping room status can be described in the following communication terms:

- Available Clean, or Ready—room is ready to be occupied
- Occupied—guest or guests are already occupying a room
- Stayover—guest will not be checking out of a room on the current day
- Dirty or On-Change—guest has checked out of the room, but the housekeeping staff has not released the room for occupancy
- Out-of-Order—room is not available for occupancy because of a mechanical malfunction

Housekeeping and the front office also communicate on the details of potential **house count** (a report of the number of guests registered in the hotel), security concerns, and requests for **amenities** (personal toiletry items such as shampoo, toothpaste, mouthwash, and electrical equipment). These issues are of immediate concern to the guest as well as to supervisors in the hotel.

Reporting of room status is handled on a face-to-face basis in a hotel that does not use a property management system (PMS). The bihourly or hourly visits of the housekeeper to the front desk clerk are a familiar scene in such a hotel. The official reporting of room status at the end of the day is accomplished with a **housekeeper's room report**—a report prepared by the housekeeper that lists the guest room occupancy status as vacant, occupied, or out-of-order. Sometimes even regular reporting of room status is not adequate, as guests may be anxiously awaiting the opportunity to occupy a room. On these occasions, the front desk clerk will have to telephone the floor supervisor to determine when the servicing of a room will be completed.

The housekeeper relies on the **room sales projections**—a weekly report prepared and distributed by the front office manager that indicates the number of departures, arrivals, walk-ins, stayovers, and no-shows—to schedule employees. Timely distribution of the room sales projections assists the executive housekeeper in planning employee personal leaves and vacation days.

The front desk also relies on housekeeping personnel to report any unusual circumstances that may indicate a violation of security for the guests. For example, if a maid or houseman notices obviously nonregistered guests on a floor, a fire exit that has been propped open, or sounds of a domestic disturbance in a guest room, he or she must report these potential security violations to the front office. The front office staff, in turn, will relay the problem to the proper in-house or civil authority. The front office manager may want to direct the front desk clerks and switchboard operators to call floor supervisors on a regular basis to check activity on the guest floors.

Guest requests for additional or special amenities and guest room supplies may be initiated at the front desk. The prompt relay of requests for extra blankets, towels, soap, and shampoo to housekeeping is essential. This is hospitality at its best.

Food and Beverage Department

Communication between the food and beverage department and the front office is also essential. Some of this communication is conveyed by relaying messages and providing accurate information on **transfers,** which are forms used to communicate a charge to a guest's account. Communication activities also include reporting **predicted house counts,** an estimate of the number of guests expected to register based on previous occupancy activities, and processing requests for **paid-outs,** forms used to indicate the amounts of monies paid out of the cashier's drawer on behalf of a guest or an employee of the hotel. These vital services help an overworked food and beverage manager, restaurant manager, or banquet captain meet the demands of the public.

Incoming messages for the food and beverage manager and executive chef from vendors and other industry representatives are important to the business operation of the food and beverage department. If the switchboard operator is given instructions on screening callers (such as times when the executive chef cannot be disturbed because of a busy workload or staff meetings, or vendors in whom the chef is not interested), the important messages will receive top priority.

In a hotel that has **point-of-sale terminals,** computerized cash registers that interface with a property management system, information on guest charges is automatically posted to a guest's **folio,** his or her record of charges and payments. When a hotel does not have point-of-sale terminals that interface with PMS point-of-sale terminals, the desk clerk is responsible for posting accurate charges on the guest folio and relies on transfer slips. Also, the night auditor's job is made easier if the transfer slip is accurately prepared and posted. The front office manager should work with the food and beverage director in developing standard operating procedures and methods to complete the transfer of charges.

The supervisors in the food and beverage department rely on the predicted house count prepared by the front office manager to schedule employees and predict sales. For example, the restaurant supervisor working the breakfast shift will want to know how many guests will be in the hotel so he or she can determine how many servers to schedule for breakfast service. Timely and accurate preparation of this communication tool assists in staffing control and sales predictions.

Authorized members of the food and beverage department will occasionally ask the front office for cash, in the form of a paid-out, to purchase last-minute items for a banquet, the lounge, or the restaurant or to take advantage of other unplanned opportunities to promote hospitality. Specific guidelines concerning cash limits, turnaround time, prior approval, authorized signatures, and purchase receipts are developed by the general manager and front office manager. These guidelines help to maintain control of paid-outs.

Figure 3-2. Front desk clerks must be able to provide immediate responses to guests' requests for information. (Photo courtesy of Radisson Hospitality Worldwide.)

Banquet Department

The banquet department, which often combines the functions of a marketing and sales department and a food and beverage department, requires the front office to relay information to guests about scheduled events and bill payment.

The front desk staff may also provide labor to prepare the **daily announcement board,** an inside listing of the daily activities of the hotel (time, group, and room assignment), and **marquee,** the curbside message board, which includes the logo of the hotel and space for a message. Since the majority of banquet guests may not be registered guests in the hotel, the front office provides a logical communications center.

The daily posting of scheduled events on a felt board or an electronic bulletin board provides all guests and employees with information on group events. The preparation of the marquee may include congratulatory, welcome, sales promotion, or other important messages. In some hotels, an employee in the front office contacts the marketing and sales department for the message.

Michael DeCaire is the food and beverage manager at the Houston Hilton, Houston, Texas. His previous experience includes positions as executive chef at the Park Hotel in Charlotte, North Carolina; executive and executive sous chef at the Pacific Star Hotel on the Island of Guam; and executive sous chef at the Greenleaf Resort in Haines City, Florida.

Mr. DeCaire relies on the front desk for accurate forecasting of arrivals, notification of VIPs and Hilton Honors Club members, communication of complaints and positive comments concerning food and service, and processing of guest bills. He also works with the front desk on obtaining a thorough knowledge of the needs and location of banquet and meeting guests through a ten-day forecast of banquet and meeting events.

The communication emphasis at the Houston Hilton is extended into a nine-week cross-training program, in which all departments (food and beverage, front desk, housekeeping, sales, etc.) participate in learning the basics of each department. This training effort allows the salesperson to appreciate the duties of a cook, the waiter or waitress to understand the duties of a front desk clerk, and the front desk clerk to value the duties of a housekeeper. Another area of cooperative training efforts is fire command post training.

Mr. DeCaire offers the following advice for students wanting to make a career in the hotel industry: take an entry-level job in the hospitality industry so you can understand the work requirements of weekends, holidays, and nights prior to investing in a college education. This effort will pay big dividends for your career growth.

The banquet guest who is unfamiliar with the hotel property will ask at the front office for directions. This service might seem minor in the overall delivery of service, but it is essential to the lost or confused guest. The front office staff must know both how to direct guests to particular meeting rooms or reception areas and which functions are being held in which rooms. Front desk clerks, as shown in Figure 3-2, must be ready to provide information for all departmental activities in the hotel.

The person responsible for paying the bills for a special event will also find his or her way to the front office to settle the city ledger accounts. If the banquet captain is not able to present the bill for the function, the front desk clerk should be informed about the specifics of food and beverage charges, gratuities, rental charges, method of payment, and the like.

Controller

The controller relies on the front office staff to provide a daily summary of financial transactions through a well-prepared night audit. This information is also used to measure management ability to meet budget targets. Since the front office provides the controller with financial data for billing and maintenance of credit-card ledgers, these two departments must relay payments and charges through the posting machine or property management system.

James Heale is the controller at the Sheraton Reading Hotel, located in Wyomissing, Pennsylvania. He processes money that comes in and expenses and taxes that are paid out. He prepares daily audits, is responsible for payroll preparation, and produces quarterly and annual financial statements. He also prepares financial forecasts and subsequent budgets.

Mr. Heale says his relationships with desk clerks, cashiers, and night auditors are important; however, his relationship with their respective managers is more important. He audits the work of the desk clerks, cashiers, and night auditors but does not directly supervise them. If they make mistakes, Mr. Heale tries to show them why. He makes sure they receive proper training, which includes letting them know the results of audits when they occur and making them aware of their individual performance.

Mr. Heale has a good relationship with the front office manager. They work together to forecast room sales and do the auditing of daily cash banks. The front office manager monitors the payroll and may ask for Mr. Heale's assistance. The front office manager is also involved in cash management problems; he and Mr. Heale alert each other to any problems and work together to solve them. The front office manager monitors accounts receivable and is required to let Mr. Heale know when a guest has exceeded his or her credit limit.

He adds that everyone in a hotel is a salesperson. Selling is a big part of his job through fostering a good relationship with local vendors. His efforts may encourage vendors to become customers of the hotel.

Maintenance or Engineering Department

The maintenance or engineering department and front office communicate on room status and requests for maintenance service. Maintenance employees must know the occupancy status of a room before attending to plumbing, heating, or air-conditioning problems. If the room is reserved, the two departments will work out a time frame so the guest will be able to enter the room or be assigned to another room. Cooperative efforts produce the best solutions to sometimes seemingly impossible situations. Figure 3-3 depicts the essential communication and planning by departmental managers to provide guest services at a time that will not interfere with delivering hospitality.

Likewise, the requests from guests for the repair of heating, ventilating, and air-conditioning units; plumbing; televisions; and other room furnishings are directed to the front desk. These requests are then communicated to the maintenance department. The front desk clerk must keep track of the repair schedule, as guests want to be informed of when the repair will be made.

Security Department

Communications between the security department and the front office are very important in providing hospitality to the guest. These departments work together very closely in maintaining guest security. Fire safety measures and emergency communication

Figure 3-3. *Coordination of maintenance service requires cooperation between the maintenance and front office departments. (Photo courtesy of Host/Racine Industries, Inc.)*

systems as well as procedures for routine investigation of guest security concerns require the cooperation of these departments.

Human Resources Management Department

The human resources management department may rely on the front office staff to act as an initial point of contact for potential employees in all departments. It may even ask the front office to screen job candidates. If so, guidelines for and training in screening methods must be provided.

Some directors of human resources management depend on the front office to distribute application forms and other personnel-related information to job applicants. The potential employee may ask for directions to the personnel office at the front desk. The human resources management department may also develop guidelines for the front desk clerk to use in initially screening candidates. For example, the guidelines may include concerns about personal hygiene, completion of an application, education requirements, experience, and citizenship status. This information will help the executives in the human resources management department interview potential job candidates.

Analyzing the Lines of Communication

This section is devoted to reviewing some situations in which communications between the front office and other departments play a role. Each situation will describe some communication problems between departments, trace the source of miscommunication, analyze the communication system, and present methods that will help improve communications. The purpose of this method of presentation is to help future professionals to develop a systematic way of continually improving communications.

Situation 1: Marketing and Sales Knows It All—but Didn't Tell Us

Mr. and Mrs. Oil Magnate are hosting a private party for 200 people in the Chandelier Room of City Hotel. On arriving at the hotel, they approach the front desk and ask if Mr. Benton, the director of marketing and sales, is available. The desk clerk checks the duty board and sees that Mr. Benton has left for the day. He responds, "Sorry, he's left for the day. What are you here for anyway?" The Magnates immediately feel neglected and ask to see the manager on duty.

Mr. Gerard, the assistant general manager, arrives on the scene and asks what he can do for the Magnates. Mr. Magnate has a number of concerns: Who will be in charge of their party? Will their two favorite servers be serving the cocktails, appetizers, and dinner? Have the flowers that were flown in from Holland arrived? Mr. Gerard says, "Gee, you'll have to speak with André, our banquet captain. He knows everything."

When André arrives on the scene, he tells the Magnates that Mr. Benton left no instructions about who will be serving the party, and he has not seen any tulips in the walk-in. Mrs. Magnate declares that this party will be a disaster. Mr. Magnate decides to proceed with the party and take up the lack of professional service later.

Later has arrived: Mr. Magnate has complained to the general manager and I. M. Owner—owner of City Hotel—and both are upset about the situation. Mr. Magnate and I. M. Owner are coinvestors in a construction project. Even if the two men were not business associates, the treatment of any guest in such a shabby way spells disaster for future convention and banquet sales.

ANALYSIS

The communications breakdown in this case was the fault of all the employees involved. Communication is a two-way process, and both senders and receivers must take active roles. As "the sender," Mr. Benton, the director of marketing and sales, did not do his homework. Assuming he was aware of I. M. Owner's relationship with Mr. and Mrs. Magnate, he should have adjusted his work schedule so that he could be there for the party. He also should have informed the front office manager of the Magnates' scheduled event, explained who they were, and asked that he be summoned immediately on their arrival. Mr. Benton should also have worked more closely with André, the banquet manager, in scheduling employees and receiving and storing the flowers. Although Mr. Gerard, the assistant general manager, would not normally be involved in the details of a party, in this case, the VIP status of the guests would be a reason for him to be aware of the presence of the Magnates in the hotel.

The "receivers" in the communication process are also at fault. These include the front office staff, the banquet manager, and the assistant general manager. At times, a member of the management team will fail to communicate the particulars of an upcoming event. However, the front office staff, the banquet manager, and the assistant general manager are responsible for reviewing the daily function board as well as the weekly function sheet. They are also responsible for learning about the backgrounds of the people, associations, and corporations that stay at and conduct business with the hotel.

Several things can be done to avoid this type of situation. First, the front office manager can ensure that the initial guest contact will be professional by reviewing the function board with each front desk employee on each shift. The manager can then help the front office staff focus on the upcoming events of the day. Weekly staff meetings may also provide an opportunity for the director of marketing and sales to give brief synopses of who will be in the hotel in the coming week. At that point, any special requests for VIP treatment could be noted.

Situation 2: Why Can't Those Room Attendants in Housekeeping Get Those Rooms Cleaned More Quickly—or, If That Guest Asks One More Time . . .

It is a busy Tuesday morning at the front desk. The Rosebud Flower Association (350 guests) is checking out of the hotel. The Franklin Actuary Society (250 guests) is beginning to arrive for registration. Yesterday, the president of Rosebud, José Rodríguez, requested a late checkout for all his members because they had to vote on an important legislative issue. The president asked a desk clerk, Samantha (a new member of the front office staff), to approve the late checkout. Samantha, unaware of any reason not to grant this request, OK'd a 2:30 P.M. checkout time.

It is 11:15 A.M., and the front office manager is on the phone with the housekeeper asking why some of the rooms have not been released. The housekeeper assures the front office manager that he will investigate the situation immediately and goes to the first, second, and third floors of the hotel to speak with the floor supervisors. They tell him that there are DO NOT DISTURB signs on the doors of the majority of the rooms. One of the guests told the supervisor on the second floor that he had permission to stay in the rooms until 2:30 P.M. When the housekeeper relays this information to the front office manager, a nasty exchange takes place between these two managers concerning the delivery of professional hospitality.

It is now 3:15 P.M., and the hotel lobby is jammed with people checking out and checking in. Only about 20 percent of the rooms needed have been released by housekeeping. The food and beverage manager arrives and suggests to the front office manager that he announce the availability of the coffee shop and lounge in the hotel to the waiting guests. The front office manager feels that this is a good idea but that, with such chaos, no one would hear the announcement. Therefore, he does not make the announcement.

At 7:20 P.M., the last guest is checked in. The front office manager breathes a sigh of relief and happens to notice a gift box addressed to Samantha. Samantha opens it and reads the card out loud: "Extra thanks to you for your kind consideration." The front office manager reminds Samantha that gifts from registered guests are not encouraged. Samantha replies that this is from a former guest—"You know, that nice Mr. Rodríguez from the flower association. All he asked for was a late checkout time for his group."

ANALYSIS

The miscommunication in this case was the fault of the front office manager. At some time during the orientation and training of new employees, the front office manager must communicate the policies, procedures, and limits of authority. Well-developed operational policies and procedures and documented training enable communications to flourish. For example, new employee orientation would include a discussion on the policy for communicating requests for late checkout to the supervisor on duty. An in-depth review of the clearance procedure that the supervisor on duty must follow would further help the new employee understand that the front office does not act alone. A decision made by one employee affects the work of many people. A typical review of procedures could include the following:

1. Consult with the reservations manager to determine the expected time of departure for the guests or groups of guests currently in the hotel and expected times of arrival of those who will be registering the next day.

2. Consult with the director of marketing and sales to determine if any special group requests concerning checkout departure on arrival times have been granted.

3. Consult with the housekeeper to determine the effect of a delayed checkout time on daily operations of the housekeeping department.

4. If the request for a delayed checkout time will conflict with another group's check-in time but the situation warrants approval of the request, ask the food and beverage

manager to set up a special snack table in the lobby for guests unable to check into their rooms.

When the front office manager takes the time to explain the policies and procedures of the department, the new employee can think through situations rather than responding with a knee-jerk reaction. The delivery of service in a hotel requires the employee to be able to meet the needs of the guests by exercising his or her authority and taking responsibility for conveying an atmosphere of hospitality.

Situation 3: I Know What You Said, and I Think I Know What You Mean

The director of maintenance, Sam Jones, has assigned his crew to start painting the fifth-floor hallway. Prior to making this assignment, he checked with the reservations manager, Keith Thomas, for approval to place the fifth-floor rooms "out of order" for four days. Keith consented because a prior reservation for 150 rooms for Photo Bugs International had been confirmed for 100.

At 1:00 P.M., Sam receives a call from Keith asking if it would be possible to reassign the painting crew to some other duty. The Photo Bugs have arrived—all 150 rooms' worth! The lobby is filled with guests, for whom there are no available rooms. Sam tells Keith to give them one hour to clean up the mess and air out the south wing. He says the north wing had not been prepared for painting, so those guest rooms are ready for occupancy.

ANALYSIS

What went right? What went wrong? This case demonstrates that cooperation between two staff members can resolve even the most unfortunate of situations. Sam was aware of the need for prior approval to take guest rooms out of service. Keith's decision to grant the request had a legitimate basis. Sam was also able to head off a nasty situation for the guests by being flexible. Then what went wrong?

The words that people use in communicating with hotel staff members must be clarified. In this case, the person who booked the convention said that there were confirmations for 100. Was this 100 guests for 50 rooms or 100 guests for 100 rooms? This lack of clarification was at the root of the problem. In some hotels, the reservations manager may require a change in reservations to be written (in the form of a letter); these written instructions are then attached to the convention contract.

These examples of day-to-day problems in a hotel underscore the importance of good communication between the front office and other departments in the hotel. Similar problems will occur again and again as you begin your career in the hospitality industry. You will grow as a professional if you adopt an analytical view of the communication system. Front office managers who actively participate in systematic communications will be more effective managers. Training employees in proper procedures for dealing with other em-

INTERNATIONAL HIGHLIGHTS

Justin, the front desk clerk on duty, cannot speak Spanish fluently but knows how to communicate phonetically with the Spanish-speaking housekeeping staff. When Victorio, the houseman, approaches the front desk to inform Justin which rooms are clean, they use the phonetic pronunciation of numerals and housekeeping status. For example:

English	*Phonetic Spanish*
Room 2180	(dough s, ooe no, oh cho, sarh o)
is	(es tah)
clean	(limp e oh)

ployees as well as their own departments will help improve the delivery of professional hospitality.

The Role of Total Quality Management in Effective Communication

Total quality management (TQM) is a management technique that encourages managers to look with a critical eye at processes used to deliver products and services. Managers must ask frontline employees and supervisors to question each step in the methods they use in providing hospitality for guests. Some examples would be "Why do guests complain about waiting in line to check out?" "Why do guests say our table service is rushed?" "Why do guests get upset when their rooms aren't ready on check-in?" Managers and their employees must then look for answers to these questions.

Total quality management was developed by W. Edwards Deming, a management theorist, in the early 1950s. His intent was to offer a new way for American manufacturers to improve the quality of their products by reducing defects through worker participation in the planning process. American manufacturers were reluctant at first to embrace total quality management, but Japanese manufacturers were quick to adopt his principles of streamlining methods to manufacture products such as automobiles. He gave managers tools such as flowcharts to analyze production by dividing the manufacturing process into specific components and then focusing on the segments of processes that produce the end product.

The most important aspect of total quality management, which results in improving products and services for guests in the hotel industry, is the interaction that occurs between frontline employees and their supervisors. The interaction of employees in a group setting and/or on a one-on-one basis to determine "what is the root of the problem" and

Figure 3-4. *Group analysis of jobs is an essential element in total quality management. (Photo courtesy of Radisson Hotels.)*

"how can we achieve the end result" thrusts employees into an atmosphere of cooperation that may not have previously existed. First-shift and second-shift employees, who usually do not understand each other's activities, find they do have common concerns about serving the guest. In the situation presented earlier, housekeeping and front desk employees would realize that a guest's request for a late checkout plays havoc with delivery of hospitality. Total quality management practices would ensure that the front office would check with housekeeping to determine room availability in such a situation. The bottom line is that interdepartmental communication is enhanced each time a team composed of members of various departments meets to analyze a challenge to the delivery of hospitality. Figure 3-4 provides a view of the interaction that is necessary to make total quality management a success.

An Example of Total Quality Management in a Hotel

Total quality management in a hotel may be applied as follows: The general manager has received numerous complaints about the messy appearance of the lobby—furniture and pillows are out of place, ashtrays are overflowing, flowers are wilted, and trash receptacles are overflowing. The front office manager recruits a total quality management team, which consists of a front desk clerk, a maid, a waiter, a cashier, and the director of

While a guest in room 421 is checking out, she indicates that there is a dripping faucet in that room. After the guest departs, the desk clerk brushes off her remark, saying to a fellow desk clerk, "There are so many dripping faucets in this hotel that one more won't mean anything."

If you were the front office manager and you heard this exchange, what would you do? How would you encourage better communication between the front office and maintenance?

marketing and sales. The team meets and discusses how the lobby area could be better maintained. The maid says her colleagues are overworked and are only allotted 15 minutes to clean up the public areas on the day shift. The front desk clerk says that he would often like to take a few minutes to go out to the lobby to straighten the furniture and pillows, but he is not allowed to leave the front desk unattended. The director of marketing and sales say that she is embarrassed when a prospective client comes into the hotel and is greeted with such a mess. She has called housekeeping several times to have the lobby cleaned but is told, "It's not in the budget to have the lobby cleaned several times a day." All of the team members realize that the untidy lobby does create a poor impression of the hotel and the situation does have to be remedied.

The team decides to look at the elements in the situation. The furniture is on wheels for ease of moving when the housekeeping staff cleans. The pillows do add a decorative touch to the environment, but they are usually scattered about. The waiter jokingly says, "Let's sew them to the back and arms of the sofa!" Might the ashtrays be removed and receptacles added for a guest to use in extinguishing a cigarette? Could a larger waste receptacle with a swinging lid be used to avoid misplaced litter? "The fresh flowers are very nice," adds one of the team members, "but many hotels use silk flowers and plants. This must save money over the long run."

The team discussion encourages each person to understand why the maid can't straighten the lobby every two or three hours and why the desk clerk can't leave his post to take care of the problem. The employees' comments concerning furniture and appointments foster an atmosphere of understanding. Team members start looking at one another with more empathy and are slower to criticize on other matters. Was the issue of the messy lobby resolved? Yes, but what's more important, the team members developed a way to look at a challenge in a more constructive manner.

Solution to Opening Dilemma

Upon initial review, the problem would seem to be that all employees should be encouraged to be more willing to assist guests in an emergency. However, in this case, the desk clerk has a "perception problem" concerning his job. This shortsightedness probably results from poor training and a dearth of opportunities for employees from various departments to exchange ideas and socialize. The front office manager should discuss the situation with the convention representative and emphasize the benefits of total quality management. Supervisors must concentrate on the guests' needs and foster employee growth and development, so that their employees will likewise concentrate on the guests' needs. These concepts are at the heart of effective interdepartmental communications.

Chapter Recap

This chapter analyzed the interdepartmental communications that must be maintained in a hotel. In particular, it focused on how the front office relates to employees in all departments—marketing and sales, housekeeping, food and beverage, banquets, controller, maintenance, security, and human resources. Guest needs are met when employees cooperate and communicate to provide hotel services. However, when these lines of communication break down, so, too, does the quality of service. The front office manager must take an objective view of these communications, considering the needs of the guest, the actions of the employees, and the policies and procedures in effect. There are times when the segments of the communication system will seem overwhelming, but the professional hotelier improves with each new challenge.

Situations illustrating communication lapses and their subsequent analysis provided insights into the complex process of communicating. Each employee must develop an appreciation for the jobs of other departmental employees to promote an understanding of how each employee's activities affect the delivery of hospitality. Well-developed operational policies and training programs will assist employees in communicating within a department and between departments.

Total quality management was introduced as a management tool that encourages interdepartmental cooperation and communication. This management technique focuses on ways everyone can work together to discuss issues and problems and resolve them as a team. This method produces the best products and services for the guest.

End of Chapter Questions

1. How do the communication efforts of front office employees help set the tone for a guest's visit? Give some examples.

2. Give some examples of how the marketing and sales department and the front office communicate.

3. Communications between the front office and the housekeeping department revolve around room status. How can each department director ensure that these communications are effective?

4. How does the banquet department interact with the front office? Do you think any of these duties should be shifted to the banquet captain's staff? Why or why not?

5. What does the controller expect of the front office on a daily basis? Why is this communication tool so important?

6. What role does the front office play in communications between the guest and the maintenance department?

7. How can the human resources department include the front office in the operations and communications process?

8. What does "tracing and analyzing the lines of communication" mean to you? Do you think this will assist you in your career in the hospitality industry?

9. What is your reaction to the use of total quality management as a means of developing better communications between departments?

10. Identify a problem area in your place of employment and develop a plan to use total quality management to resolve the issue. Whom would you place on the total quality management team? What results would you expect?

CASE STUDY 301

It is Thursday morning at The Times Hotel. The reservations manager has printed the list of reservations for the day. The front office staff has prepared 252 packets for guests who have preregistered for the Pet Owners of the Americas Conference. The Times Hotel has been designated the headquarters for the cat owners, while The Sebastian Hotel, located two blocks away, has been designated the headquarters for the dog owners. The participants in the Pet Owners of the Americas Conference are supposed to start arriving at noon.

The Times Hotel had a full house on Wednesday night. A planning group (179 rooms) for the Biology Researchers Conference was in the hotel. They held a meeting into the early hours of Thursday morning. Several of the guests posted DO NOT DISTURB signs on their doors.

Yoon-Whan Li, the executive engineer, has noticed the air-conditioning going on and off on the fifth and sixth floors. Yoon-Whan investigated the problem and estimates it will require about 12 hours of repair time. Yoon-Whan gets on the phone to the front office to report the problem, but the desk clerks are busy and fail to answer the phone. Meanwhile, another repair call comes in, and Yoon-Whan is off again. The air-conditioning situation is never reported to the front office.

The chef is busy preparing vendor orders for the day. He is also planning the food production worksheets for the Pet Owners of the Americas. The chef has left word with one of the suppliers to return his call early in the afternoon to clarify an order for the banquet tonight. The organizer for the Pet Owners of the Americas wants a special Swiss chocolate ice cream cake roll. The sales office has also included an order for two ice sculptures—one cat and one dog.

The banquet manager and several of his crew are scheduled to arrive about three hours prior to the banquet to begin setting up furniture and tabletops.

The servers will arrive about one hour before the banquet begins.

It is now 11:00 A.M., and a group of the conferees has arrived to register. They have brought along their cats and want to know where they can house them. The front desk clerk does not know where the cats are to be housed. He calls the sales department and asks for directions. The sales department says that the person who organized this conference specifically told the participants that they were to leave their pets at home. This was not to be a pet show, only a business/seminar conference.

The housekeeping staff is unable to get into the rooms (checkout time is noon). The Biology Researchers Conference attendees have not risen because of the late planning meeting. Also, two of the room attendants did not report to work this morning.

It is now 1:30 P.M., and the majority of the Pet Owners are in the lobby, with their pets, waiting to get into the rooms. With the air-conditioning out of order, the lobby is bedlam. The odor and noise are beyond description. Housekeeping calls down and says that it will need about two more hours before the first 75 rooms can be released.

The switchboard has been bombarded with telephone calls for the Pet Owners. The chef is anticipating his call from the vendor for the Swiss chocolate ice cream cake roll. He finally calls the supplier and finds out that she has been trying to call him to let him know that the supplier is out of this product, but no one answered the phone at the front desk. The

chef is beside himself and runs out of the kitchen into the lobby area. He finds the switchboard operator and verbally rips him apart. The front office manager is up to her ears in kitty litter and responds likewise to the chef. It is not the best of situations.

Just when it seems that nothing else can go wrong, a group of ten Pet Owners of the Americas arrives in the lobby with guaranteed reservations. The hotel is completely booked, and these additional reservations represent an overbooked situation. The reservationist forgot to ask if these guests were cat or dog owners. You guessed it—they all brought along Fido. The clamor in the lobby is now unbearable—dogs are barking at cats, cats are hissing at dogs, and guests are complaining loudly.

The banquet manager and his crew have finished setting up the room for the banquet. One of the crew turns on the air-conditioning; there is a dull roar, and blue smoke pours from the vents. Thinking this is only a temporary condition, he does not report it to the banquet manager. Later on, the banquet manager instructs the setup crew to take the ice sculptures from the freezer and set them in front of the podium and head table. The banquet servers will be arriving within an hour to start the preparations for the banquet.

If you were the front office manager, what would you do to solve the immediate problems at hand? After the commotion had settled down, how would you analyze the situation? List the opportunities for improving communications between the front office and other departments.

CASE STUDY 302

The following script fictionalizes a hotel general manager's weekly staff meeting. Several students should act the roles of staff members, while other students observe and analyze the communications.

Margaret Chu (*general manager*): Good morning, everyone! It's great to gather once again to discuss

our challenges and plan for the future. Let's see, Ana, you asked to have time today to discuss the issue of too few parking spaces in the hotel garage.

Ana Chavarria (*front office manager*): Yes, and this problem is causing all kinds of difficulties for my staff. At least ten guests a day threaten to cancel their next reservation if I don't find them a parking space. How am I supposed to achieve 100 percent occupancy with such a little thing as parking causing such a big problem?

Andy Roth (*parking garage manager*): Hold on there, Ana. Running a parking garage isn't an easy job. We have a lot of new monthly business customers who are helping us make plenty of money. Did you forget that those new monthly business customers paid for the property management system you just bought? You were pretty happy about that new business six months ago.

Margaret Chu: Look, folks, we have to focus on the customer right now; I think both of you have lost sight of who the customer is.

Eric Jones (*food and beverage manager*): It seems to me we have too few customers. I would like to see some of those new parking customers stop in to one of my restaurants to have lunch. We have been tracking our lunch guests with business card drawings, and so far we have only had three of them in for lunch. Let's get rid of those new parking customers and stick to the regular hotel guests.

Frank Goss (*director of maintenance*): I agree. Those new parking customers are littering all over the garage. They dump their cigarette butts and fast-food trash all over the place.

Andy Roth: I'll tell you just like I told Ana, those new parking customers bought you that fancy machine to change lightbulbs in your department. Where were all of you people when I asked Margaret Chu if we could start to market the sales of new parking garage permits? This hotel should be called Hotel Second Guess!

Eric Jones: I think we are getting carried away with this concern; the real problem we have here is the lack of cooperation with security. Ana, didn't you have two guest rooms broken into this month? It's too bad the director of security isn't here to tell us

more about it. We never seem to get any follow-up reports on what's going on or what we can do to prevent it from happening again.

Margaret Chu: Mike, that is a good point you bring up, but we have to resolve Ana's problem first. What do all of you suggest we do about the parking problem? Should we abandon a very profitable profit center or keep the hotel guests happy?

Andy Roth: Ms. Chu, if I may be so bold as to say so, the solution we need is neither of those two options but a third one. Let's lease some off-premises parking from the Reston Hotel across the street for our hotel guests during the business week. My friend Margo runs that garage, and she says it is only about 75 percent full most weekdays.

Margaret Chu: Well, Andy, I will have to check this out with the general manager of the Reston. He and I have a meeting with the City Visitors Association tomorrow.

Frank Goss: Ms. Chu, before we get to that security problem, let's discuss my need to cover the second shift over the weekend. That is an impossible request, because I am so understaffed. Do any of you have any extra employees who are handy in fixing things and would like to earn a few extra bucks?

Margaret Chu: Frank, it's not that easy. We are on a tight budget, and there are no extra dollars to pay overtime. Let's think about it and put a hold on scheduling a person for the second shift until we can resolve the issue.

Frank Goss: Sounds good to me.

Margaret Chu: OK, Frank, we can meet right after this meeting and talk about it.

Many of you do have challenges running your departments, and most of the time, you do great jobs. However, from what I am hearing today, we need to start anticipating problems before they happen. Recently I ran across a management technique called total quality management. It will help us understand one another's challenges and make us a little more patient. I will schedule a few workshops for you and your employees in the next few weeks.

As observers of this staff meeting, how do you feel the staff members interact with one another? What role is Margaret Chu playing? If you were the general manager, what role would you play? What effect do you feel the total quality management workshops will have on this group?

Key Words

amenities
banquet manager
daily announcement board
folio
guest histories
house count
housekeeper's room report
housekeeping room status
interdepartmental communication

intradepartmental communication
marquee
paid-outs
point-of-sale terminals
predicted house count
room sales projections
sales associate
total quality management (TQM)
transfers

CHAPTER 4

Property Management Systems

OPENING DILEMMA

At a recent hotel trade show, you noticed a new property management system

that seems to produce all the types of reports that your current system cannot

produce. The vendor at the show said she will set up a meeting with you in a

week or two to talk more about this system. How would you prepare for her

visit?

CHAPTER FOCUS POINTS

- Physical structure and positioning of the front desk

- Selecting a property management system (PMS)

- Using PMS applications

The first three chapters of this text provided an overview of the hotel industry, organization of the hotel, organization and management of the front office, and interdepartmental communication, which laid the groundwork for understanding how the front office fits into a network for providing service to the guest. In this chapter, we focus on the operational aspects of the front desk department, which include considering the physical structure and positioning of the front desk, selecting a property management system (PMS), and using PMS applications.

Computer applications are central to front office operations in today's modern hotels. For new properties, computers are standard pieces of equipment; for existing hotels, computers are being integrated into everyday operations to assist in providing hospitality to guests. Computer applications include routinely processing reservations as well as handling registrations, guest charges, guest checkout, and the night audit. **Interfacing,** electronic sharing of data, of hotel departments such as food and beverage and the gift shop through **point-of-sale,** an outlet in the hotel that generates income (restaurant, gift shop, spa, garage); maintenance through monitoring of energy and heating and cooling systems;

and security through control of guest keys are just a few of the applications that are explored in this chapter.

As you begin your career in the lodging industry, you will want to develop a thorough understanding of front office computer applications. This text does not refer to one particular computer hardware or software system; your training at any lodging property will include specific operating procedures to produce various reports or review information from the database. Instead, this chapter provides general information on which you can base your understanding of computer applications at the front desk. These applications are encompassed by the term **property management system (PMS)**, a generic term used to describe applications of computer hardware and software used to manage a hotel.

You will notice that PMS is not confined to the front office; it interfaces with housekeeping, food and beverage, marketing and sales, gift shop, controller, engineering, safety and security, and other departments, all of which are service departments of a hotel. Each department plays a role, along with the front office, in serving the needs of the guest—before, during, and after the guest's stay. It is the front office staff which coordinates the communications, accounting, security, and safety requirements of the guest. As the nerve center of the hotel, the front office handles most of the recordkeeping and so benefits most from a computerized system.

The first part of this chapter sets the stage for adopting a PMS. Software and hardware considerations are discussed,[1] as are other considerations in choosing a PMS. The final section of the chapter discusses the various computer modules of the PMS as they apply to the lodging industry.[2]

This revision of *Hotel Front Office Management* includes references to a student manual for a hotel front office software simulation prepared by Dr. Sheryl Fried Kline and William Sullivan. This tutorial will allow students to process reservations and registrations, post guest charges, handle customer service issues, and perform the night audit procedure. It is a great opportunity for students to practice capturing and maintaining the many details of managing the guest experience in a hotel front office and then understand how those details support the administrative function of the hotel. The application of this student manual and software simulation will begin in Chapter 5.

Physical Structure and Positioning of the Front Desk

Figure 4-1 shows the layout of a computerized front office. While manual equipment is still being used in some independent properties, the computerized system has become the system of choice, primarily because of the needs of guests, management, and owners.

Guest First Impression

The front desk has always held a pivotal position of importance in the lodging operation. It is one of the first points of contact with the guest, and, as such, its ambience sets

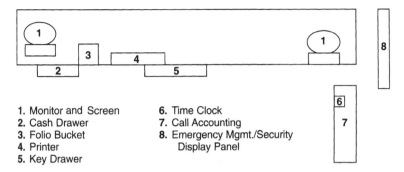

1. Monitor and Screen
2. Cash Drawer
3. Folio Bucket
4. Printer
5. Key Drawer

6. Time Clock
7. Call Accounting
8. Emergency Mgmt./Security
    Display Panel

Figure 4-1. *The layout of computerized equipment centers on guest service and employee efficiency.*

the tone for the hotel. Neatness, orderliness, attractiveness, quality, and professionalism are just a few of the impressions that the front desk should convey to a guest. The guest wants to feel important, safe, and in the hands of professionals. The impression the physical layout of the desk creates will assist the front office in creating a positive image for the operation. Providing hospitality to the guest and promoting in-house sales (covered in more detail in Chapters 11 and 13) are of great importance to the continued financial success of the operation. To provide an environment for these objectives to be met, a well-planned physical arrangement of the front desk is important.

Creating a Balance between Guest Flow and Employee Work

EQUIPMENT

The front desk should be positioned so that it accommodates the guest while enabling employees to work efficiently. Guests who wait in line for ten minutes only to be told they are in the wrong line will have a negative first impression. Likewise, a desk clerk who has to wait to use a printer or share a computer terminal will not be as efficient as possible. As you become familiar with the practice of processing guests at the front desk, you will see how easy it is to plan a layout of the physical equipment needed.

GUEST SAFETY

The position of the front desk is usually determined by the main entrance of the building and the location of the elevator. The front desk clerk and the night auditor must be able to see anyone who enters the hotel, to ensure a safe environment for the guest. Positioning the front desk on the same side as the main entrance and the elevator is not recommended. Figure 4-2 shows a few arrangements that allow entrances to be monitored. In all three settings, the front desk clerk has a view of who is coming into the hotel

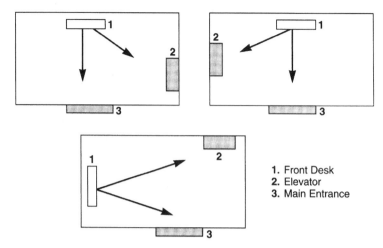

Figure 4-2. *Front office staff have a clear view of persons entering the lobby from the street entrance or elevator.*

1. Front Desk
2. Elevator
3. Main Entrance

Kevin Corprew, director of rooms operation at the Marriott in Overland Park, Kansas, is a graduate of the University of Houston in hotel and restaurant management. Mr. Corprew has worked with Marriott Hotels in various places and positions, including the Marriott Medical Center in Houston, Texas, as a desk clerk, rooms controller, and supervisor; the Airport Marriott in Houston, Texas, as a banquet manager; and the Marriott Courtyard in Legacy Park, Dallas, Texas, in rooms care (housekeeping and engineering), front office, and restaurant and bar areas. He also worked at the Hilton Washington and Towers in Washington, D.C., in sales.

Mr. Corprew indicates that setting the ambience of the front desk requires a simple, elegant appearance. Preliminary discussions of new trends in front desk structure include a walk-through for associates that will allow them to pass in front of and behind the desk to accommodate guests. Also, the front desk and lobby are to be considered together in design and function.

The organization of the front desk, with its computers and vast amounts of details, revolves around an uncomplicated guideline: keep it simple. Mr. Corprew provides plenty of key machines (electronic devices to make electronic guest room keys); ensures that all staff follow standard operating procedures, such as keeping faxes and mail in one location; and requires associates to be considerate of guests' needs. His organizational principle is continued at the time of check-in, when a 100 percent automated use of a property management system only requires the associate to swipe a credit card and to prepare and present the room key to the guest.

Kevin Corprew urges young professionals who want to make a career in the hospitality industry to lead by example with high morals and standards and not to be something that they are not. He encourages students to start in entry-level jobs so they will have a basis for dealing with employees.

International translation cards, which assist foreign guests in translating travel phrases of their native language into English, are frequently kept at front desks. Foreign visitors and hotel desk clerks find these cue cards very helpful.

from the street entrance and who is coming off the elevator. This view is essential to the night auditor, who assists security in monitoring the activities in the hotel lobby.

Selecting a Property Management System

This section focuses on the components that should be included when deciding to adopt a PMS. The decision-making process begins with understanding the importance of a needs analysis performed by a team of frontline staff members. The needs analysis should focus on the flow of the guests through the hotel and interdepartmental communication needs. A review of administrative paperwork produced by management in all areas of the hotel is also a consideration. After management has gathered relevant data concerning the operational needs, it must objectively determine whether a computer will help to improve guest service. Other important concepts covered here include software selection considerations and computer hardware terminology. A review of how people interact with computers and how a hotel must make provisions while hardware is being installed is also offered. The importance of computer training and planning a backup power source for continued computer operation is reviewed. The often overlooked maintenance agreement and the very important financial payback complete the discussion of selecting a PMS.

Importance of a Needs Analysis

Selecting new equipment for a hotel property is best done after a needs analysis is performed.[3] A **needs analysis** indicates the flow of information and services of a specific property to determine whether the new equipment—in this case, computers—can improve the flow. The bottlenecks that occur at registration or the lack of information from the housekeeping department on the occupancy status of a room can be alleviated by the use of computers at the front desk. Only after the completion of an operational flow analysis can computer applications be developed to improve the situation.

The importance of needs analysis can be most clearly seen when you consider what can go wrong if such an analysis is not made. The first area of concern for property owners and managers is cost, both initially and over the long term. As the technology evolves and the equipment becomes more common, the cost of computerizing a hotel has decreased and the payback period has shortened. However, even with these lower costs, installing and operating a PMS is not inexpensive, and the cost of installing and operating a system that does not meet the specific needs of a particular property is exorbitant.

A system that works very well for one downtown hotel may not meet the needs of a downtown hotel in another city or of a motel in the same area. All the technological gadgetry in the world will not impress a guest if the equipment fails to deliver service. The system must meet the needs of the staff as well as the guests. An inappropriate PMS will produce control reports that are not useful to management; the functions of such software therefore become limited, and the cost of the system exceeds its value. For example, a hotel owner who believes that a PMS would speed up registrations and decides to purchase a system that does not allow housekeeping staff to input room status from the guest room phone will be disappointed.

Procedure for Performing a Needs Analysis

The following list shows the procedure for performing a needs analysis.

1. Select a team to analyze needs.

2. Analyze the flow of guests through the lodging property.

   - Reservations
   - Registration
   - Guest accounting
   - Checkout
   - Night audit
   - Guest history

3. Analyze the flow of information from other departments to the front office.

4. Analyze the administrative paperwork produced in other departments.

5. Review the information gathered in steps 2, 3, and 4.

6. Evaluate the needs that have been identified—such as control reports, communication, and administrative paperwork produced in other departments—in terms of importance.

7. Combine needs to determine desired applications.

Selecting a Team

The first and most important step in performing a needs analysis for adopting a PMS in a hotel is to select a team to determine the reports and information being generated. The analysis team should include employees at both the management and staff levels.

Such a team is better able to see all aspects of the operation: management can provide input on the overall objectives, while staff is more aware of day-to-day needs. The front office manager who feels the reservation system is very inefficient may find that the desk clerk not only agrees but can offer suggestions for improving the situation. This desk clerk may not know the first thing about **flow analysis processes**—preparing a schematic drawing of the operations included in a particular function—but the hands-on information provided will assist the front office manager in evaluating the reservation system. In another instance, the general manager may request that certain additional room sales analysis reports be produced by the marketing and sales department only to find the front office manager producing that information.

Analyzing the Flow of Guests through the Hotel

The second step in the needs analysis is to analyze the flow of guests through the visit to the property, which provides a structure for this very detailed analysis process. The guest stay does not start at registration but at the time a reservation is made. (In reality, the guest stay starts even before this, because guests often select a property as a result of marketing efforts.)

Issues that can be analyzed are quite diverse. They include analyzing the ease with which the telephone system can be used, the availability of room occupancy status for guests on any specific date, the length of time it takes to complete a reservation request, the method used to confirm a reservation, the procedure used to block rooms, and the means of finding a single reservation. Also subject to analysis are the methods for gathering guest information upon check-in and the processes for ensuring the correct posting of guest charges, the time required for a guest to check out, the procedure used to resolve a guest's dispute of charges, and the process for posting meal and phone charges just before checkout. How are the daily room charges and taxes posted to the rooms? How long does it take to do this? Are there any vital statistics that are not being produced by completion of the night audit report? How is the information assembled in the night audit? How long does it take to produce this information? Also determine if guest information already on hand from reservation, registration, and guest accounting is being applied for additional visits.

Communicating Information

The third step in the needs analysis process is to look at the information coming from other departments to the front office. How is information concerning occupancy status received from the housekeeping department? How can a guest report an emergency or fire on the property? How do the food and beverage department and gift shop report guest charges? How does the marketing and sales department determine if blocks of rooms are available on certain dates? How does the engineering department monitor energy use in guest rooms? How does the security department ensure the integrity of guest keys? A good PMS can embrace all of these lines of communication.

Reviewing Administrative Paperwork

The fourth step is to review the administrative paperwork produced in the hotel that is necessary to assist management. How does the human resources department maintain personnel files and former employee records? How is direct-mail advertising generated in the marketing and sales department? How are function books and individual function sheets maintained? How are **tickler files,** files used to prompt notice of when certain events will be occurring, maintained? How are work orders processed? What method is used to devise daily menu specials?

Management Review of Information

In the fifth step of this analysis, management must take charge of reviewing the information compiled to determine if needs are being met. Is the marketing and sales department making mistakes because incorrect information concerning the inventory of available rooms was provided by the front office staff? Are desk clerks unable to check the occupancy status of a guest room because the housekeeping department is not providing immediate information? Have misquotes on room rates caused lost revenue for the hotel? Is the night auditor unable to retrieve room status information to confirm or guarantee reservations?

The significance of each need and the consequences if the need is not met are then established. Customer satisfaction and quality of service as well as financial implications are considered. How often have conventions not been booked because accurate information on room availability was not at hand? How much revenue was lost as a result? How frequently does a general manager receive complaints because a guest was sent to a room that was under repair or not cleaned? How often must the front office manager adjust a guest's room rate because of a misquote? How does the number of guaranteed reservations compare with the number of confirmed reservations? Why are guaranteed reservations not requested by the night auditor?

Assessing Needs Based on Findings

The final step in the analysis is to combine various operational and administrative needs to determine which computer applications are appropriate for the property. Often the shared use of a room inventory database is well worth the financial investment. A word-processing program to produce direct-mail letters, regular correspondence, and daily menus may also justify a particular module of a PMS. The needs analysis enables you to know what you need and what you do not need and will help you choose from the many systems available.

Choosing Software

Selecting **software,** computer-designed applications that process data such as guest information and aid in financial transactions and report generation, is more important than selecting **hardware,** computer equipment such as central processing units, keyboards, monitors, and printers. The effectiveness of a PMS depends on selecting software that allows management to increase guest satisfaction and to access financial and informational data for control purposes. The information obtained from the needs analysis will provide a framework for evaluating the numerous software packages on the market today.

Each software package offers numerous features; it is important to choose one package that is most appropriate for your needs. Software on the market today includes those guest service, accounting, and information options that are standard in the hotel industry. Investigate the guest service features, accounting options, and information applications to determine which PMS is best for your property. If you feel that the applications of a particular software package will not help you manage your property, that adding a particular guest service will not increase guest satisfaction, that no significant savings will result from producing more sophisticated accounting reports, or that the arrangement of historical information about guests will not be beneficial, then you should not adopt that particular PMS. You control the software selection; its function is to assist you in doing a better job. Only you can decide which applications are most useful in your facility. Some of the more common options for various departments are listed in Figure 4-3.

Choosing Hardware

Choosing hardware for a PMS is not as difficult as choosing software. Today most available hardware is compatible with standard computer operating systems (such as Microsoft Windows). This consideration is essential because most software programs are written to run on these standard operating systems. In short, you must choose your hardware based on its ability to handle the software; check on this with your hardware vendor.

Other technology factors to consider include the following working concepts:

Processor speed: how fast a central processing unit (CPU) makes calculations per second; expressed in MHz (the abbreviation for "megahertz")

Disk drive: a place in the computer where data is stored or read; hard or floppy—3½-inch versus Zip drive

Megabyte: 1,024 kilobytes of formatted capacity

Gigabyte: 1,024 megabytes of formatted capacity

Access time: the amount of time required for a processor to retrieve information from the hard drive; recorded in milliseconds

Internet: a network of computer systems that share information over high-speed electronic connections

I/O ports (input/output devices): keyboards, monitors, modems, mouse, joystick, light pen, printers, and track balls

Monitor: a television screen with color or monochrome capacity to view input and output data, control column width and line length of display, adjust height of character display, and allow visual control

Figure 4-3. *Common software options in a PMS.*

MARKETING AND SALES
- Client file
- Direct mail
- Guest history
- Travel agent
- Meeting room information

NIGHT AUDIT
- Room and tax posting
- Various operational reports

ACCOUNTING
- Accounts payable
- Accounts receivable
- General ledger
- Payroll
- Profit-and-loss statement
- Balance sheet

HUMAN RESOURCES MANAGEMENT
- Personnel files
- Time and attendance

ELECTRONIC MAIL

SECURITY

RESERVATIONS
- Room availability
- Yield management

FRONT DESK
- Check-in
- Room status
- Postings to guest accounts
- Guest credit audit
- Advance deposits
- Cashier

CALL ACCOUNTING
- Guest information
- Phone call posting

HOUSEKEEPING
- Room status

MAINTENANCE
- Work orders

FOOD AND BEVERAGE
- Point-of-sale
- Menu profitability
- Inventory
- Recipes

Keypad: a numeric collection of typewriter keys and function keys that allow the operator to enter numbers or perform math functions in a computer

Keyboard: a standard or Dvorak-type typewriter-style keypad that allows the operator to enter or retrieve data

Printer: computer hardware that produces images on paper:

> **Dot-matrix:** produces small dots printed with an inked ribbon on paper

> **Ink-jet:** produces small dots printed with liquid ink on paper

> **Laser:** produces photo images on paper

> **Letter-quality:** a better type of dot-matrix print

> **Draft-style:** a good type of dot-matrix print

> **Tractor-fed:** a type of printer that uses a continuous roll of paper

> **Single-sheet:** a type of printer that uses single-sheet paper

Modem: computer hardware that allows for transfer of data through telephone lines; expressed in baud—information transfer—rates

CPS (characters per second): measure of the speed with which individual characters are printed

Computer supplies: paper, forms, ribbons, ink cartridges, and floppy disks needed to operate the system

Megahertz (MHz): one million cycles per second; indicates computer speed

PPM (pages per minute): printing speed capability

Zip drive: a computer accessory that holds data; a 100-megabytes Zip drive holds an equivalent of 70 floppy diskettes

The front office manager must be aware of the operational capabilities of the PMS. Computer texts and trade journals can help you understand the various hardware options available; *Personal Computer* magazine, in particular, is very helpful for keeping up to date on hardware configurations and software applications. Visits to hospitality industry trade shows will also keep you informed on state-of-the-art systems.

The standard hardware used to operate a PMS is shown in Figure 4-4. The basic hardware requirements are organized around the various points-of-sale and customer service areas. Keyboards, monitors, disk drives, and printers constitute the basic user setup. The data manipulation and storage area is part of the mainframe, minicomputer, or personal computer.

The ability to interface among computer databases (sharing or networking of information) is very important. As computer applications become more sophisticated, sharing

Figure 4-4. *Computer hardware includes a keyboard, monitor, central processing unit, and printer. (Photo courtesy of IBM.)*

databases is essential. For example, the information secured at the time a reservation is made can be used by the marketing and sales department to generate more business.

The positioning of the hardware at workstations should be based on the same work-flow analysis used for any new process or equipment. Consider the needs of the guest (who will be the end user), the employee who will operate the equipment, and the other staff who will want access to information. The information you have gained from the needs analysis will assist you in explaining your particular needs to the computer consultants who will install your PMS.

The installation of the electronic cables that connect all of the hardware must also be analyzed. Installation and replacement of cables that run through walls and floors can be costly. The requirement for air-conditioned atmospheres for proper computer functioning should also be investigated; in guest service areas, this may not present a problem, but in other areas, it may pose difficulties.

Ergonomics, the study of how people relate physiologically to machines, is also a consideration for the front office manager. Glare and flicker from the **cursor,** a flashing point on a monitor that indicates where data can be entered, and movement on screens can cause eyestrain. In fact, it is fairly common for computer operators to require lenses to correct eyestrain. Another common complaint is neck pain due to improper positioning of the monitor. The swivel base provided on most hardware helps to eliminate these problems. Pain in the wrist may also occur if the keyboard is positioned above the waist of the operator. Carpal tunnel syndrome, compression of a nerve in the wrist and fingers, is another unfortunate result of overuse of computer keyboards. Because carpal tunnel syndrome causes extreme pain for a computer operator, the keyboard should be positioned at waist level. Also, pains in fingers and hands can occur with extensive entry of data on a keyboard.

Other PMS Selection Considerations

Other factors to consider in choosing a PMS are vendor claims, installation plans, training, backup power sources, and maintenance.

Vendor Claims

The prospective PMS purchaser should contact current users of the system being considered and ask relevant questions: How easy is it to operate this system? How useful are the reports you obtain? Has the vendor been available to help train staff and provide emergency service? Answers such as "I don't know how the property could manage without it" or "It is very difficult to operate, and the reports are awkward" may alert you to potential advantages or problems. (Remember, however, that different properties have different needs and priorities; a rave review because the system provides an option that you consider unimportant is meaningless for your purposes.) Consider the amount of time these properties spent on needs analyses. A visit to the hotel property is worth the effort invested. Learning how different features of the system work, how various departments interact with the PMS, and what kinds of forms are used will help you with part of your decision. You will also get a feeling for how guest services are affected.

Hardware Installation Plans

A careful plan for hardware installation will help the management maintain guest service and employee morale. First, it is key to determine who will install wiring or cables. Next to be determined is which hardware will be installed and at what times, followed by which departments will receive hardware first, and what methods will be required to get all departments of the property **on-line,** a term used to indicate that a computer is operational and connected with a central computer. This information should be used to develop a flowchart, which will help departments adapt and interact using on-line operations.

Computer Training Programs

The training offered by a computer company ranges from classes held at the corporate headquarters to on-the-job training sessions and informal consultant hot lines. The staff that will use the computers must be thoroughly trained if the equipment is to be put to

Figure 4-5. *Employees need time to practice using computer hardware and software. (Photo courtesy of Red Lion Hotels.)*

its best use. Training at the terminals should be preceded by an explanation of how the system will help staff members in their work. Some computer companies will lend a dummy computer setup to a lodging property so that the staff can experiment with the training modules (Figure 4-5). This allows them to make mistakes in private and to become familiar with the keyboard configuration. Documentation of procedures will also assist the staff in developing an awareness of the system's capabilities, as will individual hotel-developed step-by-step computer application cue cards.

It is also important to note that employee resistance to change can be overcome with an early buy-in to a new concept and a training program that is very user-friendly. The team concept will help employees to overcome resistance to change because they are included on the team. Members of the needs analysis team will see an idea develop from concept to fruition. Also, many employees resist change because they fear they will be unable to perform a new task. A training program that allows adequate time and practice will help introduce technology.

Backup Power Sources

What happens if the power goes out? This concern, as well as the possibility of **brownouts,** partial loss of electricity, or **blackouts,** total loss of electricity, has been addressed by computer dealers. Battery-powered temporary energy units are used when power is lost or cut, to ensure that operational data are not lost. Hotel managers who have experienced power losses are well versed in maintaining communication among the various departments and posting charges as required. Once the power returns in full, the staff can catch up on posting to the electronic folio.

Maintenance Agreement

One final consideration in adopting a PMS is the maintenance agreement, which should spell out the related costs of repair and replacement of hardware and software. Allowance for emergency service and times available for general service should also be listed. When loaner or backup equipment is available, it enhances the attractiveness of the agreement.

Financial Considerations

Purchasing or leasing a PMS for hotel use is a major financial decision. Such an investment can tie up cash flow. If the costs and benefits are not realistically projected, profits may be in jeopardy. The first part of this chapter stressed the importance of performing a needs analysis. Hotel properties that match needs with computer applications by going through this process will achieve the most realistic assessment of costs versus benefits when adopting computers.

The controller of a lodging property has usually prepared a budget in consultation with the general manager. Sales of room nights, food and beverages, and other products and services are projected. Considered with these projections are the related costs of producing those goods and services. The controller is usually aware of the specific costs in each department—the amount of overtime pay required at the end of the month to produce the monthly inventory in the food and beverage department, the extra part-time help required to staff the front desk for a busy checkout or check-in, the cost to produce a direct-mail piece for the marketing and sales office, and the fee charged by the outside accountant to produce a monthly profit-and-loss statement. This knowledge is very helpful in determining how much money can be saved if a PMS were to be introduced. The amount of money that can be saved (along with tax depreciation advantages) must be equal to or greater than the amount spent on the computer system. Sometimes management may feel that less tangible benefits, such as greater service to the guest or improved morale among employees, justify the cost even when dollar savings are not quite equal.

The decision about whether to purchase or lease must also be made. The outright cost of purchase, related finance charges (if applicable), discount for cash, and depreciation are only a few of the points to review if the hotel decides to purchase. These considerations have to be weighed against continuance of cash flow, application of lease payments to the purchase price, and tax advantages of leasing.

Determining the **payback period**—the period of time required for the hotel to recoup purchase price, installation charges, financing fees, and so forth through cost savings and increased guest satisfaction—will also assist management in deciding whether to install computers. If the controller reports a series of financial problems such as the following, the payback period becomes clearer:

- 5 percent of all local phone calls are not posted at the front desk
- 2 percent of sales are lost every month because guest checks are inaccurately totaled in the food and beverage department
- Ten hours of overtime could be saved through internal preparation of paychecks for each pay period

As the department directors go over their respective profit-and-loss statements with the controller, additional areas for cost recovery can be noted. The time invested in preparing an accurate needs analysis will pay off in the long run.

The above concerns of the controller include areas in addition to the front desk. Remember that the adoption of a PMS includes the management of all guest services and accounting functions. While the needs of the front desk alone—for a call-accounting system or the rental of a reservations system—may not justify the expense of a PMS, the needs of all departments can make such a system cost-effective.

PMS Applications

The property management system is organized around the functions needed to assist in delivering service to the guest. The software options listed earlier in this chapter are only a few of the many that are available to hoteliers. For purposes of this review, assume that the lodging property has been equipped with a state-of-the art PMS and the system is up and running. The software program **main menu** lists on the screen all the available individual programs (modules) that are included in the system. Refer to Figure 4-6.

The options shown in Figure 4-6 are similar to those previously listed in this chapter. The front desk clerk can access any of these individual programs by typing the designated keystrokes or following directions on a **touch screen,** a type of computer monitor screen that allows the operator to input data by the touch of a finger. The documentation, which consist of either printed or on-screen (monitor) instructions, explains how to operate the hardware or software that accompanies a specific PMS. This documentation will consist of written step-by-step instructions as well as a flowchart of individual programs and subprograms, all of which is very valuable in training staff. The flowcharts are comparable to the blueprints of a building. The following discussion of individual modules and subprograms will highlight the applications of these software options in a property management system.

Figure 4-6. *Main menu of a property management system.*

1. Reservations
2. Yield Management
3. Registration
4. Room Status
5. Posting
6. Call Accounting
7. Checkout
8. Night Audit
9. Inquiries/Reports
10. Back Office
11. Housekeeping
12. Food and Beverage
13. Maintenance
14. Security
15. Marketing and Sales
16. Personnel
17. Electronic Mail
18. Time Clock

Reservations

The reservations module (refer to Figure 4-7) consists of subsystems that can receive individual guest or group data, check a guest's request against a data bank of available rooms, and store this information. The guest data are received through a personal phone call or through another computer in the referral system. All of the possibilities or room types and locations, room rates, and special requests can be matched with the existing room inventories. This information can be stored for up to 52 weeks (or more) in most systems.

Information concerning guarantees with credit cards or confirmed reservations is captured at this time. Details on deposits, blocking, times of arrival and departure, VIP guest lists, projected occupancies and reports on these reservation functions assist the front office manager.

The guest who is checking out of the Limited-Service Inn in Dallas, Texas, and wants to make a reservation at the Limited-Service Inn in Chicago for that evening can have the reservation confirmed within seconds. The guest information is already available in the data bank, and through electronic transmissions, the request is verified (via a check of the existing room inventories held in the data bank for the Limited-Service Inn in Chicago) by a central computer. Similar procedures are followed by other referral agencies. (Further examples of computerized reservations options are provided in Chapter 5.)

Figure 4-7. *Reservations module.*

1. Guest Data
2. Room Inventory
3. Deposits
4. Special Requests
5. Blocking
6. Arrivals
7. Departures
8. VIP
9. Projected Occupancy
10. Travel Agents
11. Guest Messages
12. Reports

Yield Management

Yield management, a process of planning to achieve maximum room rates and most profitable guests (guests who will spend money at the hotel's food and beverage outlets, gift shops, etc.), encourages front office managers, general managers, and marketing and sales directors to target sales periods and develop sales programs that will maximize profit for the hotel. This module (Figure 4-8) shares similar databases with the reservations module—room inventory, room rates, reservation status, and guest information. If a hotel is entering a maximum demand sales period, the yield management module will allow the reservations manager to block out that time period to prevent guest requests for room reservations for less than the minimum time period. Also, the computer will prompt the reservations clerk on which room rate category to apply. Daily reports on how well the front office achieved maximum yield of **rack rates,** the highest room rate charged in a hotel, provides feedback to the general manager and owners. A history of guest sales in food and beverage also assists sales and marketing managers in determining if a group reservation has potential for profitability.

Figure 4-8. *Yield management module.*

1. Master Rate Table
2. Per-Person Increments
3. Guest Type Increments
4. Yield Management

Figure 4-9. *Registration module.*

1. Reservations
2. Guest Data/Registration
3. Room Inventory
4. Room Status
5. Security
6. Reports
7. Self-Check-in

Registration

Guest registration modules have greatly improved the check-in process. Because information has already been captured at the time of reservation, less time is required for registration. The front desk clerk need only verify the guest's request for room type, location, and rate with room inventory and room status. Provisions for walk-in guests without reservations are similarly handled. Method of payment is also established. The hard-plastic key can be issued after the security module has changed the entrance code for the room. The guest registration procedure can also be completed by the **self-check-in process,** a procedure that requires the guest to insert a credit card having a magnetic stripe containing personal and financial data into a self-check-in terminal and answer a few simple questions concerning the guest stay (Figure 4-9). (Self-check-in is discussed in more detail in Chapter 7.)

As an example of how this module works, consider the guest who flies to Chicago from Dallas, signs a guest registration form, waits until the desk clerk checks the status of the room, and receives a key—check-in is complete. All guest information was captured when the initial reservation at the Dallas Limited-Service Inn was made. The data bank of room occupancy information provided by the housekeeper is available to the front desk via the computer. The front desk clerk chooses the room the guest will occupy and issues a key. The total time required for registration is less than five minutes.

Room Status

Access to the **room status** module provides information on availability of entry to a guest room. There are two types of room status—reservation and housekeeping. Reser-

The general manager of the hotel asks you to help determine the payback period for a $20,000 PMS. How would you begin?

Figure 4-10. *Room status module.*

1. Room Inventory
2. Availability
3. Reports

vation status can be open, confirmed, guaranteed, or repair. Housekeeping status can be ready, on change, or out-of-order. Reservation status is maintained by the reservation department or reservation system, while housekeeping status is provided by the housekeeping department. The room status feature is one of the most valuable features of the PMS (Figure 4-10). It streamlines the operation problems of check-in and assists other departments as well. This module, which may share the same room data bank with reservations, provides very useful reports used by the housekeeper, front office manager and staff, maintenance engineer, night auditor, reservations clerk, and marketing and sales department. The housekeeper must know which guest rooms have been occupied and need cleaning; desk clerks must know if the guest room is reserved or open for sale; the maintenance engineer must plan in advance for routine painting and refurbishing; the night auditor must verify which rooms have been sold to complete the night audit; the reservations clerk needs information on the availability of guest rooms; and the marketing and sales department must have current information on room availability for conventions.

Posting

The **posting** module of a PMS often supplies one of the first benefits realized by the front office manager, because it allows immediate posting of charges incurred by the guests (Figure 4-11). Not only is the posting operation streamlined, but accuracy is ensured. A PMS allows the posting to occur at the point-of-sale in the restaurant, lounge,

Figure 4-11. *Posting module.*

1. Point-of-Sale
2. Room
3. Tax
4. Transfer
5. Adjustment
6. Paid-out
7. Miscellaneous Charges
8. Phone
9. Display Folio
10. Reports

or gift shop. Similarly, room and tax charges or telephone calls can be posted to the electronic folio in a very short time. Transfers and adjustments of guest charges (with approval by management) to folios are easily made. Charges incurred on behalf of the guest can be posted to the electronic folio by entering room number, amount of charge, department, and transaction type. These data are stored in memory and are retrieved after an inquiry, during report generation, or at checkout. The accuracy of these charges still depends on the employee operating the point-of-sale terminal in the restaurant. Entering an inaccurate room number (room 412 entered as 712) or a reversed amount ($32.23 entered as $23.32) will still result in an incorrect posting.

Our guest at the Limited-Service Inn in Chicago wants to charge his valet expense of $20.95 to his room account. After the desk clerk has processed the paid-out to the deliveryperson, this charge is posted to the electronic folio by entering the room number, amount of charge, department, and type of transaction. The night auditor verifies the integrity of all department totals.

Call Accounting

The **call-accounting** module of a PMS is a system that automatically posts telephone charges and a predetermined markup to a guest's folio (Figure 4-12). The individual subscriber to the telephone system (the lodging property) can charge a service fee for any local or long-distance call. The hotel can now use the telephone system to generate profit rather than to simply supply service to the guest. The ability to make a profit through adding service charges, combined with the increased frequency and accuracy of electronic posting, has made the call-accounting option very desirable. However, with the increased use of cell phones, phone cards, and personal digital assistants (PDAs), telephone revenue has declined in some properties. The PMS call-accounting feature retrieves data for time, charges, and service fee and then posts these charges to the electronic folio. The accuracy of processing telephone charges is greatly increased through the use of a PMS call-accounting feature.

Figure 4-12. *Call-accounting module.*

1. Guest Information
2. Employee Information
3. Post Charges
4. Messages
5. Wake-up Calls
6. Reports

Figure 4-13. *Checkout module.*

1. Folio
2. Adjustments
3. Cashier
4. Back Office Transfer
5. Reports
6. Guest History

Checkout

The inconvenience of guest checkout (long lines, disputes over charges) is greatly reduced with the PMS checkout feature, which prints out an accurate, neat, and complete guest folio within seconds (Figure 4-13).

Disputes over guest charges still occur at the time of checkout, but not as often. The posting of a long-distance telephone call to room 295 instead of room 296 is less likely to occur with a PMS, because the PMS interfaces with the call-accounting system and the phone charge is automatically posted to the guest's electronic folio.

Efficiency at time of checkout is also improved when the desk clerk retrieves a hard copy of the folio and presents it for review to the guest. The guest has already indicated method of payment at check-in. An imprint of the credit card has been made, or prepayment has occurred. The **floor limit,** a dollar amount of credit allowed by the credit-card agency, and **house limit,** a dollar amount of credit allowed by the hotel, have been monitored by the PMS. These controls help to avoid high **debit balances,** the amount of money the guest owes the hotel. Last-minute purchases of products or services are automatically posted at the point-of-sale terminals.

The guest completes the checkout process by confirming the method of payment. The desk clerk may suggest the possibility of making future reservations at this property or other properties in the chain or referral group. Transfers to the city ledger are made electronically at this time. Cashier activity reports are monitored as well as other information about the day's checkouts (such as number of guest departures and time of departures). A PMS can generate a **paid in advance** (PIA) listing, which monitors guests who paid cash at check-in. The PIA prevents guests from charging any products or services to their guest folio.

Guests can avoid checkout lines by using **in-room guest checkout,** a feature of the property management system that allows the guest to use a guest room television to check out of a hotel. For this process, the night desk staff slips a copy of an updated guest folio under the door the night prior to checkout. The guest enters a few digits on the television control panel to start the process. After he or she answers a few questions (regarding multiple guest accounts in the same room, accuracy of charges, and method of payment, for example), the process is complete. The guest can pick up a copy of the folio at the front desk if desired.

Figure 4-14. *Night audit module.*

1. Guest Charges
2. Department Totals
3. City Ledger
4. Cashier
5. Financial Reports
6. Housekeeping

Night Audit

The night audit has always been very labor-intensive. In addition to acting as a desk clerk and posting the room and tax charges, the night auditor must balance the guest transactions of the day. To extend credit to guests, debits and **credits,** the amount of money the hotel owes the guests, must be balanced on a daily basis. The debits originating from the various departments must be checked against the totals posted to the various guest folios. The credits, in the form of guest payments, must be accounted for by reviewing the guests' outstanding balances. Although this sounds like a simple process, the procedure can be very involved (Figure 4-14).

The PMS simplifies the night audit by producing totals from departments and guest folios. These data are assembled into standard report forms. Various financial information is then used in the daily report. The daily report is used by the management of the lodging property to determine the financial success of a particular day.

Inquiries/Reports

The **inquiries/reports** feature of the PMS allows management to retrieve operating or financial information at any time. The front office manager may want to check the number of available rooms in the room inventory for a particular night, the status of the number of guests to be checked in, the number of guests to be checked out for the day, the current room status from the housekeeping department, or the **outstanding balance report,** a listing of guests' folio balances. These reports can be produced easily on a PMS (Figure 4-15). The inquiries/reports feature of the PMS enables management to maintain a current view of operations and finances.

Back Office

The hotel's accounting office, known as the **back office,** uses the accounting module of a PMS, which assists in the overall financial management of the hotel (Figure 4-16). PMS simplifies the accounting processes. These include: the labor-intensive posting procedure of **accounts payable,** which is the amount of money the hotel owes vendors; the transfer of **accounts receivable,** which is the amount of money owed to the hotel, based

Figure 4-15. *Inquiries/reports module.*

1. Reservations
2. Registrations
3. Checkouts
4. Housekeeping
5. Credit Balances

on the guest ledger and city ledger; compilation and production of the payroll; budget preparation; the production of the **profit-and-loss statement,** which is an official financial listing of income and expenses; and the **balance sheet,** which is an official financial listing of assets, liabilities, and owner's equity at a certain point in time. For example, financial information concerning a certain vendor is entered once on a terminal located in the back office (controller's office). This information is then reflected throughout various parts of the accounting process. Likewise, the financial information produced through the night audit can be accessed for various reports. These and other features assist in streamlining the accounting process.

Housekeeping

Obtaining current information concerning guest room status has always caused problems for the front desk staff. Guests become very impatient when they are delayed in the check-in process. Desk clerks who have not received a room release from housekeeping have no choice but to remain calm and try to appease the guests. The process of obtaining ready status is quickly achieved with a PMS (Figure 4-17). The maid or houseman enters the ready status immediately through a computer terminal on the guest floor, instead of waiting to report a block of rooms to the floor supervisor. The housekeeper no longer needs to make several trips per day to the desk clerk to release blocks of rooms. The efficiency of this module depends on the continued efforts of the housekeeping staff in reporting room status.

Personnel assignments of room attendants for cleaning rooms can also be made very

Figure 4-16. *Back office module.*

1. Accounts Payable
2. Acounts Receivable
3. Payroll
4. Budgets
5. General Ledger
6. Reports

Figure 4-17. *Housekeeping module.*

1. Room Availability
2. Personnel Assignment
3. Analysis
4. Housekeeper's Report
5. Equipment/Supplies Inventory
6. Maintenance Requests

easily. Labor analysis of number of guest rooms cleaned by room attendants and amount of labor hours required to clean guest rooms is performed faster, and the daily housekeeper's report is quickly generated. Inventory of equipment and guest room supplies is also readily available.

Maintenance requests for guest rooms can be communicated through the PMS. The maintenance department staff can also check room status information to determine if the housekeeping staff noted repairs to be made. If the maintenance department wants to take a room out of service for a few days to perform repairs, this information can be relayed to the housekeeping and front desk staff through the housekeeping module.

Food and Beverage

The food and beverage module reduces paper flow (vouchers) as well as telephone calls from the restaurants and lounges to the front desk (Figure 4-18). It also facilitates the accounting process, verifying the integrity of the point-of-sale system. Cashier reports (cash, credit, room service) are easily produced. Other features include inventory control and calculation, recipe development, pricing, item profit evaluation, and sales projections. Sales production analysis and labor analysis are also possible with this module.

Figure 4-18. *Food and beverage module.*

1. Point-of-Sale
2. Posting
3. Cashier Reports
4. Food/Beverage Inventory
5. Recipes
6. Sales Control
7. Sales Production Analysis
8. Labor Analysis

Figure 4-19. *Maintenance module.*

1. Review Work Order
2. Room Status
3. Cost/Labor Analysis
4. Inventory
5. Repair Cost Analysis
6. Energy Usage Analysis
7. Guest Room Power Start

Maintenance

Using a PMS streamlines the processing of work orders. Repair orders are entered by various department members. Incomplete jobs can be prioritized, and completed jobs can be analyzed for cost. Inventories of equipment and parts can be maintained. This module is also used to track energy costs and areas of use. In fact, heating and air-conditioning in guest rooms can be activated at the front desk. This module enables the management of a hotel to analyze operational information of this vital department (Figure 4-19).

Security

Electronic key production has enhanced key control. Each guest receives an electronic key that has a unique electronic code, because the PMS changes the key configuration or combination for each new guest room. Blank key cards plastic or metal) can be coded at the front desk for each new guest.

Continual monitoring is a feature of the security module of the PMS. Fire-alarm systems in guest rooms, public areas, and operational areas are kept under constant surveillance via a **fire-safety display terminal,** a device that ensures a constant surveillance of sprinkler systems and smoke detectors. An alarm system or a voice telephone monitoring system will alert guests to a fire anywhere on the property. Elevators return automatically to the main lobby area or other designated floor. Burglar alarms are also monitored through this module. The security feature of a PMS monitors the use of security codes in other modules as well (Figure 4-20).

Figure 4-20. *Security module.*

1. Keys
2. Fire Alarm
3. Burglar Alarm
4. Security Code Transactions

Figure 4-21. *Marketing and sales module.*

1. Guest History
2. Word-processing
3. Client Files
4. Banquet Files
5. Desktop Publishing
6. Reports
7. Travel Agencies
8. Room Status—Meeting Rooms

Marketing and Sales

The marketing and sales department makes extensive use of the PMS (Figure 4-21). This department can retrieve **guest histories**—information on guests' previous stays that reveals geographic origin, telephone information, organizational affiliation, credit-card usage, personal room accommodation preferences, and the like—from reservation and registration files. The source of the reservation (secretary, group, travel agent), type of accommodation requested, and zip code of business office or personal domicile are only some of the data that can be obtained from the reservation files. Additional marketing data (newspapers read on a regular basis, radio stations listened to on a regular basis, source of recommendation) can be collected at the time of registration to give the marketing and sales department information on advertising media for target markets.

Another PMS application that the marketing and sales department can use is the ability to produce **direct-mail letters,** which are letters sent directly to individuals in a targeted market group. Individual letters advertising certain products and services, together with mailing labels, can be prepared. Weekly **function sheets,** listings of the daily events in a hotel such as meetings, banquets, receptions, and so forth, can be produced by assessing various individual **banquet sheets,** listings of the details of an event at which food and beverages are served. Information on clients can be stored and updated as required. Contracts can also be produced. Tickler files on upcoming events are a great asset in keeping an edge on the competition. In addition, monthly newsletters can be produced through the word-processing and desktop-publishing applications. This module provides a great organizational feature in maintaining reserved occupancy status of meeting and banquet rooms.

Personnel

The maintenance of personnel files is greatly enhanced by using a PMS (Figure 4-22). Information concerning job category, date of hire, record of orientation and training, rate of pay, last evaluation date, promotions, pay increases, payroll deductions, and the like will assist management in developing a well-operated human resources department. The

Figure 4-22. *Personnel module.*

1. Employee File
2. Job Control List
3. Word-processing
4. Analysis
5. Reports

amount of paper involved in employee recordkeeping can be kept to a minimum. The word-processing application is used to generate form letters, job descriptions, reports, employee procedures, and policy manuals. The PMS also permits labor analysis to be performed with ease.

Electronic Mail

The electronic mail feature, often called **E-mail,** is a communication system that uses an electronic network to send messages via computers. It is very helpful in distributing current information on policies and procedures to a large staff as well as communicating with current and former hotel guests. When E-mail is used, security codes are issued to maintain privacy. Staff members are able to check their E-mail at the computer terminal. Copies of E-mail can be printed if needed for future reference (Figure 4-23).

In a large corporation with many company-owned properties or franchises, E-mail allows for communication among establishments. In a hotel with many operating departments and thus many department heads, this feature is a great asset to the communication process.

Time Clock

Individual employees are issued a security code and an individual personal identification number. Upon entering their work area, they need only enter that number to record their start time. As they leave the work area for breaks or at a shift's end, they again need only enter that number. This information is stored and used by the controller's department when compiling the payroll. This feature saves a great deal of time in calculating the number of hours an employee worked on any given day (Figure 4-24).

Figure 4-23. *Electronic mail module.*

1. Security Codes
2. Mail
3. Hard Copy

Figure 4-24. *Time clock module.*

1. Security Codes
2. Personal Identification Number
3. Time In
4. Time Out
5. Analysis
6. Reports

Solution to Opening Dilemma

Prior to the vendor's visit, it is advisable to perform a needs analysis. Although such an analysis may have been performed five years ago, the needs of hotel guests, management, and operations change over time. Forming a team of frontline employees and supervisors will allow for a good decision. This team should analyze the flow of guests through the duration of their stay to establish a list of guest needs that could be enhanced through technology. Because the team is composed of employees from different departments, other departmental requirements, including administrative paperwork, will also need to be discussed. These discussions will enable the team to prepare a list of needs that will enhance the guest's stay, assist departments in preparing reports, and improve communications among departments. The final step is to prioritize the needs and measure them against the budget. Other considerations include verifying vendor claims, developing installation plans, discussing training programs provided by the computer company, finding out about the availability of backup power sources, and securing a reasonable maintenance agreement. Financial considerations will include cost-benefit analysis, the decision to purchase or lease, and working out a realistic payback period.

Chapter Recap

This chapter reviewed the importance of positioning the front desk to allow front office personnel a view of guests who enter the lobby from the street entrance and elevators. The guest's first impression is enhanced by the ambience, physical appearance, and orderliness of the equipment and personnel. The front office manager must establish a balance between guest service and work processing to allow for efficiency.

This chapter examined the use of computers by a hotel property, particularly in the front office. Deciding to purchase a computer system and choosing the system begins with a thorough needs analysis, a detailed procedure that allows the front office manager (and other department managers) to assess the value of automating particular systems. The process of evaluating software is a prime prerequisite in determining which computer applications best meet the needs of a particular property. The front office manager will also want to evaluate the hardware needed to operate the selected software package. The decision to adopt a system is further clarified by considering vendor claims concerning operation, installation, training, backup power sources, and the maintenance agreement. The financial considerations of purchasing or leasing will complete the computer decision. Front office managers should be aware of the computer applications—reservations, registration, room status, posting, call accounting, checkout, night audit, inquiries/reports, back office, housekeeping, food and beverage, maintenance, security, marketing and sales, personnel, electronic mail, and time clock—of a property management system as they relate to the successful operation of a front office.

End of Chapter Questions

1. When arranging equipment at the front desk, what factors should be considered?

2. Why is the position of the front desk in a hotel lobby important?

3. Describe the evolving role of computers in the hotel industry.

4. Explain in your own words what a property management system is. How does a property management system help to provide hospitality to a guest?

5. Why should a needs analysis be performed before computers are purchased? What are the components of a needs analysis?

6. Why are computer software considerations more important than computer hardware considerations?

7. If you are employed at a hotel that uses a property management system, which of the software options listed in the text do you use? Explain the advantages of these modules.

8. If you are employed in a hotel with a property management system, discuss computer hardware descriptions with your front office manager. What does your manager find most valuable? Why?

9. Why is interfacing important in a property management system? What are some examples of interfacing?

10. What is ergonomics? How does the ergonomics of computer terminals affect the front office staff?

11. How would you go about verifying vendor claims when considering the purchase of a property management system?

12. How does a well-developed installation plan for a property management system assist hotel management?

13. Why should management be sure employees are properly trained to use a property management system?

14. If the power goes out in a 200-room lodging property for four hours, how would you preserve the data in a property management system?

15. If you are employed in a hotel, ask your front office manager if there is a maintenance agreement for the property management system. What items are covered? How well has the computer company stood behind the agreement?

16. Discuss the "purchase versus lease" consideration in terms of financial profitability.

17. What does the main menu of a PMS tell an operator? How is it organized?

18. Review the computer applications described in this chapter. Explain how they are used to provide better service to the guest and to improve financial control in the hotel.

Software Simulation Exercise

Review Chapter 1, "Getting Started," of Kline and Sullivan's *Hotel Front Office Simulation: A Workbook and Software Package* (New York: John Wiley & Sons, © 2003), and work through the various concepts as presented in the chapter.

- How to Use This Demonstration Software
- Using the Innstar Program
- How to Exit Innstar
- Printing from Innstar
- Clerk ID Number
- Description of the Hotel Property
- Summary of the Basics
- System Requirements
- Chapter 1 Exercises

CASE STUDY 401

Ana Chavarria, front office manager, and Lorraine DeSantes, director of marketing and sales, have just returned from a computer conference at which they were able to take a look at the latest property management systems for hotels. Ana is very enthusiastic about updating and adopting front office applications for reservations, registration, room status, posting, call accounting, checkout, and night audit. Lorraine is sure the marketing and sales applications will help her department be more efficient.

Both realize the cost involved in obtaining modules for a property management system. What would you suggest they do prior to discussing this issue with Margaret Chu, general manager of The Times Hotel?

Assuming Ms. Chu is willing to consider the purchase of a PMS, how should Ana and Lorraine proceed? Whom should they include in developing a PMS adoption plan and why? What areas should they investigate?

CASE STUDY 402

The computer team of The Times Hotel is in the process of updating a computer needs analysis. The team is ready to decide which new modules should be adopted. Ana Chavarria, front office manager and chairperson of the committee, is seeking some consensus on whether the team should recommend the purchase of a point-of-sale module for the restaurant operation or a guest history module for the marketing and sales department. Eric Jones, food and beverage manager, says the point-of-sale module will pay for itself in six months because guests are walking out of the hotel without having their breakfast charges posted to their folios. Lorraine DeSantes, director of marketing and sales, says the purchase of the guest history module will increase business by 25 percent in the first year. The budget will allow for only one purchase. What concepts would you recommend to the team to break the stalemate?

Notes

1. CARA Information Systems, Inc,; Computerized Lodging Systems, Inc.; ECI/EECO Computer, Inc.; Hotel Information Systems; and Lodgistix, Inc.
2. Ibid.
3. Reprinted from *Hospitals* 56, no. 9 (May 1, 1982), by permission. Copyright 1982 by American Hospital Publishing, Inc.

Key Words

access time
accounts payable
accounts receivable
back office
balance sheet
banquet sheet
brownouts
call accounting

computer supplies
CPS (characters per second)
credit
cursor
debit balance
direct-mail letters
disk drive
dot-matrix

draft-style
E-mail
ergonomics
fire-safety display terminal
floor limit
flow analysis processes
function sheets
gigabyte
guest histories
hardware
house limit
ink-jet
inquiries/reports
in-room guest checkout
interfacing
Internet
I/O ports (input/output devices)
keyboard
keypad
laser
letter-quality
main menu
megabyte
megahertz

modem
monitor
needs analysis
on-line
outstanding balance report
paid in advance (PIA)
payback period
point-of-sale
posting
printer
processor speed
profit-and-loss statement
property management system (PMS)
ppm (pages per minute)
rack rate
room status
self-check-in process
single-sheet
software
tickler files
touch screen
tractor-fed
yield management
Zip drive

Reservations

OPENING DILEMMA

Two days remain before the first guest checks in for the Forest Conservation Conference. A quick review of the reservation module report indicates that several of the new desk clerks took guaranteed reservations (35 rooms) for that convention that account for 10 percent more rooms than are available.

Making reservations is a necessity for travelers and an important marketing tool for lodging establishments. Travelers in various market segments depend on a well-organized reservation system that is easily accessible through toll-free numbers or on the Internet to ensure a well-planned trip. Lodging establishments want to provide a continuous flow of guests, which will bring profits. A reservation system must ensure efficient means of accessing, processing, and confirming information (Figure 5-1). Without an efficient reservation system, all aspects of managing a hotel will be negatively affected. For example, while overbooking reservations may guarantee a full house for the hotel, it will also leave the guest who is turned away with a negative impression. This not only decreases the hope of repeat business but also ensures that the dissatisfied customer will tell others of the negative experience. This chapter examines the reservation system as an integral part of progressive front office management and discusses the operation of a well-run system.

Figure 5-1. *A reservation clerk is ready to process a guest's request for a room reservation. (Photo courtesy of Radisson Hospitality Worldwide.)*

Importance of a Reservation System

Profitable business ventures rely on effective marketing principles, which include reviewing people who are in need of hotel products and services, determining their needs, developing products and services that meet their needs, and making a profit on the sale of those products and services.

A well-organized reservation system allows hotels to ensure a steady flow of guests into their properties. Hotel chains offer their members the ability to fill 30 percent or more of available rooms on a nightly basis. Independent hoteliers have the onerous responsibility of creating exciting marketing programs to capture room business. Easy access to a hotel's data bank of rooms helps in fulfilling the customers' needs as well as in reaching a targeted daily occupancy rate, average daily rate, yield percentage, and RevPAR. A reservation system represents the primary means of producing positive cash flow and a favorable income statement.

Overview of the Reservation System

The hotel industry is powered by sales that are derived from the use of computerized reservations systems. The following information on Choice Hotels International, Six Con-

Dulcie Baker, director of sales at the Tidewater Inn, Easton, Maryland, has been in the hotel industry for more than 25 years. Ms. Baker's duties include responsibility for room sales for groups, banquet coordination, and managing the sales staff.

She began her career at the front desk, reservations, and sales at the Wilmington Hilton, Wilmington, Delaware, and continued developing her sales expertise at the Bay Valley Hotel & Resort, Bay City, Michigan; the Holiday Inn in Coral Springs, Florida; The Abbey in Lake Geneva, Wisconsin; the Holiday Inn in Greenbelt, Maryland; and the Days Inn at the Inner Harbor in Baltimore, Maryland.

The Tidewater Inn is privately owned and does not participate in a national reservations system. Its focus is on delivering quality hospitality in its trademark operation. However, it does practice yield management and works from yearly budget projections to produce the targeted volume in sales.

Ms. Baker extends her best wishes to future professionals who are studying hotel management and says, "Good luck. It's a great business if you're people-oriented."

---

tinents Hotels (formerly Bass Hotels & Resorts), Carlson Hospitality Worldwide, and Pegasus Solutions provides a concise view of the importance of computerized reservation systems to the hospitality industry.

Choice Hotels International

Choice Hotels International, with its 5,000 franchisees in 42 countries, operates under the Comfort, Quality, Clarion, Sleep, Econo Lodge, MainStay Suites, and Rodeway Inn brands. In a press release, Choice Hotels International announced its capability of offering guests reservation services through handheld computers:

> Owners of the Palm VII or Palm VIIx handheld computer can download Choice's web clipping application to their handheld by visiting www.choicehotels.com, then clicking on "wireless" on the options menu. After following the download instructions, Palm VII or Palm VIIx handheld owners with Palm.Net service are able to reserve rooms, check room availability, check on existing reservations and more. "Essentially, the application provides all of the booking capabilities available through our web site," said Gary Thomson [senior vice president and chief information officer at Choice].[1]

Six Continents Hotels

Six Continents Hotels (formerly Bass Hotels & Resorts) operates 3,200 hotels and resorts in nearly 100 countries and territories on six continents under the Inter-Continental, Crowne Plaza, Holiday Inn, Express by Holiday Inn, and Staybridge Suites brands. This corporation has 490,000 guest rooms and hosts more than 150 million guests each year. Six Continents Hotels reservations system Holidex processes more than 100 million reservations per year.[2]

Carlson Hospitality Worldwide

Carlson Hospitality Worldwide's central reservation system is called Curtis-C (pronounced "courtesy"). It services approximately 730 hotel locations and six cruise ships operating on all seven continents. For the year 2000, it processed approximately 8,900 reservations per day, with a total of 3,242,031 for that year. Brands include Regent International Hotels, Radisson Hotels & Resorts, Country Inns & Suites by Carlson, Park Plaza and Park Inn hotels in North America, and Radisson Seven Seas Cruises. It is connected to 455,000 travel agents via the global distribution system (GDS). Curtis-C interfaces with the company's hotels via HARMONY, the company's property management system, and the CustomerKARE (or Customer *K*nowledge *a*nd Relationship Enabling) system. It also interfaces with the HARMONY Database Manager, which provides access to hotel inventory (updated rates and availability) along with the ability to deliver reservations through several distribution systems; the Guest Communication Manager, a system that manages guest satisfaction information (providing a history of service problems per guest per hotel and scanning for trends and patterns); and KnowledgeNet, which provides hotels with easy access to valuable company information (corporate policies, forms, reports, hotel procedures, and newsletters) and also eliminates monthly printing of hotel reports and distribution to the properties. The benefits of this interfacing of data include creating and distributing products worldwide in seconds, making information easily accessible to customize the customer experience, allowing for synergies among applications and reducing resource requirements, and adapting to changing markets and technologies.[3]

Role of the Internet in Securing Reservations

In a *Hotel & Motel Management* article by Bruce Adams, Alan White, from the application service provider Pegasus Solutions, discusses ResView, the company's central reservation system (CRS) offered on the application-service-provider model.

"Today, you need photos," he said. "We also are pushing a shopping engine for a softer search, which wants to know what experience customers are looking for." They could search by summer and the beach, for example, or for family-oriented experiences or for winter skiing. "We want to build more intelligence into it for the more savvy consumer," he said. White said that the number of corporate customers booking through the Web has doubled in the last year. Those customers want to be able to use negotiated rates, which adds another level of complexity. "The use of negotiated rates on the Web has doubled in the last year [2000]," he said. "We see increased booking volume on the Web, which slightly erodes Global

Distribution System and voice bookings." Despite the increase there are still 1,000 Web hits for a single Web booking. For voice reservations, it is fewer than 100 calls for every booking, he said. "Our Web sites are extremely busy, so we have to use different architectures to handle all the volume," he said. "Many, many people shop on the Web and book elsewhere." "Direct to hotel is still the most popular booking channel, claiming about 62 percent of reservations," White said. Hotels using the new Web-booking model also want an increased emphasis on preferred guest handling. "They want to be able to keep track of guests, know where they are from, why they have come, how they got them and when they come back," he said. "They also want more sorting of data and delivering of extracts."[4]

This *Hotel & Motel Management* article focuses the reader on several important issues that hotel front office managers and general managers should consider in maintaining a marketing edge with reservations. The use of the Internet in making room reservations is becoming a part of the natural way of doing business. Potential business and pleasure traveler guests want to see what your hotel offers in the form of guest rooms, amenities, food and beverages, and other services as well as related prices. Likewise, the hotel managers seek feedback data on the customers who may visit their Web site and hopefully their hotel. It is interesting to note that, at the time of this writing, out of 1,000 Web hits made by consumers, only one customer sale is made, as compared to the 100 incoming calls processed for every one reservation completed. Perhaps the softer touch still has its place in hospitality.

Types of Reservation Systems

Franchisee

The **franchisee** is a hotel owner who has access to a national reservation system and receives the benefits of the corporation's management expertise, financial backing, national advertising, and group purchasing. A franchise member of a reservation system or a member of a referral system gains significant advantages from combined efforts of **interhotel property referrals,** a system in which one member-property recommends another member-property to a guest, and national advertising.

Referral Member

A **referral member** of a **reservation referral system,** a worldwide organization that processes requests for room reservations at a particular member-hotel, is a hotel developer/owner who has access to the national reservation system. Hotels that are members of the reservation system are more than able to justify these costs: for example, a chain property may obtain 15 percent to 30 percent of its daily room rentals from the national reservation system, depending on local economic and market conditions. Compared to the costs incurred by an independent property that must generate every single room sale with individual marketing and sales efforts, franchise referral costs seem minimal.

Hotel & Motel Management reports that use of the reservation system by franchises and referral properties involves various fees, such as royalty, marketing, and reservations. For example, a royalty fee could include 50 cents per day per room, or $1,000.00 plus $75.00 per room per year, or 5 percent of the gross room rate. A marketing fee may include $3.00 per room per month or a $480.00 sign fee. A reservations fee could include 25 cents per minute for use of a toll-free number or $12.00 per room per year or $5.50 per delivered reservation or 5 percent per room night booked.[5]

Sources of Reservations

Guest reservations come from a variety of market segments. Some of the more common groups include corporate clients, group travelers, pleasure travelers, and current guests who want to return to the same hotel. This is only one way of classifying guest reservations. The purpose of analyzing these segments is to understand the needs of each group and provide reservation systems to meet their needs.

Corporate Clients

The **corporate client** is a hotel guest who is employed by a business or is a guest of that business. Corporate clients provide a hotel with an opportunity to establish a regular flow of business during sales periods that would normally be flat. For example, a hotel located in an area popular with weekend tourists would operate at a loss if an aggressive marketing effort were not made to secure corporate clients from Sunday through Thursday nights. Corporate clients are usually in town to visit corporate headquarters or to attend business meetings or conventions. Visits are usually well structured in advance, with detailed agendas and itineraries. Such structured schedules suggest that the corporate guest will need reservations to ensure a productive business visit.

The reservation for the corporate guest may be initiated by a secretary or an administrative assistant. These office personnel are vital to the marketing efforts of a hotel. Many hotels offer a secretaries club, which is a powerful marketing and public relations effort aimed at this group. The program encourages the secretary or administrative assistant to make room reservations with the hotel for visiting business clients by providing incentives such as gift certificates for the person who books the most reservations, free meals for being a member, and free special-interest seminars. This system provides the basis for a very loyal contingent of secretaries and administrative assistants who think of the club's hotel first. This marketing program helps the front office manager and the reservationist get to know the various leaders in the business community in an indirect way. If such people need a quick reservation on a busy night, they feel they will receive special consideration from the hotel's management.

A toll-free phone number assists the cost-conscious corporate client by giving corporate guests calling from outside the property's area code an opportunity to save on phone bills. The independent lodging property that has installed a toll-free phone number gives itself a marketing advantage. If the person making the reservation wants to check out rates, location, amenities, related hotel services, and the like, he or she can do so without incurring an expense. The corporate client can then match travel needs with the available lodging properties.

The corporate client can also place the reservation through the reservation/referral system of the chain organization. The large chains, through their radio, television, billboard, and print advertising, offer the corporate client the opportunity to make a reservation easily through a toll-free number. The number connects the caller to a reservationist who has access to a data bank of available rooms at lodging properties that are members of the chain or referral system. The reservation can be completed in minutes. The use of a single phone number to access all properties offers the corporate client an easy, standard way to make reservations for stays in several cities with one call. In the lodging industry, this opportunity to gain repeat business is very important.

The travel agent also makes reservations for corporate clients. The travel agent who is booking air or other transportation for clients usually books room reservations as well.

The corporate client can also visit a hotel's Web site to obtain information on the hotel and make a room reservation.

Group Travelers

Group travelers are persons who are traveling as a group either on business or for pleasure. Convention guests and seminar attendees are examples of groups that travel on business. Participants in organized tours tend to pursue recreation, education, and hobbies, and special interests constitute some of the pleasure segment. The key to marketing reservations to this group is providing an efficient access method for planning details of a tour. The **group planner** is the person responsible for securing guest room accommodations, food and beverage programs, transportation reservations, meeting facilities, registration procedures, tours, and information on sightseeing, as well as maintaining a budget for group travelers. The group planner must satisfy the needs of the group in an efficient, orderly, and professional manner. The details involved in organizing a three-day convention in a large city for 700 attendees or a seven-day tour of points of interest for 44 people are quite extensive. How does the leader of group travelers begin?

Some of the options available for the tour or meeting planner include tapping into the **bus association network,** an organization of bus owners and tour operators who offer transportation and travel information to groups, using directories listing various lodging properties, communicating with hotel representatives of various lodging properties, and contacting hotel brokers. Hoteliers provide information concerning lodging facilities and tourism through these sources.

Bus associations are professional organizations on the national and state levels that provide their members with organized destination information needed for planning tours and conventions. Usually these associations organize conventions of their own by working with various hotels, tourist attractions, and travel and promotion associations in the public sector that supply facilities and points of interest to the group traveler. Through the monthly publications of these associations, members can remain current on the travel industry. The lodging operation that advertises in these publications will reach a market that is looking to add variety to a group tour.

Travel directories, organized listings of hotel reservation access methods and hotel geographic and specific accommodations information, also provide the group travel planner with the opportunity to match facilities with the needs of the group. The most common of these directories is the *Hotel & Travel Index.* Other directories include the following:

> *AAA Tour Books and Travel Guides*
> *Consortium Guide*
> *Destination-specific Directory*
> *Michelin Guide*
> *Mobil Travel Guides*
> *OAG Business Travel Planner*
> *OAG Gazetters*
> *Official Hotel Guide*
> *Official Meeting Facilities Guide North America*
> *Premier*
> *Star Service*
> *The Hotel Guide (THG)*
> *Weissmann Travel Reports*[6]

These valuable publications enable the planner to check the features of different lodging properties with great ease.

Working with a **hotel representative,** a member of the hotel's marketing and sales department who actively seeks out group activities planners, is another method the group planner may find quite appropriate. Armed with the details about the lodging facility, points of interest in the area, and community background, the hotel representative can prepare a package deal for the planner. This active solicitation of group business can prove to be very profitable for a hotel.

Another type of active solicitation for group travelers is done by the **hotel broker.** This is the person who sells hotel room prize packages to corporations, sweepstakes promoters, game shows, and other sponsors. By booking reservations in volume, a hotel broker obtains a discount for the organization that wants to offer a hotel visit as a prize. Chain and referral organizations usually have people in their corporate marketing and sales divisions who contact various organized groups or brokers to sell the hotel rooms and facilities.

As mentioned earlier, the key to securing the business of group travelers is to develop a structured access system that assists the planner in meeting the needs of the group. The more readily available the information concerning the lodging property, tourist attractions, and the community, the easier it will be for the planner to choose a property.

Pleasure Travelers

Pleasure travelers are people who travel alone or with others to visit points of interest or relatives, or for other personal reasons. These travelers, who are often unrestricted by deadlines or schedules, are more flexible in their travel plans than are corporate clients and group travelers. They are more willing to seek someplace to stay along the way; however, some of the people in this group may want to obtain guaranteed reservations to ensure a trip with no surprises. This group is very fragmented and consists of many subgroups, including singles, married couples, young families, senior citizens, and students. Some of the various methods the pleasure traveler can use to secure room reservations are travel agencies, toll-free numbers, reservation/referral systems, and the Internet.

Although using travel agents to place reservations may not be as common with pleasure travelers as it is with businesspeople, the ease of "one-stop shopping" that travel agents offer encourages hotels to develop strong business relationships with them. Melinda Bush of *Murdoch* magazines states, "Hotels are viewing [travel] agents as extensions of their sales and marketing departments."[7] The fee a lodging facility pays for accepting a reservation placed by a travel agent is usually 10 percent or more of the room rate, a minimal sum compared to the increase in volume and subsequent profits that an agent can generate for a property.

Another method used by the pleasure traveler to make reservations is the toll-free phone number. Calling these numbers, which are listed in travel guides and the phone book, provides pleasure travelers with up-to-the-minute room rates and reservation availability status.

The third method available for the pleasure traveler is the reservation/referral system. This option offers the traveler a quick way to contact a particular hotel, via a national or an international reservation/referral system. Travelers planning trips for a long period of time or visits to unfamiliar areas usually prefer some semblance of assurance that accommodations will be available, clean, safe, and comfortable. The quality assurance provided by name recognition built up over a period of time by a chain convinces the traveler to place room reservations through its reservation/referral system.

A fourth method used by the pleasure market segment to make reservations is via the Internet. Travelers can visit the Web site of the participating hotels to investigate accommodations and pricing as well as to make reservations. Considering the popularity of home computers and their connection to the Internet, this method will grow.

Current Guests

One of the often overlooked areas for attracting room reservations is through **current guests,** guests who are registered in the hotel. (Although this topic is covered in more detail in Chapter 13, it is important to mention it briefly here as a source of reservations.) This potential market is a promising source of repeat business. The people in this group have already experienced the services and facilities of a lodging property and may be quite willing to make an immediate commitment to more hospitality from the same hotel or another hotel in the same chain or referral group.

The opportunity for booking additional reservations occurs during the check-in and checkout phases of the guests stay. After registering the guest, the front desk clerk may ask if he or she will be continuing to travel after leaving the hotel. If the guest mentions plans to travel to another city, the desk clerk may inquire if a reservation is needed. Likewise, the desk clerk may ask the guest on checkout if additional reservations are needed for continuation of this trip or for future trips. The hotel that promotes its facilities to current guests in this way will be rewarded with an increase in room occupancy.

Forecasting Reservations

Forecasting or **rooms forecasts,** which involves projecting room sales for a specific period, is a natural next step after the data from the reservation process have been collected. This step includes previewing the effects of reservations on the income statement, scheduling labor, and planning for the use of facilities. In addition to presenting a practical method for preparing a rooms forecast (sometimes referred to as a "projection of room sales"), this section also indicates how such a forecast can be used as a means of communication with other departments (Figure 5-2).

One of the purposes of a rooms forecast is to preview the income statement. It enables the hotel managers to determine projected income and related expenses for a certain time period. The front office manager, who has estimated total room occupancy to be 100 rooms with an average room rate of $75 for a seven-day period, can project a revenue of $52,500 (100 × $75 × 7) from room sales. Budgeted cost-control policies allow the front office manager to allocate a certain amount of that income for front office staff. This process of projecting sales and related expenses is very important to the successful management of the front office (Figure 5-3).

The front office is not the only department that depends on a well-constructed rooms forecast. The food and beverage department, housekeeping department, and maintenance department rely on the **house count.** This refers to the number of persons registered in a hotel on a specific night. This is important for scheduling labor, using facilities, planning improvements or renovating facilities, ordering supplies, and the like. For example, if a **full house,** 100 percent hotel occupancy, is predicted and there are no scheduled banquet breakfasts, extra wait staff must be scheduled in the dining room. Employees in the housekeeping department may be refused vacation during certain periods when a full house is expected. Other contingencies include a maintenance department's need to schedule major repairs and preventative maintenance, annual cleaning, and remodeling of guest rooms when occupancy is low; a controller's need to prepare a cash flow estimate; an executive housekeeper's need to schedule adequate staff based on guest room occupancy;

Figure 5-2. *A rooms forecast assists in planning for delivery of service.*

ROOMS FORECAST FROM: ___ SUN DEC 1 ___ TO: ___ SAT DEC 7 ___										
	1	2	3	4	5	6	7			
GUAR RES	25	50	55	40	45	10	10			
CONF RES	20	25	20	20	25	10	15			
WALK-INS	80	80	80	5	5	5	5			
GROUPS	20	0	0	30	30	30	0			
TTL ROOMS	145	155	155	95	105	55	30			
TTL GUESTS	180	195	190	110	125	75	45			

COMMENTS: DEC 1/2/3 WALK-INS FROM DDS CONVENTION AT STONE HILL MANOR
DEC 4/5/6 JOHNSON TOURS FROM CANADA—
ALL MEALS IN DINING ROOM A LA CARTE

CC: HOUSEKEEPER   GENERAL MGR
FRONT OFFICE MGR   DIR MKTG AND SALES
SWITCHBOARD   FOOD AND BEV MGR
MAINT ENGR   EXEC CHEF
GARAGE MGR   BANQ MGR
RESTAURANT MGR   HOSTESS A.M./P.M.
                     LOUNGE MGR

a security department's requirement to be aware of activity projected for the hotel; and a parking garage manager's need to know if the garage can meet the auto/van space requirements for the anticipated guests. These are just a few of the uses of the rooms forecast.

The front office manager will want to determine the revenues projected by this rooms forecast. To do this, the average room rate or the specific room rate for a group may be applied. This information is very important to the controller, general manager, and owner of the hotel, who use it in managing the hotel's finances. This system can also be used to prepare quarterly or yearly financial projections.

Overbooking (Occupancy Management)

The concept of **overbooking**—accepting reservations for more rooms than are available by forecasting the number of no-show reservations, stayovers, understays, and walk-ins,

Figure 5-3. *The front office forecast is issued to all department heads in the hotel.*

TIMES HOTEL
Weekly Room Sales Forecast

	10/1	*10/2*	*10/3*	*10/4*	*10/5*	*10/6*	*10/7*
Departures	0	10	72	75	5	15	125
Arrivals:							
Confirmed	40	20	30	25	5	8	22
Guaranteed	30	18	17	90	4	2	10
Total	70	38	47	115	9	10	32
Walk-ins	20	20	30	10	10	5	50
Stayovers*	10	85	68	65	175	177	65
No-shows	5	3	5	10	2	2	3
TOTAL**	95	140	140	180	192	190	144

* Yesterday's total − departures
** Yesterday's total − departures + arrivals + walk-ins − no-shows

Notes:
10/1 Dental Committee (125 rooms), checkout 9:00 A.M.–10:30 A.M.
  Lion's Convention (72 rooms), check-in 1:00 P.M.–4:00 P.M.
10/3 Lion's Convention, checkout after 10:00 A.M. group brunch; checkout extended until 1:00 P.M.
  Antique Car Show in town. Most are staying at Hearford Hotel (only 50 reservations so far); expect overflow from Hearford, about 30 walk-ins.
10/4 Antique Car Show over today.
  Advanced Gymnastics Convention. Mostly ages 10–16.
  Check-in 4:00 P.M.–6:00 P.M.
10/7 Advanced Gymnastics checks out at 12:00 noon.
  Painters Convention in town. Headquarters is the Anderson Hotel.
  Expect overflow, 50 walk-ins.

with the goal of attaining 100 percent occupancy—is viewed with skepticism. As future hoteliers, you will face the onerous task of developing a policy on overbooking. The front office manager has the responsibility of administering this policy.

American courts seem to agree that "in many instances, overbooking to overcome the problem of no-shows and late cancellations may produce advantages by way of operating efficiencies that far outweigh the occasional inconveniences to guests and travellers." They have held hotel overbooking to be customary and justifiable practice for offsetting the losses from no-shows. Writing in February 1980, Gould et al. could find no direct statutory or administrative law governing hotel overbooking with the exception of one Florida regulation.[8] Hoteliers and front office managers who practice overbooking do so to meet an organization's financial objectives. They do not intentionally overbook to cause problems for the traveler. Rex S. Toh reports "the no-show rate is anywhere between 5 and 15% in most markets."[9]

This financial loss due to no-shows could add up to a substantial amount of money for a hotel. In a hotel that typically has 100 confirmed reservations (not guaranteed with a credit card) and experiences a 5 percent no-show rate, five rooms per night would remain unsold. With an average room rate of $70, these five rooms would cost the hotel $350 in revenue. Over a year, this would amount to $127,750. Lost revenues of this volume virtually force the hotelier to develop an aggressive occupancy management policy to manage no-shows. This policy is based on management of the various occupancy categories into which guests are placed: those with confirmed reservations, those with guaranteed reservations, stayovers, understays, and walk-ins.

Confirmed reservations, prospective guests who have a reservation for accommodations that is honored until a specified time, represent the critical element in no-shows. After that time, the hotel is under no obligation to hold a reservation. The front office manager must keep accurate records of no-shows in this group. Various types of travelers with confirmed reservations—corporate, group, or pleasure—have varying no-show rates. For example, corporate confirmed reservations may have a 1 percent overall no-show rate. Group travelers may have a 0.5 percent no-show rate, with no-shows all coming from one or two particular bus companies. Pleasure travelers may have a 10 percent no-show rate. The detailed investigation of each of these categories will suggest methods for minimizing no-show rates.

Guaranteed reservations, prospective guests who have made a contract with the hotel for a guest room, represent a less volatile group because the guest provides a credit card number to hold a room reservation. Rex S. Toh reported that the no-show rate for guaranteed reservations was 2 percent, compared to 10 percent for confirmed reservations.[10] The front office manager should investigate these no-shows to determine their sources and plan accordingly.

Stayovers are currently registered guests who wish to extend their stay beyond the time for which they made reservations. Accurate records on various traveler categories (corporate, group, or pleasure) will reveal their stayover rates. For example, employees of a corporation who travel with spouses may extend a Thursday and Friday business trip to include a Saturday. Similarly, a group conference scheduled from Monday through Thursday may encourage the attendees to stay longer to sightsee.

Understays are guests who arrive on time but decide to leave before their predicted date of departure. Pleasure travelers may find their tourist attraction less interesting than anticipated. Urgent business may require the corporate client to return to the office sooner than expected. Maintaining accurate records will help the front office manager to predict understays.

A welcome sector of the hotel market, **walk-in guests,** can enhance daily occupancy percentages when effectively managed. The front office manager must be aware of the activity in the local area. Heavy tourist seasons, special tourist events, conventions, and the like will increase the number of potential guests in the area. Awareness of such possibilities helps the front office manager plan accordingly. Walk-in numbers are often higher if the front office manager maintains good relations with the front office managers of other nearby hotels, who refer guests to other properties when theirs are fully booked. Sending guests who cannot be accommodated to nearby hotels ensures a win-win situation for guests and hotels.

When these occupancy categories have been tracked, the front office manager can more accurately predict occupancy. The front office manager can obtain the data for this formula by reviewing the property management system (PMS) reservation module, which lists the groups, corporate clients, and individual guests who have made reservations for a specific time period. Also, the front office manager should check the tourist activity in the area, business events planned in other hotels, and other special events happening locally.

The following **occupancy management formula** considers confirmed reservations, guaranteed reservations, no-show factors for these two types of reservations, predicted stayovers, predicted understays, and predicted walk-ins to determine the number of additional room reservations needed to achieve 100 percent occupancy. **No-show factors** are based on prior experience with people with confirmed or guaranteed reservations who did not show up.

$$
\begin{aligned}
&\text{total number of rooms available} \\
-\ &\text{confirmed reservations} \times \text{no-show factor} \\
-\ &\text{guaranteed reservations} \times \text{no-show factor} \\
-\ &\text{predicted stayovers} \\
+\ &\text{predicted understays} \\
-\ &\text{predicted walk-ins} \\
\hline
=\ &\text{number of additional room reservations} \\
&\text{needed to achieve 100 percent occupancy}
\end{aligned}
$$

Here is an example of how to use this formula:

1. If a 200-room lodging property has 75 confirmed reservations with a 5 percent no-show factor in that category, 71 rooms can be predicted to be occupied by guests with confirmed reservations. The no-show factor is based on historical records of this category for this property maintained and reviewed by the front office manager.

2. There are 100 guaranteed reservations, with a historical no-show rate of 2 percent. This means that 2 rooms have probably been reserved by no-show guests and may be available for sale. The policy of the hotel may or may not allow the sale of these 2 rooms. If the hotel knows of other hotels in the immediate area that have available rooms for that particular night, the front office manager might be willing to walk a guest with a guaranteed reservation to another hotel if all the guests with guaranteed reservations arrive. It is important to be extremely cautious in this category. A very

unpleasant scene can occur if an exhausted guest arrives at 3:00 A.M. with a guaranteed reservation and finds no vacancies.

3. The predicted number of stayovers at this given time—based on historical records, with considerations for the season of the year, tourist attractions, nature of the current guests (convention, tourist, or business traveler)—is 4 rooms. This number of rooms must be subtracted from the number of rooms available for sale.

4. The predicted number of understays at this given time, considering factors similar to those applied to stayovers, is 5. This number of rooms is added to the number of rooms available for sale.

5. The predicted number of walk-ins for this given time period—using historical records and available information concerning tourist events, activity at other hotels, attractions in nearby communities, and the like—is 8.

The arithmetic for this example works out as follows:

$$
\begin{aligned}
& 200 \text{ rooms available} \\
- & \ 71 \text{ confirmed reservations } (75 - [75 \times 0.05]) \\
- & \ 98 \text{ guaranteed reservations } (100 - [100 \times 0.02]) \\
- & \ \ 4 \text{ stayovers} \\
+ & \ \ 5 \text{ understays} \\
- & \ \ 8 \text{ walk-ins} \\
\hline
= & \ 24 \text{ number of additional room reservations needed} \\
& \quad \text{to achieve 100 percent occupancy}
\end{aligned}
$$

The occupancy management formula indicates to the front office manager that 24 additional rooms must be rented to achieve 100 percent occupancy. By predicting this number in advance, the front office manager has reasonable flexibility in accepting 24 additional reservations for the evening.

Yield Management

Yield management is the technique of planning to achieve maximum room rates and most profitable guests. This practice encourages front office managers, general managers, and marketing and sales directors to target sales periods and to develop sales programs that will maximize profit for the hotel. This topic is fully explored in Chapter 6. Yield management is part of successful administration of a reservation system, because it forces the front office manager to make a realistic attempt to produce a favorable income statement. Applying rate categories to specific time periods with minimum length of reservations

As front office manager of The Times Hotel, you want to project the number of additional rooms you will need to book to achieve 100 percent occupancy for the night of April 15. Use the following historical data to determine the number of additional room reservations needed to achieve 100 percent occupancy: 500 rooms available, 100 confirmed reservations with a 5 percent no-show history, 200 guaranteed rooms with a 2 percent no-show history, 15 stayovers, 10 understays, and 45 walk-ins.

and reviewing potential markets and their spending habits assist the front office manager not only in meeting the goal of 100 percent occupancy but also in achieving maximum profitability.

Processing Guest Reservations

Means of communication with the client; room inventory data banks; systems for reservation, confirmation, deposits, and cancellations; and **blocking procedures,** a process of reserving a room on a specific day, are the major components of a well-organized guest reservation processing system.

The guest who wants to secure overnight lodging accommodations must have an efficient means of communicating the room reservation to the hotel, such as a toll-free phone number, fax number, or personal computer. In turn, the hotel must have a way to check reservation requests against a data bank of available rooms. To ensure the reliability of the room reservation, the hotel establishes a deposit or guarantee system that commits the guest to the purchase of the accommodation. A cancellation process allows the guest and the hotel the flexibility necessary to function in a complex society. A blocking procedure that balances future commitments with present room requirements also helps the front office manager in providing an effective room reservation processing system.

Computerized Reservations Systems

The lodging property associated with a systemwide reservation service is connected to the system via a nationwide toll-free telephone number. The telephone number has been widely distributed by the marketing and sales departments of the corporation. The potential guest who dials this toll-free number will be greeted by an operator located at the central reservation headquarters. This operator has access to the computerized data bank of available rooms at each participating lodging property, so that, for example, a request for a certain type of room for three consecutive nights (February 15, 16, and 17) at a property in Boston can be matched through the data bank. If the participating property has rooms available for those nights, the request can be processed. If it does not have space available, the operator can suggest properties in the reservation/referral system that do have rooms available.

After the operator has determined that the guest's room request can be satisfied, he or she will ask when the arrival time will be. The many lodging properties in the industry have different policies on how long they will hold a reserved room; some will hold the room until 6:00 P.M., for example, while others will hold the reservation only until 4:00 P.M. In any case, the time of arrival is extremely important to the hotel's income. Rooms that are held for guests who do not show, and that cannot be resold, adversely affect the front office manager's ability to produce income. The maxim that "a room unsold is an opportunity lost forever" has profound implications for the profit-and-loss statement.

Because the hotel must have enough lead time to resell a no-show reservation and because guests want to ensure that their accommodations will not be resold before they arrive, a system must be in place to meet the needs of both the hotel and the guests. Both computerized and traditional reservations systems can offer various levels of reservation assurance to accomplish this goal via advanced, confirmed, and guaranteed reservations.

Outsourcing Reservations

In addition to central reservation systems (CRS) operated by hotels, there are **outsourcing** providers of central reservation systems that are available for hotel managers.

This new breed of CRS and service provider processes voice, Internet and Global Distribution System–based reservations on behalf of hotels. This hybrid group provides reservation systems to clients that want to manage closely their reservation processing, while also offering all the services of a traditional representation company. In addition, these companies offer their services through Web-enabled application-service provider [ASP] models.

SynXis Agent, a suite of reservation-management and distribution products, consists of four main components—a CRS; GDS connectivity; alternate-distribution-system connectivity; and Book-A-Rez, an Internet-booking tool. Through its suite of Internet-based applications, SynXis enables hotel operators to consolidate and control hotel inventory from all booking sources. It also provides direct access to the four major GDSes and enables consumers to book hotel reservations online through the hotel's Web site.

Sally Payze, vice president of operations at SynXis, indicates "It consolidates inventory across all booking channels into a single image of inventory. That allows all channels to have access to the last room available and there is no managing of allotments by channel. Its interface allows hotels to define and manage group profiles, administer room blocks and manage rooming lists. In addition, travel planners can enter their own rooming lists directly from the Web, which saves hotel labor, provides immediate confirmation numbers and reduces data-entry errors."[11]

Types of Reservations

ADVANCED RESERVATIONS

A guest usually chooses the advanced reservation option when he or she is in transit and is calling to determine if a property has rooms available for a particular time period. The guest does not want any commitment from the hotel to secure the room reservation. The hotel will hold the reservation until a specified time. This type of reservation has been dropped by some lodging reservation systems in favor of confirmed reservations, which specify a certain arrival deadline with no commitment by the guest to pay if he or she does not show.

CONFIRMED RESERVATIONS

The confirmed reservation is comparable to a contract that becomes void at a certain hour of a certain day. The confirmed reservation allows the hotel to project the number of guests that will check in by the deadline hour. After that deadline, the hotel is free to sell that room to walk-in guests or to accept overflow guests from another property. The hotel usually keeps track of the number of no-shows and compares them to the total number of confirmed reservations that were made; these historical records help in predicting occupancy—and revenue—accurately. (They are also used in overbooking, discussed earlier in this chapter.)

GUARANTEED RESERVATIONS

Guaranteed reservations enable lodging establishments to predict revenue even more accurately. They commit the guest to pay for a room night and the hotel to provide accommodations, regardless of arrival time. If the guest does not show up (without prior cancellation), the hotel may process a credit-card voucher for payment. Likewise, no matter when the guest arrives on the reserved night, the hotel must have the reserved accommodation available. The guaranteed reservation requires the hotel to determine the method of guest payment. The guest may secure the method of payment with a valid credit card, an advance payment, or a preauthorized line of credit (each of these methods is described in detail in Chapter 9).

Reservation Codes

Reservation codes are a sequential series of alphanumeric combinations that provide the guest with a reference for a confirmed or guaranteed reservation. (Reservation codes are also referred to as confirmation numbers.) This code indicates that accommodations have been secured for a specific date with a commitment to pay for at least the first room night. The code, which usually consists of several letters and digits that do not necessarily have any meaning to the guest, may identify the hotel in the chain/referral group, the

PROCESSING GUEST RESERVATIONS 145

person who processed the reservation, the date of arrival, the date of departure, the type of credit card, the credit-card number, the room rate, the type of room, and/or the sequential number of the reservation. The organization that develops the code will include information in the code that is appropriate for the efficient management of a particular reservation system. A guaranteed reservation code may look like this:

122-JB-0309-0311-MC-75-K-98765R

- *122*: the identification number of the property in the chain
- *JB*: the initials of the reservationist or desk clerk who accepted the reservation
- *0309*: the date of arrival
- *0311*: the date of departure
- *MC*: the type of credit card (MasterCard)
- *75*: the nightly room rate of $75
- *K*: indication that the reserved room has a king-size bed
- *98765R*: the sequential reservation number

A few things should be kept in mind when establishing a reservation code system. The amount of memory available to store the code information in a computer data bank may be limited. Therefore, a shorter code that provides less information may be necessary. The reservation code should be designed to give adequate information to the hotel property that must provide accommodations for the guest. The purpose of the code is to communicate the details of a guaranteed accommodation to the host property. The guest data have already been entered into the central computer and usually can be easily retrieved. However, there are times when these data may not be available or may be misplaced. When this happens, a reservation code allows the host property to provide appropriate accommodations.

The method of paying for a guaranteed reservation is established when the reservation is made. Credit cards or previously approved direct billing are the most common methods. Sometimes the guest will send a bank check or deliver cash to secure a reservation. A bank check is acceptable, as long as adequate time is available to process the check. The cash advance payment and bank check, however, should alert the front office manager that this guest has not established a line of credit with a credit-card organization or with the hotel. Determining how the guest will pay the total final bill is essential. The folios of guests who pay cash in advance must be monitored.

Cancellations

Cancellations due to the guest's change in plans are easily handled by a computerized reservations system. The guest calls the central reservation system or the hotel where the reservation has been made. Some lodging organizations stipulate a time period for canceling reservations. Twenty-four, 48, or 72 hours' notice may be required for the guest to be exempt from paying the first night's room rate. Policies vary among reservation systems, based on the historical frequency of cancellations (and the subsequent effect on the profit-and-loss statement) and the public relations policy (the potential of lost repeat business) of the organization.

Cancellation Codes

A **cancellation code** is a sequential series of alphanumeric combinations that provides the guest with a reference for a cancellation of a guaranteed reservation. (Cancellation codes are also referred to as cancellation numbers.) This code verifies that the cancellation has been communicated to the hotel property and assures the guest that he or she is not liable for the canceled reservation. For example, if the front office staff mistakenly processes a charge for a guaranteed reservation that had been canceled, the guest could refute the credit-card billing with the cancellation code.

A cancellation code is composed like a reservation code and consists of letters and digits that may identify the hotel property, the person who processed the cancellation, the date of arrival, the date of departure, and/or the sequential number of the cancellation. This and other information is included to ensure efficient management of room cancellations. If the guest had applied a cash deposit to the room, a credit balance on the guest folio would have to be processed. A cancellation code may look like this:

122-RB-0309-1001X

- *122*: the identification number of the property in the chain
- *RB*: the initials of the reservationist or desk clerk who accepted the cancellation
- *0309*: the date of arrival
- *1001X*: the sequential number of the cancellation

Blocking Procedure

After a reservation has been received, the reserved room is blocked in the room inventory. In a computerized reservation system, the room is automatically removed from the available-room data bank for the dates involved. For example, if each of the participating 75 hotels in the reservation/referral system has 200 rooms available, the room bank would have 15,000 rooms available to be sold on any one night. As a reservation request is processed, the room or rooms involved are blocked out of the available-room inventory. Reservation requests for 4,000 rooms on a particular night at the various participating properties require the computer to block (or reserve) those rooms at the appropriate hotels. If additional reservation requests are received for that night at a particular property and that hotel is already filled to capacity, the computer will not process the requests. It may, however, tell the computer terminal operator that a hotel in the same geographic area does have vacancies. This is undoubtedly one of the major advantages of participating in a reservation/referral system. This type of blocking is usually referred to as **blocking on the horizon**—that is, in the distant future. Another type of blocking, referred to as **daily blocking**, involves assigning guests to their particular rooms on a daily basis.

Process of Completing Reservations through a PMS

The previous discussion has focused on processing guest reservations through a central reservation headquarters. However, the individual PMS at a member hotel of a reservation/referral system is also able to process a reservation request. Chapter 4 discusses the reservation module and includes the list of applications available to the reservationist or desk clerk (shown in Figure 4-7). If the reservationist selected option 1, "guest data," the screen on the video display terminal would look like that in Figure 5-4. The clerk would enter the data into the PMS as requested. That data would then be cleared through the rooms reservations bank to confirm the availability of the room requested.

Other options in the menu would be accessed as needed. For example, option 2, "room inventory," would list the **reservation status,** a term used to indicate the availability of a guest room to be rented on a particular night, that is, OPEN (room is available for renting), CONFIRMED (room has been reserved until 4:00 P.M. or 6:00 P.M.), GUARANTEED (room has been reserved until guest arrives), and REPAIR (room is not available for guest rental) (Figure 5-5). Option 3, "deposits," would be accessed when the clerk needed to determine whether the guest had a deposit on file (Figure 5-6). The information for this option is compiled from the "guest data" option, where the clerk indicates that the guest wanted to guarantee a reservation with a credit card or send a cash (bank check) deposit. Option 4, "special requests," assists the reservationist or desk clerk in determining if rooms are

Figure 5-4. *The guest data screen prompts the reservationist to obtain information about the guest and his or her stay.*

RESERVATIONS—ENTER GUEST DATA		
NAME:		
COMPANY:		
BILLING ADDRESS:		ZIP:
PHONE NUMBER:		
DATE OF ARRIVAL:	TIME OF ARRIVAL:	DATE OF DEP.:
AIRLINE:	FLIGHT #:	TIME OF ARRIVAL:
ROOM:	# GUESTS:	RATE:
COMMENTS:		
CONFIRMATION:		
CREDIT CARD:	NUMBER:	
TRAVEL AGENCY:	AGENT:	ID #:
ADDRESS:		ZIP:

Figure 5-5. *The room inventory screen keeps track of guest room reservation status.*

ROOM INVENTORY 11 06				
ROOM	TYPE	RATE	STATUS	GUEST
101	K	65	OPEN	
102	K	65	CONF	SMITH, V.
103	K	65	CONF	GREY, R.
104	DB	55	GUAR	LITTLE, N.
105	DB	55	GUAR	THOMAS, P.
106	K	75	OPEN	
107	K	75	OPEN	
108	KSUITE	95	GUAR	DENTON, K.
109	DB	55	OPEN	
110	DB	55	GUAR	SLAYTON, J.
115	K	75	REPAIR	
116	K	75	REPAIR	
117	KSUITE	95	REPAIR	
120	SUITE	150	GUAR	STONE CO. CONV.
121	K	95	GUAR	STONE CO. CONV.
122	K	95	GUAR	STONE CO. CONV.
123	K	70	GUAR	STONE CO. CONV.
124	K	70	GUAR	STONE CO. CONV.
125	K	70	GUAR	STONE CO. CONV.

available to meet the specific needs of a guest (Figure 5-7). Facilities for handicapped guests, smoking/no smoking options, particular views, and locations near other hotel facilities are some of the features listed here. This option helps the new desk clerk provide hospitality to guests.

Option 5, "blocking," provides reports to the front office manager on which rooms are to be reserved for incoming guests on a particular day or on the horizon (Figure 5-8). This option will assign a guest or guests to a specific room. Option 6, "arrivals," lists the individuals or groups that are expected to arrive on a specific date (Figure 5-9). Option 7, "departures," indicates which guests are expected to check out on a particular date. This option is used by the front office manager or desk clerk to determine room availability for guests who wish to overstay their reserved time as well as to sell future visits (Figure 5-10). Option 8, "VIP," provides the desk clerk with information on those guests with VIP status (Figure 5-11). Even though all guests are very important persons, VIP status is granted to persons who may be regular guests and expect special treatment, or celebrities or officials who need to spend minimal time checking in. If this information is obtained with the reservation request, it will assist the desk clerk at registration.

Figure 5-6. *The guest deposits data screen displays a guest's deposit for a particular visit.*

DEPOSITS—RETRIEVE DATA

NAME: GROSSMAN, S.
MANDRAKE INSURANCE CO.
ADDRESS: 447 LANKIN DRIVE
PHILADELPHIA, PA   00000

ARRIV: 0917   CASH 75.00   FOLIO: 55598R

NAME: LINCOLN, D.
KLINE SHOE SALES
ADDRESS: 7989 VICTORY PLAZA
NY, NY   00000

ARRIV: 0917   CASH 100.00   FOLIO: 56789R

Figure 5-7. *The special requests screen assists reservationists in meeting a guest's request for various room accommodation.*

SPECIAL REQUESTS—ROOM AVAILABILITY 06 05

ROOM	TYPE	RATE	STATUS
101	DB/RAMP NEARBY	65	OPEN
108	K/RAMP NEARBY HDKP BATH	75	OPEN
109	DB/RAMP NEARBY HDKP SHOWER	75	REPAIR
115	K/HEARING & VISUAL IMP/HDKP SHOWER	75	OPEN
130	K/OCEAN VIEW	85	OPEN
133	K/OCEAN VIEW	85	OPEN
136	K/HEARING & VISUAL IMP/HDKP SHOWER	75	OPEN
201	K/HDKP TUB	75	OPEN
208	K/HDKP TUB	75	OPEN
209	DB/HDKP SHOWER	55	OPEN
211	K/POOLSIDE	75	OPEN
301	K/HDKP TUB	75	OPEN
333	K/OCEAN VIEW	85	OPEN
428	DB/MEETING ROOM	95	OPEN
435	DB/MEETING ROOM	95	REPAIR

BLOCKING REPORT 02 MONTH		
ROOM	STATUS	COMMENTS
101	GUAR	PENN CONFR
102	GUAR	PENN CONFR
103	GUAR	PENN CONFR
104	GUAR	PENN CONFR
105	GUAR	PENN CONFR
106	OPEN	
107	OPEN	
108	OPEN	
109	GUAR	0205114501
110	OPEN	
201	GUAR	PENN CONFR
202	GUAR	PENN CONFR
203	GUAR	PENN CONFR
204	GUAR	PENN CONFR
205	GUAR	PENN CONFR
206	GUAR	PENN CONFR
207	OPEN	
208	OPEN	
209	GUAR	0219BR4567
210	GUAR	0418BR4512
301	OPEN	
302	GUAR	PENN CONFR
303	GUAR	PENN CONFR

Figure 5-8. *The blocking report screen provides front office staff with room reservation status on the horizon.*

Option 9, "projected occupancy," provides the various departments in the hotel with information concerning the number of guests who will be in the hotel on a certain day (Figure 5-12). Option 10, "travel agents," allows the reservationist to maintain data on the travel agent or travel agency that initiated a reservation (Figure 5-13). This option allows speedy processing of the agent's or agency's fee for placing a reservation with the hotel. This option interfaces with the accounts payable module. Option 11, "guest messages," allows the front desk clerk to relay important information to the guests on registration (Figure 5-14). This feature is another way the hotel can convey hospitality to the guest by demonstrating attention to details. Reports concerning reservations can be obtained by the front office manager by selecting option 12, "reports."

These examples provide only a brief overview of the capabilities of a reservation module of a PMS. Your hands-on experience with a PMS will provide you with real-life applications of a very valuable management tool. Managing reservation data allows the front office manager to organize hundreds of details into usable information—informa-

Figure 5-9. *The arrival report screen lists incoming guests with reservations.*

RESERVATIONS INCOMING 02 15			
NAME	ROOM	RATE	DEP
ABERNATHY, R.	400	75	0216
BROWNING, J.	201	75	0217
CANTER, D.	104	65	0216
COSMOE, G.	105	65	0219
DEXTER, A.	125	70	0217
DRAINING, L.	405	95	0216
GENTRY, A.	202	70	0216
KENT, R.	409	70	0218
MURRY, C.	338	80	0218
PLENTER, S.	339	80	0217
SMITH, F.	301	75	0218
SMITH, S.	103	65	0216
WHITE, G.	115	75	0216

Figure 5-10. *The departures screen lists names of guests and groups for a particular day.*

DEPARTURES 03 09		
ROOM	NAME	COMMENTS
207	SMITH, V.	GREATER COMPANY
208	ANAHOE, L.	GREATER COMPANY
209		
211	LISTER, B.	MERCY HOSPITAL
215		
233	CRAMER, N.	KRATER INSURANCE CO.
235		
301	SAMSON, N.	MERCY HOSPITAL
304		
319	DONTON, M.	JOHNSON TOURS
321		JOHNSON TOURS
322	ZIGLER, R.	JOHNSON TOURS
323		JOHNSON TOURS
324	ASTON, M.	JOHNSON TOURS
325	BAKER, K.	JOHNSON TOURS
326	BAKER, P.	JOHNSON TOURS

Figure 5-11. *The VIP information screen lists details of special needs of guests.*

VIP INFORMATION

BLAKELEY, FRANK M/M
GRANITE DEVELOPMENT COMPANY
2234 WEST RIVER DRIVE
GRANITE, IN   00000
000-000-0000

LIKES SUITE 129/30 OR SUITE 145/46. PERSONAL SECURITY GUARD NEEDS ROOM 131
OR 147. ALERT HOTEL SECURITY OF THEIR ARRIVAL.

CEO/GRANITE DEVELOPMENT COMPANY WILL WANT BABY-SITTER (CHILDREN AGES
5 AND 7). CALL CHEF TO SEND WINE AND CHEESE AND CHOCOLATE CHIP OR
OATMEAL COOKIES AND MILK. CALL GIFT SHOP FOR YELLOW ROSES FOR MRS.
BLAKELEY.

DIRECT BILL (TIMES HOTEL ACCT. NO. 420G) TO GRANITE DEVELOPMENT
COMPANY, 301 THOMPSON DRIVE, GRANITE, IN 00000

Figure 5-12. *The projected occupancy screen assists front office managers in meeting projected income.*

PROJECTED OCCUPANCY 12 18

CONF RES	42 ROOMS	50 GUESTS
GUAR RES*	89 ROOMS	93 GUESTS
STAYOVERS**	50 ROOMS	85 GUESTS
WALK-INS***	35 ROOMS	50 GUESTS
TOTALS	216 ROOMS	278 GUESTS

OCCUPANCY 86%   ROOM INCOME $15,120

*   JOHNSON AEROSPACE ARRIVAL AFTER 10 P.M.
**   SMITHMILL CORP. BUFFET BREAKFAST AND BANQUET DINNER.
***   LANCER STAMP SHOW AT ST. THOMAS HOTEL.

Figure 5-13. *The travel agent screen assists hotels in keeping track of commissions paid to travel agents.*

	TRAVEL AGENT INFO			
DATE	AGENCY	AGENT	ACTIVITY	COMM STATUS
09 23	MENTING #4591 32 KAVE SIMINTON, NJ 00000 000-000-0000	BLANT, E. #4512 B	GUAR 5 @70	PD 09 30
09 30	MENTING #4591	CROSS, L. #4501 B	GUAR 10 @65	PD 10 05
02 01	MENTING #4591	CROSS, L. #4501 B	GUAR 20 @75	PD 02 10
02 05	MENTING #4591	BROWN, A. #4522 B	GUAR 10 @70	PD 02 15

tion that will help provide hospitality to guests and financial success to the lodging property.

Database Interfaces

Department managers rely on information captured at the time a reservation is made to plan their work. **Database interfaces,** which transfer shared information among computers, allow managers to retrieve this information at will. Marketing directors need current data to monitor projected sales, while sales representatives in the marketing department need immediate information on room availability for specific time periods.

Figure 5-14. *The guest message screen is available for front office staff at a moment's notice.*

MESSAGE—GUESTS
BRINKE, L. W. 01 02 12:57 P.M.
TOM WASKIN OF GEN MERCH IS NOT ABLE TO KEEP APPT ON 01 02 AT 4:00 P.M. CALL HIM TO RESCHEDULE 000-000-0000 BEFORE 7:00 P.M. 01 02. SWE
BRINKE, L. W. 01 02 1:38 P.M.
JENNIFER HOWE OF STERN ELEC WILL MEET YOU AT 5:00 P.M. IN TIMES HOTEL LOBBY AS PLANNED. BRING ALONG DATA ON RESEARCH PROJECT 21-Z. SWE

Housekeeping staff members can plan routine care and maintenance activities depending on projected occupancy. Maintenance crews can plan refurbishing and repairs when projected occupancy is low. Food and beverage directors can promote a positive cash flow by increasing food and beverage marketing programs during slow room sales periods. The controller also needs to access the reservation database in planning fiscal budgets.

True Integration

It is interesting to note that there is a technological advancement being developed that integrates a hotel's central reservations system and property management system. Rebecca Oliva reports the term **true integration,** in which the CRS and PMS use the same database for processing reservations.[12] This allows for real-time reservations, which are a perceived benefit for consumers, as well as less technology investment for the storage of data, which is a benefit for hotel investors. Hotels can access reservation data via the Internet. Current software providers include MICROS Systems, through OPERA, and AREMIS (AremisSoft Corporation).

Solution to Opening Dilemma

The override feature on a reservation module for a property management system allows individual employees to book reservations beyond the number of rooms available and beyond the occupancy management limit. This feature must be controlled by the reservations manager, front office manager, or manager on duty. However, a front office manager has to handle this challenge by having his or her staff check out the room availability in nearby hotels and notify guests that their room reservations will be handled at another hotel. In some cases, guests can't be notified prior to their arrival, and the front desk staff must be prepared to deliver customer service with utmost composure.

Chapter Recap

This chapter has addressed hotel reservation systems. As the popularity of computerized reservation systems increases, chains and referral properties have adopted them to meet the needs of the traveling public.

Reservations ensure that corporate, group, and pleasure travelers will have accommodations at their destination and provide the hotel with a steady flow of business. Determining the sources of these reservations assists the front office manager in developing procedures to satisfy the needs of the guest. The traveler can use various means to make reservations, such as toll-free telephone numbers, fax numbers, and the Internet. The rooms forecast is used to communicate occupancy status to other departments in the

Thomas Norman, CHA, is the general manager of the Holiday Inn Grenada, in Grenada, Mississippi. This hotel is a 130-room property with seating for 275 banquet guests as well as a Holidome with pool and recreational spa area. After Mr. Norman graduated with a baccalaureate degree from Henderson State University, he continued his interest in the hotel industry with various entry-level hotel supervisory positions. His résumé includes hotel general manager positions with Wilson World Hotel in Dallas, Texas; Radisson Marque in Winston-Salem, North Carolina; various Holiday Inns and Ramada Inns; The Inn at Reading in Wyomissing, Pennsylvania; and the Mountain Laurel Resort in the Pocono Mountains; as well as consulting work in Texas.

Mr. Norman, in reflecting on the manual system versus the property management system of processing and controlling reservations, feels that although the front-end cost of a computerized system is not inexpensive, the hotel recovers the cost "in a hurry," especially in a property that manages a high volume of group business. (Consider the processing of reservations for each person in a large group, with the information being individually handwritten onto reservation cards, which are then hand-filed and processed.) He estimates that the payroll work hours for reservations are cut by more than half with the implementation of a computerized system. He explains that the computerized system provides much faster call-up of information, and easier review of reservations and room availability, versus the manual system, in which a clerk must go to the proper book to locate and pull out the information.

hotel. Overbooking, used to balance no-shows and understays, can be carefully structured using the occupancy management formula. Computerized reservation systems also help front office managers to manage guest information databases, dates of arrival, length of stay, and so forth. Confirmed and guaranteed reservations assure the guest of accommodations on arrival, with various degrees of assurance based on time of arrival and willingness to prepay. These levels of assurance also affect the financial success of the hotel. All elements discussed in this chapter combine to provide means of access for the guest and a technique for marketing rooms for the hotel. The front office manager is responsible for providing this service to the guest.

End of Chapter Questions

1. How does a well-organized reservation system meet the needs of the traveler?

2. How does the lodging industry meet the needs of the traveler for assured reservations?

3. What advantages does a hotel belonging to a reservation/referral system enjoy?

4. What are some major sources of guest reservations? What information does this analysis reveal?

5. Discuss the nature of a typical corporate client's travel plans and explain how these plans are related to a well-organized reservation system. What are some reservation access methods available to the corporate client?

6. Why are tour or meeting planners important to the hotel with regard to group reservations? What are some reservation access methods available to the planner of group tours?

7. How does the pleasure traveler differ from the corporate client and group traveler? What are some reservation access methods available to the pleasure traveler?

8. If you have been or are currently employed at a front desk in a hotel, what do you think of the potential for repeat business from current guests? Does your hotel have a procedure to secure reservations on check-in or checkout?

9. Why is it necessary to prepare a rooms forecast? What are the components of this management tool? In addition to the front office manager, who else uses the room forecast?

10. What does "overbooking" mean? Discuss the legal and financial implications of this practice.

11. What are the components of an aggressive occupancy management procedure? How are they applied to the occupancy management formula?

12. What are the major steps involved in processing a guest reservation?

13. Briefly describe the method used to process a reservation with a computerized system.

14. Discuss the differences between a confirmed reservation and a guaranteed reservation. What financial implications does each entail?

15. Design a reservation code for a computerized reservation system. Why did you choose the control features in your code?

16. Develop a cancellation code for a computerized reservation system. Why did you choose the control features in your code?

17. What does blocking of rooms involve? Give some examples.

18. How do you think true integration of the central reservation system and a hotel's property management system will affect guest satisfaction and the hotel's financial success?

CASE STUDY 501

Margaret Chu, general manager of The Times Hotel, and Ana Chavarria, front office manager, are in the process of developing a policy on overbooking. The current policy prohibits the reservations manager from booking more than 100 percent of the available rooms. Reservations are composed of 60 percent confirmed and 40 percent guaranteed.

In the past six months, about 5 percent of the confirmed reservations have been no-shows, resulting in a financial loss of about 500 room nights. No analysis of the confirmed reservations that resulted in no-shows has been made because Ms. Chavarria has not

had time to organize such a study. This loss of $42,500 (500 rooms × $85 average room rate) has forced management to consider developing an aggressive occupancy management program.

Offer some suggestions to Ms. Chu and Ms. Chavarria concerning the following related concepts: the legality of overbooking, the need to maintain an accurate accounting of the financial impact of no-shows, and the management of the different reservation/occupancy categories that make up the hotel's room sales (confirmed reservations, guaranteed reservations, stayovers, understays, and walk-ins).

CASE STUDY 502

Use the following data to prepare a rooms forecast for the first week of May for The Times Hotel:

Number of rooms available = 600
Number of rooms occupied on April 30 = 300

May 1:
Departures = 200 rooms
Arrivals = 200 rooms (70 percent confirmed, 30 percent guaranteed)
Walk-ins = 40 rooms
No-shows = 0.02 percent of expected arrivals

May 2:
Departures = 50 rooms
Arrivals = 100 rooms (60 percent confirmed, 40 percent guaranteed)
Walk-ins = 10 rooms
No-shows = 0.02 percent of expected arrivals

May 3:
Departures = 200 rooms
Arrivals = 100 rooms (50 percent confirmed, 50 percent guaranteed)

Walk-ins = 20 rooms
No-shows = 0.02 percent of expected arrivals

May 4:
Departures = 50 rooms
Arrivals = 100 rooms (20 percent confirmed, 80 percent guaranteed)
Walk-ins = 10 rooms
No-shows = 0.01 percent of expected arrivals

May 5:
Departures = 300 rooms
Arrivals = 70 rooms (30 percent confirmed, 70 percent guaranteed)
Walk-ins = 25 rooms
No-shows = 0.0143 percent of expected arrivals

May 6:
Departures = 50 rooms
Arrivals = 175 rooms (92 percent confirmed, 8 percent guaranteed)
Walk-ins = 10 rooms
No-shows = 0.04 percent of expected arrivals

May 7:
Departures = 200 rooms
Arrivals = 180 rooms (10 percent confirmed, 90 percent guaranteed)

Walk-ins = 25 rooms
No-shows = 0.0223 percent of expected arrivals

Software Simulation Exercise

Review Chapter 2, "Reservations," of Kline and Sullivan's *Hotel Front Office Simulation: A Workbook and Software Package* (New York: John Wiley & Sons, © 2003), and work through the various concepts as presented in their chapter.

- Reservation Process in INNSTAR
- How to Make a Basic Reservation
- How to Retrieve and Display a Reservation
- How to Cancel a Reservation
- How to Reactivate a Reservation
- How to Make a Group Block
- How to Book a Room from a Room Block
- Analyzing Reservation Status Screens
- Special Situations
- Chapter 2 Exercises

Key Words

blocking on the horizon
blocking procedures
bus association network
cancellation code
confirmed reservations
corporate client
current guests
daily blocking
database interfaces
forecasting
franchisee
full house
group planner
group travelers

guaranteed reservations
hotel broker
hotel representative
house count
interhotel property referrals
no-show factor
occupancy management formula
outsourcing
overbooking
pleasure traveler
referral member
reservation code
reservation referral system
reservation status

room forecasts true integration
stayovers understays
travel directories walk-in guests

Notes

1. "Choice Hotels Offers Wireless Reservations via Palm Handhelds" (October 19, 2000), Choice Hotels, Silver Spring, Md.

2. Six Continents Hotels, 3 Ravina Drive, Suite 2900, Atlanta, Ga.

3. Betsy Day, Public Relations Director, Carlson Hospitality Worldwide, Minneapolis, Minn., personal communication to author, June 26, 2001.

4. *Hotel & Motel Management*, vol. 216, no. 10 (June 4, 2001), p. 50, "Second Generation of Web Bookings Offer Special Searches," by Bruce Adams.

5. "*Hotel & Motel Management*'s 2001 Franchising-Fees Guide," *Hotel & Motel Management* 216, no. 9 (May 21, 2001): 26.

6. Hotel Sales & Marketing Association International 1999 Survey of Travel Agents, North America segment.

7. Melinda Bush, "Hotel Booking—Information Is Critical," *Lodging Hospitality* 44, no. 7 (June 1988): 2.

8. Rex S. Toh, "Coping with No-Shows, Late Cancellations, and Oversales: American Hotels Out-do the Airlines," *International Journal of Hospitality Management* 5, no. 3 (1986): 122.

9. Ibid., 121.

10. Ibid., 122.

11. Bruce Adams, "Baby Grows Up," *Hotel & Motel Management* 216, no. 10 (June 4, 2001): 50.

12. Rebecca Oliva, "Singular Solution," *Hotels* 35, no. 7 (July 2001): 99.

Yield Management

OPENING DILEMMA

The assistant sales manager has left a message for the front office manager and

the food and beverage manager requesting clearance to book a conference of

400 accountants for the first three days of April. The front office manager needs

to check out some things before returning the call to the assistant sales manager.

As mentioned in earlier chapters, yield management is the technique of planning to achieve maximum room rates and most profitable guests. This concept appeared in hotel management circles in the late 1980s; in fact, it was borrowed from the airline industry to assist hoteliers in becoming better decision makers and marketers. It forced hotel managers to develop reservation policies that would build a profitable bottom line. Although adoption of this concept has been slow in the hotel industry, it offers far-reaching opportunities for hoteliers in the twenty-first century. This chapter explores traditional views of occupancy percentage and average daily rate, goals of yield management, integral components of yield management, and applications of yield management (Figure 6-1).

CHAPTER FOCUS POINTS

- Occupancy percentage
- Average daily rate
- RevPAR
- History of yield management
- Use of yield management
- Components of yield management
- Applications of yield management

Occupancy Percentage

To understand yield management, we will first review some of the traditional measures of success in a hotel. **Occupancy percentage** historically revealed the success of a hotel's

Figure 6-1. *A front office manager discusses the elements of yield management in a training session. (Photo courtesy of Hotel Information Systems.)*

staff in attracting guests to a particular property. This traditional view of measuring the effectiveness of the general manager, marketing staff, and front office staff was used to answer such questions as how many rooms were sold due to the director of sales' efforts in creating attractive and enticing direct mail, radio and television ads, billboard displays, or newspaper and magazine display ads? How effective were reservation agents in meeting the room and amenity needs of the guests? Did travel agents book a reservation? How competent were front office staff members in making the sale? While interpretations of occupancy percentage are still good indicators of the staff's efforts, in this chapter we will focus on applications of yield management.

The occupancy percentage for a hotel property is computed daily. The method used to determine it is as follows:

$$\frac{\text{number of rooms sold}}{\text{number of rooms available}} \times 100 = \text{single occupancy \%}$$

To see how this formula works, consider a hotel that sold 75 rooms with a room inventory of 100 rooms; this would yield a 75 percent occupancy percentage:

$$\frac{75}{100} \times 100 = 75\%$$

Investors also use occupancy percentage to determine the potential gross income of a lodging establishment. For example, a 100-room property with a daily average 65 percent occupancy and an $89 average daily rate generates about $2.1 million in sales annually: 100 rooms $\times$ 0.65 occupancy = 65 rooms occupied daily; 65 $\times$ $89 room rate = $5,785 revenue per day; $5,785 $\times$ 365 days in a year = $2,111,525 gross income from room sales annually.

However, it is also important not to assume that occupancy is standard each night. Variations are reflected in the following example:

A 65 percent occupancy is usually achieved on Monday, Tuesday, and Wednesday evenings. However, Thursday, Friday, and Saturday night statistics reveal a 40 percent occupancy, with Sunday night occupancy at 50 percent. Therefore:

Monday–Wednesday:	100 $\times$ 0.65 $\times$ $89 $\times$ 156 (52 $\times$ 3)	= $902,460
Thursday–Saturday:	100 $\times$ 0.40 $\times$ $89 $\times$ 156 (52 $\times$ 3)	= $555,360
Sunday:	100 $\times$ 0.50 $\times$ $89 $\times$ 52	= $231,400
		Total: $1,689,220

Double occupancy is a measure of a hotel staff's ability to attract more than one guest to a room. Usually a room with more than one guest will require a higher room rate and thus brings additional income to the hotel. This method is also traditional in determining the success of building a profitable bottom line. The method to determine **double occupancy percentage** is as follows:

$$\frac{\text{number of guests} - \text{number of rooms sold}}{\text{number of rooms sold}} \times 100 = \text{double occupancy \%}$$

If a hotel sold 100 rooms to 150 guests, then the double occupancy percentage is 50 percent, computed as follows:

$$\frac{150 - 100}{100} \times 100 = 50\%$$

Average Daily Rate

Average daily rate (ADR) is a measure of the hotel staff's efforts in selling available room rates. Such questions as why more $85 rooms than $99 rooms were sold, or whether the marketing office developed attractive weekend packages to sell the $80 rooms instead of relying on the desk clerk on duty to take any reasonable offer from a walk-in guest, are typically answered when the ADR is reviewed.

The method to compute the ADR is as follows:

$$\frac{\text{total room sales}}{\text{number of rooms sold}}$$

If a hotel has daily room sales of $4,800 with 60 rooms sold, the ADR is $80, computed as follows:

$$\frac{\$4,800}{60} = \$80$$

The ADR is used in projecting room revenues for a hotel, as previously described in the discussion of occupancy percentage. Occupancy percentage and ADR computations are essential parts of yield management, because they challenge hoteliers to maximize occupancy and room rates.

RevPAR

RevPAR (revenue per available room) was introduced in Chapter 1 to allow you to understand one of the financial determinants that hoteliers use. RevPAR is determined by dividing room revenue received for a specific day by the number of rooms available in the hotel for that day. The formulas for determining RevPAR are as follows:

$$\frac{\text{room revenue}}{\text{number of available rooms}}$$

or

hotel occupancy × average daily rate

This type of financial insight into a hotel's ability to produce income allows owners, general managers, and front office managers to question standard indicators of hotel success. RevPAR asks the question "How many dollars is each room producing?" If there are certain rooms that are always occupied because of a lower rate, attractive amenities, or other reasons, then the hotel's administration may want to duplicate those sales to similar markets. This questioning opens the door for the concept of yield management, which turns the passive efforts of hoteliers into aggressive financial strategies.

History of Yield Management

The airline industry instituted the first use of yield management after deregulation in the late 1970s.[1] The airlines blocked out certain time periods when seats on flights were priced at certain levels; the potential passenger either booked the flight at the price quoted or found other means of transportation. This bold marketing policy met with some problems but established the economic structure of airfares.

Hotels share similar operational features with airlines. Each has a fixed number of products (hotel rooms and airline seats) that, if not sold on a certain day or flight, cannot be resold. Airlines and hotels sell to market segments that have distinct needs in product and service level. Each has demand periods (holidays, weekdays, and weekends in hotels; holidays, weekdays, and time of day for airlines), which place the provider in a favorable position. Airlines and hotels have various rates from which guests can choose. Reservations are the key operational concept that allows managers to use yield management.[2] By using computers to track a database of products (hotel rooms and airline seats) and to process reservations, each has the ability to look at a sales horizon of 45 to 90 days and to set price and reservation policies that will allow managers to predict profitability.

One of the major differences in how yield management is used in airlines and hotels is that at the hotel, the guest will also spend money within the hotel for various products and services. The airline passenger usually does not have an opportunity to spend large amounts of money during a plane flight. Because of this unique difference, hoteliers have to consider the financial potential of one prospective guest over another in determining reservation policies. For example, one group that is requesting to block a group of 500 rooms with a $50,000 value may also want to book banquets and other food service events that total $25,000, while another group may want to book a block of 600 rooms with a value of only $60,000.

Use of Yield Management

The goal of yield management is twofold: to maximize profit for guest room sales and to maximize profit for hotel services. These goals are important for future hoteliers to understand, because if they set out only to maximize room sales, the "most profitable guest" may not stay in the guest room. This is the difference between airline yield management and hotel yield management.

The following information shows how yield management is used in the hotel industry. As you read through this information, note how the management staff is using technology to make informed decisions, which will reflect favorably on the bottom line. The real challenge of developing any computer application is to support the goals of the management staff. The following quote from the International Hotel Association summarizes the importance of using yield management as a business tool: "Yield Management is the must-have business planning tool for hoteliers in the 1990s and beyond. The computerized functioning [mathematical model] of yield management is complex, but the concept is simple: By using a combination of pricing and inventory control, a hotelier can maximize profits from the sale of rooms and services."[3]

So how are hotel general managers, directors of marketing, and front office managers applying this new technology to produce more profit for a hotel? Here are some examples:

OPERA—a Revenue Management System (Yield Management) is one of the smartest and most informed strategies for increasing sales and raising profits. OPERA Revenue Management System is powered by OPUS 2 Revenue Technologies, a subsidiary of MICROS Systems, Inc. By synthesizing the hospitality industry's most sophisticated technologies for sales forecasting, analysis and rate quotation in an easy-to-use format, this revolutionary revenue management system guides personnel in offering rates and dates that will maximize revenues.

Designed to work in concert with the OPERA, CRS (Centralized Reservation System), and PMS applications, Windows®-based revenue management systems are fully integrated, thereby eliminating the need for duplicate data entry. All reservation transactions are automatically and seamlessly communicated, allowing the system to deliver rate quotations every hour, so personnel can make appropriate adjustments as demand patterns shift. After gathering data from all reservation transactions, group blocks, and inventory changes, the system creates rate hurdles, which guide reservations agents to sell the most profitable stays at the most profitable rates. During high demand, for example, the rate hurdle will be high, shutting off discounted rates. During low demand, the hurdle will be lower, encouraging agents to sell to even the most price-sensitive guests. As a result, revenues are optimized while rate resistance is minimized.

OPERA Revenue Management Systems powered by OPUS 2 Revenue Technologies automatically evaluates a group's total contributions by analyzing all revenue sources including room rates, food and beverage, conference facility, equipment rentals, etc. These revenues are then compared to the net cost of the group and the impact the group may have on transient revenue, including how it may disrupt typical transient stay patterns. After analyzing these factors, if the group is considered not profitable, the system prompts the sales manager with alternative rate guidelines and stay dates in an attempt to accommodate the customer profitably, thereby gaining incremental business as opposed to turning the customer away.

The built-in incentive program is driven by the profitability of the groups that the establishment hosts. The system allows management to institute a range of incentives for sales managers based on the group business they capture. While the system is easy to use and understand, its depth of analysis allows a direct link to the performance of individual sales managers to each property's profitability.[4]

PROS Revenue Management can help hotels gain substantial incremental revenues while simplifying decision making for individual and group reservations, promotions, walk-in acceptance, network rerouting, and contract negotiations. Linked to property management and centralized reservations systems, The PROS Forecaster obtains historical and current booking information to forecast future demand by such factors as day of arrival, product (room type, rate), and length of stay. Its split history functionality defines multiple non-contiguous periods of history to use as bases for forecasting when data from a previous year reflects unusual influences. Hotels can also specify periods of the year with unique demand profiles, such as holidays and special events, to forecast from very specific history pools. The PROS Forecaster can combine such alternative data sets and incorporate data weighting to improve forecast accuracy.

The PROS Optimizer uses forecaster results to set the most revenue-beneficial room rates and allocations based on the forecast demand at each price point. Many factors influence the bid price (minimum acceptance price) for a hotel's fixed inventory. Doubles have more value than singles especially when the actual rooms are identical. Extended stays are usually preferable to one-nighters, except when the latter leaves free capacity for an upcoming high-demand period. If a hotel has a party room or ballroom, people attending a function there have added incentive to stay at the hotel, raising bid prices for rooms during that period.

Vacancies and room spoilage are serious problems in the hospitality industry. Even with credit card–guaranteed reservations, a room that goes empty for a night represents a lost opportunity. The PROS Optimizer automatically sets overbooking levels to gain the most revenue possible while avoiding denials of guests with reservations.

PROS can also assess the revenue value of prospective groups and provide minimum bid prices for their acceptance. Its systems track the rate at which preliminary requests from a travel agent or group manager become firmed reservations, and the rate these reservations materialize into paying guests at the front desk.[5]

maxim® automated revenue management system is a state-of-the-art yield management solution for the hospitality industry. It interfaces with a property management system (PMS) and/or Centralized Reservation System (CRS) to obtain up-to-date information on transient and group bookings, rates, room types and other data. Property history and current booking information is used to forecast future demand for products by arrival date, rate, room type, and length of stay. The system generates recommended yield actions, including changes to length-of-stay availabilities at the level of rate category and room type. A graphical user interface, in an easy-to-use windows environment, allows users to review the forecast and recommend revenue actions, make adjustments to the forecast if appropriate and transmit yield actions to the PMS and/or CRS. maxim®'s revenue actions can be implemented by a hotel's revenue manager, the management company's remote revenue support staff, or by the Yield Management Systems support team.

Some of the features of this system include the following.

- Forecasting accuracy achieved by incorporating activity related to the initial reservation, denied reservations, cancellations, modifications, no shows, check-ins, and check-outs.

- Identifies the mix and price of bookings that will generate maximum profits for each hotel.
- Accurately determines which customer reservation requests to accept and which to decline.
- Considers competitive pressures and economic cycles with daily analysis and updates.
- Assesses the impact of prospective groups on overall property net revenue and provides guidelines on minimum room rates for groups.
- Tracks planned and actual group block materialization and identifies deviations from forecast.
- Performs a complex optimization of data every night, processing every booking transaction and updating large forecast data sets.
- Forecasts transients up to a year and half into the future.[6]

Components of Yield Management

To understand yield management, it is important that you know its interrelated components. Each part of yield management feeds into a network, which supports the goal of maximizing profit for a hotel.

Definition of Yield

Previously occupancy percentage was presented as a traditional concept used to try to achieve 100 percent occupancy. Using this concept, a certain percentage of the rooms may have been sold, but how profitable was this venture? For example, Table 6-1 shows Hotel ABC which has 500 rooms. It sells 200 rooms at $80 and 200 rooms at $95 (rack

Table 6-1. *Occupancy Percentage Comparison*

Hotel	No. Rooms Available	No. Rooms Sold	Rate	Income	Occupancy %
ABC	500	200	$80	$16,000	
					80
		200	$95	19,000	
		400		$35,000	
XYZ	500	100	$80	$8,000	
					80
		300	$95	28,500	
		400		$36,500	

Table 6-2. *Yield Comparison*

Hotel	Revenue Realized	Revenue Potential	Yield %
ABC	$35,000	$47,500*	73.68
XYZ	$36,500	$47,500*	76.84

*500 rooms × $95 (rack rate) = $47,500

rate), earning $35,000 in room sales and achieving an 80 percent occupancy. Hotel XYZ also has 500 rooms and sells 100 rooms at $80 and 300 rooms at $95 (rack rate), earning $36,500 and achieving the same 80 percent occupancy. This additional income ($1,500) earned on a daily basis will assist hoteliers in building a better profit-and-loss statement. This process of creating additional income leads us to the definition of yield. **Yield** is the percentage of income that could be secured if 100 percent of available rooms were sold at their full rack rate. **Revenue realized** is the actual amount of room revenue earned (number of rooms sold × actual rate). **Revenue potential** is the room revenue that could be received if all the rooms were sold at the rack rate. The formula for determining yield is as follows:[7]

$$\text{yield} = \frac{\text{revenue realized}}{\text{revenue potential}}$$

Table 6-2 demonstrates the effects of yield management strategies. Both hotels have achieved an 80 percent occupancy, but Hotel XYZ has achieved a higher yield while selling the same amount of rooms.

Another example of determining yield is as follows: If The Times Hotel has 300 rooms available for sale and sold 200 rooms at $85 with a rack rate of $110, the yield is 51.51 percent.

$$\frac{200 \times \$85 = \$17,000}{300 \times \$110 = \$33,000} \times 100 = 51.51\%$$

The determination of yield provides a better measure of a hotel staff's effort to achieve maximum occupancy than the traditional view of occupancy percentage. The 51 percent yield means the staff's effort in achieving maximum occupancy could have been improved by using effective strategies to sell more $110 rooms. Thus, the goal of yield management is to sell all available rooms at the highest rate (rack rate). A later subsection of this chapter deals with the development of effective strategies to ensure maximum yield.

Optimal Occupancy and Optimal Rate

Achieving the best yield involves redefining the use of occupancy percentage and average daily rate. Although these concepts are important to the long-range potential financial picture, they take on a new meaning with yield management. **Optimal occupancy,** achieving 100 percent occupancy with room sales, which will yield the highest room rate, and **optimal room rate,** a room rate that approaches the rack rate, work together to produce the yield. The following scenario illustrates the harmony that must be achieved to maximize yield:

A 300-room hotel has sold 100 rooms at $76.00, 150 rooms at $84.00, and 35 rooms at $95.00 (rack rate). The yield for this combination is 83 percent. If yield management were in use and the daily report revealed 200 rooms sold at $90.00 and 85 rooms at $95.00, a 91 percent yield could have been realized. Not only could an additional eight percentage points have been achieved, but an additional $2,550.00 could have been earned. In both situations, an occupancy of 95 percent was achieved, but the average daily rate in the first case was $82.54, while the optimal room rate in the second case was $91.49. The $91.49 optimal room rate more closely approaches the $95.00 rack rate.

Strategies

E. Orkin offers a simple policy for developing strategies to implement yield management: when demand is high, maximize rates; when demand is low, maximize room sales.[8] These concepts are portrayed in Table 6-3. Orkin also offers some specifics on developing strategies. He says that when demand is high, "restrict or close availability of low-rate categories and packages to transients [guests], require minimum length of stays, and commit rooms only to groups willing to pay higher rates. When demand is low, provide reservation agents with special promotional rates to offer transients who balk at standard rates, solicit group business from organizations and segments that are characteristically rate sensitive, and promote limited-availability low-cost packages to local market."[9] Restricting or closing availability was indeed a challenge because most front office managers were familiar with the "sell out the house" operating procedure and were unsure if this aggressive marketing tactic would work. Some hoteliers were setting reservation policies that required minimum length of stay during heavy demand periods. The procedure rec-

Table 6-3. *Yield Management Strategies*

Demand	Strategy
High	Maximize rates, require minimum stays
Low	Maximize room sales, open all rate categories

ommended for low demand (special promotional rates and soliciting group and local business) was the strategy used during any demand period. As yield management continues to be tried and tested in hotels, various combinations of maximizing room rates and room sales will continue to challenge hoteliers.

Forecasting

An important feature of yield management is forecasting room sales. Orkin suggests using a daily-decision orientation rather than a seasonal decision-making scheme in developing a particular strategy.[10] Accurate forecasting of transient demand will assist hoteliers in developing strategies to maximize sales to this group. For example, if a hotel has group business reservations for 95 percent of available rooms, seeking transient business with special promotional packages during that time period would not be advisable. If the period following the group business is low, then advance knowledge of this information will allow time for marketing and sales to develop special promotional packages aimed at the transient and local markets.

Block-Out Periods

The strategies just discussed for high-demand periods require front office managers to block out certain days when potential guests who seek reservations must commit to a minimum length of stay. If a guest requests a reservation for October 25, but that date falls in a block-out period of October 24, 25, and 26, the reservation agent will have to refuse the request. If the guest is willing to commit to all three days, then the reservation can be processed. This process of establishing block-out periods will allow a hotel to develop standardized reservation operating procedures for a 24-hour-a-day reservation system. Forecasting of these time periods is an essential feature of yield management.

Systems and Procedures

Orkin suggests that a front office manager who implements yield management use an automated system that will process reservations, track demand, and block out room availability during certain time periods.[11] The details of operating a reservation system for a 500-room hotel on a 365-day basis that uses yield management would be overwhelming if left to manual calculation. He also advises initiating specific rate-setting policies that will ensure profitability. Establishing block-out periods will require an ongoing marketing effort by the hotel to ensure sales in projected low-demand periods. He also urges front office managers to develop a well-trained staff, who will understand and use yield management procedures. Training is another key element in making a very complicated system workable (Figure 6-2).

Those of you who have experience in the hotel industry will appreciate Orkin's last

Figure 6-2. *A front office manager encourages discussion of the application of yield management in a training session. (Photo courtesy of IBM.)*

caution—be adaptable to changes in demand. If a four-day convention has booked 90 percent of the rooms for arrival on April 5 and 25 percent of those reservations have canceled by March 30, the front office manager should drop the restrictions for a four-day stay and encourage reservation agents to offer promotional packages to transient guests.

Feedback

Feedback on decisions employed in yield management is essential in any new venture in management. A record of the date and amount of turnaway business is vital for hoteliers to assess the viability of yield management and to update yield management and marketing strategies for the future.[12] A general manger who reviews the report of a recent five-day block-out period, as depicted in Table 6-4, would find that the period restricted for a five-day minimum length of stay worked well for May 1–3, but 178 room reservations were lost for May 4–5. The director of marketing and sales will have to research the contracts the hotel had with the various groups involved. Also, the front office manager should ask if the front desk clerks, bell staff, or cashiers heard any guest comments on why they checked out earlier than scheduled. The turnaway business on May 3–5 might also indicate that the convention events scheduled on these days were more interesting or that the members of this group did not want to commit to a five-day stay and wanted reservations for only the last three days of the convention.

Table 6-4. *Turnaway Business Report*

Date	Yield %	No. Rooms Turned Away	Dollars Lost [@ $95 Rack Rate]
May 1	98	35	3,325
May 2	96	20	1,900
May 3	93	60	5,700
May 4	50	90	8,550
May 5	50	88	8,360

HOSPITALITY PROFILE

Doug Gehret is the director of rooms at the Waldorf=Astoria in New York City. Prior to his graduation from Penn State in hotel, restaurant, and institutional management in the early 1990s, he did an internship with Walt Disney World. His first job after graduation was with the Hilton Short Hills in Short Hills, New Jersey, as a management trainee in the front office.

Mr. Gehret relates that he uses yield management "every hour of every day" with a revenue management department at the Waldorf=Astoria. This interaction focuses on its room pricing versus the competition's room pricing and the number of confirmed and number of regrets that are based on price and availability. Reviewing this data allows the Waldorf=Astoria to maximize business. He also says that the key to understanding the rooms operation is to understand the components of yield management. In today's hotel business, you have to increase topline revenues such as room sales because there is minimal opportunity to reduce expenses in order to grow profit levels.

Mr. Gehret interacts with other departments in the hotel by supporting the activities of the sales and convention team. The efforts of his front desk staff in delivering quality communications and service promote repeat business with groups. Housekeeping depends on the front office in preparing accurate room blocks and changes to those blocks of rooms as well as accurate forecasting of room sales for preparation of employee scheduling.

Mr. Gehret is responsible for delivering VIP service to various guests. The Waldorf=Astoria has created a "Diamond Reception" service for VIP guests and Diamond Travelers. This service consists of reception service that is similar to boutique hotels— seated registration and a personal staff who assist guests in acclimating themselves to the new environment.

Mr. Gehret urges students of hospitality management to think of the "big picture" as you develop your career by taking jobs and positions that will broaden your experience and prepare you for positions of responsibility and authority. He advocates commitment and gaining every possible bit of knowledge so you can learn about the business and yourself.

Management Challenges in Using Yield Management

An enormous problem facing hotels that employ yield management is alienation of customers.[13] Potential guests who have a reservation refused because they do not want to comply with minimum-stay requirements or who feel they are victims of price gouging may not choose that hotel or any hotel in that chain the next time they are visiting that particular area. It is important that employees be well trained in presenting reservation policies to the public.

Considerations for Food and Beverage Sales

The previous discussion on yield management focused on rates, room availability, minimum stay, and the like. However, there is another issue that assists hoteliers in setting yield management policies that cannot be overlooked—potential food and beverage sales.[14] Certain market segments have a tendency to purchase more food and beverages than other segments. This factor must be taken into consideration to determine the most profitable customer to whom to offer the reservation.

Let's review Table 6-5 to determine which potential group would bring in the most income to the hotel. Group B, with projected income of $92,500 due to projected food and beverage costs (perhaps guests with larger expense accounts or scheduled banquet meals), will bring more projected income to the hotel, even though the room rate for group B is lower than for group A.

Some hoteliers will debate the food and beverage issue because the profit from food and beverage sales is not as great as that from room sales. Other debates in applying yield management center on the type of guests who request reservations and the subsequent effects on room furnishings and use of hotel facilities. For example, group B may be a conference group of high school students who may damage hotel facilities, while group A may be senior citizens who are attending a conference. Developing effective yield management policies, which identify groups who may yield additional income (or expense), is necessary to make yield management work. This is indeed a challenge to you as you begin your career as a hotelier.

Table 6-5. *Considerations of Food and Beverage Income in Setting Yield Management Strategies*

Group	No. Rooms	Rate	Room Income	Food and Beverage Income	Projected Income
A	350	$110	$38,500	$18,750	$57,250
B	300	$100	30,000	62,500	92,500

Applications of Yield Management

The best way to understand yield management is to apply it to various situations. Try your hand at the following scenarios to become familiar with the basics of yield management.

Scenario 1

A front office manager has reviewed the daily report, which reveals that 240 rooms were sold last night. The hotel has 300 rooms and a rack rate of $98. Using the following breakdown of room sales, determine the yield for last night:

85 rooms at $98
65 rooms at $90
90 rooms at $75

Scenario 2

The general manager has asked you to develop a block-out period for the October Annual Weekend Homecoming event at The Times Hotel. There is a definite possibility of 100 percent occupancy, but the general manager is concerned that several of the alumni will dine off-premises. He would like a package rate, which will include a kickoff breakfast and a dinner after the game. How will you proceed?

Scenario 3

A representative from the Governor's Conference has requested a block of 200 rooms for three days at a $75 rate. This conference is attended by people who know how to entertain, and the projected food and beverage expenditure per person is quite significant. During that same three-day time period, there is a jazz concert scheduled in the city. In the past, reservations from this group plus walk-ins have allowed you to achieve 100 percent occupancy (200 rooms) at a $135 rate (rack rate is $95). However, the jazz enthusiasts do not have a positive history of large food and beverage purchases. What would you do, and on what would you base your decision?

Solution to Opening Dilemma

The front office manager will want to check the room availability for this time period in the reservation module. She will want to determine if any block-out periods already exist and, if so, what minimum room night restrictions are in force. The front office manager

Randy Randall graduated from Cornell University's School of Hotel Administration in 1968. He served as director of operations for Wintergreen Resort in Wintergreen, Virginia. He also spent six years with the Sea Pines Resort company as director of operations for Palmas del Mar resort in Humacao, Puerto Rico; was manager of the Hilton Head Inn; and held a variety of other management positions at the Sea Pines resort in Hilton Head Island, South Carolina. In 1986, he moved to the corporate office as a senior vice president of operations at Richfield Hospitality Management, Denver, Colorado. In 1994, he became general manager of the Eldorado Hotel in Santa Fe, New Mexico. He is responsible for all aspects of the day-to-day operation of the hotel.

Mr. Randall decided to use yield management in managing his reservation system. He feels yield management maximizes revenue at times when demand is low because it allows the hotel to sell rooms at a lower rate and when demand is high because it allows it to sell rooms at the highest rate. Since 1994, the average rate in the hotel has increased by $34.49 through 2000, with an increase experienced every year. This represents a 23.3 percent increase. With regard to the Santa Fe, New Mexico, market, it has seen a $6.42 increase for the same period, which represents 5.8 percent. The average rate for downtown Santa Fe properties that are directly competitive to the Eldorado Hotel has increased $20.54, for 15.7 percent. He attributes this performance ahead of the market in large part to the successful implementation and consistent use of the yield system. The hotel also includes all availability in the global distribution system (GDS), a travel agent system, which gives the travel agency more ability to sell its rooms. Many other hotels restrict availability in the GDS and Internet sales locations, hoping to avoid commissions, and as a result tend to lose overall occupancy and rate.

He forecasts the desired average rate and the number of occupied rooms for individual and group business for every day of the year. Once a week, his staff inputs the actual bookings, and he updates them on a rolling six-month system. They make a strategic rate decision for every day—either high, medium, low, or D (for "disastrous")—or close out certain dates. This gives the hotel's reservations office the flexibility to play a rate game. It factors together the current bookings and room sales forecast. The yield management strategy session occurs every week and includes the general manager, front office manager, director of sales and marketing, leisure sales manager, and rooms division manager.

Mr. Randall relates that some of the initial challenges included learning the system and learning to rely on it. The staff had to stop second-guessing it. It took about 90 days to get comfortable with the system, and overall it was relatively painless. He urges all general managers to adopt yield management. He feels that those who do not use it can't make effective rate decisions and maximize revenue. For example, he says that Santa Fe is a destination location and he often gives complimentary rooms to meeting planners and charities. But now he doesn't give away a room unless he knows there will be one available.

---

will check with the food and beverage manager, who will want to determine the availability of banquet facilities and food services and the financial implications that may influence the decision. If the decision leans toward rejection of the offer, the assistant sales manager should consider public relations implications.

The controller of the hotel has asked the front office manager to project room sales for 45 days in the future. This is necessary for the controller to estimate cash flow for a payment on a loan that is due in 30 days. How will the use of yield management assist the front office manager in making an accurate projection?

Chapter Recap

This chapter discussed the traditional concepts of occupancy percentage and average daily rate in determining the effectiveness of management's efforts to achieve a positive income statement. RevPAR was used to answer the question "How many dollars is each room producing?" Yield management was introduced as a new tool hoteliers can use in developing guest room sales strategies and evaluating potential food and beverage purchases, which will ensure a higher profit. Yield management was borrowed from the airline industry, which shares a common operational design with the hotel industry. Components of yield management include revenue realized, revenue potential, optimal occupancy and optimal rates, strategies, block-out periods, forecasting, systems and procedures, feedback, and challenges front office managers face in implementing and using yield management.

End of Chapter Questions

1. Explain in your own words the concept of yield management.

2. What does occupancy percentage tell the owner of a hotel? Discuss the shortcomings of this concept in measuring the effectiveness of a general manager.

3. Similarly, discuss the use of occupancy percentage in determining the effectiveness of a general manager versus the concept of average daily rate (ADR). What impression does quoting only the ADR give the owner of a hotel?

4. How can the use of RevPar assist hotel managers in measuring the effectiveness of front desk staff and marketing managers?

5. What similarities in operational design do the airline industry and the hotel industry share?

6. What are the goals of yield management? If you are employed at a front desk in a hotel, do you see these goals being achieved?

7. Determine the yield for a hotel that has 200 rooms available for sale with a rack rate of $80 and sold 200 rooms at $55.

8. Determine the yield for a hotel that has 275 rooms available for sale with a rack rate of $60 and sold 150 rooms at $55.

9. Determine the yield for a hotel that has 1,000 rooms available for sale with a rack rate of $135 and sold 850 rooms at $100.

10. Discuss the concepts of yield and occupancy percentage as revealed in questions 7, 8, and 9.

11. Discuss strategies to use when demand is high.

12. Discuss strategies to use when demand is low.

13. Why should a front office manager set daily rate strategies as opposed to general period rate strategies?

14. Explain in your own words the term *block-out period.*

15. Why is training front office staff in the use of yield management so essential for it to succeed?

16. What role does the transient guest play in the success of achieving yield?

17. What information can be obtained by reviewing the breakdown of rooms sold by rate category in the daily report? What should a hotel staff do with this information?

18. Why should turnaway business be reviewed on a daily basis? What should a hotel staff do with this information?

19. What role do potential food and beverage sales play in yield management? What are your thoughts on rejecting the role of this concept in achieving yield?

CASE STUDY 601

Ana Chavarria, front office manager at The Times Hotel, has completed a yield management seminar at Keystone University and is preparing an argument to adopt this concept at The Times Hotel to present to Margaret Chu, general manager. She begins by compiling a history of room occupancy and ADRs, which she hopes will reveal areas in which yield management could help. She prepares an electronic spread-sheet that lists rooms sold with corresponding room rates and correlates the data to tourism activities in the area. Ana sends an analysis of revenue realized and revenue potential to Ms. Chu for review prior to their discussion.

After reviewing the analysis, Ms. Chu concludes, "This is just another scam; the industry is slow to adopt this," and disregards the entire report. She knows that occupancy percentage, ADR, and RevPAR are all that you need to be efficient today, so why change?

Ana passes Ms. Chu in the lobby, and Ms. Chu indicates her distrust of the yield management con-cept but says she will listen to Ana's presentation to-morrow.

What tips could you give Ana to help her present a sound case for adoption of yield man-agement?

CASE STUDY 602

Suggest yield management strategies to use under the following circumstances at The Times Hotel:

Situation 1: The Train Collectors are coming to town from November 10 through November 15 and will draw 50,000 people. Every room in town is expected to be taken for that time period. What policy should the hotel develop for guests who want to reserve a room for the following time periods?

- November 10 only
- November 10 and 11 only
- November 10, 11, and 12 only

- November 11, 12, and 13 only
- November 12, 13, and 14 only
- November 13, 14, and 15 only
- November 13 and 14 only
- November 14 and 15 only
- November 15 only

Situation 2: The last two weeks of December are usually a very slow period for room sales, but a local Snow and Ice Festival will attract visitors who may request reservations for single overnight accommo-dations. What policy should the hotel develop for accepting room reservation?

Notes

1. S. E. Kimes, "Basics of Yield Management," *Cornell Hotel and Restaurant Administration Quarterly* 30, no. 3 (November 1989): 15.

2. Ibid, 15–17.

3. "The ABCs of Yield Management," *Hotels: International Magazine of the Hotel and Hotel Restaurant Industry* 27, no. 4. (April 1993): 55. Copyright *Hotels* magazine, a division of Reed USA.

4. MICROS systems, Inc., 7031 Columbia Gateway Drive, Columbia, MD 21046–2289.

5. PROS Revenue Management Inc., 3100 Main Street, Suite 900, Houston, TX 77002.

6. Yield Management Systems, (YMSI, L.C.C), 2626 N. Lakeview Avenue, Suite 3009, Chicago, IL 60614.

7. E. Orkin, "Boosting Your Bottom Line with Yield Management," *Cornell Hotel and Restaurant Administration Quarterly* 28, no. 4 (February 1988): 52.

8. Ibid., 53.
9. Ibid., 54.
10. Ibid., 53
11. Ibid.
12. Ibid., 56.
13. Kimes, "Basics of Yield Management," 19.
14. Ibid., 18–19.

Key Words

average daily rate (ADR)

double occupancy percentage

occupancy percentage

optimal occupancy

optimal room rate

revenue potential

revenue realized

yield

Guest Registration

OPENING DILEMMA

The group leader of a busload of tourists approaches the front desk for check-in. The front desk clerk acknowledges the group leader and begins the check-in procedure only to realize that there are no clean rooms available. The desk clerk mutters, "It's now 4:00 P.M., and you would think someone in housekeeping would have released those rooms by now." The group leader remarks, "What's holding up the process?"

- Importance of the first guest contact
- Capturing guest data
- Guest registration procedures
- Registration with a property management system

One of the first opportunities for face-to-face contact with a hotel occurs when the guest registers. At this time, all the marketing efforts and computerized reservation systems should come together. Will the guest receive what has been advertised and promised? The front desk clerk who is well trained in the registration process must be able to portray the hotel in a positive manner. This good first impression will help ensure an enjoyable visit.

The first step in the guest registration process begins with capturing guest data such as name, address, zip code, length of stay, and company affiliation, which are needed during his or her stay and after departure. Various departments in the hotel require this information to provide service to the guest. The registration process continues with the extension of credit, room selection, room rate application, the opportunity to sell hotel services, room key assignment, and folio processing. Continually efficient performance of the registration process is essential to ensuring hospitality for all guests and profitability for the hotel.

Importance of the First Guest Contact

The first impression a guest receives of a lodging facility during registration is extremely important in setting the tone for hospitality and establishing a continuing business relationship. The guest who is warmly welcomed with a sincere greeting will respond positively to the hotel and will expect similar hospitality from other hotel employees. If the guest receives a half-hearted welcome, he or she will not be enthusiastic about the lodging facility and will be more likely to find fault with the hotel during his or her visit. Today's guest expects to be treated with respect and concern, and many hotels make the effort to meet those expectations—those that do not should not expect the guest to return.

What constitutes a warm welcome of hospitality? This varies from employee to employee. It begins with the employee's empathizing with the feelings of the traveler, someone who has been away from familiar surroundings for many hours or many days. He or she may be stressed by the frustrations of commercial travel, delayed schedules, lost luggage, jet lag, missed meals, unfamiliar surroundings, unclear directions, or unfamiliar public transportation. The hotel employee who is considerate of the traveler under these circumstances will be more likely to recognize anxiety, restlessness, and hostility and respond to them in a positive, understanding manner.

A typical scenario might be as follows: Mr. Traveler arrives at 9:15 A.M. at the registration desk of a hotel. He is visibly upset because he is late for a very important presentation to a group of investors. He wants to get into his room, drop off his luggage, and get public transportation to the corporate center. The desk clerk knows there are no clean rooms available at this time. The desk clerk rings for a bellhop to escort Mr. Traveler to the luggage storage area. When the bellhop arrives, the desk clerk relates Mr. Traveler's situation. The bellhop calls the doorman to obtain a taxi, gives Mr. Traveler a receipt for his luggage, and then escorts him to the main entrance of the hotel. Then he takes Mr. Traveler's luggage to the storage area. These few time-saving practices allow Mr. Traveler to arrive at the presentation within a reasonable amount of time. When Mr. Traveler returns to the hotel later that day, he expresses his appreciation to the desk clerk on duty. The stage has been set for an enjoyable, hospitable stay.

However, the situation could have gone like this: When Mr. Traveler arrives, the desk clerk tells him, "Checkout time is not until 12 noon, and we don't have any rooms available yet. Check back with us after 4:00 P.M." Mr. Traveler searches for the luggage room, drops off his luggage (losing minutes because of a long line), manages to find his way back out to the main entrance, and asks the doorman to hail a cab (losing another ten minutes because it is rush hour). Mr. Traveler arrives late for the presentation because of the delay at the hotel and heavy traffic. Because Mr. Traveler is unaware of the availability of other room accommodations in the area, he returns after the presentation and waits in the hotel's lobby or lounge until 4:00 P.M. This time, the stage is set for an unpleasant visit. Mr. Traveler will probably choose another hotel the next time he has business in the area.

These two scenarios are repeated frequently in the hospitality industry. The latter, too often the norm, gives rise to discussions of overpriced accommodations and unfriendly and unhelpful hotel staff. A system must be in place to ensure that all travelers are extended hospitality as a standard operating procedure. The first guest contact is too essential to the delivery of a well-managed guest stay to leave it to the personal discretion of an individual.

Components of the Registration Process

The registration process is one of the many points of interaction with the guest and ultimately the cornerstone of delivering service before, during, and after the guest stay. Early in this section, we discuss the importance of capturing guest data that is confirmed from the previous reservation process or initiated with a walk-in guest. While guests are in our care, we can communicate with them, maintain an accurate accounting record, and later on respond to any inquiries with regard to financial concerns or follow up on service.

The registration process follows a rather succinct procedure of offering guest hospitality, retrieving a reservation, reviewing the registration card for completeness, extending credit, selecting a room to meet the needs of the guest, checking room status, confirming room rates, promoting additional room sales, assigning room keys, and processing the guest folio. All these steps occur within the space of several minutes, but the organization behind the scenes of the registration process is essential. Let's take a look at how the hotel operational policies and procedures are developed to support the ease of a smooth registration process.

Capturing Guest Data

It is important to note at the outset the value of capturing guest data at registration. This information is used by many employees in the hotel to provide service and hospitality to the guest. It will be used to transfer messages to the guest, to inform the staff of the guest's needs, to check credit background, and to process charges.

Guests will undoubtedly receive phone calls, phone messages, mail, and/or fax transmissions that the hotel must deliver. Recording the proper spelling of a guest's name, including the middle initial, during registration will assist the telephone operator and bellhop in locating the correct guest. A person with a common last name such as Smith should not miss an important message just because more than one Thomas Smith is registered at the hotel.

Hotel employees also need to know who each person is in the hotel so standard operating procedures can be carried out. For example, the director of security will want the housekeeping staff to be on the alert for unusual circumstances that indicate that more people are staying in a room than are registered for that room. Not only will this information assist in providing security to registered guest, but it will provide the hotel with additional income.

Guests' special needs—such as certain room furnishings (cribs or rollaway beds), facilities for the physically challenged, separate folios for guests splitting costs, wake-up calls, or requests for rooms on lower floors that were not indicated when the reservation was made—should be noted and communicated to the appropriate hotel staff. Guests who are members of a group must have their registrations handled in a special manner to expedite the process. However, it is still important that the tour leader of the group provide individual guest information and room assignments. This information is necessary so that the hotel staff can locate a specific guest or deliver messages as they are received.

The front desk clerk who accepts a guest's credit card as a means of payment must check the validity of the card and the available credit balance. Obtaining credit information from walk-ins or guests with confirmed reservations will aid in the process of extending credit, billing, and collecting charges on checkout.

Guest Registration Procedure

The guest registration procedure involves several steps that, if followed accurately, will allow management to ensure a pleasant, efficient, and safe visit. The guest registration process involves the following steps and will be discussed generally as these steps relate to effective front office management. Later in this chapter, use of a PMS (property management system) method of registration is discussed.

1. Guest requests to check into the hotel.

2. Front desk clerk projects hospitality toward the guest.

3. Front desk clerk inquires about guest reservation.

4. Guest completes registration card.

5. Front desk clerk reviews completeness of registration card.

6. Front desk clerk verifies credit.

7. Front desk clerk makes room selection.

8. Front desk clerk makes room assignment.

9. Front desk clerk assigns room rate.

10. Front desk clerk discusses sales opportunities for hotel products and services with guest.

11. Front desk clerk provides room key.

Guest Hospitality

The registration process begins when a guest requests to check into the hotel. The guest may arrive alone or with a group. The front desk clerk begins the check-in process with a display of hospitality toward the guest; important elements include eye contact, a warm smile, an inquiry regarding travel experience, an offer to assist the guest in a dilemma, and the like. As mentioned earlier, the importance of a warm welcome to a guest's positive impressions of the hotel and its staff cannot be overemphasized. Most travelers expect common courtesy along with a quality product and a well-developed delivery system.

Inquiry about Reservation

After the front desk clerk has welcomed the guest, he or she asks if a reservation has been placed. If the guest responds affirmatively, the reservation is retrieved (called up on the computer). If the guest is a walk-in, the front desk clerk must check the availability of accommodations. If accommodations are available, the next step is to complete the registration card.

Completion of Registration Card

The **registration card** provides the hotel with guest's billing information and provides the guest with information on checkout time and room rates (Figure 7-1). Even if the guest has a reservation, the completion of the registration card is important, as it verifies the spelling of names, addresses, phone numbers, anticipated date of departure, number of people in the party, room rate, and method of payment.

The top portion of the registration card supplies information about the guest so the hotel has an accurate listing of registered guests. With this information, phone calls, messages, and the like can be relayed as they are received. This record is also used for billing purposes. If the hotel has parking facilities, the garage manager will want information on the guest's car for security and control purposes. Obtaining complete and accurate information is very important in hotels that use a PMS, this form is preprinted.

Review Completeness of Registration Card

The front desk clerk should quickly review the completeness of the registration card. For example, handwriting should be legible. If the card needs a corrected printed revision, it should be done at this time. The guest may forget to fill in a zip code, which is often used by the marketing and sales department to analyze market demographics as well as by the controller's office to process invoices. If a guest does not know a license plate number or other auto information, the desk clerk should indicate to the guest that this

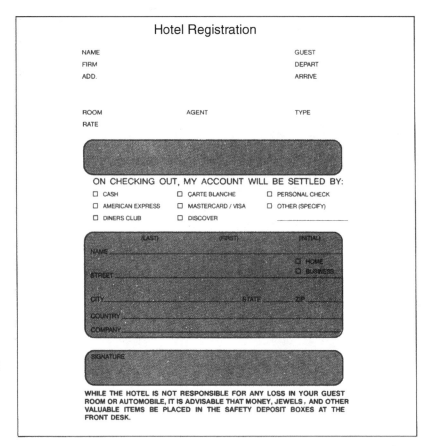

Figure 7-1. *A registration form is used in a PMS and is often preprinted for guests who have reservations.*

information is necessary for security. If the desk clerk follows up this statement with a phone call to the garage attendant to obtain the necessary information, the effort will be appreciated by the guest, security officer, and garage manager.

Any areas on the registration card that remain blank should be called to the guest's attention. Such omissions may be oversights, or they may be an effort by the guest to commit fraud. The guest who does not supply a credit card and gives a weak excuse ("I forgot it in my car" or "It is in my suitcase, which the airline is delivering in three hours"), combined with a front desk clerk who accepts these reasons, sets the stage for fraud. A busy front desk clerk will more than likely forget to obtain this information later in the day.

Extension of Guest Credit

Front desk clerks must perform a few basic procedures to extend credit to guests. These include accepting the designated credit card from the guest, using credit-card processing equipment, interpreting information from the credit-card validation machine, and verifying the cardholder's identification.

CREDIT CARDS

Credit cards are grouped according to the issuing agency. The major groupings are bank cards, commercial cards, private label cards, and intersell cards. As their name suggests, **bank cards** are issued by banks; Visa, MasterCard, and JCB are three bank cards. **Commercial cards** are issued by corporations; Diners Club is an example. **Private label cards** are generally issued by a retail organization, such as a department store or gasoline company. Their use is usually limited to products sold by the issuing organization, but they may be acceptable for other purposes. **Intersell cards** are similar to private label cards but are issued by a major hotel chain. This type of card is acceptable at all properties of the chain and any of its subsidiaries.

Each of these issuing agencies has verified the credit rating of the person to whom the card was issued. This enables the hotel to extend credit to the person who offers the credit card for future payment; this is a very important option for hotels. Hotels extend credit to guests as a basis for doing business. Without this preestablished certification of credit, a hotel would have to develop, operate, and maintain a system of establishing customer credit. Hotel chains that accept intersell cards have done this, as have smaller hotels that are willing to bill to an account.

All credit cards are not equal from a hotel's financial point of view. The hotel may have a standing policy to request a bank credit card first or its own intersell card and then a commercial credit card. The reason for this is the **discount rate**, a percentage of the total sale that is charged by the credit-card agency to the commercial enterprise for the convenience of accepting credit cards, the issuing agency requires. The discount rate depends on the volume of sales transactions, amount of individual sales transaction, expediency with which vouchers are turned into cash, and other factors. Each general manager, in consultation with the controller and front office manager, works with each credit-card–issuing agency to determine a rate that is realistic for the hotel.

The commercial credit card may require a 10 percent discount of the sale to be returned to the credit-card agency, while one bank credit card requires 4 percent and another bank credit card requires 3 percent. The effect on the profit-and-loss statement is shown in the following illustration:

	Commercial	Bank Card 1	Bank Card 2
Guest bill	$200	$200	$200
Discount rate	×.10	×.04	×.03
Amount of discount	$20	$8	$6
Guest bill	$200	$200	$200
Amount of discount	−20	−8	−6
Hotel revenue	$180	$192	$194

Even though Bank Card 2 seems more profitable, it may not be the credit card preferred by the hotel. The Bank Card 2 credit-issuing agency may stipulate a seven-day turnaround time, so that the hotel will not have access to the money until seven days have passed. Bank Card 1 may give the hotel instant access to the money on deposit of the vouchers.

In 2000, JCB (an international credit card company) reported annual sales volume of ¥4,827 billion (approximately U.S. 44 billion) in 7.96 million merchant outlets in the United States, Germany, the Netherlands, Spain, Switzerland, the United Kingdom, Australia, China, Hong Kong, Indonesia, Japan, Korea, the Philippines, Singapore, Taiwan, Thailand, New Zealand, and Malaysia, with 38.08 million cardholders.[1]

The cash flow requirements of the hotel must be thoroughly investigated and income and expenses must be projected before management can decide which credit cards it prefers.

Guests choose their credit cards for a variety of reasons, but sometimes they simply offer the first one pulled from a wallet. If the desk clerk is alert to the guest who displays several major credit cards, a request for the desired card may be acceptable to the guest. This small procedure could mean more profit for the hotel over a fiscal year.

Credit-Card Processing

The **credit-card imprinter,** a machine that makes an imprint of the credit card the guest will use as the method of payment, and the **credit-card validator,** a computer terminal linked to a credit-card data bank that holds information concerning the customer's current balance and security status, are basic pieces of equipment at the front desk in many hotels; however, some hotels with a PMS or computerized credit-card processing equipment do not require this equipment. The front desk clerk uses the credit-card imprinter to imprint the cardholder's name, card number, and card expiration date onto a preprinted voucher. The credit-card validator enables the front desk clerk to establish approval for a certain amount of money to be deducted from a guest's credit line. The credit-card company provides an approval code for authorization of the charge.

The data programmed into a credit-card validator by the credit-card issuing agencies differ from company to company. Some may only indicate that a card is current. Some indicate that the credit card is valid and the amount of the sale will not cause the guest to exceed his or her credit limit; conversely, the information may indicate that the amount of the sale will cause the guest to exceed the limit. For example, a guest's bill, estimated to be $300 for a three-day stay, may not be covered by an available credit line of $173. In that case, the front desk clerk will have to ask for another credit card to establish credit. The information received from the credit-card validator may also indicate that this credit card has been reported stolen and should be retained by the hotel. Established procedures for handling fraud will indicate how hotel security should be alerted in this case.

Proof of Identification

Some hotels require proof of identification when a credit card is presented, whereas others demand none. When the hotel policy does require the guest to produce identification, a valid driver's license with a photo is usually acceptable. Alteration of the nonphoto identification is all too common, making it less than reliable. Hotel security departments must work with the front office in training desk clerks and cashiers to be alert to fraudulent identifications.

BILL-TO-ACCOUNT

The credit card is the most often used form of establishing credit in a hotel. However, there are other means of extending credit to the guest. The **bill-to-account** requires the guest or the guest's employer to establish a line of credit and to adhere to a regular payment schedule. The guest or the employer would complete a standard credit application. The controller would evaluate the completed form, considering outstanding financial obligations, liquid financial assets, credit-card balances, and other credit concerns. If the applicant is deemed creditworthy, then the controller establishes a line of credit. The bill-to-account client is informed of the billing schedule and payment schedule.

When offering bill-to-account credit to the guest, the hotel takes on the responsibility of bill collecting. It must anticipate the effect of the billing and payment schedule on the profit-and-loss statement and the cash flow of the hotel. The controller's office is responsible for the accounting process of the bill-to-account clients. This can involve many hours of clerical work and computer processing time. This extra labor should be evaluated when deciding if the 3–10 percent discount charged by the credit-card–issuing agency is more cost-effective than internal accounting of guest charges. Since some of the credit-card–issuing agencies offer immediate cash tender to the hotel's bank account, some hotels may prefer this method of payment so they can meet immediate financial obligations (employee payroll, vendor accounts, tax payments, and the like).

Room Selection

Part of the registration process includes the front desk clerk's selection of a guest room, which can be confusing for the front desk clerk and frustrating for the guest. This selection involves blocking guest rooms prior to a guest's arrival, meeting the guest's needs, and maintaining a room inventory system. If the guest is assigned a room that does not meet his or her personal requirements, the guest then requests a different room. The front desk clerk responds with a list of available options that seem to satisfy the guest's request.

BLOCKING PROCEDURE

The blocking procedure is very important in ensuring an even flow of processing guests who want to check in. Blocked rooms allow the front desk clerk to immediately assign a room to a guest without searching through confirmed and guaranteed reservations as well as available room inventory. Otherwise, desk clerks would have to review reservations and available rooms at the guest's arrival.

The blocking procedure begins with a review of confirmed and guaranteed reservations as well as expected checkouts for a particular day. For example, if a 200-room hotel has

125 rooms occupied on the night of November 1 with 25 room checkouts scheduled for the morning of November 2, the front office manager would determine that 100 rooms are available for guests to use on November 2, as follows:

$$
\begin{array}{rl}
& 200 \text{ rooms available in the hotel} \\
- & \underline{125} \text{ rooms occupied on Nov. 1} \\
= & 75 \text{ rooms available for sale on Nov. 1} \\
+ & \underline{25} \text{ room checkouts on Nov. 2} \\
= & 100 \text{ rooms available for sale on Nov. 2}
\end{array}
$$

From this 100-room inventory, the front office manager or a designated front office staff person is able to determine which room should be assigned to which guest reservation.

Continuing with the previous example, if there are 90 guest reservations for the evening of November 2 and 35 of them have indicated an early arrival of 10:00 A.M., then the person who is blocking the rooms for November 2 will block their rooms from the rooms unoccupied on November 1. The remaining 55 reservations can have their rooms blocked into the remaining available room inventory. In some hotels, no specific match is made between a guest reservation and guest room. Instead, the person who is blocking rooms will provide a list to front desk clerks that indicates that certain rooms with two double beds, king-size bed, facilities for the handicapped, and the like, are held for guests with reservations. Hence, the first-come, first-served concept of matching reservation with available room is followed.

Meeting Guest Requests

Guests' needs usually include bed requirements, room location, floor plan arrangements, ancillary equipment, rooms designed and equipped for special needs, immediate availability, and price. If the guest has a reservation, the room selection will be blocked prior to the guest's arrival. The walk-in guest presents opportunities to the front desk clerk to optimize a sale and meet the needs of the guest. Opportunities to sell are discussed later in this section.

SPECIAL ACCOMMODATIONS

The first issue in room selection is meeting the guest's requests for special accommodations. The general trend in designing hotel rooms includes placing two beds, usually king-size, queen-size, or double, in one room, which can accommodate the single guest, businesspeople sharing a room, a family of two adults and three children, and various other guest parties. This design permits the front desk clerk more freedom in assigning a room, since so many different needs can be met. Hotels with some rooms containing two twin beds or one twin bed and one double bed or one king-size bed with no room for a rollaway restrict the front desk clerk in assigning rooms and therefore affect the bottom-line income from each room. New hotels offer more opportunities for front desk clerks to meet guests' requests for various bed arrangements and maximize room income. The hotelier must provide the front desk clerks with several options offering various bed sizes and rate flexibility. The front office manager who discusses guest preferences with the reservationist and the front desk clerks and reviews guest comment cards is able to determine which bed accommodations should be made available.

LOCATION

Guests often request a certain room location: on the lower level of a hotel, near the parking lot, away from the elevator shaft, in the corner of the building, far from a convention. Also, certain views of the area may be requested—for example, ocean, bay, lake, or city square. Rooms with special views are usually priced higher, as the guest is willing to pay more, feeling this will enhance the visit. Although these rooms are limited by the design and location of the building, they add a certain character to a lodging property. The marketing and sales department will usually promote these rooms very heavily. Sometimes, guests' requests for specific locations or views can be easily met; other times, a lack of available rooms will force the guest to compromise.

LAYOUT AND DECOR

The guest may request a certain floor plan or room decor. If a businessperson wants to use the room as a small meeting room as well as a sleeping area, a room with a **Murphy bed,** a bed that is hinged at the base of the headboard and swings up into the wall for storage (such as the SICO brand wallbed), should be assigned, if available. A guest who is on an extended business trip may request a room with a kitchenette. Several people sharing a room for a visit may appreciate a room in which the sleeping and living areas are separate. The newly revived suite design meets various guest needs. Rooms with balconies or various themes and decors are often requested to enhance a special occasion.

EQUIPMENT

Guests also request various ancillary equipment and amenities. Although cable television and telephones are now standard room furnishings, large-screen televisions, video-cassette recorders, satellite reception, computer and Internet jacks, extra telephone jacks, and more than one telephone may be requested. Some hotels provide computers, **fax machines,** equipment for facsimile reproduction via telephone lines, and/or convertible desks, which accommodate a businessperson's need for work space. (Figure 7-2). The availability of upscale amenities—such as terrycloth robes, fragrant soaps and shampoos, well-stocked honor bars and snack bins, complimentary local and national newspapers, and popular weekly magazines—often plays a role in the guest's decision to stay at a hotel. If guests are not sure you offer these amenities, they may request them.

Figure 7-2. *This room is equipped with such amenities as a computer and in-room fax to facilitate the business guest's stay. (Photo courtesy of Westin Hotels and Resorts.)*

SPECIAL NEEDS

Guests often request rooms designed and furnished with equipment to meet special needs. Rooms equipped for the hearing-impaired and guests in wheelchairs are very common. Advances in hotel marketing, building design and construction, and electronic safety features allow the guest with a physical disability to enjoy the facilities of the hotel. Hotel owners who maintain aggressive marketing and sales departments realize the growing number of active people in the labor force who are physically challenged and who travel. Legislation may also constitute an impetus to provide accommodations for the physically challenged. Ramps, specially designed bathroom facilities, and electronic visual devices that alert the hearing-impaired to fire danger can be located on the lower floors of a hotel. Smoking and nonsmoking guest rooms are also frequently requested by guests.

AVAILABILITY

Immediate availability is of great concern to most guests. Usually the traveler has spent many hours in transit and wants to unload luggage, freshen up, and move on to other activities. For other guests, registration is the last stop before collapsing from a wearying day of travel and activity. The guest is very vulnerable at this time, often willing to accept a room with a higher rate that meets his or her immediate needs. Nevertheless, the front desk clerk should do all that is possible to locate a room that is ready for occupancy before trying to pitch a higher-priced room.

Long lines of people waiting to register and delayed availability of rooms can make room selection very difficult for the front desk clerk. A delay by the housekeeper in releasing rooms for occupancy often causes guests to wait. Sometimes the desk clerk must inquire of the housekeeping department whether rooms are ready for occupancy. Guests who insist they be admitted to a room—any room—because of special circumstances make the front desk clerk's room selection decision very complex. When the reputation of the hotel is at risk, a quick conference with the front office manager may speed up the decision-making process for the front desk clerk (if desk clerks have not been empowered to make such decisions). In such a case, the front office manager and the general manager should assist the housekeeping department in working out any rough spots and streamline the communication system between housekeeping and the front office.

PRICE CONSTRAINTS

Price is often another guest concern. Guests with budget constraints may request a room for the lowest price; this is their primary concern. Room location, floor plan, room arrangements, ancillary equipment, and immediate occupancy play lesser roles in their room selection. When guests request the least expensive room available, a front desk clerk should try to accommodate them from the available inventory of rooms. Depending on the projected occupancy for the night, the front office manager may instruct the front desk staff to accommodate all such guests within reason; a sale that brings in 10–20 percent less than the designated rates is better than several rooms left unsold. Communication between front desk clerks and front office managers and the training of front desk clerks to sell rooms underlie the effectiveness of providing guests with acceptable room rates.

Room Inventory

Maintaining a room inventory system involves constantly updating and checking a database that specifies **housekeeping status,** a term that indicates availability of a room, such as OCCUPIED (guest or guests are already occupying a room), STAYOVER (guest will not be checking out of a room on the current day), DIRTY or ON CHANGE (a guest has checked out of the room, but the housekeeping staff has not released the room for occupancy), OUT-OF-ORDER (the room is not available for occupancy because of a mechanical malfunction), and AVAILABLE, CLEAN or READY (the room is ready to be occupied). This facet of registration requires constant communication efforts among front office, housekeeping, maintenance, and reservation staffs.

The following lists of reservation statuses (from Chapter 5) and housekeeping statuses are offered as a review and a means to differentiate housekeeping status from reservation status.

RESERVATION STATUS	HOUSEKEEPING STATUS
Open	Available, Clean or Ready
Confirmed 4 P.M.	Occupied
Confirmed 6 P.M.	Stayover
Guaranteed	Dirty or On Change
Repair	Out-of-order

Accurate, up-to-date room status reports are vital to the operation of a front desk for providing guest hospitality and financial viability. The desk clerk who assigns a dirty room to a guest conveys incompetence. Assigning a room that already has occupants creates hostility and embarrassment for both the new and the current guests. Conversely, a room that is thought to be occupied but in fact is vacant is defined as a **sleeper.** This is a lost sales opportunity that cannot be re-created the next day.

The housekeeping department must communicate the housekeeping status in an accurate, orderly, and speedy manner. The floor supervisor of the housekeeping department must inspect each room to determine if guests have indeed vacated the room, to ensure the cleanliness and servicing of the room, and to note any physical repairs that are needed before the room is released to the front desk for rental. An orderly system whereby the housekeeping department transfers this information to the front desk—through regularly scheduled communications from the floor supervisor, maid, or houseman via the telephone, PMS, or personal visits to the front desk—is necessary to maintain the integrity of the system. Delays in transferring this information will slow down the process of providing hospitality to the guest.

The reservations staff must also be aware of the need to coordinate the immediate requirement of a businessperson for a small meeting room at the last minute with that of an incoming guest for a sitting room for a small gathering, the latter requiring confirmation when the reservation is made. Adequately meeting these requests is important to delivering hospitality to the guest. When the guest arrives to register and finds that these essential facilities are unavailable, hostility toward the hotel—specifically directed at the front desk clerk—results. Standard operating procedures must be established to ensure the accuracy of room status.

Room Rates

The marketing plan of a hotel will include pricing programs for room rates, based on many intricate and market-sensitive factors. Courses in hospitality marketing and hotel operations will help you develop an understanding of their relationship to price. This introduction to room rates discusses the importance of establishing and monitoring effective room rates to ensure maximization of profit.

Figure 7-3. *Room sales projections are based on room rates and market sensitivity to these rates.*

SPRING TIME HOTEL PROJECT—ROOMS SALES PROJECTION

	J	*F*	*M*	*A*	*M*	*J*	*J*	*A*	*S*	*O*	*N*	*D*
Rooms avail.	200	200	200	200	200	200	200	200	200	200	200	200
% occ.	40	40	60	70	70	80	90	100	70	70	50	40
Rooms sold/ day	80	80	120	140	140	160	180	200	140	140	100	80
Days/mo.	31	28	31	30	31	30	31	31	30	31	30	31
Proj. rooms sold	2,480	2,240	3,720	4,200	4,340	4,800	5,580	6,200	4,200	4,340	3,100	2,480

TOTAL ROOMS PER YEAR = 47,680

47,680	47,680	47,680
$\times$ $70 rate	$\times$ $85 rate	$\times$ $90 rate
$3,337,600	$4,052,800	$4,291,200
	−10%	−15%
	(loss in sales because of higher rate)	(loss in sales because of higher rate)

ESTABLISHING ROOM RATES

The rental charge for a room provides income to pay for hotel expenses generated in other areas, such as administrative costs, overhead, and utilities. Often students try to compare the efficiencies (control of food cost and labor costs, marketing techniques, etc.) of a freestanding restaurant with the sometimes seeming inefficiencies of a hotel restaurant. In a hotel, the general manager may plan for some of the profit from room rental to be applied to food and beverage operations. In a freestanding restaurant, the manager does not have that luxury.

When hotel real estate developers perform feasibility studies, they base the profitability of the enterprise on sales projections and other related factors, such as investment opportunities, investment portfolio balance, and current income tax laws. A consulting firm will survey market demand for room sales and room rates, which will form a basis for a room sales projection. Of course, adjustment of market demand because of the entrance of this new hotel into the market is calculated. An example of a room sales projection is shown in Figure 7-3.

The three room sales projections at various average room rates shown in Figure 7-3 give the real estate developers some idea of room income, provided management and operations are able to produce and service the sales. The investors in the Spring Time Hotel project will want to determine projected sales in all departments (such as food and beverage, garage, gift shop, athletic facilities, and rentals). This total income figure will provide the basis for total projected sales. Further consideration must be given to related expenses, such as food and beverage costs, furnishings, labor, administrative costs, loan repayments, overhead, utilities, and advertising. These costs are assembled in a standard profit-and-loss statement. With the computer application of electronic spreadsheets, it is easy to determine whether anticipated income will be adequate to cover incurred costs and provide profit. If the projected income is inadequate, the investors will manipulate the average room rate—raising it, for example, from $70 to $75 or from $90 to $95— and analyze the results. While the income generated may seem favorable, the price-sensitive market where the hotel will be located may not be able to produce the number of projected sales at the higher room rates.

Clearly, room rates involve many factors, including manipulation of projected sales and related expenses along with realistic considerations of market competition, marketing and sales efforts, operations, price sensitivity, and tax investment opportunities. The room rate set for one season may be adjusted up or down for a different season. If a competitor lowers or raises room rates, the front office manager will have to consult with the owners, general manager, and other department heads. The decision to lower or raise rates or offer a special package will depend on the effect this action will have on the profit-and-loss statement. In areas saturated with hotel rooms and experiencing a slowdown in tourism or business activity, price wars can spell disaster to a hotel operation. Projecting a hotel's financial success using room sales alone does not take into account the possibility of oversaturation of rooms in an area at a later time. When room rates are adjusted to compete with those of other hotels, hotel revenues will be affected. Other hotel operations that are not cost-effective will then drain the profits from the total operation.

Several methods are used to establish room rates. Each provides guidelines for the hotel real estate developer. These are *only* guidelines and should be reviewed with the previous discussion in mind. The front office manager must stay in touch with the general manager and controller to monitor room rate effectiveness. The general **rule-of-thumb method for determining room rates** stipulates that the room rate should be $1 for every $1,000 of construction costs. (This figure is from the 1960s; the current figure is $2 for every $1,000 of construction costs.) For example (using the $1 for every $1,000 of construction costs formula), if a new hotel is constructed at a cost of $45,000 per room, the room rate would initially be $45 per night. Clearly, this is a very general method of guesstimating room rates and should not be relied on alone.

The **Hubbart formula** considers such factors as operating expenses, desired return on investment, and income from various departments in the hotel to establish room rates. This method relies on the front office to produce income that will cover operating expenses, overhead, and return on investment for the hotel operation. The following example applies these factors:

A hotel with $4,017,236 of operating expenses (various departmental operating expenses and overhead), a desired return on investment of $1,500,000 and additional

Figure 7-4. *A room rate survey compares room rates of competing hotels.*

ROOM RATE SURVEY—WEEK OF 0215

	RACK		CORP.		GROUP			
Number of Persons in Room	1	2	1	2	1	2	3	4
Hotel								
SMITH LODGE	$70	$80	$68	$68	$65	$65	$65	$65
WINSTON ARMS	$72	$80	$68	$70	$60	$65	$70	$75
HARBOR HOUSE	$75	$85	$70	$75	$60	$60	$65	$65
THOMAS INN	$80	$90	$75	$80	$75	$75	$80	$80
ALLISON INN	$100	$110	$89	$95	$80	$80	$85	$90
GREY TOWERS	$85	$95	$80	$80	$75	$75	$75	$80
JACKSON HOTEL	$78	$85	$73	$78	$63	$65	$68	$70
TIMES HOTEL	$90	$100	$80	$89	$75	$75	$80	$85

income of $150,000 from other sources (food and beverage, rentals, telephone) with projected room sales of 47,680 room nights would set its room rate at $113.

$$\frac{(\text{operating expenses} + \text{desired ROI}) - \text{other income}}{\text{projected room nights}} = \text{room rate}$$

$$\frac{(\$4,017,236 + \$1,500,000) - \$150,000}{47,680} = \$113$$

Once again, these methods are guidelines only. Room rates must be constantly monitored with regard to market conditions of supply and demand. The front office manager will have to actively survey the room rates of competing hotels to determine the competitiveness of the hotel's rates. Figure 7-4 is an example of a weekly room rate survey.

This subsection on room rates is presented to show you, firsthand, the complexities of establishing a room rate. The market factors, construction costs, operating expenses, desired return on investment, efficiencies of operations, and marketing programs combine to produce a very complex concept. Front office managers must constantly monitor the effects of established room rates on the profit-and-loss statement. Other department managers in the hotel must also be aware of their importance to the overall financial success of the hotel.

TYPES OF ROOM RATES

Hotels have developed various room rate categories to attract different markets. These rates will depend on seasons, number of potential sales in a market, and other factors.

Providing constant feedback on the effectiveness of room rates in attracting business and evaluating the continued need for each of these categories are the responsibilities of the front office manager and director of marketing and sales. Commonly used room rate categories are rack rate, corporate rate, commercial rate, military/educational rate, group rate, family rate, package rate, American plan, half-day rate, and complimentary rate.

A **rack rate,** the highest room rate charged by a hotel, is the rate given to a guest who does not fall into any particular category, such as a walk-in who requests a room for the night. Rack rates are usually the highest rates charged by the hotel, but they do not necessarily produce the most income for the hotel (see Chapter 6). Charging a group $5 less than the rack rate to encourage repeat business may garner more income for the hotel in the long run.

Corporate rates are room rates offered to businesspeople staying in the hotel. This category can be further broken down into businesspeople who are frequent guests (a specified number of visits per week or per month) and guests who are employees of a corporation that has contracted for a rate that reflects all business from that corporation.

Commercial rates are room rates for businesspeople who represent a company and have infrequent or sporadic patterns of travel. Collectively this group can be a major segment of hotel guests and thus warrants a special rate. The **peddler's club,** a marketing program to encourage repeat business by frequent business guests, was developed to encourage businesspeople who do not have any set schedule for visiting a city to stay at a specific hotel. A card is issued, which is validated with each visit. After a specified number of visits, the guest is awarded a free room night. Currently, there are many variations of this concept. Marketing and sales departments of large hotel corporations have developed sophisticated frequent-visitor marketing programs to encourage guests to stay with them.

Military and educational rates are room rates established for military personnel and educators, because they travel on restricted travel expense accounts and are price-conscious. These groups are a source of significant room sales because their frequent visits may supply a sizable amount of repeat business.

Group rates are room rates offered to large groups of people visiting the hotel for a common reason. The marketing and sales department usually negotiates this rate with a travel agency or with a professional organization. For example, a travel or tour agent may be granted a group rate for a bus group of 40 tourists. A meeting planner may request a group rate for 400 convention delegates. This is a very lucrative source of potential business for a hotel.

Family rates, room rates offered to encourage visits by families with children, are offered during seasonal or promotional times. For example, children under a certain age are not charged if they stay in a room with an adult. Franchise organizations have promoted this concept very well through television and display advertising.

Package rates, room rates that include goods and services in addition to rental of a room, are developed by marketing and sales departments to lure guests into a hotel during low sales periods. A bridal suite package may include complimentary champagne, a cheese-and-cracker basket, flowers, and/or a complimentary breakfast. A Weekend in the

City package may include lunch in the hotel dining room, tickets to the theater, a late-night snack, and/or tickets to an art gallery or a sporting event. If these packages are advertised and promoted, they will become a regular source of business for low-volume weekends.

A variation of the package rate is the **American plan,** a room rate that includes meals—usually breakfast and the evening meal—as well as the room rental. The **modified American plan,** a room rate that offers one meal with the price of a room, is very common in resorts, where there is a more leisurely pace. (The system in which food and beverages are kept separate from room charges is called the **European Plan.**)

A frequently used rate classification is the **half-day rate,** a room rate based on length of guest stay in a room, which is applied to guests who use a room for only three or four hours of a day (not overnight) to rest after sightseeing or shopping or between air flights. Businesspeople may want to rent a room for a short business meeting. Lawyers may want to rent a room to maintain privacy while taking a deposition from a witness. The room is then rented again that evening. If a hotel has guaranteed reservations for late arrivals, the front desk clerk can accept half-day guests for those rooms from 1 through 5 P.M. A good communication system with the housekeeping department is essential, so the room can be cleaned for the guest with a guaranteed reservation. The hotel that offers a half-day rate must establish reservations blocking procedures that indicate which rooms are available for half-day rentals. If rooms will be needed by a convention group in the early afternoon following another convention group that checked out that morning, this type of sale is not recommended.

The final rate category is a **complimentary rate (comp),** a rate for which there is no charge to the guest. The management of the hotel reserves the right to grant comp rooms for various reasons. Guests who are part of the hotel's management hierarchy or personnel group may receive a comp room as a fringe benefit. Management may offer comp rates to tour directors and/or bus drivers of the tour group, travel agents, tour operators, and local dignitaries who are vital to the public relations program of the hotel. This rate does cost the hotel, but the cost is usually outweighed by the goodwill generated.

These rate categories have variations in all hotels. The purpose of the rate categories is to attract groups of guests who will supply repeat business and help ensure full occupancy.

MAXIMIZING ROOM RATES

The front desk clerk and reservationist have the opportunity to present various room rates in a manner that reflects the positive features of the product. Guests who are assigned a room at the highest or lowest rate without any choice are not given the opportunity to participate in the sales decision. Guests who may want to enjoy the best accommodations might look as though they could afford only the lowest-priced room. Other guests who look as though they could afford the Governor's Suite may have budgeted only enough for the lowest-priced room. Reservations that are placed by telephone do not bias the reservationist according to the personal appearance of the future guest. A preplanned sales pitch to maximize room rates for all guests must be formulated and taught to the front office staff.

Knowledge of room furnishings, special features, layout, and rate ranges is necessary to establish a room rate maximization program. In addition, these features should be described in a way that enhances them and tempts the guest. The most important part of this program is to ensure that the front desk staff can carry it out; not everyone enjoys selling, and the staff must be encouraged to develop the proper attitude toward sales. Employee incentive programs are helpful in motivating front desk staff.

The desk clerk or reservationist who handles the walk-in guest, the guest with a reservation, or a guest making a reservation must be extremely knowledgeable about the product being sold. Familiarity with room furnishings, special features, floor plans, views, and rate ranges is obtained through experience and training. The training of a new person in the front office must include visits to the various guest rooms and public areas of the hotel. These visits should be reinforced with written copies of general categories of room inventories that note the various room furnishings, special features, and floor diagrams. Room rate ranges may be printed on special brochures for the guests. However, applying room rates in special cases must be supported by clear policies and communicated to the special staff. The front office manager must develop case studies that illustrate exceptions to the stated rate ranges. Situational applications appropriate to periods of low projected occupancy, 100 percent occupancy, and an overbooked house can be of great assistance in training.

The staff not only must know the hotel's features but should be able to entice guests with positive descriptions. A room described as "decorated in pastels; contains two king-size beds with comforters, overstuffed chairs, and a well-stocked minibar and refreshment cabinet; overlooks the bay side of the Charles River; and provides complete privacy" tempts the guest to want this luxurious experience.

Not everyone, of course, is a born salesperson. Indeed, most people are generally shy about selling. Desk clerks who are not comfortable selling rooms must be encouraged to develop these skills by practicing them until they become natural. How can a front office manager foster such skills?

People are reluctant to sell because they feel they are pushing the buyer to purchase something. They can be made more comfortable in selling when they believe they are offering a service or product that will benefit the guest. Each of the room's features should be highlighted as a reason for the guest to select the room. This reason will relate to guest satisfaction. For example, if the clerk promotes a guest room with an additional small meeting room (at a higher rate) as an attractive feature, the person who is registering may be grateful to learn about this valuable option, because he or she can conduct corporate business without renting two rooms.

Front desk clerks should be trained to recognize subtle clues to a guest's needs. Clues are usually present in both face-to-face situations and during telephone calls. Not all people recognize these clues because they are not trained to listen for them. A training procedure should be developed and presented to the front office staff. When the front desk clerk feels comfortable in being able to satisfy the guest's needs with a certain type of room, then a good sales attitude has been fostered. The idea that "I have to sell" is replaced with "I want to make the guest's experience the best it can be." If a caller mentions that a reservation is an anniversary gift to her parents, the reservationist may want to suggest "a bayside room that overlooks the Charles River or a room that looks out on or the beautiful mountain ranges of the Poconos in Pennsylvania."

A front office manager should also devise an incentive program for the staff to maximize room rates. Incentives should be related to the needs of the employee. If money is the motivator, then a financial reward (based on the average daily rate achieved for the evening above the standard average daily rate) is presented as a bonus to the desk clerk. This bonus could also consist of preference in scheduling, additional vacation or personal days, or consideration for promotions. If employees know that their individual efforts in achieving room rate maximization will be recognized, they will be more enthusiastic about selling. As with all incentive programs, the financial expenditures for the rewards must be cost-effective.

The staff with the proper knowledge, vocabulary, and attitude will maximize room rates better than the staff that is simply told to sell from the **bottom up,** a sales method that involves presenting the least expensive rate first, or from the **top down,** a sales method that involves presenting the most expensive rate first. These principles are important in achieving a maximum room rate. However, if the desk clerk or reservationist is armed with facts about the product (rooms), familiar with words that accentuate the positive features of the product, and comfortable with selling as a procedure that improves the guest's stay, then he or she is likely to generate higher room rates and encourage repeat business.

Sales Opportunities

The front desk clerk has an unparalleled opportunity to promote the services of the hotel during guest registration. The front office manager who has adopted a marketing as well as a front office focus will understand the benefits of developing a front office staff that is comfortable with salesmanship. The discussion here focuses on additional room reservations that can be garnered at registration and the promotion of additional room reservations.

FUTURE RESERVATIONS

The front office manager should consider developing procedures for front desk clerks to follow that encourage a guest to book additional reservations during the check-in process. Suggesting additional reservations during registration may remind the businessperson of the need for room accommodations the following week, when he or she will visit a city with a hotel that is affiliated with the same chain. It may inspire the traveler who has not made reservations for the rest of his or her trip and finds your rates very attractive to stay in a chain member property. This promotion of member properties can be a very profitable marketing concept. Front office managers in independent hotels will also find this concept profitable. Independent hotels have the advantage of offering unique

As front office manager of a hotel, you have noticed that several of your desk clerks don't offer a warm display of hospitality at check-in times. They are a nice group of people and mean well, but they don't have that spark that they used to display several months ago. How would you handle this situation?

---

lodging experiences. Guests who are frequent visitors to a city may want to secure reservations for their next trip. Unless the request for a future reservation is made, it probably will not be received.

Developing a Plan for Promoting Future Reservations

Maximizing sales opportunities also requires a program in which the front desk clerks actively participate, making it profitable for the hotel. The previous discussion on sales opportunities also applies to developing a plan for promoting future reservations.

The front office manager who wants to develop a plan to sell rooms at the time of guest registration must consider the opportunities for booking additional rooms, salesmanship skills, incentive plans, and effects on the profit-and-loss statement. During registration, the front desk clerk should ask guests if they will need additional reservations for the remainder of their trips. Again during the checkout, the front desk clerk should inquire if the guests need additional reservations. If these inquiries are reinforced with printed materials in guest rooms and elevators that advertise the value and offer an incentive to make additional reservations, or if repeat business is rewarded with a frequent-visitor incentive program, then the possibility of securing additional reservations is realistic. If desk clerks encourage future reservations because they believe they are helping the guest with travel plans, they will be more comfortable and successful in persuading guests to make reservations.

The front office manager should develop an incentive program that will assist desk clerks in trying to achieve additional reservations at the time of registration. The effects of such a plan on the profit-and-loss statement are usually easy to determine. Additional room sales will generate additional income. The controller of the hotel will notice the increase in sales. The costs of administering the incentive program should be compared to the income produced by the additional reservations; such costs may include financial bonuses and additional vacation.

Assigning Room Keys

During the guest registration process, a room key is issued to the guest. This is a fairly simple task; however, the process does involve security and maintenance of keys. Later in this chapter, the computerized method of room key assignment is discussed.

After the front desk clerk has determined the room assignment and the guest has agreed to the room rate, the key or keys are obtained for the guest. The key being issued must be checked against the room number assigned on the registration card before it is handed to the guest. A key for room 969 can look like 696 if it is viewed upside down. The key for room 243 could mistakenly be picked up for room 234. These errors occur when the front desk staff is busy checking people in and out. Giving the room key to the guest should be handled with utmost discretion, for the guest's safety. The front desk clerk should not loudly announce, "Here is your key to room 284." It is better to say, simply, "Here is your key" or "Your room number is written on the inside of your check-in packet." It is also important to instruct a guest on the procedure for using an **electronic key,** a plastic-key with electronic codes embedded on a magnetic strip. If there is a special waiting period or a certain-colored indicator light on the guest room door, this should be pointed out.

Security of the Key System

Maintaining the security of the keys requires that they be stored in a safe place. The familiar pigeonhole key and mail rack system is still common in some hotels. Some have adopted a key drawer, located beneath the front desk. Other hotels with electronic locking systems produce a new key for each new guest. The electronic combination is changed each time at the front desk. Guests who lose their keys during a stay may ask for a duplicate. Proof of identification and proof of registration should be required. This protects the guest who is registered in the room as well as other guests of the hotel. Most guests do not mind providing these proofs of identification. They are usually satisfied to know their security is a priority at the hotel.

Maintaining the Key System

The maintenance of a hard-key system requires the front office staff and housekeeping staff to return keys to their storage area, a time-consuming job when several hundred keys must be returned to their pigeonholes or slots in a **key drawer** (a drawer located underneath the counter of the front desk that holds room keys in slots in numerical order) after a full house has checked out. If the housekeeping staff notices a key left in a room after a guest has checked out, it should be returned to the front desk. Some hotels use a **key fob,** a decorative and descriptive plastic or metal tag attached to a **hard key** (a metal device used to trip tumblers in a mechanical lock) that lists the name and address of the hotel, to encourage the finder of a key to mail it back (Figure 7-5). Other hotels do not attach such a key fob because they believe that if a key is found (or actively sought) by a person with criminal intentions, guest security is at risk. Keys and locks that have become worn must be replaced, a responsibility of the maintenance department. Replacement of room keys and locks can be done only with an authorized purchase order from the controller, initiated by the front office or maintenance department. The security department maintains control of key replacement activity.

Maintaining the electronic locking system is much simpler than maintaining the hard-

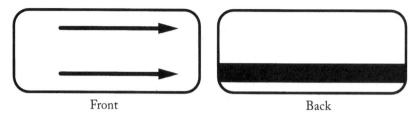

Front   Back

MAGNETIC STRIP CARD

Figure 7-6. *Electronic key cards are used to protect guests.*

Figure 7-5. *A key fob and guest room key are used in hotels with mechanical locks.*

key system. On checkout, when the guest's folio is cleared in the PMS, the plastic key is rendered invalid (Figure 7-6). When the next guest registers for that room, a new electronic combination will be set and an electronic key will be issued. Encoding the electronic combination on a magnetic strip on a credit-card–type key is also possible.

After the guest receives the room key, the front desk clerk should ask if the guest needs help carrying luggage and other personal effects to the room. If help is needed, a bellhop is summoned to escort the guest to the room. If the guest does not require assistance, the front desk clerk should provide clear directions to the room.

Registration with a PMS

As you learned in Chapter 4, property management systems have many capabilities, including registration. To review, the basic applications of the PMS registration module are as follows:

- Retrieving reservation form
- Checking room inventory option
- Checking room status option
- Verifying room rate
- Issuing room key

Figure 7-7. *A completed reservation screen on a PMS provides information on a guest's requests for a visit.*

RESERVATIONS—ENTER GUEST DATA

NAME: BLACKWRIGHT, SAMUEL
COMPANY: HANNINGTON ACCOUNTING
BILLING ADDRESS: 467 WEST AVENUE   ARLINGTON, LA   ZIP: 00000
PHONE NUMBER: 000-000-0000

DATE OF ARRIVAL: 0309   TIME OF ARRIVAL: 6 PM   DATE OF DEP.: 0311

AIRLINE: AA   FLIGHT #: 144   TIME OF ARRIVAL: 3:45 PM

ROOM: # GUESTS: 1   RATE: 80

COMMENTS:

CONFIRMATION #: 122JB03090311MC80K98765R

CREDIT CARD: MC   NUMBER: 00000000000000000000

TRAVEL AGENCY: AGENT: ID #:
ADDRESS: ZIP:

Retrieving Reservation Form

The registration module is put to use before the guest arrives at the hotel to register. The guests who have placed reservations with the hotel have already had their data entered into the PMS database. Figure 7-7 shows a completed version of the blank guest data screen illustrated in Figure 5-4. The guest information is now available for registration. The PMS is able to produce advance registration forms for guests, like that shown in Figure 7-8, with an interface between the registration module and the reservation module database. The PMS preselects a room for the guest from the room inventory for the day of arrival. When the guest arrives, the advance registration form already will have been printed the night before by the second- or third-shift front desk clerks. After the advance registration forms have been printed, they are filed alphabetically at the front desk. Some operations choose not to preprint the forms but instead have the guest complete a standard registration card. Having preprinted advance registration forms available when guests arrive is invaluable in registering guests quickly, particularly when a full house is checking in or when the front desk is operating with less than its full staff.

When a guest with a reservation arrives at the front desk to register, the front desk clerk greets him or her and then inquires whether the guest has a reservation. The desk clerk retrieves the preprinted advance registration form from the file. If no form is available, the desk clerk retrieves this information from the reservation module by entering the guest's last name or confirmation number. The guest information is then available for registration.

Figure 7-8. *An advance registration form is prepared prior to a guest's arrival.*

ARRIV	RESV	DEP	CONF NO	ROOM ASMT	RATE
03-09	6 PM	0311	122JB03090311MC80K98765R	722	80.00

GUEST INFO	NO. GUEST	CREDIT CARD
Blackwright, Samuel Hannington Accounting 467 West Ave. Arlington, LA 00000 000-000-0000	1	MC 00000000000000000000

Guest Signature

The registration module can also handle the registration of groups, allowing advance registration information for entire groups of guests to be preprinted. Figure 7-9 shows how registration details for a group can be controlled. With further processing of this information, including preassignment of rooms, group preregistration packets, like those shown in Figure 7-10, can be prepared, making the registration of groups very simple for the tour director and the front office.

Checking Room Inventory Option

What happens if there is a name missing from the reservation data bank for a person or group? If the guest cannot produce a confirmation number and no reservation can be found, the front desk clerk will try to provide accommodations. The room inventory and room status options of the registration module are checked to determine if rooms are available. The room inventory option indicates the availability of rooms (Figure 7.11). It informs the desk clerk which rooms are being held for reservations (GUAR for guaranteed and CONF for confirmed), which have been taken out of inventory because of a needed repair (REPAIR), and which are available to rent for the night (OPEN). Additional information is provided about the features of the rooms, such as king-size bed (K), a room suitable for holding a conference (CONF), a room with two king-size beds (2K), a room with one double bed (DB), a room with a bay view (BAY), a room with a kitchenette (KITCH), a room with a studio couch (STUDIO), adjoining rooms (/), or a room with a conversation area and other amenities (SUITE). The rate per room for a single guest is indicated.

Checking Room Status Option

The desk clerk also needs to know which rooms are ready for occupancy, which can be determined by activating the room status option of the PMS (Figure 7-12). This option

Figure 7-9. *The group registration option keeps track of members of a group.*

<table>
<tr><td colspan="4" align="center">GROUP REGISTRATION</td></tr>
<tr><td colspan="4">NAME OF GROUP: JOHNSON HIGH SCHOOL DEBATE TEAM</td></tr>
<tr><td colspan="4">DATE IN: 0109   DATE OUT: 0112   NO. ROOMS: 8</td></tr>
<tr><td colspan="4">NO. GUESTS: 15   RATE: 57/S 64/D</td></tr>
<tr><td colspan="4">BILLING INFO: DIRECT BILL R. SIMINGTON, 401 MADISON DR., OLIVER, DE 00000</td></tr>
<tr><td colspan="4" align="center">21 DAYS. EACH PAYS INCIDENTALS AT CHECKOUT.</td></tr>
<tr><td>ROOM NO.</td><td>NAME</td><td>RATE</td><td>COMMENTS</td></tr>
<tr><td>201</td><td>VERKIN, S.</td><td>32</td><td></td></tr>
<tr><td>201</td><td>LAKEROUTE, B.</td><td>32</td><td></td></tr>
<tr><td>202</td><td>SIMINGTON, R.</td><td>57</td><td>ADVISER</td></tr>
<tr><td>203</td><td>CASTLE, N.</td><td>32</td><td></td></tr>
<tr><td>203</td><td>ZEIGLER, R.</td><td>32</td><td></td></tr>
<tr><td>204</td><td>DRAKE, J.</td><td>32</td><td></td></tr>
<tr><td>204</td><td>DRAKE, A.</td><td>32</td><td></td></tr>
<tr><td>205</td><td>LENKSON, C.</td><td>32</td><td></td></tr>
<tr><td>205</td><td>SMITH, B.</td><td>32</td><td></td></tr>
<tr><td>206</td><td>HARMON, T.</td><td>32</td><td></td></tr>
<tr><td>206</td><td>LASTER, H.</td><td>32</td><td></td></tr>
<tr><td>207</td><td>AROWW, C.</td><td>32</td><td></td></tr>
<tr><td>207</td><td>THOMPSON, N.</td><td>32</td><td></td></tr>
<tr><td>208</td><td>JONES, K.</td><td>32</td><td></td></tr>
<tr><td>208</td><td>SAMSET, O.</td><td>32</td><td></td></tr>
</table>

Figure 7-10. *A group preregistration packet helps achieve quick registration for groups.*

TIMES HOTEL

(GROUP REGISTRATION)

Welcome to our hotel. Your registration has been preprocessed. You have been assigned to room __. Your tour guide has arranged to make final payment for room charges. Questions concerning other charges to your room account can be answered by dialing "3" on your room phone.

Thank you,
Front Desk Manager

Figure 7-11. *The room inventory screen of a PMS tells front desk staff the reservation status.*

ROOM INVENTORY 1225				
ROOM	TYPE	COMMENTS	RATE	AVAILABILITY
109	K	BAY	68	GUAR
201	K	KITCH	75	REPAIR
202	K		65	CONF
203	K		65	CONF
204	K		65	CONF
205	K		65	OPEN
206	CONF	STUDIO	80	OPEN
207	K	/208	65	OPEN
208	K	/207	65	OPEN
209	K	BAY	68	GUAR
210	K	KITCH	75	GUAR
301	2K	SUITE	100	REPAIR
302	2K	SUITE	100	GUAR
303	DB		55	OPEN
304	K	KITCH	75	OPEN
305	K		65	OPEN
306	CONF	STUDIO	80	GUAR
307	K	/308	65	GUAR
308	K	/307	65	OPEN
309	K	BAY	68	OPEN
310	K	KITCH	75	GUAR
401	K	KITCH	75	GUAR

is similar to the room inventory option but does not include rates and has a column on status, telling the desk clerk which rooms are being cleaned and serviced by housekeeping (ON CHG), which are being repaired (OUT OF ORDR), which are occupied by another guest (OCC), and which are available for guest occupancy (READY). The integrity of this information is maintained with constant input and updates from the housekeeping and maintenance departments.

If a room is available and the front desk clerk is fairly sure that the hotel will not be full that night, the guest without a confirmation number or reservation would be handled as a walk-in guest. The guest data option of the registration module allows the front desk clerk to enter guest registration information (Figure 7-13). Note that this option prompts the desk clerk to inquire if the guest needs additional reservations for future visits.

A guest may present a confirmation number when there are no rooms available. When overbooking has produced more guests than there are rooms available, a guest will be

Figure 7-12. *The room status screen of a PMS tells front desk staff the housekeeping status.*

ROOM STATUS 0722				
ROOM	**TYPE**	**COMMENTS**	**AVAILABILITY**	**STATUS**
109	K	BAY	GUAR	ON CHG
201	K	KITCH	REPAIR	OUT OF ORDR
202	K		CONF	ON CHG
203	K		CONF	ON CHG
204	K		CONF	READY
205	K		OPEN	READY
206	CONF	STUDIO	OPEN	READY
207	K	/208	OPEN	ON CHG
208	K	/207	OPEN	ON CHG
209	K	BAY	GUAR	READY
210	K	KITCH	GUAR	ON CHG
301	2K	SUITE	REPAIR	OUT OF ORDR
302	2K	SUITE	GUAR	READY
303	DB		OPEN	READY
304	K	KITCH	OPEN	READY
305	K		OPEN	ON CHG
306	CONF	STUDIO	GUAR	READY
307	K	/308	GUAR	ON CHG
308	K	/307	OPEN	ON CHG
309	K	BAY	OPEN	ON CHG
310	K	KITCH	GUAR	ON CHG
401	K	KITCH	GUAR	ON CHG

walked to another hotel, where the guest is provided with accommodations. Although, when **walking a guest with a reservation,** the hotel is under no obligation to provide cab fare, pay for the room at the other property, provide telephone calls to allow the guest to notify people of a change of venue, pay for a meal, or provide a complimentary future stay, some hotels will try to accommodate the guest to ensure positive guest relations. While the guest is usually not satisfied with this situation, he or she may accept the alternative accommodations as better than nothing. When the front office staff realizes that an overbooking situation is fast approaching, they should telephone nearby hotels to establish projected occupancy.

Verifying Room Rate

The guest may remember a verbal quoted rate at the time of registration that is not on the confirmation form or in the PMS. It is wise to discuss any discrepancies with the

Figure 7-13. *A blank registration screen in a PMS is activated to register a walk-in guest.*

REGISTRATION—ENTER GUEST DATA

NAME:

COMPANY:

BILLING ADDRESS: ZIP:

PHONE NUMBER:

CREDIT CARD: TYPE: NUMBER: EXP. DATE:

AUTO MAKE: MODEL: LIC. PLATE: STATE:

TYPE OF ROOM: NO. GUESTS: RATE:

DATE IN: DATE OUT: CLERK:

FUTURE RESERVATION?   DATE: TYPE ROOM: NO. GUESTS:

HOTEL ID NO.:   CONF: YES   NO   GUAR: YES   NO

CONF NO.:

---

guest to avoid problems at checkout. The guest who thought she was being charged for an $85 room rate when in fact it was a $125 room rate could be embarrassed at checkout if she doesn't have adequate financial resources to pay. Desk clerks should have guests acknowledge the room rate by asking guests to initial the room rate on the registration form. It is also important to discuss room taxes or any local municipal charges, which may be added to the room rate.

Issuing Room Key

If the guest can be accommodated, the new key for the guest room is prepared with an electronic key preparation device (Figure 7-14). This device produces a new "key" (the size of a credit card, composed of plastic) encoded with an electronic combination for each new guest. The combination for the door lock is controlled through the hotel's security system.

Obtaining Reports from the PMS

The PMS can also produce an alphabetical listing of the guests and their room numbers. This option, a variation of the registered guests report option shown in Figure 7-15, is available to the switchboard operator.

The front office manager can access various report options of the registration module for effective front office management. The registration module options just discussed provide the basis for gathering and organizing information the front office manager needs to monitor. For example, the guest arrivals report option informs the front office manager

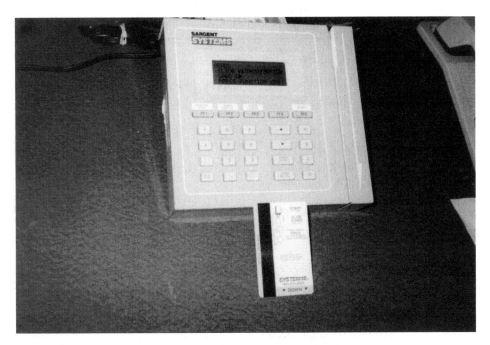

Figure 7-14. *An electronic device is used to prepare new electronic room keys for guests. (Photo courtesy of Lincoln Plaza Hotel and Conference Center, Reading, Pennsylvania.)*

of the guests with reservations who are expected to arrive (Figure 7-16). The group arrivals report option lists the various groups with reservations that are expected to arrive (Figure 7-17).

These data can be arranged by different categories—room number, date of registration, checkout date, room rate, guest name—according to the front office manager's needs. These report options, often referred to as **data sorts,** which indicate groupings of information, vary depending on the type of software used for the PMS. The room inventory report option, which gives the front office manager a quick listing of the rooms that are still vacant (Figure 7-18), is useful in achieving maximum occupancy. Variations of this option might include listings of all vacant, occupied, on-change, or on-repair rooms, sorted by type—with king-size beds, on the first floor, with a bay view, in a certain rate range. The room status report option provides a quick listing of which rooms are available for occupancy (Figure 7-19). Variations of this option would sort all rooms that are ready, on change, occupied, or out of order.

Self-Check-in

The PMS allows guests to check themselves in with a credit card. The guest with a reservation guaranteed by a credit card can use a designated computer terminal (Figure 7-20) that guides him or her through the registration procedure. This option assists in

Figure 7-15. *Registered guests can be listed alphabetically with a PMS.*

		REGISTERED GUESTS 0215				
ROOM	NAME	ADDRESS	DATE IN	DATE OUT	RATE	NO. GUESTS
205	ARRISON, T.	RD 1 OLANA, AZ 00000	0215	0216	75	2
312	CRUCCI, N.	414 HANOVER ST., CANTON, OH 00000	0205	0217	70	1
313	DANTOZ, M.	102 N FRONT ST., LANGLY, MD 00000	0213	0216	70	1
315	FRANTNZ, B.	21 S BROADWAY, NY, NY 00000	0211	0216	75	2
402	HABBEL, B.	BOX 56, LITTLEROCK, MN 00000	0215	0217	75	2
403	IQENTEZ, G.	HOBART, NY 00000	0213	0216	70	1
409	JANNSEN, P.	87 ORCHARD LA., GREATIN, NY 00000	0215	0222	90	1
410	ROSCO, R.	98 BREWER RD., THOMPSON, DE 00000	0213	0221	70	1
411	SMITH, V.	21 ROSE AVE., BILLINGS, TN 00000	0215	0218	70	1
501	ZUKERMEN, A.	345 S HARRY BLVD., JOHNSTOWN, CA 00000	0215	0219	85	2

Figure 7-16. *An alphabetical listing of guests who will arrive can be prepared by a PMS.*

	ARRIVALS—INDIVIDUAL GUESTS 0918			
NAME	RESV	DATE IN	DATE OUT	CONF NO.
BLAKELY, K.	GUAR	0918	0920	09180920JCB75K9334L
BROWN, J.	CONF	0918	0919	09180919JCB75K9211L
CASTOR, V.	GUAR	0918	0922	09180922V75K8456L
CONRAD, M.	GUAR	0918	0921	09180921MC75K8475L
DRENNEL, A.	GUAR	0918	0921	09180921V80K8412L
FESTER, P.	CONF	0918	0925	09180925JCB75K8399L
HRASTE, B.	GUAR	0918	0919	09180919JCB75K8401L
LOTTER, M.	GUAR	0918	0922	09180922V80K8455L

Figure 7-17. *A PMS can list names of groups that will arrive by date of arrival.*

ARRIVALS—GROUPS 0918					
NAME	DATE IN	DATE OUT	NO. ROOMS	RATE	NO. GUESTS
HARBOR TOURS	0918	0922	02/1	55/1	42
			20/2	65/2	
JOHNSON HS BAND	0918	0921	02/1	45/1	54
			13/4	60/4	
MIGHTY TOURS	0918	0919	02/1	55/1	42
			20/2	65/2	

streamlining registration at a busy front desk. The owners, general manager, and front office manager must weigh the capital expenditures, decreased labor costs, increased speed of registration, delivery of hospitality, and opportunity for selling additional hotel services within the hotel when deciding whether to provide this option. Hotels with a high occupancy percentage may choose to install this technology to keep the registration lines moving. However, it is important to consider room status, such as the possibility of a room's being "on change" when a guest is waiting to enter the room. The efficiency of the housekeeping department in cleaning and servicing rooms must also be considered. If a guest does not need to enter a room immediately, then a self-check-in system may be cost-effective in providing the guest with an additional service.

Figure 7-18. *This screen on a PMS helps front office staff to determine which rooms are vacant.*

ROOM VACANCIES 0701		
ROOM	ROOM	ROOM
103	402	701
104	411	710
109	415	800
205	503	813
206	509	817
318	515	823
327	517	824
333	605	825

Figure 7-19. *This screen on a PMS provides the housekeeping status of guest rooms.*

ROOM STATUS 0524			
ROOM	**STATUS**	**ROOM**	**STATUS**
101	ON CHG	114	ON CHG
102	ON CHG	115	READY
103	ON CHG	116	ON CHG
104	ON CHG	117	ON CHG
105	READY	118	ON CHG
106	ON CHG	119	OCC
107	ON CHG	120	OCC
108	OUT OF ORDR	201	READY
109	OCC	202	READY
110	OCC	203	READY
111	OCC	204	ON CHG
112	READY	205	OUT OF ORDR
113	OUT OF ORDR	206	READY

Figure 7-20. *A guest may choose to use the self-check-in option of a property management system. The process is initiated with a credit card. (Photo courtesy of Hyatt Hotels and Resorts.)*

J udy Colbert reports in *Lodging* how to deliver hospitality to international visitors:

> To make foreign guests feel comfortable, the hotel [New York Hilton and Towers] has a multilingual staff that speaks 30 different languages. Each wears a lapel pin in the colors of the country flag for the language he or she speaks. Brochures, local information, and in-room materials are available in several languages. And an AT&T Language Line, which provides assistance in 140 languages, is accessible from every guestroom.
>
> Hyatt Hotels is working on an educational program to train the staff to the nuances of international visitors. These materials include world culture and trends, learning a dozen or so basic phrases in foreign languages, and preparing signage and in-room pieces in multiple languages.[2]

An article by Rick Bruns in *Lodging* magazine describes the latest technology that is being tried in hotels to streamline the registration process:

> Walk into the lobby of the Wyndham Garden Hotel–Dallas Market Center, and before you reach the front desk, an employee greets you, holding a special wireless communications device. She types in your name, swipes your credit card and encodes your magnetic room key card. The 250-room, full service property is the final test site for the Dallas-based chain's next step in creating the handheld hotel.
>
> "We'll be the first hotel group by far to have wireless check-in and key cards with our handheld device," says a Wyndham International spokesperson.
>
> It's already possible for travelers to make reservations at any Wyndham using a Web-enabled PDA [personal digital assistant], like a Pocket PC, or an internet-enabled cell phone. Members of Wyndham's By Request frequent guest program can also log onto its website from a PDA, check their account status, and change their preferences.[3]

Solution to Opening Dilemma

Good communication between the housekeeping and front office departments relies on constant efforts by both departments to determine the progress in releasing rooms. There are times when the housekeeping department is short-staffed or extremely busy, and its communication of the release of rooms can be delayed. In those cases, the front office staff should make an extra effort to stay in close touch with the floor supervisors in order to determine how soon rooms will be released for sale by floor supervisors. In some hotels, housekeeping staff members can release rooms via the property management system.

Chapter Recap

This chapter has described, in detail, the process of registering hotel guests. The process begins with emphasizing to the staff the importance of making a good first impression on the guest, which sets the stage for an enjoyable guest stay. Obtaining accurate and complete guest information during registration serves as the basis for a sound communication system for all the departments in the hotel that provide services to the guest. Registering the guest involves extending credit to the guest, selecting a room, constructing and applying room rates, selling hotel services, and assigning a room key.

End of Chapter Questions

1. How important do you think the guest's first contact with the hotel is in providing hospitality? Give some examples from your experiences as a guest in a hotel.

2. Why is obtaining guest data accurately during the registration process so important? Who uses these guest data besides the front office? Give some examples of how incorrect data can affect the guest and the hotel.

3. What are the major parts of the guest registration process? How will knowledge of this system help you as you progress in a management career in the hotel?

4. Why is the choice of credit cards important to the profit-and-loss statement of the hotel? Give some examples.

5. What are some of the hidden costs involved in using a bill-to-account system? When do you think a hotel is justified in adopting a bill-to-account system?

6. Identify some of the requests a guest will have with regard to room selection. How can a front desk clerk be attuned to the needs of a guest?

7. Why are establishing and monitoring room rates so essential to the hotel's profit-and-loss statement?

8. What are the rule-of-thumb method and the Hubbart formula for establishing room rates? How effective do you feel each one is in ensuring profit for a hotel?

9. Describe a system of monitoring room rates. If you are employed at a front desk, do you see your supervisor or manager using such a system? How often? How effective do you feel this is in maintaining effective room rates?

10. Describe the various types of room rates. If you were asked by the front office manager to determine which room rates should be eliminated and whether any new types of room rates should be initiated, how would you proceed?

11. What do you think of the room rate maximization program described in the chapter? How does it affect the profit-and-loss statement? What are the important components of this program?

12. What are some opportunities for the desk clerk to sell hotel services as discussed in this chapter? If you are employed at the front desk of a hotel, do you see this being done? What effect does this have on the profit-and-loss statement?

13. What pointers would you give a new desk clerk on room key assignment?

14. Explain how to use the PMS to register a guest with a reservation. Note any inefficiencies.

15. Discuss the advantages and disadvantages of registering guests with a PMS.

CASE STUDY 701

Ana Chavarria, front office manager of The Times Hotel, has been meeting with the owner and general manager for the past several weeks to discuss the upgrade of the hotel's PMS. The owner is reluctant about the purchase; the capital investment, although reasonable, is still significant and will affect the cash flow. Margaret Chu, the general manager, was previously employed by a hotel that upgraded its PMS, and she was somewhat perplexed by the advertised benefits versus the real benefits in terms of improved customer service. Ms. Chavarria, in contrast, had a very encouraging experience with a PMS upgrade. The owner asks Ana to prepare a report to justify the upgrade of the PMS at The Times Hotel.

What concepts should Ana use to justify the upgrade purchase to achieve improved customer service in registration? Consider such aspects of the registration process as registering individuals and groups, determining room status, and issuing room keys.

CASE STUDY 702

Margaret Chu, general manager of The Times Hotel, has finished reviewing the latest batch of comment cards from this past weekend. Several of the glitches in guest service centered on the "It took too long to get into my room" syndrome. Ms. Chu thought she had this worked out with Ana Chavarria, front office manager, and Thomas Brown, executive housekeeper. Both of these managers developed a plan and shared it with him just one week ago. "What could have gone wrong?" wondered Ms. Chu. She has set up a meeting with Ana and Thomas for this afternoon. Provide a brief outline of points Ms. Chu should discuss.

Software Simulation Exercises

Review Chapter 3 of Kline and Sullivan's *Hotel Front Office Simulation: A Workbook and Software Package* (New York: John Wiley & Sons, 2003) and work through the various concepts as presented in their chapter.

- What Is the Registration Process?
- How to Register a Guest with a Reservation
- How to Register a Guest without a Reservation (Walk-in)
- How to Find and Change a Reservation for a Future Date for a Guest Who Arrives Today
- Chapter 3 Exercises

Review Chapter 5, "Guest Services," of Kline and Sullivan's *Hotel Front Office Simulation: A Workbook and Software Package* (John Wiley & Sons) and work through the various concepts as presented in their chapter.

1. Housekeeping

2. Work Orders

3. Telephone Services

4. Chapter 5 Exercises

Notes

1. JCB International Credit Card Co., Ltd., 626 Wilshire Boulevard, Suite 200, Los Angeles, California 90017.
2. Judy Colbert, "The Do's and Don'ts of Attracting International guests," *Lodging* 25, no. 8 (April 2000): 33–34.
3. Rick Bruns, "Long Awaited Wireless Checks In," *Lodging* 26, no. 8 (April 2001): 103.

Key Words

American plan	complimentary rate (comp)
bank cards	corporate rates
bill-to-account	credit-card imprinter
bottom up	credit-card validator
commercial cards	data sorts
commercial rates	discount rate

electronic key
fax machine
European plan
family rates
group rates
half-day rate
hard key
housekeeping status
Hubbart formula
intersell cards
key drawer
key fob
military and educational rates

modified American plan
Murphy bed
package rates
Peddler's Club
private label cards
rack rate
registration card
rule-of-thumb method for determining
　room rates
sleeper
top down
walking a guest with a reservation

Processing Guest Charge Payments

OPENING DILEMMA

The night auditor has been unable to track down a $35.50 shortage in balancing

the night audit. He suspects that it occurred because of a posting error on a

paid-out on behalf of a guest or food service department staff person.

The lodging industry has always prided itself on its ability to maintain up-to-date records of outstanding guest balances (Figure 8-1). The front office processes a multitude of charges and payments on any given day, requiring a well-organized bookkeeping system to process the guests' bills and maintain the integrity of the hotel's financial records. This chapter addresses how those guest charges are processed.

Common Bookkeeping Practices

Knowledge of basic bookkeeping methods enables the front office manager to understand the reasons for following particular procedures when handling financial transactions. This ability will greatly assist the front office manager in training front desk clerks and night auditors. Instead of teaching the staff which keys to press on the keyboard to process a transaction, explaining why a charge must be posted in a certain way will facilitate bookkeeping procedures. Many of you have already taken a basic accounting course or have had experience with a bookkeeping system. However, this chapter does not assume any previous knowledge of accounting procedures.

Figure 8-1. *The electronic folio displays all the data on a guest's stay that is held within the PMS. (Photo courtesy of Lincoln Plaza Hotel and Conference Center, Reading, Pennsylvania.)*

The concept of assets refers to items that have monetary value. The concept of liabilities refers to financial or other contractual obligations or debts. These two concepts provide the basics for a bookkeeping system. Examples of assets include items such as ownership of a class ring, a textbook, or two tickets to a concert. Examples of liabilities include a contract to pay for the class ring in three months, a contract to pay for a car, or a promise to pay a friend for typing a term paper. Guest charges are financial obligations that are owed to a hotel; these are considered an asset for the hotel. If a guest prepays an account, this is a liability to the hotel because the hotel will have to return the money to the guest at the time of checkout.

Assets and liabilities are increased and decreased by an organized set of accounting practices. These are called **debits,** which refer to an increase in an asset or a decrease in a liability, and **credits,** which refer to a decrease in an asset or an increase in a liability. Debits and credits provide a basis for the hotel bookkeeping system. They provide the power (mechanical means) to increase and decrease assets and liabilities for the guest and the hotel. These effects of debits and credits on assets and liabilities are shown in Table 8-1.

While this definition may be easy to remember, it is sometimes difficult to apply. However, if you apply these definitions with regard to the type of account, you should have no problem. The following examples demonstrate how to apply debits and credits.

Table 8-1. *Effects of Debits and Credits on Assets and Liabilities*

	DEBIT	CREDIT
ASSETS	increases	decreases
LIABILITIES	decreases	increases

If a guest charges $100 on a credit card for goods and services in the hotel on any one day, the individual charges would be processed as a debit (an increase) to the guest account, an asset to the hotel's accounts receivables. A credit (an increase) of an equal value would be applied to the respective departmental sales accounts (**a revenue account,** part of owner's equity).

If a guest pays $100 in advance to reserve a room, this amount would be processed as a credit (an increase) to the guest account (the hotel's advance payments, a liability). A debit (an increase) of an equal amount would be applied to the hotel's cash account (an asset).

Forms Used to Process Guest Charges and Payments

The folio, transfers, and paid-out slips are documents that allow for the documentation and transfer of charges and payments to a guest's account (Figure 8-2). In a property management system, the electronic folio is stored in the computer memory until a hard copy is required. The hard copy of the electronic folio is a standard folio that lists the date of transaction, item, transfer slip number for referral, debit or credit amount, and updated balance. The **transfer slip** allows the desk clerk to transfer an amount of money from one account to another while creating a paper trail. A **paid-out slip** (a prenumbered form that authorizes cash disbursement from the front desk clerk's bank for products on behalf of a guest or an employee of the hotel) documents the authorized payment of cash to a vendor or an employee for a quick purchase of materials for the hotel. In a hotel with a PMS that interfaces with the various point-of-sale departments, the transfer of charges incurred by the guest or the transfer of a portion of one guest's bill to another guest's folio is done automatically.

The front desk clerk uses these forms in posting charges and payments, which is the process of debiting and crediting charges and payments to a guest folio. The night auditor can then track the procedures that the front desk clerk used in posting. These forms assist in maintaining control of bookkeeping activities in the front office.

Account Ledgers

The guest ledger is a collection of **folios** (guests' records of charges and payments) of current guests of the hotel. The city ledger is a collection of folios of unregistered hotel

Figure 8-2. *The front desk clerk will post a credit-card payment on a guest's folio. (Photo courtesy of The Breakers.)*

guests who maintain accounts with the hotel. These guests may submit cash advances for a future purchase of the hotel's goods and services, such as a deposit on a banquet or on a reservation. The hotel may also offer personal billing accounts to businesspeople in the city, who are also part of the city ledger. These unregistered hotel guests may keep open accounts for entertaining clients, for example. The **folio well,** a device that holds the individual guest folios and city ledger folios, or bucket provides the physical dimensions of the guest ledger and city ledger.

The accurate and timely processing of all these accounts assists the front office manager in maintaining hard copies of guests' financial transactions with the hotel. These accounts are collectively referred to as the hotel's **accounts receivable**—what guests owe the hotel. The accounts receivable consist of two categories, the guest ledger and the city ledger.

Tracking a guest stay, from initial reservation through checkout, provides examples of the many charges and payments that affect the guest ledger (Table 8-2). Likewise, following the activities of the nonregistered guest shows how city ledger accounts are affected (Table 8-3).

Table 8-2. *Transactions Affecting the Guest Ledger*

Stage in Guest Cycle	Type of Transaction
Reservation	• Deposit on future reservation • Return of deposit on reservation due to cancellation
Registration	• Prepayment of account
Guest stay	• Charge for room and tax • Charge for food and beverages and gratuities • Charge for purchases in gift shop • Charge for parking • Charge for valet • Charge for phone calls • Charge for in-room movies • Charge for cash advance
Checkout	• Payment of outstanding balance • Return of credit balance to guest • Transfer of charges to another account • Correction of posting errors

Table 8-3. *Transactions Affecting the City Ledger*

Nonregistered Guest Activity	Type of Transaction
Food and beverage	• Deposit on upcoming function • Return of deposit due to cancellation • Charge for food and beverages • Payment for food and beverages
Business/entertainment	• Charge for food and beverages • Payment for food and beverages
Office and retail rental	• Rental charge • Payment of rental charge
Parking rental	• Parking charge • Payment of parking charge

Posting Guest Charges and Payments

As mentioned earlier, processing guest charges and payments is referred to as "posting" (increasing and decreasing assets and liabilities). Posting adds or subtracts guest charges and payments to the guest's individual account. Again, the accurate and timely posting of guest charges and payments is important in maintaining accurate financial records, as the guest may decide to check out at any time during the day and will require an accurate statement of transactions.

Posting charges and payments in a hotel with a PMS greatly increases the accuracy of the posting. Each of the PMS posting module options, as listed in Figure 4-11, allows the front desk clerk to post the various charges and payments that a guest incurs during his or her stay. With relative ease, the guest's electronic folio can be updated at the time of purchase of various goods and services. Figure 8-3 is an example of an electronic folio to which charges and payments have been posted with a PMS.

Point-of-Sale

The point-of-sale option allows the front office computer to interface with the computers in the various departments in the hotel. In a hotel, when the front office interfaces with the restaurant, the front office computer terminal accepts and automatically posts charges made in the restaurant (the point-of-sale) to a guest's folio. Any department (gift shop, recreational facilities, room service, and telephone) in the hotel that can serve as a point-of-sale (the place where a product or service is purchased) must be able to interface with the front office to post charges to the guest's account. This electronic transfer ensures that the charge is posted to the guest folio in a timely manner and increases the accuracy of the posting. (See Figure 8-4.)

Room and Tax

The room option of the posting module has been described as a "blessing" by front office employees who used to work with a mechanical posting machine. In a mechanical front office system, the desk clerk or night auditor physically removed each guest folio from its file, placed the folio into the posting machine, depressed the correct keys, removed the folio from the posting machine, and then refiled it. In a hotel with a PMS, the desk clerk can automatically post the charges to the individual electronic folios by activating the room option. While the PMS is posting room charges, the clerk is free to do other tasks.

The tax option is often activated with the room option, because most properties are required by state or local laws to charge and to collect sales and occupancy taxes from the hotel guests. The tax option posts the appropriate taxes to the guest folio when the room charge is posted.

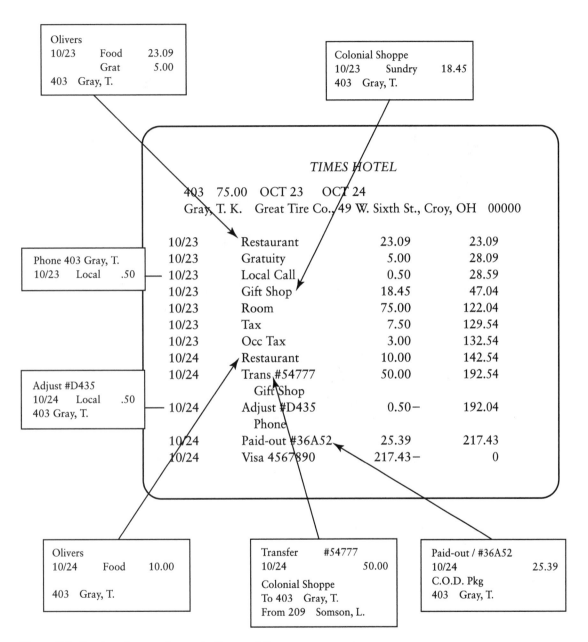

Figure 8-3. *Posting charges electronically to a folio.*

Figure 8-4. *Guests who incur charges in the dining room will have these charges immediately posted electronically to their guest folios via the point-of-sale terminal. (Photo courtesy of Omron Systems, Inc.)*

Transfers and Adjustments

The transfer and adjustment options enable front office personnel to correct errors in and make requested changes to the guest folio. The charges posted to a guest's electronic folio will at times have to be transferred to another folio, or adjustments to the amounts will have to be made. For example, a guest may discover that his or her hotel bill will be picked up by a corporation in the city. The bill had been guaranteed with the guest's credit card. The front desk clerk must transfer the guest's charges from the folio in the guest ledger to the corporation's house account in the city ledger. Another guest may claim that a charge from room service should have been charged to the person who was sharing the

A guest in the hotel has reviewed her account and says the person who was sharing the room incurred the $12.15 phone charges. The guest wants you to take care of this. How would you proceed?

room. In this case, the front desk clerk would adjust (remove) the charge from one guest folio and transfer it to the other guest folio.

There will be times when a guest questions charges for a phone call, movie viewing, or other services. The desk clerk can immediately adjust the account, depending on the authorized financial correction flexibility policy. Such a policy spells out the guidelines that a desk clerk can use in adjusting a guest's account. For example, a guest may refuse to pay for a charge for a telephone call because it should have been posted to the folio of the guest who was sharing the room. Otherwise, the front office shift supervisor or front office manager will authorize the adjustment. It is important to remember that immediate correction of errors may influence a guest's perception of a hotel's service. The policy on authorized financial correction flexibility reflects the quality of service the hotel wants to deliver.

All of these transfers and adjustments can be made easily with a PMS. Also, the adjustments are at once reflected in all the guest and departmental accounts affected by the change, with very little paperwork. This system makes the night auditor's job of verifying the integrity of accounts much easier.

Paid-out

The paid-out option is used to track authorized requests for cash paid out of the desk clerk's cash drawer. Desk clerks may be required to pay immediately for goods and services on behalf of guests, such as delivery of flowers, valet services, and COD (cash on delivery) packages. These charges are usually preauthorized by the hotel on behalf of the guest. The amount paid out can be charged to the guest's folio and reflected in the desk clerk's cash balance and the departmental account in one process. This saves the tedious effort of initiating a paper trail and also avoids the possibility of human error.

Miscellaneous Charges

The miscellaneous charges option is included in a PMS to allow the desk clerk to post charges that are atypical to the majority of hotel properties. If a hotel has, for example, a recreational facility that does not have a point-of-sale terminal, this option may be engaged. This feature can also be used to post miscellaneous charges to the city ledger accounts.

Phone

The phone option is included in a PMS for those properties that do not have an interface with the call-accounting system. With the call-accounting interface, the charges for local and long-distance phone calls, plus surcharges, will be posted automatically. Without the interface, the desk clerk must manually post the phone charge on the electronic folio.

Display Folio

The display folio option permits the front desk clerk or other authorized members of the management staff to view a guest's electronic folio at any time. If a guest requests the current balance on his or her folio, the desk clerk can produce a hard copy of the folio with a few keystrokes. After the guest has reviewed the hard copy, he or she may indicate that a certain charge is in error. This discrepancy can be resolved prior to checkout.

Reports

The reports option allows the front office manager to organize data in a way that is useful to the controller and the management team. The night auditor can cross-check departmental totals from the restaurant, phone service, gift shop, or recreational facility with the amounts charged to the guest folios. These data can be shared with the various department managers to provide feedback for evaluating marketing programs and cost-control efforts. Figure 8-5 illustrates the types of reports that can be obtained.

Transferring Guest and City Ledgers to Accounts Receivable

The debits and credits incurred by guests and future guests of the hotel are maintained as back office accounts receivable (monies owed to the hotel). Once the guest has received the goods and enjoyed the services of the hotel, then this financial record must be transferred to the master accounts receivable for the hotel. If a guest's folio shows a debit balance (an amount the guest owes to the hotel) of $291 and the guest wants to pay that off by charging $291 to his MasterCard, then the amount is transferred to the MasterCard accounts receivable.

Another type of transaction involves the **back office accounts payable,** amounts of money that have been prepaid on behalf of the guest for future consumption of goods or services (sometimes referred to as back office cash accounts), such as when a guest deposits a sum of money for a future stay. For example, the personal check a guest sends to the hotel, dated February 5, for a stay on December 21 must be credited first to the

Figure 8-5. *Reports created with the posting module.*

OLIVERS RESTAURANT 1/28 2,315.92

M	Total	Room CHG	V	M/C	JCB	DC
B	750.25	125.90	67.50	35.87	234.00	.00
L	890.67	25.00	124.50	340.00	150.00	75.00
D	675.00	235.00	56.98	75.00	221.75	125.00

GRAYSTONE LOUNGE 1/28 1,496.48

1.	780.09	121.00	.00	.00	45.00	.00
2.	456.98	75.00	35.80	87.30	89.60	75.40
3.	259.41	12.90	.00	.00	.00	.00

COLONIAL SHOPPE 1/28 1,324.72

1.	571.97	153.98	.00	76.43	121.56	.00
2.	752.75	259.93	82.87	83.76	25.71	.00

ROOM 1/28   4,529.56

TAX 1/28   452.95

ADJUST 1/28   66.04

OLIVERS	23.98	#X4567
OLIVERS	5.98	#X4568
PHONE	.50	#X4569
PHONE	.50	#X4570
OLIVERS	27.54	#X4571
PHONE	7.54	#X4572

PAID OUT 1/28   143.20

OLIVERS	45.00	#45A41-SUPPLIES
OLIVERS	12.00	#45A42-SUPPLIES
ROOM 701	32.45	#45A43-FLOWERS
ROOM 531	3.75	#45S44-COD
ADMIN	50.00	#45A45-SUPPLIES

PHONE 1/28   578.15

LD	450.61
LOC	127.54

hotel's back office accounts payable or back office cash account and then to the guest's folio. This amount of money will be held for the guest's arrival on December 21. When the guest arrives on December 21, the guest folio will be brought to the front of the folio well and activated upon registration.

These examples demonstrate that the activities in the guest ledger and city ledger are not isolated. They are reflected in the back office account. The guest ledger and city ledger are temporary holding facilities for the guest's account. The back office accounts are the permanent arenas for financial processing.

Importance of Standard Operating Procedures for Posting and the Night Audit

Standard operating procedures for processing charges and payments are used for the night audit, which is performed to balance the day's financial transactions. The financial activities recorded in the guest ledger, city ledger, and various departments within the hotel must be processed accurately. It is not uncommon for a night auditor to spend many hours looking for a small or large dollar amount to correct a discrepancy in the accounts. This error can usually be traced to a front desk clerk who transposed a dollar amount ($35.87 entered as $53.87) or transferred a charge to an incorrect account ($20.50 valet charge as a $20.50 restaurant charge). However, it is very difficult to detect if a desk clerk used an incorrect folio (room 626 instead of room 625). An experienced night auditor can usually pinpoint the error and resolve discrepancies caused by transposing figures or picking up incorrect accounts.

Because of the tedious effort required to resolve such errors, front office managers must thoroughly train front office personnel to process guest charges and payments correctly. This training program must include a statement of behavioral objectives, preparation and demonstration of detailed written procedures to follow when posting charges and payments, preparation and discussion of theoretical material that explains debits and credits, explanation of all related backup paperwork, clarification of the relationship of front office accounting procedures to back office accounting procedures, and delivery of hands-on training on the PMS. Such training efforts will pay off in reduced bookkeeping errors and better customer service.

Solution to Opening Dilemma

The night auditor should check paid-out slips with accompanying invoices from floral shops, dry cleaners, specialty shops, and the like or receipts from suppliers to determine if posting figures were transposed.

Chapter Recap

This chapter described procedures for processing guest charges and payments in a front office that uses a property management system. This process is based on knowledge of basic bookkeeping concepts—assets, liabilities, debits, and credits—as they apply to the guest ledger and city ledger. Folios, transfers, and paid-out slips provide a communication system to track the charges and payments from the various departments and guests. The interface of the property management system with the point-of-sale was presented as it affects the guest bookkeeping system. Transferring accounting data from the guest ledger and city ledger to the back office accounts was also discussed. The importance of adhering to standard operating procedures in processing guest charges and payments for the night audit was emphasized. The preparation of a training program for new front office personnel was also mentioned as a way to ensure that this goal is achieved. These operating procedures are essential to maintaining the integrity of the guest's bill and streamlining the bookkeeping process for the hotel.

End of Chapter Questions

1. List some assets that a student may hold. List some liabilities that a student may incur. What differentiates the two terms?

2. In your own words, define the bookkeeping terms *debit* and *credit*. What power do they have in a bookkeeping context?

3. What forms are used in the various departments and the front office to provide records of a guest's charges and payments? Describe each. What are the purposes of these forms?

4. What is an electronic folio? How would you describe this to a front desk clerk who just started to use a PMS?

5. What is the guest ledger? Give an example of something included in it. Describe how you would post a check for prepayment of two nights' room rate.

6. What is the city ledger? Give an example of something included in it. Describe how you would post a check for prepayment of a social reception.

7. Give examples of the various financial transactions that may occur during a guest stay.

8. Give examples of the various financial transactions in which the nonregistered guest may be involved.

9. If you are employed in a hotel that uses a property management system that interfaces with a point-of-sale department, describe the procedure for posting a guest charge or payment.

10. Why are the guest and city ledgers considered only temporary holding areas for financial transactions? Where are such records permanently maintained?

11. Why is careful and accurate posting of charges and payments so important to the night audit? How can a front office manager ensure that posting is done correctly?

CASE STUDY 801

Ana Chavarria, front office manager, has just finished talking with Cynthia Restin, the night auditor, who has spent the majority of her shift trying to track down three posting errors totaling $298.98. Last Tuesday night, a charge of $34.50 was posted to the wrong department in the city ledger; on Wednesday night, a paid-out in the amount of $21.85 had no financial document attached to the paid-out slip; and on Thursday, a $250.00 prepayment on a social event was credited to a city ledger account as $520.00. Cynthia told Ana that she has been at The Times Hotel for more than ten years, and in her experience, these mistakes are usually the result of improper training of new front desk clerks. Ana thanked Cynthia for the information and told her that she would look into the matter.

Ana called Mary Yu, lead person on the first shift, into her office. Mary trained the new front desk clerks, Henry Yee and Tony Berks. Both Henry and Tony were good trainees and seemed to understand all the tasks involved in operating the property management system. Ana asked Mary to relate the procedure she used to train these new recruits.

Mary says she described the property management system to them and then let them post some dummy charges on the training module. Then she had them correct each other's mistakes. After they had practiced for 15 minutes, the front desk became very busy, and they had to turn the training mode off and activate the regular operating mode. Henry posted several paid-out charges and transfers. Tony was a little more reluctant to touch the machine, but after the coffee break, he wanted to try to post guest payments.

Ana realizes that the development of a training program is her responsibility, and she has let that responsibility slip. How would you help Ana prepare an effective training program that teaches new front desk clerks why and how to post guest charges and payments?

CASE STUDY 802

Ana Chavarria, front office manager of The Times Hotel, has gathered her front office staff at a meeting to discuss the current policy on adjusting guest charges. Several guests have completed and returned guest comment cards indicating that requests for adjustments on their accounts have been delayed.

Luis Jimenez recalls that one guest had requested that a $10.25 phone call be removed from his account because he did not make that call. Another guest wanted an $8.95 movie charge deducted from her bill because she did not watch the movie. Luis said he referred these guests to the front office supervisor on duty, which made both guests very angry. The guests who were waiting in line for service were also annoyed.

Lavina Luquis had a similar situation, but she decided to just deduct the disputed $32.95 lunch charge without approval. The front office supervisor on duty reprimanded Lavina and told her, "All adjustments are handled by me."

Ana wants to update the hotel's policy on authorizing adjustment of guest accounts. Give her some guidelines on dollar amounts that can be adjusted without the supervisor's approval and describe some situations in which adjustments can be applied.

Key Words

accounts receivable
assets
back office accounts payable
credit
debit
folio well

liabilities
paid-out slips
posting
revenue account
transfer slip

Guest Checkout

OPENING DILEMMA

The general manager of the hotel indicated at the staff meeting today that the budget allows for the purchase of an additional module in the property management system. She suggests that the guest history module might be just what the hotel needs to increase room sales. The general manager has scheduled a visit from the PMS vendor tomorrow and wants you (the front office manager) and the director of marketing and sales to prepare a list of questions for the vendor that will help you determine whether the purchase of the guest history module for the hotel is justified.

CHAPTER FOCUS POINTS

- Organization of late charges to produce an accurate guest folio

- Procedures necessary to perform the guest checkout

- Transfer of guest accounts to the back office

- Checkout reports available with a property management system

- Guest histories

Guest checkout can indeed be a time of confusion, short tempers, and long lines, a test of the patience of both the guest and the cashier. Think of the last time you checked out of a hotel. How did it go? Was the cashier courteous and hospitable? If not, were you angry because of his or her indifference? Always remember what it is like to be a guest. It will serve you well throughout your career in the hospitality industry.

This chapter will assist you in developing a thorough understanding of the guest checkout process. It is not a difficult procedure to understand and implement; however, it does require planning in order to organize the details of this part of the guest's stay.

The use of the checkout module of a PMS is discussed throughout the chapter. Recall from Figure 4-13, the checkout module, that the options available include folio, adjustments, cashier, back office transfer, reports, and guest history.

Organizing Late Charges to Ensure Accuracy

As you have learned in earlier chapters, throughout the guest's stay, various charges for room, tax, food and beverages, valet, and other services are posted to the guest folio as they are incurred when a hotel utilizes all modules in the PMS. At the time of checkout, **late charges,** guest charges that might not be included on the guest folio because of a delay in posting by other departments, can result in substantial loss of income, as Table 9-1 indicates.

Failure to post telephone charges for local or long-distance calls made by the guest prior to checkout is another area for lost revenue. For example, a lodging property that fails to post 20 phone calls per day, at an average cost of fifty cents each, would lose $3,650 per year.

Front offices with property management systems that can interface the posting module with the point-of-sale departments and the call-accounting system can post late charges easily. As soon as the charge is incurred at the point-of-sale or through the call-accounting system, it is posted to the electronic folio. Without this interface, the point-of-sale cashier must telephone the front desk clerk prior to the guest's checkout. The telephone operator and front desk clerk must have a good reporting system to record all phone calls. When a PMS is not used, the front office manager and other department managers should initiate a communication program for their employees that will ensure a quick and accurate relay of information about last-minute charges.

Table 9-1. *Revenue Loss Caused by Failure to Post Charges*

Lost Breakfast Charges	
Average number of charged breakfasts per day	100
Percentage of lost charges	× .03
Number of lost charges per day	3
Average check	× $5.00
Amount lost per day	$15.00
Days per year	× 365
Amount lost per year	$5,475

Guest Checkout Procedure

If front office personnel have collected and posted guest late charges in an appropriate and timely manner, then the guest checkout can proceed without any bottlenecks. However, when the cashier or front desk clerk must make several phone calls to the restaurant, gift shop, and switchboard to verify charges, delays and disputes can occur.

The guest checkout involves the following steps:

1. Guest requests checkout.

2. Desk clerk inquires about quality of products and services.

3. Guest returns key to desk clerk.

4. Desk clerk retrieves hard copy of electronic folio.

5. Desk clerk reviews folio for completeness.

6. Guest reviews charges and payments.

7. Guest determines method of payment.

8. Guest makes payment.

9. Desk clerk inquires about additional reservations.

10. Desk clerk files folio and related documents for the night audit.

11. Desk clerk communicates guest departure to housekeeping and other departments in the hotel if necessary.

The objective of the checkout process is to process the guest's request for settlement of his or her account as quickly and efficiently as possible. The lodging establishment also wants to maintain a quality-control system for both the guest and the hotel: posting errors can mean erroneous charges for the guest and lost money for the lodging establishment.

Throughout your career in lodging management, you will be called on to develop operational procedures. First set your objectives and keep them simple. Accommodate guests and maintain necessary data to provide the lodging establishment with information for the income statement. The steps outlined for guest checkout show how easy it is to establish operational procedures when you keep these goals in mind. The narratives that follow elaborate on each step in the guest checkout.

Inquiring about Quality of Products and Services

When the guest arrives at the front desk to check out, the cashier should inquire about the guest's satisfaction with the accommodations, food and beverages, and miscellaneous services provided by the hotel (Figure 9-1). Cashiers should be alert to possible problems.

Figure 9-1. *Guest checkout is a time for inquiring about guest services and determining method of payment. (Photo courtesy of Lincoln Plaza Hotel and Conference Center, Reading, Pennsylvania.)*

Incidental comments about a cold room, low water pressure, leaky plumbing, or damaged furniture should be noted and passed along to the appropriate department heads.

Because guests often do not verbalize complaints or compliments, all lodging properties should have guest comment cards available as an optional source of communication. In many leading lodging chains, the chief executive officer answers these cards personally. The general manager of an independent lodging property can provide a similar personal touch by acknowledging negative comments. A good public relations program can be enhanced by addressing any minor problems experienced by the guest that might indicate lack of concern. Also, concern for guest satisfaction impacts the financial success of the hotel.

Retrieving the Room Key

Lodging properties that use a hard-key system must request the return of the hard key. The security of the guest as well as the financial investment in the hard-key system mandates that this procedure be a part of the guest checkout. Guest security is jeopardized if keys are lost or not returned. A 200-room property with approximately five keys per room that must be constantly replaced will find that a great deal of money is being spent

Upon checkout, a front desk clerk asks a guest if his accommodations were acceptable. The guest says that the heater in the room didn't work last night. Since the hotel has a 100 percent satisfaction guarantee, the desk clerk is obliged to comp the room. If you were the front office manager, what would you do to follow up on this incident?

to maintain the key supply. Some properties require a key deposit, returnable upon guest checkout.

The hotel with a PMS and/or an electronic key system can easily change the electronic code on a key for future entrance to the guest room. Although the initial financial investment in such a system is substantial, security is the ultimate objective in adopting this technology.

Retrieving and Reviewing the Folio

In a front office with a PMS, the cashier uses the folio option of the checkout module to retrieve the electronic folio by entering the guest's name or room number. A hard copy is printed for the guest.

The guest and the cashier should both review the folio. The cashier reviews the obvious charges: room fee and tax for the number of nights spent in the hotel (day of arrival through last night), incidentals (such as movie rental, personal phone calls, or purchases at the gift shop) paid for by the individual rather than a corporation, and the like. The cashier must inquire if late charges were incurred at the restaurant or any other hotel department or if any last-minute phone calls were made.

The guest must also be shown a copy of the folio for a final review. The front office manager should provide cashiers with a list of procedures to follow if charges are questioned. Typical questions concern charges for phone calls that were not made, meals that were not eaten, gifts that were not purchased, flowers that were not received, laundry that was not sent out, or in-room movies that were not viewed. Using the list provided by the front office manager, the front desk clerk or cashier may adjust these charges up to a certain dollar amount. A thorough cost-control procedure to track the total adjustments by each employee can help to keep such adjustments in line. Large dollar amounts that are questioned by the guest should be referred to the front office manager. The adjustments option of the checkout module in a property management system can be used to make these changes.

In-Room Guest Checkout

Before proceeding further with the guest checkout procedure, it is important to note the guest's option to use **in-room guest checkout,** a computerized procedure that allows guests to settle their accounts from their rooms (Figure 9-2). In some PMSs that feature in-room guest checkout, the guest can initiate the guest checkout the night before departing by following instructions located near the television set in the guest room. The guest can view a final version of the folio on the television screen on the morning of checkout. This expedites the process by alerting the front office to have a hard copy ready for payment. If the guest has indicated that he or she will pay by credit card or direct billing (bill-to-account), the guest does not have to stop by the front desk to check out. A control procedure is built into the PMS to prevent a cash customer from using in-room checkout. A guest who is going to pay with cash has not established a line of credit with the hotel.

Figure 9-2. *This hotel guest is reviewing his folio on the television screen in his room prior to finalizing guest checkout. (Photo courtesy of ITT Sheraton Corporation.)*

Determining Method of Payment and Collection

During registration, the guest indicated the method of payment he or she planned to use. Possibilities include credit cards, direct billing (bill-to-account), cash or personal check, traveler's checks, or debit cards. During checkout, the guest confirms the method of payment.

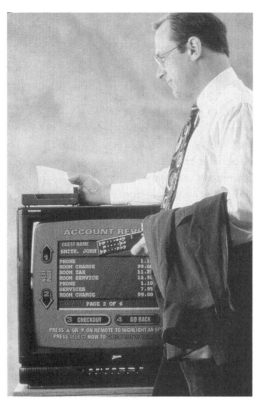

Credit Cards

Today's business and pleasure travelers usually pay with a credit card. "Plastic money" has advantages for the cardholder as well as for the hotel. The cardholder is assured instant credit to satisfy debts incurred. The extensive travel required of some businesspeople would make the almost constant requests for cash advances by corporate employees difficult to manage. The advantage for the lodging establishment is that payment is assured (less a discount paid to the corporation issuing the credit card). It is important to note that with the increased use and advances of computers in the business world, the reimbursement period can be reduced to none—the hotel is immediately credited with payment. As these advances occur, the ready acceptance of various credit cards will change.

The front office, in cooperation with the controller, usually establishes a priority system for accepting credit cards, based on cash flow requirements and the effect of the discount rate offered. The average guest will probably not be aware of the discount rate and may be willing to use whatever credit card the front desk clerk requests.

Processing a credit card in an automated hotel follows

a standard procedure. The objectives of the procedure include accurate recording of the amounts of charges and tax, name (address and phone number of cardholder are optional), verification of the credit-card dollar limit, and capture of fraudulent credit cards. The procedure might include the following steps:

1. Note the credit-card expiration date.

2. Enter the approval of the amount of the charge on the PMS checkout screen.

3. Verify the credit limit available by using the credit-card validator.

4. Allow the guest to review folio and sign.

5. Check the guest signature on the folio against the signature on the card.

6. Give the card and the guest copy of the folio to the guest.

Once the procedure has been developed, it must be followed to the letter, without exception. The fraudulent use of credit cards takes a great toll on the profits of the hotel. An incentive system for cashiers and front desk clerks can be built into the procedure for processing credit cards to encourage the capture of fraudulent cards. The small monetary reward is nominal compared to the cost of a hotel bill that may never be recovered. However, it is important to note that hotels should develop a procedure for retrieval of fraudulent credit cards. Safety of front desk staff is extremely important in this procedure.

Bill-to-Account (Direct Billing)

Hotel guests, both corporate representatives and private guests, may also use the **bill-to-account,** a preauthorized account that allows guests to have their charges processed on a regular billing cycle without the use of a credit card (sometimes referred to as "direct billing") to settle an account. Direct billing requires prior approval of the credit limit of an organization (corporate representatives) or an individual (private guest). Usually the corporation requesting direct billing will complete an application for credit approval. The controller in the lodging establishment will then perform a credit check to determine a credit rating and a credit limit. This **house limit** of credit, a credit limit set by an individual hotel, can vary, depending on the amount of projected charges and the length of time allowed for charges to be paid. The credit rating of the corporation in question will play a large part in assigning a credit limit.

The application usually will list people who are authorized to use the account as well as authorized positions within the corporation. Identification cards with an authorization number are issued by the hotel. It is the responsibility of the corporation applying for credit to monitor the authorized use of the credit. The cashier must verify identification of the corporate guest.

The bill-to-account option should be reviewed with an eye toward cost-effectiveness. Although the hotel will not have to pay a 3–8 percent discount rate to the credit-card agency, the cost incurred by the controller's office (credit checks, billing, postage, collection of bad debts) must be considered. The question of cash flow—almost immediate payment from the credit-card agency versus a four- to eight-week waiting period for corporate accounts—should also be considered. The marketing implications of direct billing also deserve attention. The status conferred by this option may be very desirable to corporate representatives and private guests.

The following procedure is used to process a bill-to-account payment:

1. Request corporate or personal identification.

2. Check to be sure the individual is authorized by the account holder to bill to the account.

3. Note any credit limit per employee.

4. Note any red flags on the credit file due to nonpayment of bills.

5. Note authorized signature.

6. Enter charges into the point-of-sale terminal along with bill-to-account identification. Once this information is entered into the POS, it becomes entered into an electronic folio in the city ledger of PMS.

Cash and Personal Checks

When guests indicate during registration that they will pay their bills with cash or a personal check, the front desk clerk should immediately be on the alert. Such a guest may very well charge everything during his or her stay (perhaps only one day in length) at the hotel and then exit without paying. Consequently, most hotels require cash in advance from guests who choose this method of payment, since the guest has not established any credit rating with the hotel. In addition, close monitoring by the night auditor and front desk clerks of the guest's charge activity is in order. Such guests will not be allowed charge privileges at other departments in the hotel. In properties with a PMS, the guest name and room number will be entered to block charges at point-of-sale areas. In a hotel without food and beverage, gift shop, and health club POS terminals, the front office will have to alert those departments that this guest has not been extended charge privileges.

To process a cash payment, the following procedure can be used:

1. Check the daily currency conversion rate when converting foreign into national currency. Take time to ensure that math is accurate.

2. Retain the amount tendered outside the cash drawer until the transaction is completed.

3. Maintain an orderly cash drawer, with bills separated by denomination.

4. Develop an orderly procedure to make change from the amount tendered.

5. Count the change out loud when giving it to the guest.

6. Perform only one procedure at a time. Refuse to make change for another bill of a different denomination if a previous transaction has not been completed.

7. Issue a receipt for the transaction.

Most lodging properties simply do not accept personal checks; there is too great an opportunity for fraud. This policy often comes as a surprise to guests, who may protest that this is the only means of payment they have. However, there are commercial check authorization companies that a hotel can employ and credit-card companies that will guarantee a guest's personal check.

The procedure for processing personal checks is as follows:

1. Request a personal check-cashing card.

2. Refer to the list of persons who are *not* allowed to present checks as legal tender.

3. Compare the written amount of the check with the figures to be sure they match.

4. Note low-numbered checks. Low numbers may indicate a newly opened, unestablished account, and the check will require a supervisor's approval.

5. Request identification (a valid driver's license and a major credit card) and record the numbers on the back of the check. Compare the name and address imprinted on the check with a valid driver's license.

6. Compare the signature on the check with the requested identification.

7. Validate the amount of the check and the credit rating of the guest with a commercial check authorization company or credit-card company.

Traveler's Checks

Traveler's checks are prepaid checks that have been issued by a bank or financial organization; they have been an acceptable form of legal tender for many years. These checks are a welcome method of payment in the lodging industry. Traveler's checks are processed like cash. Proof of credit has already been established, and there is no payment of a percentage of the sale to a credit-card agency by the hotel, as the guest has paid a percentage of the face amount of the traveler's check to the issuing agency. However, checking proof of identification (a valid driver's license or major credit card) should be a standard traveler's check–cashing policy. The guest should sign the traveler's check in the cashier's presence, and that signature should be compared with the signature already on the check. The list of traveler's check numbers that are not acceptable, supplied regularly by the check-issuing agency, must be consulted to ensure that the checks are valid.

Debit Cards

Debit cards or check cards are embossed plastic cards with a magnetic strip on the reverse side that authorize direct transfer of funds from a customer's bank account to the commercial organization's bank account for purchase of goods and services. Some examples of debit cards are MAC, NYCE, MOST, and PLUS. These are similar to credit cards in that they guarantee creditworthiness, against which the hotel charges the bill; however, the payment is deducted directly and immediately from the guest's personal savings or checking account and transferred to the hotel's account rather than being billed to the guest on a monthly basis. Debit cards continue to gain in popularity as the use of credit cards becomes more costly to the guest. However, the concept of **float,** the delay in payment after using a credit card, may remain a more attractive benefit for some guests. Some debit cards have a credit-card logo embossed on the plastic card, which indicates they are acceptable at places that accept that particular credit card and are processed through a credit-card financial organization. Debit cards are processed similarly to credit cards.

To process a debit-card payment, the following procedure is used:

1. Insert debit card into validation machine.

2. Have guest enter personal identification number.

3. Process debit-card voucher as a cash payment on the guest folio.

Assisting the Guest with Method of Payment

Guests may experience a situation in which they are short on cash or are otherwise unable to pay their bill due to an expensive emergency, overextension of credit-card limits, or theft. When these situations occur, the front desk clerk or cashier will want to be ready to offer the following services.

Money Wire

Western Union provides **money wire,** an electronic message that authorizes money from one person to be issued to another person; this service has been available to travelers for many years, with a fee charged by Western Union. This convenient service should be well established as an option for a guest. The front office manager should develop and communicate a procedure that includes the phone number and address of the nearest money wire center.

Travelers Aid Society

The Travelers Aid Society was founded for the purpose of aiding the truly down-and-out traveler beset by an unexpected emergency in an unfamiliar city. The phone number and address of this organization must also be established and communicated to the front office staff as an option of payment.

Auto Clubs

The auto clubs—AAA (American Automobile Association) being the best known—and private gasoline companies offer their members immediate cash advances in case of an emergency. Again, a listing of phone numbers of auto clubs for guest use not only helps the guest but ensures the lodging establishment that it will be paid.

The method of payment in the end can affect your bottom line. The "preapproval" criterion for credit-card and debit-card holders is an important requirement when a hotel is extending credit to a guest from check-in to checkout. The discount rate charged by the issuing agency, which takes a percentage of the gross charges, affects the income statement as well. It is also important, however, to show concern for the guest whose luck has taken a turn for the worse (serious accident, theft, unexpected illness, etc.). The front office should be equipped to offer information on alternatives such as auto clubs and money wires, which can be perceived as a display of genuine hospitality.

International Currency Exchange

When an international guest presents a credit card for payment at checkout, the credit-card–issuing agency will process the payment according to the current exchange rate between countries. If a guest wants to pay in his or her national currency, the cashier will have to compute the exchange. The daily international exchange rate can be found by calling a bank or other financial institution or reviewing the international exchange rates published in the *Wall Street Journal* in the Currency Trading section. Exchange rates for the U.S. dollar, pound, euro, peso, yen, and Canadian dollar are listed.

On January 1, 1999, the **euro** became the accepted currency for the following 11 member states of the European Community: Belgium, Germany, Spain, France, Ireland, Italy, Luxembourg, the Netherlands, Austria, Portugal, and Finland. In January 2001, Greece adopted the euro, and in January 2002, euro coins and bills were introduced. Also, the euro will provide ease in traveling throughout Europe, since a traveler will not have to exchange currency at each participating country.

The goal in computing the exchange is to determine how much of the international visitor's national currency is required to pay the bill in our country. With that goal in mind, here is a simple procedure to follow. If a Canadian guest at a U.S. hotel wants to pay a $500.00 hotel bill in Canadian dollars with an exchange rate of $0.80 Canadian to $1.00, then the cashier would use the following formula to compute the exchange of Canadian dollars for U.S. dollars:

$$\frac{\text{U.S. } \$500.00}{\text{U.S. } \$0.80} = 625.00 \text{ Canadian dollars required to pay the bill at a U.S. hotel}$$

A guest from Europe has changed her mind about using a credit card to pay the outstanding folio balance and wants to pay with English pounds. How would you proceed?

If an English guest at a U.S. hotel wants to pay a $500.00 hotel bill in pounds with an exchange rate of £1 to U.S. $2.00, then the cashier would use the following formula to compute the exchange of English pounds for U.S. dollars:

$$\frac{\$500.00 \text{ U.S.}}{\$2.00 \text{ U.S.}} = 250 \text{ English pounds required to pay the bill at a U.S. hotel}$$

It is important to consider the "float" time of the international currency collected and presented to a bank for deposit in a hotel's account; that is, it will take several days or weeks before the currency is credited to the hotel's account. Also, a different rate of exchange may be in effect at the time of the currency exchange transaction. For example, a U.S. hotel may deposit 10,000 English pounds from an English tour group thinking it will receive U.S. $20,000.00 (2.00 U.S. dollars for each English pound), but three weeks later, when the transaction occurs, the exchange rate may be U.S. $1.90 for 1 English pound. In this case, the U.S. hotel would receive approximately U.S. $19,000.00 (10,000 × 1.9 = 19,000.00) instead of the U.S. $20,000.00 originally computed at the time of deposit. To compensate for this, the hotel must consider adding a surcharge to the rate used that day as well as a transaction fee charge by banks. For example, in the case in which a U.S. hotel anticipates receiving U.S. $20,000.00 for a deposit of 10,000 English pounds based on a current exchange rate of 1 English pound for each U.S. $2.00, it may be better for the hotel to use 1 English pound for each U.S. $1.90 to cover a volatile exchange rate and a banking fee. The U.S. hotel would collect £10,526 (U.S. $20,000.00 ÷ 1.90 = (£10,526) at the time of checkout to compensate for the float time of the international currency.

Obtaining Future Reservations

Checkout, the last contact point with the guest, provides the best opportunity for securing additional reservations. It is at this time that the cashier or front desk clerk can best assist the marketing and sales department. The front office manager should develop a standard procedure for the front office staff to follow, which may include these steps:

1. At the beginning of the checkout procedure, inquire about the guest's stay. Maintain good eye contact and listen very closely.

2. Ask if the guest will be returning to this area in the near future or if he or she will need a reservation for a property in the hotel's chain or referral group. If so, ask whether he or she would like to make a reservation for that visit. Because all the guest data are already on file, a confirmation of the reservation can be sent at a later time. If the guest is in a hurry, the reservation staff can follow up later. Your role is to plant the seed for a future sale as well as to accommodate a guest.

3. Continue to check out the guest. Again, make eye contact. If the guest has not responded positively to the first inquiry, offer a departure brochure or directory that includes information about making additional reservations at the hotel's property or those properties within the chain or referral group.

4. Bid the guest farewell.

5. Report to the shift supervisor any negative comments from the guest concerning his or her stay.

6. Process any future reservations or alert the reservation clerk to these requests.

This standard procedure should be part of the desk clerk's training program. As with other sales efforts at the front office, selling additional reservations at checkout should be rewarded through an employee incentive program. This procedure gives the front office personnel a basic structure to use in pitching the sale and accommodating the guest. The employee still has the opportunity to adapt the pitch using his or her own style.

Filing Documents

The paperwork documenting the day's transactions must be in place when the night auditor's shift begins. Guest folios, transfers, paid-out slips, and the like must be filed according to a standard system. This may seem like a simple task, but at a busy front desk, with many checkouts and check-ins, it is easy to misplace documents. Care must be taken to provide the night auditor with all the necessary proof of origination of charges and trail of payment options.

Relaying Guest Departures to Other Departments

It is essential that other departments be notified after a guest has checked out to ensure smooth operation of the hotel. The PMS allows the front desk clerk and the housekeeping employees to inform one another of guest departures, stayovers, room availability status, and other occupancy details as they occur. As mentioned earlier in the text, once the electronic folio is cleared from active memory after checkout, the guest departure will be indicated on all other modules of the system. The front desk clerk does not have to telephone the housekeeper to say that room 203 is vacant; the housekeeper need not spend hours reporting room availability status to the front desk clerks. Backup phone calls are still made for situations for which current information is needed from the maintenance department. The maid or houseman can inform the front desk clerk electronically of room availability status.

In addition to informing the food and beverage department of guests who have checked out, other departments where guests can incur charges must be notified as well to prevent acceptance of unauthorized guest charges. Other departments, such as gift shops, recreational activity centers, and valet service, will also be notified so that a guest who has already checked out will no longer be able to charge a closed account. A system for notifying other departments, perhaps not interfaced in the PMS, of guest checkouts should be a basic operating procedure of the front office.

The entire communication system between the front office and other departments is further enhanced by employees who care about doing their jobs right. Desk clerks will want to ensure that rooms showing a ready-to-be-occupied status are indeed available. Housekeeping personnel must report when rooms are ready to be occupied. Careful screening of job candidates and proper training, which includes an explanation of the importance of maintaining communication with other departments, are vital to smooth operations. When everyone works together, the guest is satisfied, the lodging establishment receives a fair return on its investment, and the employee's career opportunities are enhanced.

Removing Guest Information from the System

In hotels with a PMS, removing guest information requires closing the electronic folio. This deletes the guest name and room number from the electronic guest database and the call-accounting system. This data is stored for future processing by the accounting office (see the following section) as well as the marketing and sales department for developing guest histories (discussed later in the chapter).

Transfer of Guest Accounts to the Back Office

Some methods of payment require transferring folio balances to the back office for further processing. Credit-card payments will be processed and added to the master credit-card account according to type (such as Visa or JCB). The controller maintains this account as accounts receivable. Bill-to-account charges must also be transferred to the back office accounts receivable. The controller will process the account according to standard operating procedures, which are handled electronically in a property management system. The back office transfer option enables the controller or front office staff to transfer accounts that require special handling or adjustments.

Checkout Reports Available with a Property Management System

The front office manager will want to review and analyze various data produced during checkout. Most of this information is financial. The data can be grouped into categories as the front office manager desires: method of payment and the respective amounts, total room sales, total room count, and total room sales by type are some sorting options. Room status and occupancy availability can also be tracked. The number of guests who actually checked out versus the number who should have checked out can also be compared. An analysis of guests who understayed or overstayed their reservations can be made. The reports option of the checkout module in the PMS allows the front office manager, director of marketing and sales, controller, and other department heads to review these statistics. Figures 9-3, 9-4, 9-5, and 9-6 are examples of the reports available from this module.

Guest Histories

Guest histories are marketing analyses of guests' geographic and demographic information that also provide information about guest activities while staying at the hotel. This

Figure 9-3. *Method of payment report option of a PMS.*

2/15 Method of Payment		
Type	Gross	Net
V	$ 456.98	$ 431.56
MC/	598.01	565.20
JCB	4,125.73	3,202.11
Direct bill	105.34	105.34
Cash	395.91	395.91
TOTALS	$5,681.97	$4,700.12

Figure 9-4. *Room sales report option of a PMS.*

9/22 Room Sales				
Type	Occupied	Available	Sales	Guests
K	35	37	$2,698.12	42
KK	50	50	2,965.09	65
KS	10	15	1,000.54	11
DD	45	50	2,258.36	68
TOTALS	140	152	$8,922.11	186

analysis is simplified by the use of a PMS. The guest history option of the checkout module assists the front office manager in preparing reports of such data for the director of marketing and sales. The particulars of guest histories can also be obtained from registration cards and the reservation system.

The most useful part of the marketing data is the **zip or postal code,** an individual local postal designation assigned by a country. It provides the person who is developing marketing strategies with geographic indicators of populations who have tried the products and services of a particular lodging establishment. This geographic information can be matched with communications media, such as Web site, radio, television, and newspapers, that are available in that area and with demographic (age, sex, income, occupation, marital status, etc.) and psychograpic (lifestyle) data. Matching, web site, radio stations, television stations, and newspapers to a group that constitutes the hotel's prime

Figure 9-5. *Room status report option of a PMS.*

11/1 2:19 P.M. Room Status			
DD	K	KK	KS
104 OCC	101 ON CHG	201 ON CHG	108 ON CHG
204 READY	102 ON CHG	202 ON CHG	109 READY
209 READY	103 ON CHG	203 OOO	205 READY
210 ON CHG	105 READY	206 READY	208 READY
211 ON CHG	106 OUT OF ORDR	207 READY	301 OCC
304 ON CHG	107 ON CHG	303 OCC	308 READY
309 READY	302 OCC	307 OCC	
310 READY	305 OUT OF ORDR		
311 READY	306 ON CHG		

Figure 9-6. *Understay reservation report option of a PMS.*

	Week beginning: 2/01				
	2/1	2/2	2/3	2/4	2/5
No. reservations	125	54	10	5	2
No. completed	125	50	7	3	1
Variation	0	4	3	2	1
Lost revenue	0	$480	$630	$480	$300
TOTAL LOST SALES:	$1,890				

market as well as developing well-structured direct-mail campaigns can be a very profitable marketing strategy. Defining the market for continued business is part of a sound business plan.

The front office manager who reviews the registration cards and reservation cards for group affiliations will find potential data for development of potential guests by the marketing and sales department. Follow-up by the marketing and sales department to various representatives of organizations that have stayed in the hotel may lead to the booking of future conventions and conferences.

The constant demand for meeting facilities does not just happen. Corporate clients that book facility space want to be assured that all details will be handled professionally. Trust in a hotel begins with the hotel's establishing a good track record in handling the small details of hospitality—efficiency in processing reservations, registrations, checkout procedures, and in the maintenance of clean and attractive facilities. This trust (along with a good room rate and adequate meeting space) increases room sales to small conferences.

The guest history will also provide information about the method of advertising that helped to secure the reservation and registration (Figure 9-7). If guest histories reveal that a large number of reservations originated with a particular travel or tour agency, then the marketing and sales department will want to maintain a strong relationship with that agency and to develop relationships with other agencies within that particular point of origin as well. **FAM (familiarization) tours**—complimentary visits sponsored by the lodging property that host representatives of travel organizations, bus associations, social and nonprofit organizations, and local corporate traffic managers—can produce an increase in future room revenue. During these tours, representatives can see firsthand what the property has to offer.

A lodging property that has a 70 percent corporate client market might also want to review who makes the reservations for these business professionals at the corporate client's office. The administrative assistant, traffic manager, or executive secretary is probably the person who makes the reservation. If this is the case, the lodging establishment

Figure 9-7. *Referral sources analysis option of a PMS.*

1/1–6/30 Guest History Analysis of Method of Referral		
Method	**No.**	**%**
Direct mail	300	19
Billboard	121	8
Reservation system	420	26
Local referral	89	5
Car radio	35	2
Newspaper	35	2
Web site	600	38

should put in place a program that encourages these people to call it. Incentive programs that reward those who make a certain number of reservations over a specified time period are an example.

Walk-in guests can also provide valuable marketing data. If guests indicate that "the billboard on Route 777N" was the means by which they learned about your hotel, you will have an idea about the cost-effectiveness of this type of advertising. If guests are being referred by the local gasoline station or convenience store, consider providing brochures and other information to these businesses. Perhaps complimentary dinners or escape weekends for the personnel would be effective.

Data from the guest histories concerning frequency of visits will also reveal some areas for follow-up (Figure 9-8). The frequent guest, defined as a person who stays at the establishment more than a specified number of times per month or year, might be offered a free accommodation as either a business or a personal guest. This person and his or her company should be entered into the database for follow-up with advertising promotions designed to attract that market segment.

The guest history is also useful in determining the types of rooms requested. Are rooms with two double beds being requested more often than rooms with one king-size bed? Are rooms designated as nonsmoking being requested more often than rooms designated as smoking? Are suites with cooking facilities being requested by corporate clients for long-term guests? Such hard, quantifiable data are what hotel owners use to make construction and purchasing decisions.

Reviewing room rates can also assist the controller and director of marketing and sales in forecasting profit-and-loss statements. The frequency with which certain price categories of rooms are rented will indicate the price sensitivity of certain market segments. If price sensitivity is an indicator of room occupancy, then marketing programs that maximize profits in that area must be implemented.

Examining occupancy patterns will help the front office manager to schedule person-

Figure 9-8. *Corporate guest data option of a PMS.*

1/1–1/31 Guest History—Corporate Guest Frequency		
Corporate Guest	Frequency	No. Rooms
Anderson Corp.	1/4	10
Anderson Corp.	1/7	2
Anderson Corp.	1/15	5
Dentson Co.	1/5	9
Dentson Co.	1/23	1
Hartson College	1/4	16
Montgomery House	1/20	7
Norris Insurance Co.	1/14	50
Norris Insurance Co.	1/15	65
Norris Insurance Co.	1/16	10
Olson Bakery	1/18	10
VIP Corp.	1/2	10
VIP Corp.	1/9	10
VIP Corp.	1/25	14
VIP Corp.	1/26	17
VIP Corp.	1/28	5
VIP Corp.	1/30	23

INTERNATIONAL HIGHLIGHTS

Hotels that provide service to international visitors must prepare front desk staff to deal with various languages, cultures, money exchanges, and the like. The U.S. Department of Commerce, with the support of DRI-WEFA, a global insight company with products and services that include data and software, economic and industry analysis, and consulting made the following predictions for total visitors from various countries by 2004: visitors from Europe are expected to surpass 13 million; from Asia, almost 9.3 million; from South America, 3.6 million; from the Caribbean, 1.5 million; and from Central America, nearly 1 million.[1]

The implications of this report are that students who are preparing for a career in the hotel industry must become familiar with the needs of international visitors during checkout. Studying foreign languages, common cultural concerns, and differences in legal tender will help students become valuable members of the hotel team. A hotel employee who can assist an international guest in understanding the guest folio and determining the rates of currency exchange will greatly improve the chances that this guest will return.

nel. In selected corporate-market properties, the hotel may be full from Sunday through Thursday nights but be nearly empty on Friday and Saturday. A lodging establishment with a large volume of tourist business on weekends will experience just the opposite. The front office manager will want to schedule staff accordingly.

The guest history of the PMS checkout module gives the front office manager a sophisticated method of drawing upon these data from a database of reservations and registrations. It is easy to group marketing patterns. The concepts already discussed will help in developing the data that are readily available.

Solution to Opening Dilemma

The following list of questions to ask the vendor may help to justify the purchase of the guest history PMS:

- Does this module allow us to track registrations by zip code?
- Can we match zip code and media indicated upon registration, such as radio, television, newspaper, billboard, web site, and direct mail?
- Can we print a list of guest business affiliations?
- Can we print a list of persons who initiate the reservations for corporate clients?
- Are we able to track frequency of individual guest reservations?
- Is there a means of showing how many times our suites are rented versus how many times our standard deluxe rooms are rented?
- Can that list of suite and standard deluxe room rentals be sorted by groups, such as corporate, tourist, government, or commercial?
- Can we track the number of denials we have had to issue because a certain type of room was not available?
- Does this module show our occupancy patterns by week, month, and year?

Chapter Recap

This chapter introduced the concepts and procedures required to organize and operate a guest checkout system in a hotel. The importance of communicating late charges to the front office and of notifying various point-of-sale areas about checkouts was discussed. The procedure for checking out a guest was reviewed, with attention given to sales and hospitality aspects of the procedure. The chapter emphasized the importance of communication among the housekeeping department, the food and beverage department, and the front office to strengthen service and to ensure the profitability of the lodging property. The guest history, from which guest data are grouped and analyzed, was presented as an important source of marketing feedback.

End of Chapter Questions

1. Why should a front office manager be concerned about compiling a guest's late charges? Give an example of losses that can result if late charges go unpaid.

2. Why should a front desk clerk ask a guest who is checking out about the quality of products and services? Who needs this information?

3. Why is the retrieval of a room key so important to the guest? To the hotel?

4. Do you feel a guest should review the guest folio during checkout? Why?

5. If you have used an in-room guest checkout system while you were a guest in a hotel, describe the procedure you followed. Do you feel it was a convenience or a novelty?

6. Discuss the various methods of payment available to the guest. Why does the hotel not consider these payment options financially equal?

7. Discuss the various types of credit cards. Explain their advantages to the guest and to the hotel.

8. What does bill-to-account mean? What are the hidden costs involved with this method of payment?

9. Why is cash not an eagerly sought method of payment?

10. What is a debit card? How does it differ from a credit card?

11. Summarize the procedures to follow when accepting credit cards, bill-to-accounts, cash, checks, and traveler's checks as methods of payment.

12. A guest wants to pay her account of U.S. $439 in Canadian dollars. How would you proceed?

13. How do you feel about obtaining a reservation at the time of checkout? What steps would you suggest to a front office manager to secure future reservations?

14. Why will the night auditor want all paperwork in order before beginning the night audit?

15. Why must the front office communicate a guest's departure to the various point-of-sale areas not interfaced with a PMS?

16. What types of guest accounts would be transferred to the back office?

17. List the various reports that can be generated by the checkout procedure and explain how they can assist management.

18. Discuss the role of the guest history in developing strategies by the marketing and sales department.

CASE STUDY 901

Margaret Chu, general manager of The Times Hotel, has received a phone call from the Service Feedback Agency, which she employs to provide feedback on customer service. The agent from this service said that 6 of 15 former guests indicated that there was a lengthy delay in checkout and that the holdup in service was due to a desk clerk who repeatedly had to call for the supervisor to clarify how to operate the PMS. On another point of service, none of the 15 former guests was asked to make a future reservation.

Ms. Chu calls Ana Chavarria, front office manager, into the office to discuss this report. Ana finds the service feedback report disturbing and promises to rectify the matter. Later that day, she calls Vicente Ramirez, head cashier, into her office. She asks him to write a step-by-step procedure for checking out a guest, with particular attention to use of the PMS. She also calls Angelo DeSalo, head reservation agent, into her office and asks why no future reservations are being requested at the time of checkout. Angelo indicates that desk clerks are busy and they just don't have time to request another reservation.

What steps do you think Vicente Ramirez will include in the procedure for checking out a guest? What suggestions can you give Ana Chavarria to motivate her desk clerks to ask for an additional reservation at checkout?

CASE STUDY 902

Margaret Chu, general manager of The Times Hotel, has returned from a meeting of the local hotel association. There was a presentation by the head of the state government agency on international tourism, who asked the attendees to support the state's efforts to secure international visitors to the area. He said that recent reports indicate that foreign visitors to the state will increase by 25 percent in the next two years. The economic impact of this tourism could mean more than $100 million to the local economy.

Ms. Chu calls her hotel professor friend Monica Blair at the local university and asks if Dr. Blair has a student or two who might want to take on a project of outlining concepts to use in preparing a front desk staff for international visitors. The students would work with Ana Chavarria, front office manager.

Prior to visiting Ms. Chavarria, the students are instructed to prepare an outline focusing on the question "What does the international guest need to know to have a successful visit to our town?"

Help these two students develop a list of questions to use in their meeting with Ana Chavarria.

Software Simulation Exercise

Review Chapter 4, "Posting and Folio Management," of Kline and Sullivan's *Hotel Front Office Simulation: A Workbook and Software Package* (New York: John Wiley and Sons, © 2003) and work through the various concepts as presented in their chapter.

- Posting to a Folio Directly from the PMS
- Posting to a Folio via an Interface

- Correction to a Posting
- Transfer of a Posting
- Check-out
- Cashier End-of-Shift Reporting
- Chapter 4 Exercises

Note

1. "[U.S.] Commerce Department Predicts Record-Setting Travel to U.S. This Year" (June 13, 2001), http://tinet.ita.doc.gov/tinews/archive.

Key Words

bill-to-account
debit cards
euro
FAM (familiarization) tours
float
guest histories

house limit
in-room guest checkout
late charges
money wire
traveler's checks
zip or postal code

Night Audit

OPENING DILEMMA

The front office manager has asked you to train a new night auditor. You are required to prepare an outline of concepts that you will use in training. The outline is due tomorrow.

CHAPTER FOCUS POINTS

- Importance of the night audit in a hotel
- Night audit process
- The daily flash report

The hotel's financial management starts in the front office. Of course, this responsibility is shared with the controller's office, but it begins with the accurate and timely processing of guest accounts. This chapter addresses the assembling and balancing of all financial transactions in the guest accounts and hotel departments for each day of the year. This can be a very time-consuming process for the night auditor, but it provides a balance of debit and credit entries to guest and **departmental accounts,** which include income- and expense-generating areas of the hotel (e.g., restaurants, gift shop, banquets) (Figure 10-1).

Importance of the Night Audit

The **night audit** is the control process whereby the financial activity of guests' accounts is maintained and balanced. This process tracks charges and payments (debits and credits) and the departmental receipts and charges on a daily basis. This working definition en-

Figure 10-1. *The night auditor provides a financial check on guest folios and departmental activities. (Photo courtesy of Lincoln Plaza Hotel & Conference Center, Reading, Pennsylvania.)*

compasses not only the mechanical proofing of totals of charges and payments but the further review of account activity by management. The front office manager will be able to monitor the credit activity of guests, project daily cash flow from room sales, and monitor projected and actual sales for the various departments.

Learning the process of the night audit can provide valuable information for someone who plans to continue in the hotel industry. It will also provide the necessary objective overview to evaluate the hotel's financial activity. Students will become aware of the role of the general manager, as the night audit allows a review of all the financial activity that takes places in a hotel in one day. Based on that review, the general manager must determine how it should be adapted to meet the expenses and profit goals for the accounting period. It also allows the general manager to see if marketing plans and operational activities have accomplished their stated profit goals. The night audit provides insight into how each department must be monitored to produce an acceptable income statement. It pulls together the plans and operations of a hotel on a daily basis, not just at the end of an accounting period. Ultimately, the night audit allows general managers to make good financial decisions based on current and cumulative data.

The Night Auditor

The night auditor has many responsibilities in addition to preparing the night audit report. This position also includes checking in and checking out guests who arrive or depart after 11:00 P.M., processing reservations, performing the duties of security guard, monitoring fire safety systems, acting as cashier for banquet functions, and performing the duties of manager on duty. The night auditor acts as a communication link between the guest and hotel operations during the 11:00 P.M. to 7:00 A.M. shift. This is a very important position within the front office.

The Night Audit Process

The night audit is *not* one of those reports that is put on the shelf and forgotten. Management uses it to verify the integrity of the guest accounts and to review the **operational effectiveness,** which is the ability of a manager to control costs and meet profit goals. Therefore, accuracy is extremely important.

The six basic steps involved in preparing a night audit are:

1. Posting room and tax charges

2. Assembling guest charges and payments

3. Reconciling departmental financial activities

4. Reconciling the accounts receivable

5. Running the trial balance

6. Preparing the night audit report

This listing will help guide you through the seemingly endless proofing of totals and cross-checking of entries, and expedite the completion of the process.

The night audit process described in this chapter provides information on performing the night audit with a property management system. It is important to note that learning the mechanical or "hand method" of doing the night audit will assist the front office manager in understanding the intricacies of following a paper trail of guest and depart-

Todd Sheehan is the managing partner of Lincoln Plaza Hotel & Conference Center in Reading, Pennsylvania. Previous to this position, he held supervisory positions in reservations, the controller's office, banquets, and food and beverage at The Inn at Reading, Wyomissing, Pennsylvania, as well the position of general manager of three Hampton Inns located in Reading and Allentown, Pennsylvania, and Flint, Michigan.

Mr. Sheehan summarizes the night auditor's role as one that is very important to maintain the financial success of the hotel. Although this person's role as night auditor is routine, his or her efforts to produce the trial balance provide feedback on each department's financial activities.

Each morning, Mr. Sheehan looks at the reports that are included in the night audit. The weekly flash report provides a cumulative review of rooms, average daily rate, food and beverage counts, banquet business, and so forth. The daily flash report provides period-to-date and month-to-date financial review of individual department cost centers. The trial balance report focuses on totals of receivables (how much guests owe the hotel) with regard to front desk, advance deposits, and checkouts. The revenue report shows more of a breakdown of various revenue-producing centers. There is also an adjustment report, which assists in maintaining control over financial adjustments that may seem insignificant but can add up over time. The cash deposit report allows him to maintain the integrity of banking activity by the hotel staff. Then there is the 14-day forecast report, which assists him and his sales staff in developing yield management actions to address slow periods and peak periods, with regard to room availability and rates. Also included in the night audit report is the housekeeping report, which assists him in gaining insight into room activity, such as rooms that are out of order. This report also ensures that each room occupied has a credit card responsible for payment. He uses the guest summary to determine how long guests are staying, what company they represent, and if correct rates have been applied. A detailed restaurant report is included, which centers on sales data and checks these amounts on inventory pars. This report also reviews the corrections that would have been made to guest checks as well as a check against the banquet business for the day. And finally, he reviews the accounts receivables report to retain control on amounts of money that people owe the hotel.

In summary, Mr. Sheehan indicates, "The night audit report gives you operational tools to maximize revenues on a daily basis. This effort allows you to spot revenue shortages and inefficiencies in sales activities."

mental transactions. Undoubtedly, the more modern method of performing the night audit on a PMS will be used, but you should also be familiar with the components up close and personal.

Posting Room and Tax Charges

After the night auditor has reviewed any messages from other front office staff, reviewed guests who checked out of the hotel, extended any guest stays, reviewed all room rates, and printed a variance report, his or her first task is to post room and tax charges to all accounts. The PMS can easily post room and tax charges to the electronic folios, with the room and tax options.

Assembling Guest Charges and Payments

The various modules in a PMS (food and beverage, call accounting, gift shop, etc.) allow for ease in assembling guest charges and payments. The following is a typical list of point-of-sale departments for which income will be reported:

- Restaurant 1 (breakfast)
- Restaurant 2 (lunch)
- Restaurant 3 (dinner)

- Room service 1 (breakfast)
- Room service 2 (lunch)
- Room service 3 (dinner)

- Lounge 1 (lunch)
- Lounge 2 (happy hour)
- Lounge 3 (dinner)
- Lounge 4 (entertainment)

- Valet
- Telephone
- Gift shop
- Spa and pool
- Parking
- Miscellaneous

Note how the restaurant, room service, and lounge paperwork is further classified by meal or function, to facilitate recordkeeping. General managers can review the income-generation activity of each of these departments when they are reported separately.

The guest charges option of the night audit module in a property management system can sort and total all departmental charges and payments that have been posted to the electronic folios from the point-of-sale systems that interface with the PMS. These data are accurate as long as the person entering the charges at the point-of-sale terminal keys them in accurately.

Reconciling Departmental Financial Activities

The departmental totals option of the night audit module in the PMS will report the totals of sales by department, as shown in Figure 10-2. These totals are compared to posting information received from the point-of-sale system.

Another departmental total that must be verified is the cash tendered by guests at the front office. Hotels vary in their cash-processing policies. Some front offices process restaurant guest checks from cash customers or other departments in the hotel, because management wants to centralize the cash transactions. In other hotels, this policy would be a great inconvenience because of the distance of the various restaurants, lounges, and

Figure 10-2. *The departmental totals option of a PMS lists amounts generated by each department. (Information courtesy of Lincoln Plaza Hotel Conference Center, Reading, Pennsylvania.)*

Departmental Totals

Department	Amount
Room	
Tax	
Local Telephone	
Long Distance Telephone	
Paidout	
Beverage	
Write off credit	
Restaurant Breakfast	
Restaurant Lunch	
Restaurant Dinner	
Lounge Beer	
Lounge Wine	
Lounge Liquor	
Restaurant Tips	
Restaurant Merchandise	
Restaurant Tax	
Room Service	
Room Service Tips	
Gift Shop	
Movie	
Vending	
Parking	
Dry Cleaning	
Newspaper	
Rollaway	
Gift Certificates	
Copies	
Faxes	
Stamps	
Adv. Deposit Refund	
Banquet Food	
Banquet Beverage	
Banquet Service Charge	
Banquet Wine	
Banquet Liquor	
Banquet Beer	
Banquet Meeting Rooms	
Banquet Tax	
TOTAL	

Figure 10-3. *The cashier's report maintains a control on cashier activity. (Courtesy of Lincoln Plaza Hotel & Conference Center, Reading, Pennsylvania.)*

Cashier Report

Department	*Amount*

Front Desk
  Cash Received
  Write Off
  Travel Agent Commission
  Checks
  Employee Discount Fee
  Credit Card Received
    MasterCard
    Visa
    Diners Club
    JCB
  Hotel Gift Certificate

Restaurant
  Cash Received
  Credit Card Received
    Visa
    MasterCard
    Diners Club
    JCB
  Gift Certificate Redeemed
  Lounge
  Room Service
  Discounts
  Welcome Discount Coupon

Banquets
  Cash Received
  Credit Card Received
    Visa
    MasterCard
    Diners Club
    JCB
  Allowances
TOTAL

Deposit Summary
    Cash/Foreign Currency
    Other Payment Methods
    Deposits Subtotal
    A/R Total
    Paid Out
    Total Deposit

Actual Deposit
Over/Short

A front desk clerk was $2.75 over on her cashier's report for the shift. What do you think is the source of the overage? How would you proceed to correct the error?

gift shops from the front office. It also requires additional personnel in the various departments to carry the guest checks with the cash or credit cards to the front office.

The cashier option of the night audit module in the PMS will report the amount of cash, credit cards, and coupons received and discounts processed during the shift, as shown in Figure 10-3. The total amount of cash received by each cashier who has been issued a cash drawer must be verified against the total money deposited for that shift.

Reconciling Accounts Receivable

The city ledger is an accounts receivable held at the front office. As noted in Chapter 2, the city ledger is a collection of guest accounts of persons who are not registered with the hotel. They have either received approval for direct-billing privileges or paid a deposit on a future banquet, meeting, or reception. The night auditor will treat these accounts just like the accounts on the guest ledger for registered guests. He or she must assemble the charges and verify their accuracy. The cash received from these accounts is reflected in the cashier's report.

The figures in a city ledger can be quite large. A hotel that promotes direct billing as a customer service may have outstanding guest debit charges of $10,000 to $50,000. The hotel may hold a **credit balance,** amounts of money a hotel owes guests in future services, of $25,000 to $150,000 or more from deposits on future receptions and meeting room rentals. The controller of the hotel must closely watch the balances of these accounts to ensure effective cash flow management.

The **master credit card account**—an account receivable that tracks bank, commercial, private label, and intersell credit cards such as Visa, MasterCard, and JCB—is held at the front office. Depending on the size of the hotel, the services offered to the guest, and the speed of reimbursement from the credit-card agency, this figure may also be quite large. It is not uncommon for a medium-size hotel to have an outstanding credit balance of $30,000 to $50,000 at any one time. As checks are received from the credit-card agency,

The front office manager asks you to retrieve a total for the VISA credit card balance in the accounts receivable. How would you proceed?

this figure is reduced. It will rise again when new charges are posted to a guest's folio. When the checks from the credit-card agency are received, they are posted to the respective credit card's account receivable, and a current balance is calculated.

The city ledger and accounts receivable options of the night audit module of a PMS will produce a report of the activity on the city ledger and master credit-card accounts.

Running the Trial Balance

A **trial balance** (Figure 10-4 is a first run on a set of debits to determine their accuracy against a corresponding set of credits. The trial balance helps the night auditor focus on accounts in which charges may have been posted or reported incorrectly. For that reason, it is important that the night auditor compare the departmental totals against any transfers and paid-out slips for each department processed by desk clerks and cashiers.

Goal of Preparing the Night Audit Report

Students studying hotel front office management may ask, "Why should the night audit report be prepared?" It offers a massive amount of daily operational financial feedback that provides an immediate opportunity for managers to react and respond. The night audit report is key in maximizing the efficiency of a hotel. The daily figures regarding room occupancy, yield percentage, average daily rate, and revenue per available room (RevPAR) provide managers with daily opportunities to improve a slow sales period. Guests who demand an accurate folio complete with guest charges can be helped more efficiently as a result of this process.

As you begin your career in the hotel industry, take the opportunity to review the financial statistics generated by the night audit report. It will provide a capsule review of the importance of departmental financial activities and their role in delivering hospitality. This background will also provide you with insight into the decision-making process, which, in turn, helps various departments adhere to their budgets.

Preparing the Night Audit Report

The night audit report is usually organized to meet the needs of a specific lodging establishment. Some general managers might require more financial data than others. Figure 10-5 is a sample of a night audit report of all financial activities of the day. You may want to note the columns headed "Budget" and "Goal." The budget figure is the target amount of sales planned for that day. The goal figure shows what percentage of the budgeted figure was actually achieved. If a larger amount was budgeted than was realized, then some part of the operation is not functioning as expected. Some hotel managers

Figure 10-4. *A trial balance report lists the debit and credit activity of the front desk, receivables, and payables. (Courtesy of Lincoln Plaza Hotel & Conference Center, Reading, Pennsylvania.)*

Trial Balance

Front Desk Activity	*Amount*
Opening Balance	
Total Debits (Room and Tax)	
Total Credits (Various Methods of Payments)	
Deposits Transfer (Payments Collected on Banquets or Room Deposits)	
Closing Balance	

Advance Deposits (Current Amounts in System)	*Amount*
Opening Balance	
Total Credits	
Applied/Canceled	
Closing Balance	

Receivables	*Amount*
Opening Balance	
Total Debits (General Ledger Accounts of corporations and individuals)	
Total Credits (Various Methods of Payments)	
Closing Balance	

Payables	*Amount*
Opening Balance	
Total Debits (Travel Agent Fees Paid by the Hotel)	
Total Credits (Various Methods of Payments)	
Closing Balance	

want a cumulative figure reported each day, to gain a more comprehensive overview of the achievement of financial goals.

It is important that managers approach this report as a functional tool that provides daily operational financial data. Its major components may seem overwhelming when perceived as a whole. With experience, you learn to view this seemingly complicated document in separate parts, each of which provides feedback on daily operational per-

Figure 10-5. *Night audit report.*

Night Audit	$ Actual	$ Budget	Goal (%)	Date _____
ROOM	4,500.00	7,500.00	60.00	
TAX	450.00	750.00	60.00	
Restaurant 1 *Breakfas*	750.00	825.00	90.91	
Restaurant 2 *Lunch*	1,200.00	1,500.00	80.00	
Restaurant 3 *Dinner*	2,000.00	1,500.00	133.33	
TOTAL RST SALES	3,950.00	3,825.00	103.27	
SALES TAX	197.50	191.25	103.27	
Rest Tips 1 *Break*	112.50	123.75	90.91	
Rest Tips 2 *Lunch*	180.00	225.00	80.00	
Rest Tips 3 *Dinn*	300.00	225.00	133.33	
TOTAL RST TIPS	592.50	573.75	103.27	
Room Srv 1 *Break*	125.00	350.00	35.71	
Room Srv 2 *Lunch*	150.00	300.00	50.00	
Room Srv 3 *Dinner*	300.00	250.00	120.00	
TOTAL ROOM SRV	575.00	900.00	63.89	
SALES TAX	28.75	45.00	63.89	
Room Srv 1 Tips *Break*	25.00	70.00	35.71	
Room Srv 2 Tips *Lunch*	30.00	60.00	50.00	
Room Srv 3 Tips *Dinner*	60.00	50.00	120.00	
TOTAL ROOM SRV TIPS	115.00	180.00	63.89	
Banq Bkfst	0.00	350.00	0.00	
Banq Lunch	200.00	500.00	40.00	
Banq Dinner	4,300.00	6,500.00	66.15	
TOTAL BANQ	4,500.00	7,350.00	61.22	
Banq Bkfst Tips	0.00	63.00	0.00	
Banq Lunch Tips	36.00	90.00	40.00	
Banq Dinner Tips	774.00	1,170.00	66.15	
TOTAL BANQ TIPS	810.00	1,323.00	61.22	
Banq Bar Lunch	125.00	200.00	62.50	
Banq Bar Dinner	485.00	400.00	121.25	
TOTAL BANQ BAR	610.00	600.00	101.67	
ROOM RENTAL	200.00	250.00	80.00	
Lounge 1	125.00	85.00	147.06	
Lounge 2	780.00	950.00	82.11	
Lounge 3	500.00	450.00	111.11	
Lounge 4	600.00	575.00	104.35	
TOTAL LOUNGE SALES	2,005.00	2,060.00	97.33	
Lounge Tips 1	12.50	8.50	147.06	
Lounge Tips 2	78.00	95.00	82.11	
Lounge Tips 3	50.00	45.00	111.11	
Lounge Tips 4	60.00	57.50	104.35	
TOTAL LOUNGE TIPS	200.50	206.00	97.33	
VALET	350.00	250.00	140.00	

Figure 10-5. *(Continued)*

	$ Actual	$ Budget	Goal (%)
Tele Local	110.00	125.00	88.00
Tele Long Dist	295.00	300.00	98.33
TOTAL PHONE	405.00	425.00	95.29
GIFT SHOP	212.00	350.00	60.57
GIFT SHOP SALES TAX	10.60	17.50	60.57
VENDING	125.00	100.00	125.00
SPA	450.00	500.00	90.00
PARKING	500.00	350.00	142.86
TOTAL REVENUE	20,786.85	27,746.50	74.92
Less Paid-outs			
Valet	120.00		
Tips	0.00		
TOTAL PAID-OUTS	120.00		
Less Discounts			
Room	0.00		
Food	25.00		
TOTAL DISCOUNTS	25.00		
Less Write-offs			
Rooms	75.00		
Food	15.00		
TOTAL WRITE-OFFS	90.00		
Total Paid-out and Noncollect Sales	235.00		
Total Cash Sales	4,028.45		
Today's Outstd A/R	16,758.40		
Total Revenue	21,021.85		
Yesterday's Outstd A/R	75,985.12		
TOTAL OUTSTD A/R	92,743.52		
CREDIT CARD REC'D A/R	37,500.12		
Cash Rec'd A/R	5,390.87		
Bal A/R	49,852.53	75,000.00	66.47
ANALYSIS OF A/R			
City Ledger	12,045.15		
Direct Bill	3,958.55		
Visa	19,681.01		
MC	13,788.24		
JCB	4,939.03		
Total A/R	54,411.98		

[Handwritten annotations: "yesterdays + todays Acc Receivable", "these subtracted from =", "Should match shows descrepency"]

Figure 10-5. *(Continued)*

BANK DEPOSIT		ANALYSIS OF BANK DEPOSIT	
Cash	9,419.32	Total Cash Sales	$4,028.45
Visa	22,967.98	Credit Card Rec'd A/R	37,500.12
MC	11,687.05	Cash Rec'd A/R	5,390.87
JCB	2,845.09		
TTL BANK DEP	$46,919.44		$46,919.44
AMT TR A/R	$16,758.40		

Cashier's Report

	Actual Amount	POS Amount	Difference
Shift 1			
Cash	$907.25	$907.29	−$0.04
Cr Cd	29,750.67	29,750.67	$0.00
TOTAL 1	$30,657.92	$30,657.96	−$0.04
Shift 2			
Cash	$7,884.81	$7,883.81	$1.00
Cr Cd	7,000.45	7,000.45	0.00
TOTAL 2	$14,885.26	$14,884.26	$1.00
Shift 3			
Cash	$628.22	$628.22	$0.00
Cr Cd	749.00	749.00	0.00
TOTAL 3	$1,377.22	$1,377.22	$0.00
TOTALS	$46,920.40	$46,919.44	$0.96

Analysis Cash Report

Cash Sls	$4,028.45
Cr Cd A/R	37,500.12
Cash A/R	5,390.87
TOTAL	$46,919.44

(handwritten notes: Avg rate; Room income / # rooms Available = Revpar; formula for duble occupance; # of gues − # of rooms / # of rooms)

Manager's Report

	Actual	Budget	Difference
ROOMS AVAIL	100	100	0
ROOMS SOLD	65	85	20
ROOM VAC	30	15	−15
ROOMS OOO	0	0	0
ROOMS COMP	0	0	0
OCC %	65.00%	85.00%	20.00%
DBL OCC %	15.38%	11.76%	−3.62%
YIELD %	52.94%	88.24%	35.30%
REVPAR	$45.00	$75.00	$30.00
ROOM INC	$4,500.00	$7,500.00	$3,000.00
NO. GUESTS	75	95	20
AV. RATE	$69.23	$88.24	$19.01
RACK RATE	$85.00	$85.00	$0.00
NO-SHOWS	3	1	−2

(handwritten notes: out of order; noce then are; guest/room; yiely formula; todays Rev = Rooms Avail × Rack rate)

formance. Daily review of the reported figures will allow management the opportunity to be flexible in meeting financial goals.

Departmental Totals

Each department in the hotel is required to provide a daily sales report to the front office. These figures are listed and compared to the budget goal. General managers of hotels use these figures to determine the profitability of income-generating departments and the success of marketing programs.

Bank Deposit

Bank deposits are also part of the night audit. In large hotels, bank deposits are made several times a day to satisfy security concerns. The bank deposit includes both cash and credit-card deposits. It is important to note that cash, business checks, and checks from credit-card companies are received several times throughout the business day. After these are received and recorded, they are turned over to a cashier at the front desk to post them to the corresponding guest or city ledger account.

Accounts Receivable

The accounts receivable is an ongoing listing of outstanding amounts owed to the hotel. As mentioned in Chapter 8, these potential sources of revenue are essential to providing positive cash flow. Managing and updating these accounts, by reviewing them daily, is a primary responsibility of the controller and general manager.

Cashier's Report

Some hotels have the traditional three shifts (7:00 A.M.–3:00 P.M., 3:00 P.M.–11:00 P.M., and 11:00 P.M.–7:00 A.M.) for cashiers. In larger hotels, there may be several cashiers per shift. No matter how many cashiers there are per shift, each is responsible for actual cash and credit cards received, which are compared to PMS totals. The **cashier's report**, discussed earlier in the chapter, lists cashier activity of cash and credit cards and PMS totals and is an important part of the financial control system of a hotel. The front office manager and the controller will review this part of the night audit and look for discrepancies between the actual amount received and the PMS total. They will also assess the cashier's accuracy.

Manager's Report

The **manager's report** is a listing of occupancy statistics from the previous day, such as occupancy percentage, yield percentage, average daily rate, RevPAR, and number of guests. Data such as these are necessary for monitoring the operation of a financially viable business. The general manager, controller, front office manager, and director of marketing and sales will review these statistics on a daily basis.

Formulas for Balancing the Night Audit Report

The following formulas will provide you with an understanding of how to balance the night audit.

Formula to Balance Guest Ledger	*Formula to Balance City Ledger*
total revenue	yesterday's outstanding A/R
− paid-outs and noncollect sales	+ today's outstanding A/R income
= daily revenue	= total outstanding A/R
− total cash income	− credit card received and applied to A/R
− today's outstanding A/R income	− cash received and applied to A/R
= 0	= balance of A/R

Formula to Balance Bank Deposit

total bank deposit

− total cash sales

− credit card received A/R

− cash received A/R

= 0

Room and Tax

The **room sales figure** represents the total of posted daily guest room charges. The night auditor obtains this figure from the PMS by activating the **cumulative total feature,** an electronic feature that adds all posted room rate amounts previously entered into one grand total. This figure is only as accurate as the posting of daily room rates. If a desk clerk transposes figures, then the total room sales amount will be incorrect. Since a large portion of room income is considered profit, management will watch this figure closely. The room sales figure is verified by the housekeeping report, which lists the occupancy status of each room according to the housekeeping department. The corresponding tax total is obtained by activating the **tax cumulative total feature,** an electronic feature of a PMS that adds all posted room tax amounts previously entered into one grand total. This figure is necessary for tax collecting and reporting.

Total Restaurant Sales and Sales Tax

The **total restaurant sales figure** comprises all sales incurred at restaurants or food outlets in the hotel. Restaurant 1 may represent breakfast sales; 2, lunch sales; and 3, dinner sales. Or Restaurant 1 may represent all food sales from Restaurant A; 2, food sales from the pool snack bar; and 3, sales from Restaurant B. These figures are verified against the **daily sales report,** a financial activity report produced by a department in a hotel that reflects daily sales activities with accompanying cash register tapes or point-of-sale audit tapes from each of the restaurants or food outlets. The sales tax figure is also obtained from the daily sales reports.

Tips for Restaurant, Room Service, Banquet, and Lounge Employees

Tips paid out to service employees represent an important control feature. Not only is management required to report this amount to state and federal agencies, but the tips may be paid out from the desk clerk's cash drawer or the restaurant cash drawer. In any case, tips charged to the guest's account on restaurant guest checks, tips paid immediately to service employees from the desk clerk's cash drawer on paid-out slips, room service guest checks, and charged tips on credit-card vouchers are used to verify this total.

Room Service

Some hotels report room service sales as a separate figure from total restaurant sales. If a hotel has organized a special marketing and merchandising campaign to increase room service sales or feels that careful monitoring of this potentially profitable service is necessary, then the night auditor will report this figure. Room service 1 may represent breakfast sales only; 2, lunch sales; and 3, dinner sales.

Banquet Sales

Hotels with large banquet operations will report the banquet sales figure separately from restaurant sales. These figures are a total of the guest checks, which tally the individual banquet charges. The night auditor will also check the daily function sheet to ensure that all scheduled functions have been billed.

The general manager can use banquet sales figures to determine how effective the food and beverage manager is in controlling related expenses for this division. They also indicate how effective the director of marketing and sales is in generating business. Banquet breakfast, banquet lunch, and banquet dinner figures are reported separately because they provide marketing information on which areas are successful and which could be more successful. The banquet sales figures (and the room sales figure) also provide information on the cash flow activity of the hotel. If the hotel has scheduled $25,000 of banquet business and $25,000 of rooms business for a weekend, it can meet various financial obligations due on Monday, depending on method of payment. The controller in a hotel will therefore watch room and banquet sales very closely.

Banquet Bar and Total Lounge Sales

The sales figures for the banquet bar and lounge areas originate from the point-of-sale cash registers. The total sales figures from the various outlets that serve alcoholic beverages are reported to the front office on a daily sales report after each shift. Each report is accompanied by the cash register tapes or audit tapes.

These sales figures from the various lounges and banquets are reported separately because the food and beverage manager will want to determine how well cost-control efforts have been maintained for that department, and the director of marketing and sales may want to know how successful certain marketing and merchandising campaigns have been.

Room Rental

The charges for room rental—these are not guest rooms but meeting and function rooms—are reported on special room rental guest checks. The night auditor will cross-check these guest checks against the daily function sheet to be sure the banquet manager has charged room rentals to the appropriate guests.

This figure is reported separately at those hotels that charge fees for the rental of facilities when no food or beverage is ordered. For example, banquet rooms may be rented for seminars, meetings, demonstrations, and shows. Since room rental represents a potentially large profit area (especially during slow banquet sales periods), general managers will want to know how effective the marketing and sales department has been in maximizing this profit center.

Valet

One of the services a hotel offers is dry cleaning and laundry. This feature must be closely monitored because the hotel pays cash to the off-premises dry cleaner or laundry service when the clothing is returned. These costs, plus a markup for hotel handling charges, are posted to the guests' folios. Some hotels maintain a valet or dry cleaning/laundry journal indicating valet tags, control numbers, processing dates, vendor charges, handling charges, posting activity, daily totals, and the like. Transfer slips are prepared to indicate the charges for valet service. The charges on these transfer slips are then posted to the guests' folios. The total of the transfer slips comprises the valet total for the night audit.

Telephone Charges

After the telephone industry was deregulated in the early 1980s, call accounting became a standard practice in hotels. This allowed hotels to set individual **surcharge rates,**

rates for adding service charges for out-of-state long-distance telephone service. The telephone department became a very profitable area in the hotel business. Since all phone calls are charged to the guest folio, an accurate accounting of the charges is necessary. In a hotel with a call-accounting system that interfaces with a property management system, this tally is electronically obtained.

Gift Shop Sales and Tax

The gift shop in a hotel prepares a daily sales report for the front office. Cash register tapes or point-of-sale audit tapes will accompany the report. The general manager will want to examine the financial activity of this profit center. This is another area in which cash flow potential is monitored. Recording the tax collected on gift shop sales and reporting this figure is a necessary accounting procedure.

Vending

Hotels that maintain their own vending machines will monitor the daily collection of cash. If a facility has a large number of vending machines, the food and beverage manager assigns one person to collect and count the money and prepare a daily sales report. These reports provide the total sales figure for vending.

Spa

The use of health facilities at a hotel may be provided free to guests. However, other products and services—such as swimsuits, health-related products and equipment, the services of a masseur or masseuse, sports lessons, and rental of equipment—are sold to the guest. These costs will usually be charged to the guest folio. A daily sales report will be prepared at each of the health/recreation facilities. Some hotels offer their health/recreation facilities for a fee to the general public. Transfer slips for charges to the guest accounts for future billing in the city ledger provide a total against which total spa charges are verified.

Parking

A hotel that offers valet parking or parking spaces to guests and the general public will acquire large amounts of cash during a business day. Cash, business checks, and debit- and credit-card payments are collected throughout the day for general parking, long-term business parking, and parking valet services. Guests in the hotel who are charged for parking services will have this amount charged to their accounts. The parking garage manager will prepare a daily report of the cash and charge activities for each shift of the day. Supporting documentation, including parking tickets, cash register tapes, transfer slips, and monthly parking permit renewals, accompany the daily report. The night auditor will prepare a summary total of this account from these reports.

Total Revenue and Total Write-offs

The total revenue and total write-off figures represent all the cash and charge transactions for the day, reflecting all the previously reported figures. General managers will compare the actual and budgeted figures to determine how well operations have met the financial goals of the hotel.

Throughout the business day, the front office manager will authorize paid-out slips (for valet service, tips, supplies, and the like), discounts (for rooms or restaurant charges, for example), and adjustments (room, telephone, and restaurant, for example) in the form of write-offs to guest accounts. The general manager will maintain strict control over these figures. These amounts are verified with authorized paid-out slips and transfer slips.

Cash Sales and Accounts Receivable Balance

The total revenue represents both cash and charge guest sales. A separate figure is reported for total cash sales for the day. This figure represents the totals reported and received from the various departmental daily reports and is also required to justify the daily bank deposit.

Charge sales are reflected in the outstanding accounts receivable (Today's Outstd A/ R). This is the amount that remains to be received from the guests. Total paid-outs, total discounts, and total write-offs have been subtracted from that figure. Today's outstanding accounts receivable figure is added to yesterday's outstanding accounts receivable (Yesterday's Outstd A/R) to obtain a cumulative balance of outstanding accounts receivable (Total Outstd A/R).

Credit Cards and Cash Applied to Accounts Receivable

Throughout the business day, the controller of the hotel will request front desk clerks or cashiers to post business checks and cash received from credit-card companies, direct-billing accounts, and city ledger accounts. The charges from these groups were previously moved to accounts receivable. These checks and cash payments represent charges from previously held banquets, guest room rentals, and the like. The general manager of the hotel watches this figure to determine cash flow activity. Again, the outstanding balance of accounts receivable is updated.

Analysis of Accounts Receivable

The front office manager maintains an analysis of the accounts receivable balance. It will indicate the source of the account receivable—city ledger, direct billing, or various credit cards. (It is important to note here that city ledger accounts may have a credit balance but are maintained as an account receivable. For example, if a guest pays a $500 deposit on a future banquet, a credit balance will be maintained on the account. When this credit balance is computed with other debit balances, a debit balance is realized.)

The controller will use this information to track the **aging of accounts,** determining the stage of the payment cycle—such as 10 days old, 30 days overdue, 60 days overdue—and to operate an overdue payment collection program.

Bank Deposit and Amount Transferred to Accounts Receivable

The cash, credit-card vouchers, and charges received during the business day from cash, charge, and accounts receivable transactions must be deposited in the hotel's bank accounts or transferred to the hotel's internal accounts receivable. The night auditor will provide a summary of the components of the bank deposit. Bank deposits are made throughout the business day. Those individual totals make up the total bank deposit (TTL BANK DEP). Credit-card totals are listed here because, in some circumstances, the credit-card voucher is considered cash at the time of deposit. The cash and various credit-card totals that have been deposited must match the total cash sales plus the cash received and applied to outstanding accounts receivable (Cash Rec'd A/R) minus total paid-outs. The total actual cash and credit-card payments received, which are reported on the cashier's report, will match the total bank deposit figure. The amount transferred to accounts receivable (AMT TR A/R) will correspond to today's outstanding accounts receivable (Today's Outstd A/R).

Cashier's Report

In some hotels, the front desk clerk or cashier is responsible for proofing and collecting the various departmental daily reports. In those situations, the cash and credit-card vouchers are added into the individual cashier's shift report. Also included in that report are the amounts of cash and credit-card checks received for application to accounts receivable. Each cashier's shift report is verified by departmental daily reports, cash and credit-card vouchers, and accounts receivable cash and credit-card check transactions. These figures must be verified in the daily bank deposit.

The cashier's report will also note any variances in actual totals and PMS totals. Usually, the hotel will set a policy regarding the front desk clerk or cashier's liability for these variances. For example, if the actual amount collected is one cent to one dollar less than the amount obtained in the cashier's report, the front desk clerk or cashier is not liable for the difference. Amounts significantly larger than one dollar will be investigated to see

FRONTLINE REALITIES

 The PMS is down, and the night auditor has to prepare the night audit report. How would you suggest the night auditor proceed?

if such losses are regular occurrences. When the actual amount collected is more than the amount obtained in the cashier's report, the extra money will be maintained in a house fund to compensate for undercollections. These amounts should also be investigated as to regularity and source. Substantial overages and shortages must be investigated for proper debiting and crediting of a guest's account.

Operating Statistics

The night auditor will prepare the daily operating statistics for the general manager and the various department directors. This quick summary provides a review of the day's activities and the hotel's success in meeting financial budget targets. Hotel general managers rely on these statistics as operational feedback mechanisms because they provide information on the need to modify existing operational procedures and offer insight into budgeting for future operational procedures. Also, these figures become part of the hotel's historical operations record.

The rooms sold, rooms vacant, and rooms out of order are determined by assessing the housekeeping module (Figure 4-17) and the housekeeper's report (Figure 10-6). The number of complimentary rooms (rooms comp) is determined by reviewing guest reservations, registration cards, and folios. A quick method used to determine occupancy percentage, double occupancy percentage, yield, average daily rate, and RevPAK is shown in Figure 10-7.

Room income for the day is obtained from the total room charges that were posted after a certain time in the evening (between 11 P.M. and midnight) and any half-day rate charges. The number of guests is provided by the PMS registration module. The number of no-shows is compiled by tallying the number of reservations with a confirmed status that did not show. Not included in this figure are guaranteed reservations, which are processed with a credit-card number regardless of whether the guest showed.

The preparation of a night audit report can be very time-consuming. However, with a great deal of cooperation, planning, and organization, combined with the use of a PMS that interfaces with a point-of-sale system, the time can be greatly reduced. The accurate preparation of the night audit report provides an essential control and communication tool for management.

Daily Flash Report

The **daily flash report**, a PMS listing of departmental totals by day, period to date, and year to date, is a very useful report for general managers and department managers and supervisors. This report is reviewed on a daily basis to indicate how successful a department manager was the previous day in achieving sales. This tool is important in discussing strategies for the successful achievement of financial goals. Figure 10-8 provides an illustration of the major components of a flash report.

Figure 10-6. *The housekeeper's report provides a verification of the number of rooms occupied on a particular night.*

Housekeeper's Report				Date _____	
Room	*Status*	*Room*	*Status*	*Room*	*Status*
101	O	134	OOO	167	V
102	O	135	O	168	O
103	O	136	V	169	O
104	O	137	V	170	O
105	V	138	O	171	O
106	V	139	O	172	O
107	O	140	V	173	O
108	O	141	O	174	O
109	O	142	O	175	O
110	O	143	O	176	O
111	O	144	OOO	177	OOO
112	O	145	OOO	178	OOO
113	O	146	O	179	O
114	O	147	O	180	O
115	O	148	V	181	V
116	V	149	V	182	O
117	O	150	O	183	O
118	O	151	O	184	O
119	O	152	O	185	O
120	O	153	O	186	O
121	V	154	O	187	V
122	V	155	V	188	V
123	V	156	V	189	V
124	O	157	O	190	O
125	O	158	O	191	V
126	O	159	O	192	V
127	O	160	V	193	O
128	O	161	V	194	V
129	O	162	V	195	O
130	O	163	O	196	V
131	O	164	O	197	O
132	O	165	O	198	V
133	V	166	V	199	V
				200	V

O: Occupied   V: Vacant   OOO: Out of order

Figure 10-7. *These formulas offer an easy method for determining operating statistics.*

Statistic	Method
Occupancy percentage	$\dfrac{\text{number of rooms sold}}{\text{number of rooms available}} \times 100$
Double occupancy percentage	$\dfrac{\text{number of guest} - \text{number of rooms sold}}{\text{number of rooms sold}} \times 100$
Yield	$\dfrac{\text{number of rooms sold} \times \text{average daily rate}}{\text{number of rooms available} \times \text{rack rate}} \times 100$
Average daily rate	$\dfrac{\text{room income}}{\text{number of rooms sold}}$
RevPAR	$\dfrac{\text{room revenue}}{\text{number of available rooms}}$
	or
	$\text{hotel occupancy percentage} \times \text{average daily rate}$

Solution to Opening Dilemma

It is important to prepare a training outline that will maximize the front office manager's efforts in training the night auditor. The session can begin by explaining that the objective of the night audit is to evaluate the hotel's financial activity and that the night audit process monitors departmental financial activity. The outline should cover the major concepts of posting room and tax charges, assembling guest charges and payments, reconciling departmental financial activities, reconciling the accounts receivable, running the trial balance, and preparing the night audit report. The front office manager should explain the formulas used to balance the night audit: formula to balance guest ledger, formula to balance city ledger, and formula to balance bank deposit, as well as formulas to compute operating statistics.

Chapter Recap

This chapter demonstrated the importance of producing an accurate summary of the financial transactions that occur in a hotel on any given day. The components of the night audit were listed and described. These include posting room and tax charges, assembling

Figure 10-8. *The daily flash report is reviewed each morning by the general manager and various department managers to determine the financial success of the previous day and current status in achieving other financial goals. (Information courtesy of Lincoln Plaza Hotel & Conference Center, Reading, Pennsylvania.)*

Daily Flash Report			Date _____
	Daily Totals	*Period to Date*	*Year to Date*
Revenue Types			
Room			
Telephone			
Food & Beverage			
Selected Departmental Totals			
Restaurant Breakfast			
Restaurant Lunch			
Restaurant Dinner			
Lounge Beer			
Lounge Wine			
Lounge Liquor			
Banquet Food			
Banquet Beverage			
Banquet Wine			
Banquet Liquor			
Banquet Beer			
Occupancy Totals			
Total Rooms			
Occupied Rooms			
Single Rooms			
Double/Plus Rooms			
Complimentary Rooms			
Day Rooms			
Group Rooms			
Transient Rooms			
O-O-O Rooms			
Occupancy %			
Average Daily Rate			
RevPAR			
Yield			
Arrivals			
Departures			
Stay Overs			
6 pm no shows			
Guar no shows			
Walk-ins			
Arrivals Canceled			
Reservations Taken			
Reservations Canceled			

guest charges and payments, reconciling departmental financial activities, reconciling the accounts receivable, running the trial balance, and preparing the night audit report. Finally, the preparation of a night audit report and manager's report were illustrated as well as the daily flash report, and their management implications were discussed. The accurate preparation of the night audit report and follow-up on the data assembled allow the hotel's management team to adjust financial plans.

End of Chapter Questions

1. Why does a hotel have to balance its financial transactions each day?

2. What is the night audit? What are the steps involved in preparing it?

3. What is the manager's report? What does each statistic tell the general manager?

4. Why must the night audit be prepared systematically?

5. What is a trial balance? What information does it provide the night auditor?

6. Why must the accounts receivable be included in the night audit? What do the accounts receivable comprise?

7. Discuss the importance of the night audit to the daily management of a hotel. Who reviews the night audit? Why would they be interested in these financial data?

8. Why should the accounts receivable be analyzed?

9. Why should the bank deposit and amount transferred to accounts receivable be listed on the night audit? What does each figure represent?

10. How can the front office manager control the cash in the front office cash drawer?

11. Why is it important to prepare hotel operating statistics?

12. Discuss the procedure to determine occupancy percentage, double occupancy percentage, and average daily rate.

13. Discuss the procedure to determine yield. How important is this to the general manager?

14. Discuss the procedure to compute RevPAR.

15. What use is the daily flash report to a general manager? To a front desk manager? To a food and beverage manager?

CASE STUDY 1001

The Times Hotel has collected the following data, which represent the financial transactions in the hotel today. Assemble this information into a night audit report, using the format shown in Figure 10-9 (a blank worksheet for you to fill in, which follows the data).

Departmental Daily Sales Report

Date _____

	$ Actual	$ Budget	Goal (%)
Restaurant 1	300.00	825.00	
Restaurant 2	500.00	1,500.00	
Restaurant 3	1,200.00	1,500.00	
SALES TAX (rate = 5%)			
Rest Tips 1	45.00	123.75	
Rest Tips 2	75.00	225.00	
Rest Tips 3	180.00	225.00	
RST TIPS (rate = 15%)			
Room Srv 1	45.00	350.00	
Room Srv 2	200.00	300.00	
Room Srv 3	135.95	250.00	
SALES TAX (rate = 5%)			
Room Srv 1 Tips	9.00	70.00	
Room Srv 2 Tips	40.00	60.00	
Room Srv 3 Tips	27.19	50.00	
ROOM SRV TIPS (rate = 20%)			
Banq Bkfst	0.00	350.00	
Banq Lunch	675.00	500.00	
Banq Dinner	3,021.45	6,500.00	
Banq Bkfst Tips	0.00	63.00	
Banq Lunch Tips	121.50	90.00	
Banq Dinner Tips	543.86	1,170.00	
BANQ TIPS (rate = 18%)			
Banq Bar Lunch	85.00	200.00	
Banq Bar Dinner	587.25	400.00	
ROOM RENTAL	100.00	250.00	
Lounge 1	165.00	85.00	
Lounge 2	346.75	950.00	
Lounge 3	295.00	450.00	
Lounge 4	420.00	575.00	

Departmental Daily Sales Report *(Continued)*

	$ Actual	$ Budget	Goal (%)
Lounge Tips 1	16.50	8.50	_____
Lounge Tips 2	34.68	95.00	_____
Lounge Tips 3	29.50	45.00	_____
Lounge Tips 4	42.00	57.50	_____
LOUNGE TIPS (rate = 10%)			
VALET	45.00	250.00	_____
Tele Local	125.00	125.00	_____
Tele Long Dist	87.90	300.00	_____
GIFT SHOP	150.68	350.00	_____
SALES TAX (rate = 5%)	7.53	17.50	_____
VENDING	86.25	100.00	_____
SPA	211.00	500.00	_____
PARKING	397.50	350.00	_____
Paid-outs			
Valet	85.00	_____	
Tips	0.00	_____	
Discounts			
Room	0.00	_____	
Food	15.00	_____	
Write-offs			
Rooms	0.00	_____	
Food	122.89	_____	
Total Cash Sales	2,906.98	_____	
Today's Outstd A/R	12,513.56	_____	
Yesterday's Outstd A/R	43,900.11	_____	
CREDIT CARD REC'D A/R	7,034.76	_____	
CASH REC'D A/R	2,098.63	_____	
BAL A/R	47,280.28	75,000.00	_____
ANALYSIS OF A/R			
City Ledger	3,078.00		
Direct Bill	5,901.00		
Visa	15,623.01		
MC	15,540.45		
JCB	7,137.82		
BANK DEPOSIT			
Cash	$5,005.61		
Visa	$3,532.98		

Departmental Daily Sales Report *(Continued)*

	$ Actual	$ Budget	Goal (%)
MC	$1,656.69		
JCB	$1,845.09		

Cashier's Report

	Actual Amount	POS Amount	Difference
Shift 1			
Cash	$3,754.21	$3,755.21	
Cr Cd	5,276.07	5,276.07	____
TOTAL 1	$9,030.28	$9,031.28	____
Shift 2			
Cash	$1,001.12	$1,002.50	
Cr Cd	$1,406.95	1,406.95	____
TOTAL 2	$2,408.07	$2,409.45	____
Shift 3			
Cash	$250.28	$250.28	
Cr Cd	$351.74	$351.74	____
TOTAL 3	$602.02	$602.02	____
TOTALS	$12,040.37	$12,042.75	____

Analysis Cash Report

Cash Sls	$2,906.98
Cr Cd A/R	7,034.76
Cash A/R	2,098.63
TOTAL	$12,040.37

Manager's Report

	Actual	Budget	Difference
ROOMS AVAIL	125	125	0
ROOMS SOLD	60	85	25
ROOMS VAC	65	40	−25
ROOMS OOO	0	0	0
ROOMS COMP	0	0	0
ROOM INCOME	$4,500.00	$7,500.00	$3,000.00
ROOM TAX	$450.00	$750.00	$300.00
NO. GUESTS	93	95	2
RACK RATE	$80.00	$80.00	$0.00
NO-SHOWS	1	1	0

BANK DEPOSIT ANALYSIS OF BANK DEPOSIT

Cash	$5,005.61		
VISA	$3,532.98	Total Cash Sales	$2,906.98
MC	$1,656.69	Credit Card Rec'd A/R	7,034.76
JCB	$1,845.09	Cash Rec'd A/R	2,098.63
			$12,040.37

Figure 10-9. *Times Hotel night audit.*

Night Audit		Date _____	
	$ Actual	*$ Budget*	*Goal(%)*
ROOM	_____	7,500.00	_____
TAX	_____	750.00	_____
Restaurant 1	_____	825.00	_____
Restaurant 2	_____	1,500.00	_____
Restaurant 3	_____	1,500.00	_____
TOTAL RST SALES	_____	3,825.00	_____
SALES TAX	_____	191.25	_____
Rest Tips 1	_____	123.75	_____
Rest Tips 2	_____	225.00	_____
Rest Tips 3	_____	225.00	_____
TOTAL RST TIPS	_____	573.75	_____
Room Srv 1	_____	350.00	_____
Room Srv 2	_____	300.00	_____
Room Srv 3	_____	250.00	_____
TOTAL ROOM SRV	_____	900.00	_____
SALES TAX	_____	45.00	_____
Room Srv 1 Tips	_____	70.00	_____
Room Srv 2 Tips	_____	60.00	_____
Room Srv 3 Tips	_____	50.00	_____
TOTAL ROOM SRV TIPS	_____	180.00	_____
Banq Bkfst	_____	350.00	_____
Banq Lunch	_____	500.00	_____
Banq Dinner	_____	6,500.00	_____
TOTAL BANQ	_____	7,350.00	_____
Banq Bkfst Tips	_____	63.00	_____
Banq Lunch Tips	_____	90.00	_____
Banq Dinner Tips	_____	1,170.00	_____
TOTAL BANQ TIPS	_____	1,323.00	_____
Banq Bar Lunch	_____	200.00	_____
Banq Bar Dinner	_____	400.00	_____
TOTAL BANQ BAR	_____	600.00	_____
ROOM RENTAL	_____	250.00	_____
Lounge 1	_____	85.00	_____
Lounge 2	_____	950.00	_____
Lounge 3	_____	450.00	_____
Lounge 4	_____	575.00	_____
TOTAL LOUNGE SALES	_____	2,060.00	_____
Lounge Tips 1	_____	8.50	_____
Lounge Tips 2	_____	95.00	_____
Lounge Tips 3	_____	45.00	_____
Lounge Tips 4	_____	57.50	_____
TOTAL LOUNGE TIPS	_____	206.00	_____
VALET	_____	250.00	_____

Figure 10-9. (*Continued*)

	$ Actual	$ Budget	Goal(%)
Tele Local		125.00	
Tele Long Dist		300.00	
TOTAL PHONE		425.00	
GIFT SHOP		350.00	
SALES TAX		17.50	
VENDING		100.00	
SPA		500.00	
PARKING		350.00	
TOTAL REVENUE	15,470.54	27,746.50	
Less Paid-outs			
Valet	85		
Tips	0		
TOTAL PAID-OUTS	85		
Less Discounts			
Room	0		
Food	15		
TOTAL DISCOUNTS	15		
Less Write-offs			
Rooms	0		
Food	122.89		
TOTAL WRITE-OFFS	122.89		
Total Paid-out and Noncollect Sales	222.89		
Total Cash Sales	2,906.98		
Today's Outstd A/R	12,513.56		
Total Revenue	15,643.43		
Yesterday's Outstd A/R	43,900.11		
TOTAL OUTSTD A/R	56,413.67		
CREDIT CARD REC'D A/R	7034.76		
CASH REC'D A/R	2098.63		
BAL A/R	47,280.28	75,000.00	
ANALYSIS OF A/R			
City Ledger	3,078		
Direct Bill	5,901		
Visa	15,623.01		
MC	15,540.45		
JCB	7,137.82		
Total A/R	47,280.82		

Handwritten annotations: "in departmental sales", "added should =", "todays + yesterdays", "subtracted from total outstanding A/R"

BANK DEPOSIT

		ANALYSIS OF BANK DEPOSIT	
Cash	5005.61	Total Cash Sales	2906.98
Visa		Credit Card Rec'd A/R	7034.76
MC		Cash Rec'd A/R	2098.43
JCB			12,040.37
TTL BANK DEP			
AMT TR A/R	12,513.56		

Figure 10-9. *(Continued)*

Cashier's Report

	Actual Amount	*POS Amount*	*Difference*
Shift 1			
Cash	_____	_____	_____
Cr Cd	_____	_____	_____
TOTAL 1	_____	_____	_____
Shift 2			
Cash	_____	_____	_____
Cr Cd	_____	_____	_____
TOTAL 2	_____	_____	_____
Shift 3			
Cash	_____	_____	_____
Cr Cd	_____	_____	_____
TOTAL 3	_____	_____	_____
TOTALS	_____	_____	_____

Analysis Cash Report

Cash Sls	_____
Cr Cd A/R	_____
Cash A/R	_____
TOTAL	_____

Manager's Report

	Actual	*Budget*	*Difference*
ROOMS AVAIL	175	_____	_____
ROOMS SOLD	60	_____	_____
ROOMS VAC	45	_____	_____
ROOMS OOO	0	_____	_____
ROOMS COMP	0	_____	_____
OCC %	_____	_____	_____
DBL OCC %	_____	_____	_____
YIELD %	_____	_____	_____
REVPAR	_____	_____	_____
ROOM INC	_____	_____	_____
ROOM TAX	_____	_____	_____
NO. GUESTS	_____	_____	_____
AV. RATE	_____	_____	_____
RACK RATE	_____	_____	_____
NO-SHOWS	_____	_____	_____

[Handwritten annotations: "will prob be given"; "Total Rev / Potential Rev"; "Total Rev / # of Rooms"; "Total Rev / Rooms sold"; "# of guests # of Rooms sold / # of Rooms sold"; "will prob have to do this"]

CASE STUDY 1002

The Barrington Hotel has collected the following data, which represent the financial transactions in the hotel today. Assemble this information into a night audit report, using the format shown in Figure 10-10 (a blank worksheet for you to fill in, which follows the data).

Departmental Daily Sales Report

Date _____

	$ Actual	$ Budget	Goal (%)
Restaurant 1	500.00	475.00	105
Restaurant 2	650.00	755.00	86
Restaurant 3	1,905.00	2,100.00	90.7
SALES TAX (rate = 5%)			
Rest Tips 1	75.00	71.25	105
Rest Tips 2	97.50	113.25	86
Rest Tips 3	285.75	315.00	90.7
RST TIPS (rate = 15%)			
Room Srv 1	235.00	300.00	78
Room Srv 2	120.00	250.00	
Room Srv 3	458.00	700.00	
SALES TAX (rate = 5%)			
Room Srv 1 Tips	47.00	60.00	
Room Srv 2 Tips	24.00	50.00	
Room Srv 3 Tips	91.60	140.00	
ROOM SRV TIPS (rate = 20%)			
Banq Bkfst	579.00	250.00	
Banq Lunch	2,458.00	3,500.00	
Banq Dinner	5,091.00	7,250.00	
Banq Bkfst Tips	104.22	45.00	
Banq Lunch Tips	442.44	630.00	
Banq Dinner Tips	916.38	1,305.00	
BANQ TIPS (rate = 18%)			
Banq Bar Lunch	326.00	450.00	
Banq Bar Dinner	2,987.50	3,950.00	
ROOM RENTAL	725.00	1,000.00	
Lounge 1	350.00	400.00	
Lounge 2	2,104.00	2,000.00	
Lounge 3	581.00	675.00	
Lounge 4	695.50	850.00	

Departmental Daily Sales Report *(Continued)*

	$ Actual	$ Budget	Goal (%)
Lounge Tips 1	35.00	40.00	_____
Lounge Tips 2	210.40	200.00	_____
Lounge Tips 3	58.10	67.50	_____
Lounge Tips 4	69.55	85.00	_____
LOUNGE TIPS (rate = 10%)			
VALET	210.00	350.00	_____
Tele Local	68.00	125.00	_____
Tele Long Dist	201.00	300.00	_____
GIFT SHOP	277.00	450.00	_____
SALES TAX (rate = 5%)	13.85	22.50	_____
VENDING	121.00	100.00	_____
SPA	293.00	500.00	_____
PARKING	417.00	350.00	_____
Paid-outs			
Valet	132.00	_____	
Tips	0.00	_____	
Discounts			
Room	0.00	_____	
Food	32.00	_____	
Write-offs			
Rooms	0.00	_____	
Food	87.97	_____	
Total Cash Sales	2,906.98	_____	
Today's Outstd A/R	28,259.21	_____	
Yesterday's Outstd A/R	57,880.11	_____	
CREDIT CARD REC'D A/R	12,091.50	_____	
CASH REC'D A/R	3,522.65	_____	
BAL A/R	70,525.17	80,000.00	_____

ANALYSIS OF A/R

City Ledger	13,278.00
Direct Bill	15,999.00
Visa	25,623.01
MC	11,487.34
JCB	4,137.82

BANK DEPOSIT		**ANALYSIS OF BANK DEPOSIT**	
Cash	$6,429.63	Total Cash Sales	$2,906.98
Visa	$7,509.34	Credit Card Rec'd A/R	12,091.50
MC	$2,828.00	Cash Rec'd A/R	3,522.65
JCB	$1,754.16		
			$18,521.13

Departmental Daily Sales Report *(Continued)*

Cashier's Report

	Actual Amount	*POS Amount*	*Difference*
Shift 1			
Cash	$4,822.22	$4,822.50	_____
Cr Cd	9,068.63	9,068.63	_____
TOTAL 1	$13,890.85	$13,891.13	_____
Shift 2			
Cash	$1,285.93	$1,286.00	_____
Cr Cd	2,418.30	2,418.30	_____
TOTAL 2	$3,704.23	$3,704.30	_____
Shift 3			
Cash	$321.48	$321.48	_____
Cr Cd	604.58	604.58	_____
TOTAL 3	$926.06	$926.06	_____
TOTALS	$18,521.14	$18,521.49	_____

Analysis Cash Report

Cash Sls	$2,906.98
Cr Cd A/R	12,091.50
Cash A/R	3,522.65
TOTAL	$18,521.13

Manager's Report

	Actual	*Budget*	*Difference*
ROOMS AVAIL	143	143	0
ROOMS SOLD	92	112	20
ROOMS VAC	51	31	−20
ROOMS OOO	0	0	0
ROOMS COMP	0	0	0
ROOM INC	$6,500.00	$8,200.00	$1,700.00
ROOM TAX	$650.00	$820.00	$170.00
NO. GUESTS	100	160	60
RACK RATE	$95.00	$95.00	$0.00
NO-SHOWS	2	1	−1

Figure 10-10. *Barrington Hotel night audit.*

Night Audit			Date _____
	$ Actual	*$ Budget*	*Goal (%)*
ROOM	6500	8,200.00	_____
TAX	650	820.00	_____
Restaurant 1	800	475.00	_____
Restaurant 2	450	755.00	_____
Restaurant 3	1,905.00	2,100.00	_____
TOTAL RST SALES	3055	3,330.00	_____
SALES TAX	152.75	166.50	_____
Rest Tip 1	75	71.25	_____
Rest Tip 2	97.90	113.25	_____
Rest Tip 3	285.75	315.00	_____
TOTAL RST TIPS	458.25	499.50	_____
Room Srv 1	235	300.00	_____
Room Srv 2	120	250.00	_____
Room Srv 3	458	700.00	_____
TOTAL ROOM SRV	813	1,250.00	_____
SALES TAX	40.65	62.50	_____
Room Srv 1 Tips	48	60.00	_____
Room Srv 2 Tips	24	50.00	_____
Room Srv 3 Tips	91.60	140.00	_____
TOTAL ROOM SRV TIPS	162.6	250.00	_____
Banq Bkfst		250.00	_____
Banq Lunch		3,500.00	_____
Banq Dinner		7,250.00	_____
TOTAL BANQ		11,000.00	_____
Banq Bkfst Tips		45.00	_____
Banq Lunch Tips		630.00	_____
Banq Dinner Tips		1,305.00	_____
TOTAL BANQ TIPS		1,980.00	_____
Banq Bar Lunch		450.00	_____
Banq Bar Dinner		3,950.00	_____
TOTAL BANQ BAR		4,400.00	_____
ROOM RENTAL		1,000.00	_____
Lounge 1		400.00	_____
Lounge 2		2,000.00	_____
Lounge 3		675.00	_____
Lounge 4		850.00	_____
TOTAL LOUNGE SALES		3,925.00	_____
Lounge Tips 1		40.00	_____
Lounge Tips 2		200.00	_____
Lounge Tips 3		67.50	_____
Lounge Tips 4		85.00	_____
TOTAL LOUNGE TIPS		392.50	_____
VALET		350.00	_____

Figure 10-10. *(Continued)*

	$ Actual	*$ Budget*	*Goal (%)*
Tele Local		125.00	
Tele Long Dist	_____	300.00	_____
TOTAL PHONE	_____	425.00	_____
GIFT SHOP	_____	450.00	_____
SALES TAX	_____	22.50	_____
VENDING	_____	100.00	_____
SPA	_____	500.00	_____
PARKING	_____	350.00	_____
TOTAL REVENUE	_____	39,473.50	_____
Less Paid-outs			
Valet			
Tips	_____		
TOTAL PAID-OUTS	_____		
Less Discounts			
Room			
Food	_____		
TOTAL DISCOUNTS	_____		
Less Write-offs			
Rooms			
Food	_____		
TOTAL WRITE-OFFS	_____		
Total Paid-out and Noncollect Sales	_____		
Total Cash Sales	_____		
Today's Outstd A/R	_____		
Total Revenue	_____		
Yesterday's Outstd A/R	_____		
TOTAL OUTSTD A/R	_____		
CREDIT CARD REC'D A/R	_____		
CASH REC'D A/R	_____		
BAL A/R	_____	80,000.00	_____
ANALYSIS OF A/R			
City Ledger	_____		
Direct Bill	_____		
Visa	_____		
MC	_____		
JCB	_____		
Total A/R	_____		

BANK DEPOSIT		**ANALYSIS OF BANK DEPOSIT**		
Cash		Total Cash Sales		
Visa	_____	Credit Card Rec'd A/R	_____	
MC	_____	Cash Rec'd A/R	_____	
JCB	_____			
TTL BANK DEP	_____			
AMT TR A/R	_____			

Figure 10-10. *(Continued)*

Cashier's Report

	Actual Amount	*POS Amount*	*Difference*
Shift 1			
Cash	_____	_____	_____
Cr Cd	_____	_____	_____
TOTAL 1	_____	_____	_____
Shift 2			
Cash	_____	_____	_____
Cr Cd	_____	_____	_____
TOTAL 2	_____	_____	_____
Shift 3			
Cash	_____	_____	_____
Cr Cd	_____	_____	_____
TOTAL 3	_____	_____	_____
TOTALS	_____	_____	_____

Analysis Cash Report

Cash Sls	_____
Cr Cd A/R	_____
Cash A/R	_____
TOTAL	_____

Manager's Report

	Actual	*Budget*	*Difference*
ROOMS AVAIL	_____	_____	_____
ROOMS SOLD	_____	_____	_____
ROOMS VAC	_____	_____	_____
ROOMS OOO	_____	_____	_____
ROOMS COMP	_____	_____	_____
OCC %	_____	_____	_____
DBL OCC %	_____	_____	_____
YIELD %	_____	_____	_____
REVPAR	_____	_____	_____
ROOM INC	_____	_____	_____
ROOM TAX	_____	_____	_____
NO. GUESTS	_____	_____	_____
AV. RATE	_____	_____	_____
RACK RATE	_____	_____	_____
NO-SHOWS	_____	_____	_____

CASE STUDY 1003

The Canton Hotel has collected the following data, which represent the financial transactions in the hotel today. Assemble this information into a night audit report, using the format shown in Figure 10-11 (a blank worksheet for you to fill in, which follows the data).

Departmental Daily Sales Report

Date _____

	$ Actual	$ Budget	Goal (%)
Restaurant 1	850.00	650.00	
Restaurant 2	1,034.00	1,200.00	
Restaurant 3	2,896.00	3,200.00	
SALES TAX (rate = 5%)			
Rest Tips 1	127.50	97.50	
Rest Tips 2	155.10	180.00	
Rest Tips 3	434.40	480.00	
RST TIPS (rate = 15%)			
Room Srv 1	456.87	500.00	
Room Srv 2	355.00	450.00	
Room Srv 3	760.75	1,000.00	
SALES TAX (rate = 5%)			
Room Srv 1 Tips	91.37	100.00	
Room Srv 2 Tips	71.00	90.00	
Room Srv 3 Tips	152.15	200.00	
ROOM SRV TIPS (rate = 20%)	314.52	390.00	
Banq Bkfst	890.00	450.00	
Banq Lunch	1,785.71	2,500.00	
Banq Dinner	4,951.76	7,500.00	
Banq Bkfst Tips	160.20	81.00	
Banq Lunch Tips	321.43	450.00	
Banq Dinner Tips	891.32	1,881.00	
BANQ TIPS (rate = 18%)	1,372.94	1,881.00	
Banq Bar Lunch	508.75	350.00	
Banq Bar Dinner	1,907.25	2,500.00	
ROOM RENTAL	2,000.00	500.00	
Lounge 1	495.00	500.00	
Lounge 2	2,951.50	3,500.00	
Lounge 3	724.75	450.00	
Lounge 4	805.00	750.00	

Departmental Daily Sales Report *(Continued)*

	$ Actual	$ Budget	Goal (%)
Lounge Tips 1	49.50	50.00	_____
Lounge Tips 2	295.15	350.00	_____
Lounge Tips 3	72.48	45.00	_____
Lounge Tips 4	80.50	75.00	_____
LOUNGE TIPS (rate= 10%)	497.63	520.00	_____
VALET	350.00	400.00	_____
Tele Local	85.00	150.00	_____
Tele Long Dist	241.00	350.00	_____
GIFT SHOP	650.00	500.00	_____
SALES TAX (rate = 5%)	32.50	25.00	_____
VENDING	190.00	250.00	_____
SPA	293.00	650.00	_____
PARKING	627.00	750.00	_____
Paid-outs			
Valet	256.00		
Tips	0.00		
Discounts			
Room	85.00		
Food	46.95		
Write-offs			
Room	0.00		
Food	0.00		
Total Cash Sales	3,759.32		
Today's Outstd A/R	36,851.24		
Yesterday's Outstd A/R	64,258.18		
CREDIT CARD REC'D A/R	22,681.15		
CASH REC'D A/R	5,390.97		
BAL A/R	73,037.30	90,000.00	_____
ANALYSIS OF A/R			
City Ledger	14,671.05		
Direct Bill	12,784.09		
Visa	29,712.01		
MC	10,254.81		
JCB	5,615.34		
Total A/R	73,037.30		

BANK DEPOSIT		**ANALYSIS OF BANK DEPOSIT**	
Cash	$9,150.29	Total Cash Sales	$3,759.32
Visa	$15,685.26	Credit Card Rec'd A/R	$22,681.15
MC	$4,230.88	Cash Red'd A/R	$5,390.97
JCB	$2,765.01		
			$31,831.44

Departmental Daily Sales Report *(Continued)*

	$ Actual	*$ Budget*	*Goal (%)*

Cashier's Report

	Actual Amount	*POS Amount*	*Difference*
Shift 1			
Cash	$6,862.72	$6,861.05	_____
Cr Cd	17,010.86	17,010.86	_____
TOTAL 1	$23,873.58	$23,871.91	_____
Shift 2			
Cash	$1,830.06	$1,829.83	_____
Cr Cd	4,536.23	4,536.23	_____
TOTAL 2	$6,366.29	$6,366.06	_____
Shift 3			
Cash	$457.51	$457.51	_____
Cr Cd	1,134.06	1,134.06	_____
TOTAL 3	$1,591.57	$1,591.57	_____
TOTALS	$31,831.44	$31,829.54	_____

Analysis Cash Report

Cash Sls	$3,759.32
Cr Cd A/R	22,681.15
Cash A/R	5,390.97
TOTAL	$31,831.44

Manager's Report

	Actual	*Budget*	*Difference*
ROOMS AVAIL	200	200	0
ROOMS SOLD	135	150	−15
ROOMS VAC	65	50	−15
ROOMS OOO	0	0	0
ROOMS COMP	0	0	0
ROOM INC	$10,500.00	$11,200.00	700
ROOM TAX	$1,050.00	$1,120.00	70
NO GUESTS	155	225	70
RACK RATE	$105.00	$105.00	$0.00
NO-SHOWS	4	2	−2

Figure 10-11. *Canton Hotel night audit.*

Night Audit			Date _____
	$ Actual	*$ Budget*	*Goal (%)*
ROOM	_____	11,200.00	
TAX	_____	1,120.00	_____
Restaurant 1	_____	650.00	_____
Restaurant 2	_____	1,200.00	_____
Restaurant 3	_____	3,200.00	_____
TOTAL RST SALES	_____	5,050.00	_____
SALES TAX	_____	252.50	_____
Rest Tips 1	_____	97.50	_____
Rest Tips 2	_____	180.00	_____
Rest Tips 3	_____	480.00	_____
TOTAL RST TIPS	_____	757.50	_____
Room Srv 1	_____	500.00	_____
Room Srv 2	_____	450.00	_____
Room Srv 3	_____	1,000.00	_____
TOTAL ROOM SRV	_____	1,950.00	_____
SALES TAX	_____	97.50	_____
Room Srv 1 Tips	_____	100.00	_____
Room Srv 2 Tips	_____	90.00	_____
Room Srv 3 Tips	_____	200.00	_____
TOTAL ROOM SRV TIPS	_____	390.00	_____
Banq Bkfst	_____	450.00	_____
Banq Lunch	_____	2,500.00	_____
Banq Dinner	_____	7,500.00	_____
TOTAL BANQ	_____	10,450.00	_____
Banq Bkfst Tips	_____	81.00	_____
Banq Lunch Tips	_____	450.00	_____
Banq Dinner Tips	_____	1,350.00	_____
TOTAL BANQ TIPS	_____	1,881.00	_____
Banq Bar Lunch	_____	350.00	_____
Banq Bar Dinner	_____	2,500.00	_____
TOTAL BANQ BAR	_____	2,850.00	_____
ROOM RENTAL	_____	500.00	_____
Lounge 1	_____	500.00	_____
Lounge 2	_____	3,500.00	_____
Lounge 3	_____	450.00	_____
Lounge 4	_____	750.00	_____
TOTAL LOUNGE SALES	_____	5,200.00	_____
Lounge Tips 1	_____	50.00	_____
Lounge Tips 2	_____	350.00	_____
Lounge Tips 3	_____	45.00	_____
Lounge Tips 4	_____	75.00	_____
TOTAL LOUNGE TIPS	_____	520.00	_____
VALET	_____	400.00	_____

Figure 10-11. *(Continued)*

	$ Actual	*$ Budget*	*Goal (%)*	
Tele Local	_____	150.00	_____	
Tele Long Dist	_____	350.00	_____	
TOTAL PHONE	_____	500.00	_____	
GIFT SHOP	_____	500.00	_____	
SALES TAX	_____	25.00	_____	
VENDING	_____	250.00	_____	
SPA	_____	650.00	_____	
PARKING	_____	750.00	_____	
TOTAL REVENUE	_____	45,293.60	_____	
Less Paid-outs				
Valet	_____			
Tips	_____			
TOTAL PAID-OUTS	_____			
Less Discounts				
Room	_____			
Food	_____			
TOTAL DISCOUNTS	_____			
Less Write-offs				
Rooms	_____			
Food	_____			
TOTAL WRITE-OFFS	_____			
Total Paid-out and Noncollect Sales	_____			
Total Cash Sales	_____			
Today's Outstd A/R	_____			
Total Revenue	_____			
Yesterday's Outstd A/R	_____			
TOTAL OUTSTD A/R	_____			
CREDIT CARD REC'D A/R	_____			
CASH REC'D A/R	_____			
BAL A/R	_____	90,000.00	_____	
ANALYSIS OF A/R				
City Ledger	_____			
Direct Bill	_____			
Visa	_____			
MC	_____			
JCB	_____			
Total A/R	_____			

BANK DEPOSIT		**ANALYSIS OF BANK DEPOSIT**	
Cash		Total Cash Sales	
Visa	_____	Credit Card Rec'd A/R	_____
MC	_____	Cash Rec'd A/R	_____
JCB	_____		_____
TTL BANK DEP	_____		
AMT TR A/R	_____		

Figure 10-11. *(Continued)*

Cashier's Report

	Actual Amount	*POS Amount*	*Difference*
Shift 1			
Cash	———	———	———
Cr Cd	———	———	———
TOTAL 1	———	———	———
Shift 2			
Cash	———	———	———
Cr Cd	———	———	———
TOTAL 2	———	———	———
Shift 3			
Cash	———	———	———
Cr Cd	———	———	———
TOTAL 3	———	———	———
TOTALS	———	———	———

Analysis Cash Report

Cash Sls	———
Cr Cd A/R	———
Cash A/R	———
TOTAL	———

Manager's Report

	Actual	*Budget*	*Difference*
ROOM AVAIL	———	———	———
ROOMS SOLD	———	———	———
ROOMS VAC	———	———	———
ROOMS OOO	———	———	———
ROOMS COMP	———	———	———
OOO %	———	———	———
DBL OCC %	———	———	———
YIELD %	———	———	———
REVPAR	———	———	———
ROOM INC	———	———	———
ROOM TAX	———	———	———
NO. GUESTS	———	———	———
AV. RATE	———	———	———
RACK RATE	———	———	———
NO-SHOWS	———	———	———

Software Simulation Exercise

Review Chapter 6, "Night Audit," of Kline and Sullivan's *Hotel Front Office Simulation: A Workbook and Software Package* (New York: John Wiley and Sons, © 2003) and work through the various concepts as presented in their chapter.

- Room Rate Report
- Post Room and Tax
- Postings Report
- Revenue Report
- Check-out Report
- No-Show and Cancellation Report
- Comp Rooms Report
- Deposit Report
- Maintenance Report
- Message Reports
- File Maintenance
- Chapter 6 Exercises

Key Words

aging of accounts
cashier's report
credit balance
cumulative total feature
daily flash report
daily sales report
departmental accounts
manager's report

master credit card account
night audit
operational effectiveness
room sales figure
surcharge rates
tax cumulative total feature
total restaurant sales figure
trial balance

Managing Hospitality

OPENING DILEMMA

Upon check-in, a guest indicates that the national reservation agent misquoted

his room rate at $95 when it should have been $85 per night. The front desk

clerk responds, "Sir, you will have to discuss that with the cashier when you

check out in three days. I can only register you with the rate that was entered

into the computer. What's $30 to a businessperson on a budget?"

CHAPTER FOCUS POINTS

- Importance of hospitality to the hotel guest and the hotel entrepreneur
- Managing the delivery of hospitality
- Total quality management (TQM) applications
- Developing a service management program

The concept of **hospitality,** the generous and cordial provision of services to a guest, is at the heart of our industry. These services, in the hotel industry, can include room accommodations, food and beverages, meeting facilities, reservations, information on hotel services, information on local attractions, and the like. Hospitality is a very subjective concept, and the degree of hospitality a guest perceives has implications for the overall financial success of the hotel. Guests who feel they are not treated with respect or have not received full value for their dollar will seek out others who they believe do provide hospitality. This chapter is intended to instill in you, the future professional in the hospitality industry, a sense of responsibility for providing professional hospitality. As you prepare for a career in an industry that may differentiate its product by continual and efficient delivery of professional hospitality service, these basic rudiments will serve as a primer for your development (Figure 11-1).

This chapter was inspired by a book entitled *Service America!* (Dow Jones–Irwin, 1985), by Karl Albrecht and Ron Zemke. These management consultants were early proponents of the service concept in business. Their writings, as well as my own profes-

Figure 11-1 *A well-informed hotel staff contributes to an enjoyable guest stay. (Photo courtesy of Lincoln Plaza Hotel & Conference Center, Reading, Pennsylvania.)*

sional experience in hotels and restaurants, are the basis of this chapter. A chapter devoted to hospitality seems essential, since the staff of the front office very often represents the only direct contact the guest has with the hotel.

Importance of Hospitality

Hospitality is a very important consideration for both the guest and the hotel entrepreneur. Every guest expects and deserves hospitable treatment. Providing hospitality to meet guests' needs involves not only a positive attitude but an array of services that make the guest's stay enjoyable. If the market being served by a hotel is composed of business travelers, a hotel staff will find that their needs revolve around schedules and flexible delivery of hotel services. The business traveler may arrive late and leave early. The hotel restaurant must be organized to provide a healthy and quick breakfast. Wake-up services must be located within the room or provided by an efficient staff. The hotel should also offer office services, such as word-processing capabilities, advanced telephone systems, fax and photocopying facilities, and computers. The guest who is associated with a convention may want early check-in, late checkout, and a full range of hotel services. If the convention starts at noon on Tuesday, the guest may arrive at 9 A.M. wanting to unload and set up before the noon starting time. If the convention ends on Thursday at 3 P.M., the guest may want to retain occupancy of the room beyond the normal checkout time. While the guest is in the hotel, he or she may require flexible scheduling hours of the swimming pool, health club facilities, lounge and live entertainment, gift shops, coffee shop, and other hotel services. International guests may require assistance with using electrical appliances, converting their national currency into local currency, or interpreting geographic directions.

The success or failure in providing hospitality often determines the success or failure of the hotel. Capitalizing on opportunities to provide hospitality is essential. The failure to make the most of these chances directly affects the hotel's financial success, as Albrecht and Zemke indicate in *Service America!*:

> The average business never hears from 96% of its unhappy customers. For every complaint received the average company in fact has 26 customers with problems, 6 of which are "serious" problems. Complainers are more likely than noncomplainers to do business again with the company that upset them, even if the problem isn't satisfactorily resolved. Of the customers who register a complaint, between 54 and 70% will do business again with the organization if their complaint is resolved. That figure goes up to a staggering 95% if the customer feels that the complaint was resolved quickly. The average customer who has had a problem with an organization recounts the incident to more than 20 people. Customers who have complained to an organization and had their complaints satisfactorily resolved tell an average of five people about the treatment they received.[1]

What do these issues of delivering hospitality to the guest mean to the entrepreneur? They emphatically imply that the guest who is not treated with hospitality (remember that the definition of hospitality is very subjective) will choose to do business with a competitor and may also influence others not to try your hotel for the first time or not to continue to do business with you. The entrepreneur who is aware of the competition realizes that this negative advertising will severely affect the profit-and-loss statement. Albrecht and Zemke extended their concept mathematically. Let's examine the cumulative effects of poor service in the following example.

If a hotel does not provide the desired level of service to 10 guests on any given day, only 1 of the guests will bring the complaint to the attention of the hotel staff. If the complaint is resolved quickly, this person will almost surely do business again with the hotel. He or she will also have occasion to influence 5 people to use your hotel. On the other hand, the 9 guests who did not bring their complaints to the attention of the hotel staff will probably not do business with the hotel again, and each of them may tell approximately 20 people—a total of 180 people will hear their negative account of the hotel. If this model is extended to cover a whole year of dissatisfied guests, 68,985 people will have a negative impression of the hotel ([180 people told + 9 original dissatisfied customers] × 365 days in a year), and 2,190 will have a positive impression ([5 people told + 1 original satisfied customer] × 365 days in a year).

The financial ramifications of so many people negatively impressed with your hotel

Hotels throughout the world differ in the level of service they offer their guests. Some hotels provide the basic elements of service within standard operating procedures, while other hotels focus their efforts on delivering service. Much of the explanation for the differences relates to a nation's culture of service. Cultures of countries that regard service as subservience may produce employees who operate within standard operating procedures. But when service is viewed as a profession, the culture will produce professionals as well as employees who welcome the opportunity to minister, to attend, to facilitate, and to care for the guest. Hotels that operate in countries where service is not part of the culture have to develop systems that support employee success in the delivery of hospitality.

are clearly disastrous. Hospitable treatment of guests must be more than just an option; it must be standard operating procedure. It is a concept that must be adopted as a corporate tenet and organized for effective delivery.

Managing the Delivery of Hospitality

It is not enough for the front office manager to decide that the members of the front office staff should provide good service and display hospitality to guests. To provide satisfactory hospitality to all guests at all times, front office managers must develop and administer a **service management program,** which highlights a company's focus on meeting customers' needs and allows a hotel to achieve its financial goals. This program must be based on sound management principles and the hotel's commitment to meeting those needs.

Management's Role

This may seem an odd place to start a discussion of delivering hospitality. After all, aren't the front desk clerks, switchboard operators, and bellhops the people who meet and greet guests and fulfill their needs at the front desk? Yes, these employees do provide hospitality directly, but management must work behind the scenes to develop a plan that ensures that the employees' efforts are continuous and professional. For example, management may decide to implement one or two specific, immediate changes on learning that a guest's needs have been overlooked. Management may feel that the negative impact of the rude, lazy, or careless employee has unnecessarily caused bad public relations. If a group of employees is not performing to management's standards, the cumulative effects of the group will be perceived negatively by guests. This negative impression will take a toll in the long run. Although one or two directives may correct an individual guest's problems, that hotel will reap only short-lived gains. A comprehensive program aimed at meeting the needs of a hotel's prime market—guests who continue to do business with the hotel—provides the foundation for long-term successful delivery of hospitality. This is what will make a hotel profitable.

Management's commitment to a service management program must be as integral to the organization as effective market planning, cost-control programs, budgeting, and human resources management. In fact, service management is the most visible responsibility because it affects all the other objectives of the hotel. Often the people in staff positions in hotels become so involved with their day-to-day paper shuffling and deadlines that they forget why they are in business. They may not necessarily mean to forget, but it happens all too often. Service management ensures that there is a commitment to a long-range effort by appointing someone within the organization to be responsible for developing, organizing, and delivering it.

John W. Young, executive vice president of human resources at the Four Seasons Hotels, tells us:

> We expect our general managers to respect the dignity of every employee, to understand their needs and recognize their contributions, and to work to maintain their job satisfaction with us—and to encourage their growth to the maximum extent their ability and desire allows. General measurement is based on detailed employee attitude surveys, conducted by an outside firm as well as such factors as employee turnover, employee promotions, both within the hotel and to other hotels. Also specific people-related goals are set according to the hotel's needs or the manager's personal needs, and measured, e.g., implementing a planned change in response to concerns in an attitude survey.[2]

The front office manager usually supervises service management efforts. Other key department heads who supervise employees who deal with guests, such as the food and beverage manager and director of marketing and sales, rely on the organizational leadership of the front office manager. It is important to note that the responsibility of delivering hospitality to the guest in each department is always a part of the job of each supervisor or **shift leader,** the person responsible for directing the efforts of a particular work shift. The organizational efforts provided by the front office manager serve as the basis for a homogeneous plan for the hotel.

The owner and general manager must make a financial commitment to ensure the success of the program. An important component of the program is motivating employees to deliver hospitality on a continual basis through incentive programs. **Incentive programs**

 The daughter of an international guest approaches a front desk clerk and indicates that her mother is experiencing chest pains. What hospitality opportunities are available for the front desk clerk?

are management's organized efforts to determine employees' needs and develop programs to help employees meet their needs and the needs of the hotel. Such programs reward employees for providing constant and satisfactory guest service and often involve money, in the form of bonuses, which must be budgeted in the annual projected budget. These incentives may involve the employees' choice of a monetary bonus, higher hourly rates, shift preference, or additional holiday or vacation days.

Mark Heymann, managing partner of UniFocus, based in Irving, Texas, indicates that customer satisfaction and employee satisfaction (in hotels) should be considered simultaneously. He says, "Given today's extraordinarily tough labor market, dissatisfied workers don't stick around. So a happy staff is the key to happy campers." Mr. Heymann also reports on feedback from hotel property clients with UniFocus, saying, "Money is not the key driver when it comes to holding on to staff. It's the interaction with management and the environment."[3]

The goal of any lodging establishment should be to extend the same degree of hospitality to a guest who arrives on a busy Monday morning and to a guest who arrives on a slow Saturday night. Management's ideological and financial commitment, along with the organizational efforts of the front office manager, will ensure that both of these guests are treated equally.

Figure 11-2 *Owners and managers must commit financial resources and establish priorities for the operation of a successful service management program. (Photo courtesy of Radisson Hospitality Worldwide.)*

The Service Strategy Statement

To produce an effective service management program, management must devise a **service strategy statement,** a formal recognition by management that the hotel will strive to deliver the products and services desired by the guest in a professional manner. To accomplish this, management must first identify the guest's needs.

Those of you who may have taken entry-level jobs in a hotel as a bellhop, desk clerk, switchboard operator, table attendant, or clerk in a hotel gift shop may have some feel for what guests want. They want quick and efficient service. They want to avoid long lines. They want to find their way around the hotel and the immediate vicinity. They want the products and services in the hotel to work. They want to feel safe and secure while residing in the hotel. If you use these observations as a baseline for beginning to understand guests' needs while they are away from home, you will be able to better satisfy their needs.

John Young, of the Four Seasons Hotels, reports, "Market research, internal guest comments and our regular employee attitude surveys all confirm that what has set and will continue to set Four Seasons apart from our competitors is personal service."[4]

As Eric Johnson and William Layton note, "It is only through the eyes of a customer that a definition of service quality can be obtained. Senior management cannot adequately determine what is desired at the customer level until a comprehensive evaluation of customer preference is established through a systematic consumer research study."[5] Thus, in addition to identifying generally what guests want, management should survey guests about the particular property to determine what services they expect and how they want these services delivered. The general manager of the hotel may assign this task to the marketing and sales director, who may start by reviewing and summarizing customer comment cards, which are usually held on file for six months to a year. A review of the areas in which the hotel has disappointed its guests, like that shown in Figure 11-3, will provide a basis for determining where to begin a guest survey. The problem areas identified from this study are then used as the focus of a simple survey form similar to Figure 11-4.

The survey may be administered by a member of the marketing and sales department at various times during the day. This information, as well as that gleaned from the comment cards, will give a general indication of what the guest wants. Sometimes pinpointing guest needs is not easy, because they change over time. In the example shown in Figure 11-3, speed of service delivery, high prices, poor selection of products, low-quality products, and rude personnel are problem areas in which the hotel failed to meet guest expectations. These areas, then, should be the focus of the service strategy statement, as they appear to be the primary guest concerns.

Ernest Cadotte and Normand Turgeon have analyzed a survey concerning the frequency and types of complaints and compliments received from guests of members of the National Restaurant Association and the American Hotel & Motel Association. They report:

Figure 11-3. *This report highlights areas of customer service and customer feedback.*

Times Hotel CUSTOMER COMMENT CARD SUMMARY, SEPT.–DEC.				
Product/Service	*Sept.*	*Oct.*	*Nov.*	*Dec.*
Overbooked	41	20	8	20
Slow check-in	50	31	12	25
Slow checkout	10	15	10	4
Room rate too high	10	7	9	8
Delay getting into room	35	12	18	5
Slow room service	90	3	3	10
Poor food in restaurant	6	10	2	8
Poor selections on menu	2	5	7	12
High prices on menu	2	10	10	20
Dirty room	3	4	8	15
Poor selection of amenities	—	—	5	—
Bedding insufficient	10	10	12	5
Lack of response from housekeeping	9	15	7	9
Rudeness from bell staff	1	—	5	—
Rudeness from dining room staff	1	—	10	—

The data seem to fall into a four-fold topology that compares how likely an attribute is to garner compliments versus the frequency of complaints.

1. Dissatisfiers—complaints for low performance, e.g., parking.

2. Satisfiers—unusual performance apparently elicits compliments, but average performance or even the absence of the feature will probably not cause dissatisfaction or complaints, e.g., atrium-type lobbies.

3. Critical variables—capable of eliciting both positive and negative feelings, depending on the situation, e.g., cleanliness, quality of service, employee knowledge and service, and quietness of surroundings.

4. Neutrals—factors that received neither a great number of compliments nor many complaints are probably either not salient to guests or easily brought up to guest standards.[6]

Albrecht and Zemke also identify general guest expectations as follows:

• Care and concern from service providers
• Spontaneity—people are authorized to think

Figure 11-4. *This individual hotel guest survey asks guests for their opinions on delivery of service.*

Times Hotel
Guest Survey

1. List and rate the services provided by the bell staff.

   _____   excellent good fair poor
   _____   excellent good fair poor

2. List and rate the services provided by the front desk.

   _____   excellent good fair poor
   _____   excellent good fair poor
   _____   excellent good fair poor

3. List and rate the services provided by housekeeping.

   _____   excellent good fair poor
   _____   excellent good fair poor

4. List and rate the services provided by the food and beverage department.

   _____   excellent good fair poor
   _____   excellent good fair poor
   _____   excellent good fair poor

- Problem solving—people can work out the intricacies of problems
- Recovery—will anybody make a special effort to set a problem right[7]

Their conclusions add another dimension to the service strategy statement. In addition to certain recognizable products and services delivered at a certain speed and level of quality, guests expect employees to accept the responsibility for resolving problems. The guest should not encounter unconcerned staff or be bounced from employee to employee in order to have a problem solved. Management must develop a staff that can think and solve problems. This dimension to the service strategy statement will make the delivery of professional hospitality a challenge!

DEVELOPING THE SERVICE STRATEGY STATEMENT

Once management has identified what guests want, it can develop a service strategy statement. The statement should include:

- A commitment to make service from top-level ownership and management a top priority in the company

- A commitment to develop and administer a service management program
- A commitment to train employees to deliver service efficiently
- A commitment of financial resources to develop incentives for the employees who deliver the services

These directives will serve as guidelines in the development of a service management program. More important, they force management to think of service as a long-range effort and not as a quick fix.

John W. Young states that the service strategy of the Four Seasons Hotels centers on offering

exceptional levels of personal service. People are our most important asset. Each person has dignity and wants a sense of pride in what they do and where they work. Success in delivering excellent service depends on working together as a team and understanding the needs and contributions of our fellow employees. [We must] train and stimulate ourselves and our colleagues. [We must] deal with others as we would have them deal with us. [We must] avoid compromising long-term goals in the interest of short term profit.[8]

Here is one example of a service strategy statement:

The owners of The Times Hotel, management, and staff will combine forces to establish a Service to Our Guests program, administered by management and delivered by staff. Delivery of service to our guests is crucial to the economic viability of our hotel. The owners of the hotel will provide financial support to the people who deliver hospitality on a daily basis.

Another version of the service strategy statement is as follows:

The hotel, in its continual efforts to maintain a leadership position in the hotel industry, will develop a VIP-Guest Service program. The administration and delivery of this program are essential to the financial success of the hotel. This program will include incentives and has received a priority budget line for this fiscal year.

These statements, however worded, convey the message from owners and management that a successful service management program depends on the support of all levels of management and staff.

Financial Commitment

Throughout the previous discussion on service management, financial commitment from management was stressed. Managers who want to develop and deliver a successful service management program must provide adequate staff time to think through a plan and to develop methods to motivate their employees. Scheduling time for planning and strategy

A general manager has proposed a service management program to the owner of her hotel. The front office manager has developed a plan with a $7,500 budget that includes incentives for employees. The owner of the hotel likes the program but wants the budget scaled down to $0. The owner feels that employees should be responsible for their own motivation. If you were the front office manager, how would you justify the budget in your plan?

sessions can increase the labor budget. Determining and offering motivational opportunities will also increase the financial investment. Often, lack of planning for these financial considerations will impede the desire to implement a service management program.

Total Quality Management Applications

The previous discussion of developing a background for managing the delivery of hospitality is essential for adopting total quality management (TQM) practices, as discussed in Chapter 2. Hotel owners and managers who fail to develop a clear service strategy statement and make a financial commitment to delivering hospitality experience extreme difficulty in applying the principles of TQM. TQM requires an immense commitment of labor to analyze guest and employee interaction, reallocation of responsibilities and authority to foster an improvement in services, and a long-term commitment for learning a new method of management. Preparation for adopting TQM is a requisite for success.

W. Edwards Deming's principles of TQM[9] have many aspects that can be applied to front office management practices. Deming's principles require managers to focus on a distinct level of service at the front office. Managers and frontline employees must view the interaction between customers and service providers. A front office team develops a **flowchart,** an analysis of the delivery of a particular product or service, to illustrate what occurs after a customer has verbalized a request for a product or service. Analysis of this interaction by the group of people who deliver the product or service allows for suggestions for improvement. A key component of TQM is a commitment to continuous analysis of the delivery of guest services and plans for improvement.

Developing a Service Management Program

Employee involvement in planning a service management program is as important as obtaining a financial commitment from owners in establishing such a program. Too often, when the employees are not included in the planning stages, they look at the final plan

Patrick Mene is vice president of quality for The Ritz-Carlton Hotel Company, L.L.C. His organization is the winner of the 1992 and 1999 Malcolm Baldrige Award. After he graduated from college, Mr. Mene went to work as a management trainee at Hilton. He has also worked in management positions at Hyatt, Westin International, Omni, Portman Hotel in San Francisco, and L'Ermitage Hotels. He has performed a great deal of research, particularly on the teachings of Joseph Juran.

Mr. Mene states that in addition to the Malcolm Baldrige Award's being a prestigious recognition of excellence in overall performance, leadership, profitability, and competitiveness, the participation in the competition for the award provided great feedback for the hotel. He continues by explaining that the hotel was organized vertically; it is now organized horizontally to concentrate more on the critical processes that drive the company and to provide more employee empowerment. For example, a traditional hotel may have 30 departments, while the Ritz-Carlton has only four; each one is run by a horizontally organized team. One team focuses on the pre-arrival process (customer contact with the sales office; making reservations; preplanning meetings, conferences, or banquets), one team focuses on

arrival (laundry, housekeeping, front desk), one team runs the restaurant, and one team is responsible for banqueting. This horizontal structure creates a "leaner, linked, empowered organization." Mr. Mene describes the managers in this type of organization as "coaches and advisers," while managers in traditional organizations are more "chief technicians and problem solvers."

Mr. Mene reports that customer dissatisfaction has decreased. The new structure has resulted in fewer breakdowns and less need for rework. In the past, the hotel experienced problems with incorrect or late honor-bar billings; guest rooms were always clean but were sometimes missing supplies; and at times, when guests called for information or assistance, agents were not available and calls went unanswered. These problems have been dramatically reduced.

He states that quality management science is a whole new branch of knowledge. Traditional methods of management that concentrate on selling hard, raising prices, and forcing a profit cannot identify and eliminate waste. He adds that, in any hotel, 30 percent of expenditures are the result of quality failures and are unnecessary. He feels that for those organizations that participate in TQM and make it work, it is the most effective way to achieve revolutionary results.

and remark, "This is ridiculous; not for me. Let the people in marketing and sales worry about it." In many cases, service is perceived as just another fancy concept proposed by management. Management needs to address that attitude from the outset. When employees are involved early, they are much more likely to buy into the program, since they are already a part of it.

Guest Cycle

The front office manager responsible for developing an effective service management program, along with other department directors, should first take a look at the employees they supervise. Representatives from all job categories and various shifts should be in-

Figure 11-5 *This TQM team is analyzing the delivery of a particular service to a guest. Managers and frontline employees provide an objective review. (Photo courtesy of Radisson Hospitality Worldwide.)*

cluded on the planning committee. Planning by committee can be cumbersome (scheduling, planning meetings, incurring additional payroll, etc.), but it can ensure that an effective program is developed. It allows the plan to be altered in the planning stages by those who must implement it and ensures clear, workable operational methods. It gives the employees time to adjust to the new concept while allowing time to develop adoption procedures. At each planning phase, employees learn how they will benefit from the program. This is a realistic approach to focus management's efforts in adopting this important concept.

Once the members of the planning committee have been chosen, the next step is to analyze the guest's perception of the hospitality system:

> Visualize your organization as dealing with the customer in terms of a cycle of service, a repeatable sequence of events in which various people try to meet the customer's needs and expectations at each point. It may be the instant at which the customer sees your advertisement, gets a call from your sales person, or initiates a telephone inquiry. It ends only temporarily, when the customer considers the service complete, and it begins anew when he or she decides to come back for more.[10]

Figure 11-6 illustrates the **cycle of service,** the progression of a guest's request for products and services through a hotel's departments. This outline is presented only as a

Figure 11-6. *This review of the cycle of services that the guest may encounter provides the basis for developing a service management program.*

Marketing
- Customer surveys (before and after stay)
- Advertising: billboards, direct mail, radio, television, print, Internet; incentive promotions, solo and with other hospitality organizations

Reservations
- Toll-free numbers, fax, national reservation system (ease of access), Internet
- Telephone manner of reservationists
- Cancellation policy (reasonable restrictions)
- Credit-card acceptance
- Accommodation availability (value and cost considerations)
- Complimentary services/products (value and cost considerations)
- Information on hotel shuttle and public transportation

Registration
- Hotel shuttle and public transportation
- Greetings (doorman, bell staff, front desk personnel)
- Assistance with luggage
- Check-in procedure (length of time in line, ease of check-in with preprinted registration cards or self-registration machine)
- Room accommodations (value and cost considerations)
- Credit-card acceptance
- Complimentary services/products (value and cost considerations)
- Room status/availability
- Information on other hotel services
- Cleanliness and interior design of lobby, elevators, room
- Operation of air-conditioning, heat, television, radio, plumbing in room
- Amenities available

working tool for front office managers to use in analyzing the hotel services the guest will encounter. It is not intended as a complete listing. It is important to remember that these services are provided by the employees of the hotel. In developing a list for a specific hotel property, employee input will be very useful.

Another benefit of analyzing the cycle of service is that it may highlight inefficiencies built into the system. Rectifying these inefficiencies will assist in delivering first-rate hospitality, as the following example, reported by Nancy J. Allin and Kelly Halpine of the quality assurance and training department at the Waldorf=Astoria in New York, indicates:

> While there can be many reasons to combine the positions of registration clerk and cashier, and many aspects were considered at the Waldorf=Astoria, the decision was driven by a desire to improve guest service where its impact is most obvious—at

Guest Stay

Other hotel departments:

- Food service department (menu offerings, hours of operation, prices, service level, ambience)
- Gift shop (selection, souvenirs, value/price)
- Lounge (prices, entertainment, hours, service level)
- Room service (menu offerings, prices, hours of availability, promptness in delivery and pickup of trays)
- Valet service (pickup and delivery times, prices, quality of service)
- Housekeeping services (daily room cleaning, replenishment of amenities, cleanliness of public areas, requests for directions in hotel)
- Security (24-hour availability, fire safety devices, anonymous key blank and distribution, key and lock repair service, requests for directions in hotel)

Front office:

- Requests for information and assistance (wake-up calls, hours of operation of other departments, transmittal of requests to other departments)
- Telephone system (assistance from staff)
- Update of guest folio
- Extension of stay

Checkout

- Reasonable and flexible checkout time deadlines
- Assistance with luggage
- Elevator availability and promptness
- In-room video checkout
- Length of time in line
- Immediate availability of guest folio printout; accuracy of charges
- Additional reservations

the front desk. Cross-trained employees speed the check-in and checkout process by performing both functions, as the traffic at the desk dictates. Registration clerks can cash checks and cashiers can issue duplicate room keys, in many cases eliminating the necessity of having the guest wait in two lines.[11]

Moments of Truth in Hotel Service Management

Central to the development of a guest service program is the management of what Albrecht and Zemke call **moments of truth:** "episode[s] in which a customer comes into contact with any aspect of the company, however remote, and thereby has an opportunity to form an impression."[12] Every time the hotel guest comes in contact with some aspect of the hotel, he or she judges its hospitality. Guests who are told by a reservationist that

FRONTLINE REALITIES

Shortcomings in providing guest services at the front office in The Times Hotel have become critical in one particular aspect—knowledge of special events in the local area. Guests have complained that front desk clerks do not give clear directions, estimates of travel time, information on timing of events, cost of admission, or suggestions for public transportation. Guests approach desk clerks and are given a brief response to their questions.

The front office manager has decided to use total quality management principles to resolve this situation. The hotel has stated a commitment to service and a financial commitment to this goal.

If you were the front office manager, how would you proceed?

---

they must "take this room at this rate or stay elsewhere" will not feel that hospitality is a primary consideration at this hotel. When a potential guest calls and asks to speak with Ms. General Manager and the switchboard operator answers, "Who is that?" the guest will expect the same kind of careless, impersonal treatment when (or if) he or she decides to stay at the hotel. The guest who is crammed into an elevator with half the housekeeping crew, their vacuum cleaners, and bins of soiled laundry will not feel welcomed. All these impressions make the guest feel that service at this hotel is mismanaged.

These examples are only some of the moments of truth that can be identified from an analysis of the guest service cycle. Whether a guest considers an event a moment of truth or barely notices, it is a cumulative review of the delivery of hospitality. Albrecht and Zemke tell us that each guest has a "report card" in his or her head, which is the basis of a grading system that leads the customer to decide whether to partake of the service again or to go elsewhere.[13] If a guest is to award an A+ to the hotel's hospitality report card, it is essential that these moments of truth be well managed. This challenge is not to be viewed as mission impossible but rather as an organized and concerted effort by owners, management, and employees. Keep this "customer report card" concept in mind as you develop your ideas about service management.

Employee Buy-in Concept

As Albrecht and Zemke note, "in any kind of retail or service business, the factor that has the biggest effect on sales is the 'last four feet.' It's up to the people in the store to take over at the last four feet."[14] In other words, all the sophisticated marketing programs, well-orchestrated sales promotions, outstanding architectural designs, degreed and certified management staff form only the backdrop for the delivery of hospitality. The frontline employee is *the* link in the service management program. He or she must deliver the service. It's a simple fact that still amazes many people. How can front office managers ensure that frontline employees deliver a consistently high level of service?

Albrecht and Zemke offer the following suggestions:

To have a high standard of service, it is necessary to create and maintain a motivating environment in which service people can find personal reasons for committing their energies to the benefit of the customer. People commit their energies to the extent that what they do brings them what they want. What they want may be psychological—a feeling, a status, or an experience. Or it may be material—greenbacks are an excellent form of feedback. In any case the job of management is to engineer a motivating environment.[15]

John W. Young, of the Four Seasons Hotels, echoes their ideas: "The challenge is to motivate your employees to deliver the required level of service to your customers, and do it consistently. . . . If we are to succeed in delivery of exceptional service, we have to convince every new employee of the benefit of 'buying in' to our philosophy and standards."[16]

In short, a consistently high level of service will be provided only by employees who are committed to the service management program. This commitment is fostered by management. It is such commitment that allows the front desk clerk to tell the newly registered guest about the special musical combo group playing in the lounge or to ask how the traffic coming in from the airport was or to suggest consulting the concierge in the lobby for directions to points of interest in the city. Chapter 12 further discusses employee motivation, and those concepts are crucial to the development and administration of a service management program.

Consider each employee in each hotel and determine how to stimulate their commitment to service. If money will motivate them, financial incentive programs that reward positive expressions of hospitality are in order. Employee stock ownership programs also provide an incentive for employees to realize financially the importance of delivering a consistently high level of hospitality. Other reward systems may include preferential treatment in scheduling shifts, longer vacations, and extra holidays. Long-range rewards may include promotion opportunities.

Screening Employees Who Deliver Hospitality

Another factor to consider in developing a service management program is the employee character traits needed to provide hospitality. When evaluating candidates for frontline service positions, interviews should be structured to screen out employees who are not able or willing to deal with the demands of guest service. Albrecht and Zemke offer these considerations for choosing frontline employees: "A service person needs to have at least an adequate level of maturity and self-esteem. He or she needs to be reasonably articulate, aware of the normal rules of social context, and be able to say and do what is necessary to establish rapport with a customer and maintain it. And third, he or she needs to have a fairly high level of tolerance for contact."[17] And John W. Young, of the Four Seasons Hotels, notes:

The motivation process begins with the selection of employees, which is all important. The average person applying for a job is interviewed by at least four people. When Four Seasons opens a property every single employee hired is interviewed by the hotel general manager. First we look for people who are already motivated. Our compensation policies have been designed to support and reinforce our efforts in hiring, training, and development. We look on them not only as a motivator, but as a way of sending signals to our employees consistent with our philosophy and business strategy—almost as an employee communication program itself.[18]

Group discussions among the managerial staff will help to highlight the attributes of a person who will be able to deliver hospitality. These discussions should lead to a rather informal procedure for screening employees. Questions that determine whether candidates display maturity and self-esteem, are articulate, possess social graces, and have a high level of tolerance for continued guest contact can be discussed in group settings. Managers who are aware of what they are looking for in employees are better able to secure the right people for the right jobs.

Empowerment

Empowerment—management's act of delegating certain authority and responsibility to **frontline employees,** those people who deliver service to guests as front desk clerks, cashiers, switchboard operators, bellhops, concierge, and housekeeping employees—is one of the rudiments of service management programs. The process of empowering employees requires front office managers to analyze the flow of guest services and determine how the frontline staff interact with the guest. Are there any points of service at which the guest may request variations in the level of service provided? Might there be times when a guest may question standard operating procedures, such as billing, guest room access, or room accommodations? Do frontline employees constantly inform guests, "I don't have the authority to rectify this matter. You'll have to see the manager"? If the review of the guest cycle reveals opportunities for delegating responsibility and authority, then empowerment should be exercised.

ADOPTING EMPOWERMENT INTO FRONT OFFICE MANAGEMENT

Front office employees who are not accustomed to solving problems and are not treated as members of the management team may be reluctant to suddenly take charge and make decisions. Employees who have become comfortable with having their managers solve all the problems may see no need to change the established routine. However, it is becoming increasingly apparent to front office managers that a supervisory style that does not allow for employees to be involved in the decision-making process will not be successful. The challenge to the front office manager, then, is to begin to introduce empowerment into the front office.

The analysis of the guest flow (described earlier in this chapter) is the best way to start

A guest in room 284 calls to the front desk and wants to order pizza from room service, but there is no room service menu in the guest room. The desk clerk relays the request to housekeeping, only to have the phone call go unanswered. Next, the desk clerk calls the restaurant and asks the hostess to call the guest and take care of the request. What underlying total quality management efforts are working in this situation?

the empowerment process. However, this analysis must be performed by the front office manager in conjunction with frontline employees. If input from frontline employees is not included in the analysis, valuable data may be overlooked and an opportunity for employee ownership will be lost. The opportunity for an employee to participate in the decision-making process will ensure positive initiation of empowerment.

PARAMETERS OF EMPLOYEE EMPOWERMENT

The authority and responsibility that underlie employee empowerment must be fully articulated and communicated to employees. If an analysis of the guest flow reveals opportunities for a guest to question a billing amount, then the billing amount needs to be discussed. If the amount in question is less than $5, do cashiers have the authority to credit the guest account for that amount? What if the amount in question is less than $25; do cashiers have the authority to credit the guest account for that amount? Or what if the amount in question rises to more than $25; do cashiers have the authority to credit the guest account for that amount? Along with setting parameters for employee empowerment is a management feedback system that provides information on cashier financial activity and guest satisfaction. For example, a cumulative tally as well as individual tallies of a front desk clerk's authorization of refunding charges that have been disputed by guests should be reviewed by front office managers. Financial totals that exceed the parameters of employee empowerment should be questioned.

TRAINING FOR EMPOWERMENT

Employees need training sessions to prepare for empowerment. Some issues that training sessions will cover include the feeling that management has abandoned its responsibility by asking employees to resolve guest concerns. Employees may also experience anxiety in dealing with guests who are upset. Front office managers will need to develop flexible but relatively routine methods for employees to use to achieve a uniform delivery of service.

Training for empowerment begins by asking employees how they feel about providing guests with good service. Front office managers might ask employees how they think the hotel can make the guest feel most comfortable in this environment. Questions that pertain to some of the employees' recent personal experiences at the time of check-in or checkout may initiate some opportunities for discussion. Training continues with a list of empowerment policy standards, which describe the authority and responsibility that are included in their job description. Employee-manager dialogue about these standards will help clarify employee understanding and concerns and identify manager communication issues. The manager will want to demonstrate and have employees go over the use of empowerment policy standards. Managers will also want to have follow-up training sessions with review of employee performance and opportunities for employee feedback.

Training for Hospitality Management

Part of a service management program involves employee training to deliver hospitality. Just as managers discuss what they want in an employee, managers decide what must be done to convey hospitality to travelers who are away from home. Of course, this discussion is not performed in isolation and requires input from employees. Using the guest service cycle (see Figure 11-6), the planning group determines what each frontline employee must do at each point to extend hospitality.

> The key to making training pay off is knowing what we want the trainees to be able to do when they have finished the program. An effective training process starts with a performance analysis. We must analyze the various jobs to be done in serving the customer well, and then spell out the knowledge, attitudes, and skills required of the person doing the job.[19]

You cannot take it for granted that the desk clerk knows to maintain eye contact with the guest during the check-in procedure while using a computer, that the switchboard operator knows to alert a security supervisor when a guest mysteriously hangs up in the middle of a call for information, or that a bellhop knows to check the operating conditions of the heating, ventilating, and air-conditioning unit and television when he or she brings the guest's luggage to the room. The communications of hospitality must be identified, so that each employee can be trained to convey them.

Evaluating the Service Management Program

Any program requires methods for evaluating whether the program has successfully achieved its goals. This chapter opened by defining hospitality as the generous and cordial provision of service to a guest. How do the owners and managers of a hotel know that hospitality is being delivered?

Albrecht and Zemke base the development of a sound evaluation procedure on identifying the guest's moments of truth.[20] Figure 11-6 outlines the moments of truth in the guest service cycle. This outline can serve as a guideline for what should be evaluated. The more research put into identifying the components of the guest service cycle for a specific hotel property, the more effective managers and employees will be in evaluating service delivery. Specific desired behaviors can be identified and measured. For example, if part of the registration process depends on a prompt hotel shuttle van to pick up and deliver guests to the hotel, then complaints from guests about late or slow service will tell the owners, managers, and employees that frontline employees are not delivering the necessary service correctly. Customer comment cards provide one of the ways hotel management and staff can receive feedback. However, not all satisfied or dissatisfied guests complete these cards. Owners, managers, and employees who are committed to a service management program will develop additional methods for determining guest satisfaction.

One other method that can be used to obtain useful feedback is by having frontline staff, such as a desk clerk, inquire about the guest's visit during checkout. Simply asking "Was everything all right?" is not sufficient. If the guest folio indicates the guest charged meals, beverages, room service, long-distance calls, or valet services, the front desk clerk should inquire about the delivery of service for each: "Was your food delivered hot, on time, removed from the hallway promptly?" or "How did you enjoy the live entertainment in the lounge?" A method of communicating guest responses to the appropriate departments, which can rectify the errors or reward the frontline employee, will complete the process of evaluating the success of a service management program. For example, a quick call to the manager on duty that relates the information received from the guest can assist in remedying a potential guest service problem.

An inquiry from the desk clerk at checkout provides feedback about service quality after the fact. Supervisors of the dining room, lounge, bell staff, housekeeping department, maintenance crew, and the like must develop communication procedures with their employees to monitor the guest's experience as it occurs. The host or hostess must develop a sensitivity to a guest's reaction to menu items and prices; the bellhop must constantly be aware of the guest's needs for information, directions, or assistance with luggage; while the housekeeping employee must be aware of the guest's needs for additional amenities, linens, or cleanliness of the public areas. All feedback must be communicated to the frontline employee for continuous improvement of service.

Follow-through

Vital to any service management program is the continued implementation of the program over time. In the hospitality industry, continued implementation can be very difficult. A hotel operates every hour of every day, and innumerable jobs are involved in keeping it running smoothly and profitably. Management can begin a service management program with the best of intentions, but too often it is dropped or neglected in the day-to-day flurry of operations. Albrecht and Zemke remind us that "isolated change and improvement programs tend to run their course and then to run downhill toward the performance levels that existed before the program. The difference between a program and continuous commitment is management."[21] Management is the key to implementing an effective guest service program. The commitment to hospitality is not a casual one; it requires constant attention, research, training, and evaluation. Only with this commitment can a hotel ensure hospitality every day for every guest.

Interfacing with Other Departments in Delivering Hospitality

One of the many benefits of employing total quality management is the participant's ability to understand fellow team members' job responsibilities. Teams that are composed of various departments in the hotel provide opportunities for insights into fellow members' jobs. Sometimes the process of TQM can seem like a maze of charts, processes, interactions, and the like, which tend to confuse the uncommitted. But from that process rises a thorough understanding of how the guest moves through the hospitality system and the jobs of the providers of these services. Participants in TQM come to realize that the delivery of hospitality is not the responsibility of any one person. This may come as a startling revelation to some employees because they feel alone in bearing the responsibility for guest satisfaction. TQM allows all participants the opportunity to see how each employee from the other departments shares in the hospitality activity.

The "that's not my job" syndrome is a very easy attitude to adopt in a management system in which TQM is not used. Employees who feel they have distinct job duties within and between departments and are not paid to venture beyond those guidelines may contribute to the delivery of unacceptable service. Department managers who use TQM have the opportunity to prioritize service concepts and methods to deliver service with employees. This interaction gives managers and employees the occasion to air concerns about how restrictions resulting from narrowly written job descriptions affect their ability to provide service to the guest.

A typical TQM team will assign representatives from various departments in a hotel to work on improving a particular guest service. For example, guests may complain that there are not enough towels in a guest room. This complaint, especially after housekeeping has closed down for the evening, causes a reduction in guest satisfaction and additional work for the lone front desk clerk on duty.

At the outset, the answer may be to "just put a few more towels in each guest room." The controller of the hotel may see this as additional costs of inventory purchase and laundry. Housekeepers realize that excess supplies in guest rooms have a tendency to vaporize and result in an increase in costs. However, a team approach to this seemingly simple problem will provide a list of possible solutions that an individual employee might overlook. A team of desk clerks, housekeepers, bellhops, servers, cooks, switchboard operators, cashiers, and supervisors will review this particular service and how it is delivered. Objective analysis of the components of the service will give employees insight into how departments interact to accomplish their tasks. Brainstorming sessions identify

---

FRONTLINE REALITIES

 A guest in room 1104 has requested that housekeeping tidy up after a cocktail reception in his room. He is expecting additional business guests within two hours. He wants you to ensure that the housekeeping department will respond within the next half hour. What should you do?

possible improvements that can be debated by team members. Additional meetings will find team members crystallizing concepts and gaining insights and respect for jobs performed by team members.

The team may decide to have front desk clerks alert the housekeeping staff when more than two people check into a guest room. The housekeeping staff can then routinely bring additional towels. This decision not only solves the problem of guest dissatisfaction caused by too few towels but provides an opportunity for frontline employees to develop and deliver a guest service. It is no longer a front desk problem or a housekeeping problem, but a team effort to produce a satisfied guest.

An example of a service management program is Hilton's "Hilton Pride Program," which recognizes exceptional hotel performance and customer satisfaction. "The Pride Program reinforces our pledge to maintain exceptional levels of customer satisfaction while building pride in the workplace. This sense of pride enables us to crate a level of service that brings our customers back, said Dieter H. Huckestein, executive vice president, Hilton Hotels Corporation and president, hotel operations owned and managed.

"The performance criteria include the following items:

- Customer satisfaction tracking studies
- Guest comment card responses
- Mystery shopper evaluations
- Team member surveys
- EBITDA (earnings before interest, taxes, depreciation, and amortization)
- Room RevPAR
- RevPAR index
- Brand management and product standard"[22]

Delta Hotels received the Canada Awards for Excellence Trophy 2000 from the National Quality Institute (NQI). Mr. John Johnston, president, Delta Hotels, remarked, "Not only does this award recognize our ongoing commitment to excellence, but more importantly our commitment to our guests." The selection process included "[NQI] assessors [who] visited six Delta hotels and the Corporate office to review examples of quality in action. Delta Hotels met the rigorous criteria in the Excellence Framework by demonstrating outstanding continuous achievement in Leadership, Planning, Customer Focus, People Focus, Supplier Focus, and Performance." Prior to this award, Delta Hotels established an internal quality control program—Quality Business Assessment. "With this process, Delta Hotels trains internal assessors to conduct individual hotel assessments and develop a quality improvement plan. Every two years, a hotel will undergo an initial three-day assessment and a subsequent five-day assessment to ensure that ongoing quality measures are incorporated into Delta's culture and all aspects of [its] operations. External assessors are also invited to conduct assessments, ensuring that assessments meet the professional standards of NQI." Mr. William Pallett, senior vice president, people and quality, says, "Our goal is to ensure a seamless approach to quality, so that it is part of our culture. Problem Solving Teams regularly monitor process for improvement opportunities." Tangible results of Delta's program include a one-minute check-in guarantee for guests and a guarantee for employees "to receive their review within 30 days of their anniversary date or receive one week's vacation with pay."[23]

Solution to Opening Dilemma

An immediate response to correct this guest service situation is to have the desk clerk register the guest at $95 per night, discuss the situation with the supervisor after the guest departs from the front desk, and then have the front desk clerk call the guest to confirm the room rate. However, a more effective way to handle future situations is to work with the general manager and owner to develop a service strategy statement and obtain financial resources to support a service management program. Exploration and application of employee motivation and empowerment are necessary to make a service management program work. Total quality management teams will help employees determine tasks required to deliver service. New front office managers should not take the delivery of good service for granted. Quality service is planned—not happenstance.

Chapter Recap

This chapter has stressed the importance of delivering continuous quality service in hotels, as defined by the guest. Successful extension of hospitality starts with management's commitment to a service management program. Preparing a service strategy statement will focus the planning efforts of the owners, management, and employees. Principles of total quality management provide a manager with an opportunity to involve frontline employees in analyzing the components of delivery of service and methods to improve existing services. The development of the service management program requires the involvement of frontline employees, discussion of the guest cycle, moments of truth, employee buy-in concept, screening of potential employees prior to hiring, empowerment, training, evaluation of the service management program, follow-through, and interfacing with other departments in delivering hospitality. A long-term commitment to a successful service management program is necessary.

End of Chapter Questions

1. How important do you think hospitality is to a guest in a hotel? If you are employed in a hotel, ask your manager how he or she feels about the importance of providing hospitality to a guest.

2. How would you develop a service strategy statement? Why is this an important first step in the planning process?

3. Why should frontline employees be involved in the development of a service management program?

4. How would you apply TQM to a particular situation at your place of employment? What challenges do you think will be presented in the application of this management concept? What suggestions will you make to your manager to resolve these challenges?

5. If you are employed in a hotel, prepare an outline, similar to that in Figure 11-6, of the guest service cycle at your place of employment.

6. What are "moments of truth"? How can a front office manager identify them?

7. Why must an employee "buy in" to a service management program? What would you do to ensure employee commitment?

8. Discuss some techniques that are useful in determining whether prospective employees have the attributes needed to extend hospitality.

9. Why is training an important component of the service management program? How could a front office manager begin to identify the skills needed for delivery of hospitality? If you are employed in a hotel, did you receive training in delivering hospitality?

10. How can a front office manager measure the effectiveness of a service management program?

11. Why is follow-through so necessary in the continued delivery of hospitality?

CASE STUDY 1101

The new owners of The Times Hotel have just boarded a plane at a city in Asia. Their stay in the Mandrian Hotel was superb. The attention to service was excellent, and they felt quite pampered. During the flight, one of the owners reads an article in a popular magazine concerning the mediocre service in hotels in the United States. The article details the lack of concern for the guest in many properties, the high cost of hotel rooms, and the abrupt attitudes of the hotel staff. The owners think of their hotel and realize that many of the problems mentioned in the article can be found at The Times Hotel.

The next day, at the general staff meeting, the owners share their concerns with the management staff. As the group listens attentively, they cannot help but think, "We have heard this before—another idea from the owners that will make more work for our already overworked staff." However, this time, the owners declare they don't know where to begin; they feel overwhelmed by the size of the problem. "Let's develop a plan," they suggest. All managers must do some research on this topic and return for a brainstorming session in two weeks.

The front office manager, Ana Chavarria, finds

this to be a challenge! She has read some of the articles on service management in the trade journals and decides to do more research on the topic.

Through her reading, Ms. Chavarria learns that there must be a financial commitment by the owners and a managerial commitment by the staff to make this work. If the employees become involved in the planning stages, it should work just fine. She thinks that getting the cooperation of the employees will be easy if the owners pledge their financial commitment. She guesses that the rest of the management staff will probably halfheartedly go along with the project—if it is forced on them.

At the scheduled brainstorming session, Ana outlines her findings. The owners are reluctant to incur additional expenses to motivate employees. The owners respond, "Let's find some more creative ways." The other managers suggest preparing posters with photos of employees who do a good job, placing names of employees who do a good job on the marquee, and placing a suggestion box in the employee lunchroom. Continued focus on the financial aspects distracts the group from discussing the content of a service management program. After two hours of futile effort, the owners decide to table the service management program.

If you were the front office manager, what would you have included in your presentation for developing an effective service management program?

CASE STUDY 1102

Ana Chavarria, front office manager of The Times Hotel, and Lorraine DeSantes, the hotel's director of marketing, learn that their city will be hosting the next Olympic Games. The city council and the tourism board are planning to meet to work on a program to ensure that quality service will be delivered by all agencies, private and commercial, to the many guests. There will be individual groups (hotels, restaurants, public transportation, etc.) that will meet and decide on a course of action. Margaret Chu, general manager of The Times Hotel, wants Ana and Lorraine to represent the hotel on the Hotel Hospitality Commission. Since the next games are several years away, there is ample time to involve various constituencies in developing a plan for implementation.

After a few meetings with the commission, the group feels it should break into smaller teams to discuss developing specific components of delivering quality service. Ana and Lorraine are heading the "Service to the International Visitor" planning team. What suggestions would you give Ana and Lorraine as they lead this team? Prepare an agenda for the first meeting of their team.

Notes

1. Karl Albrecht and Ron Zemke, *Service America!* (New York: Dow Jones—Irwin, 1985), 6–7.

2. John W. Young, "Four Seasons Expansion into the U.S. Market" (paper delivered at the Council on Hotel, Restaurant and Institutional Education, Toronto, Canada, July 30, 1988; edited July 17, 2001), 29.

3. Cheryl Hall, "Data Crunchers at Irving-based UniFocus Help Hotels Improve Customers Service, Maintain Employee Morale," *Dallas Morning News*, July 16, 2000. Reprinted with permission of the *Dallas Morning News*.

4. Young, "Four Seasons," 22.

5. Eric J. Johnson and William G. Layton, "Quality Customer Service, Part II," *Restaurant Hospitality* (October 1987): 40.

6. Ernest R. Cadotte and Normand Turgeon, "Key Factors in Guest Satisfaction," *Cornell Hotel Restaurant Administration Quarterly* 28, no. 4 (February 1988): 44–51.

7. Albrecht and Zemke, *Service America!,* 33–34.

8. Young, "Four Seasons," 9–10.

9. Don Hellriegel and John W. Slochum, *Management* (New York: Addison-Wesley, 1991), 697.

10. Albrecht and Zemke, *Service America!,* 37–38.

11. Nancy J. Allin and Kelly Halpine, "From Clerk and Cashier to Guest Agent," *Florida International University Hospitality Review* 6, no. 1 (spring 1988): 42.

12. Albrecht and Zemke, *Service America!,* 27.

13. Ibid., 32.

14. Ibid., 96–97.

15. Ibid., 107–108.

16. Young, "Four Seasons," 14, 35.

17. Albrecht and Zemke, *Service America!,* 114.

18. Young, "Four Seasons," 25–26.

19. Albrecht and Zemke, *Service America!,* 112–113.

20. Ibid., 139.

21. Ibid., 144.

22. Jeanne Datz, "Hilton Hotels Corporation Selects 16 out of More Than 300 U.S. Hilton and Hilton Garden Inn Hotels for the 2000 Hilton Pride Customer Satisfaction Awards," Hilton Hotels Corporation, Beverly Hills, Calif., April 16, 2001.

23. Catherine Mattice, "Delta Hotels Receives Canada Awards for Excellence Trophy 2000," Delta Hotels, Toronto, Ontario, September 26, 2000.

Key Words

cycle of service
empowerment
flowchart
frontline employees
hospitality

incentive program
moments of truth
service management program
service strategy statement
shift leader

Training for Hospitality

OPENING DILEMMA

Enrique Garcia, a hotel general manager, has heard the last complaint about his staff! He is so tired of writing letters of apology and comping guest stays because of poor delivery of service. Recently, a guest complained that after he left the front desk area in his wheelchair, one desk clerk was overheard making an unkind remark. Two days before that, another hotel employee took 45 minutes to respond to a guest's request for assistance in moving a heavy box from his room to the lobby area, and that same person said it took 10 minutes to go through the check-in process. Mr. Garcia wants to contact an advertising agency that will assist him in cleaning up the hotel's image.

Determining Employee Hospitality Qualities

Assessing personnel needs requires identifying the skills and character traits required to do a particular job. Frequently, the front office manager can recite a list of problems with front desk personnel but cannot identify their strengths. The ability to recognize positive traits—skills of present employees as well as skills a potential employee should have—helps not only in choosing the right candidate for a particular position but in assigning tasks to employees that match their abilities. If you do not know the skills of your current staff and the skills that potential staff will need, you cannot assemble a staff that will meet your needs or make effective use of their skills.

A front office manager should begin by preparing job analyses and descriptions of each position in a department. Identify the responsibilities and objectives of each and then consider the personal qualities, skills, and experience needed to perform those duties. For example, a front office manager may want front desk clerks to sell the more expensive suites or rooms and other services of the hotel. To accomplish this objective, an individual must have a very outgoing personality or be willing to accept new responsibilities as a challenge or an opportunity to grow. Or the front office manager may wish the front desk clerks to be more efficient in handling clerical duties neatly and accurately. These qualities may be found in a person with prior experience in other clerical or sales positions. Previous experience outside the labor force—for example, as an officer in a service club or a community group—may provide some idea about the person's leadership skills and ability to organize projects. These and other traits should be viewed as a whole. The motivational concepts discussed later in the chapter will help a front office manager identify and develop an employee's positive attributes.

A front office manager must think about some character traits necessary to deliver hospitality on a daily basis. These traits include maturity, an outgoing personality, and patience, as well as a willingness to accept constructive criticism. The employee should also feel comfortable selling, as he or she will be promoting the hotel's services.

When employees have outgoing personalities, in most cases they are able to seek out other individuals and to make the initial effort to set a relationship in motion. Employees who are extroverts will enjoy meeting guests and will make them feel welcome. This is the type of employee who in many cases can turn a potentially impossible situation into a challenge. For example, if a guest says there is no way he or she will be walked to another hotel—"After all, a reservation is a commitment"—an outgoing person may be better at persuading the guest that the alternative hotel will surely "meet your highest standards."

Mature employees will be able to assess "the big picture" and quickly analyze a situation before acting. Instead of reacting to a situation, this type of employee allows a guest to vent his or her concerns before offering a response. Mature employees also possess and exhibit patience in situations that require that guests be allowed time to think or carry out a request. Guests may be confused about understanding geographic directions in an unfamiliar surrounding, but a mature employee will repeat and offer written directions or sketches to allow the guest time to absorb the information.

Employees who possess a positive attitude toward constructive criticism will prosper and progress in a hotel career. Employees who are able to learn and practice their job tasks will occasionally make errors in judgment and not meet standards. Employees who want to continue to learn will seek a supervisor's insights into why a particular situation resulted from their actions.

Front desk clerks who are comfortable with practicing promotional skills while at the front desk are a great asset to a front office manager. This type of person will accept the challenge to sell products and services throughout the hotel and seek ways to meet or exceed sales quotas. This quality will allow a front desk clerk to understand the total effort necessary to produce a profit for a hotel.

Screening for Hospitality Qualities

Composing questions prior to interviewing to determine if an applicant has the personal qualities needed to fulfill a job's requirements is usually very effective. The interview will have some structure but will be flexible enough for both the interviewer and the applicant to freely express their concerns.

The front office manager begins to develop a list of questions based on the job description to guide the interview. He or she wants to determine if the candidate has an outgoing personality, patience, the ability to accept constructive criticism, and the ability to sell. These are only a few of the qualities for which a front office manager will want to screen in an interview.

An Outgoing Personality

The first question attempts to determine if the applicant is outgoing. Although observing the person during the interview will give some indication of how he or she deals with others, you could get more insight with this question: "Tell me about the last time you went out to dinner. What did you like about the host or hostess?" A response that indicates appreciation for a friendly welcome shows the candidate is aware of the concept of hospitality.

Patience

To obtain some insight into the level of patience a job candidate possesses, ask a question such as, "Tell me about your recent participation in an event (sporting, social, work) at which you received less than what you had expected." A response that indicates

---

FRONTLINE REALITIES

 You have scheduled three job interviews for tomorrow. In the past six months, you have lost six front desk clerks. As a front office manager, how will you prepare for the interviews to ensure that you choose the best employee?

that small details were overlooked but overall the experience was rewarding may indicate the person is willing to be a team player.

Ability to Accept Constructive Criticism

To gain some insight into a candidate's ability to accept constructive criticism, a question such as "At your previous job, how did your manager handle a situation in which you did not meet stated goals?" may be used. A candidate's response to this will reflect the degree of understanding the interviewee had about why he or she was reprimanded, and how the situation was corrected may indicate how this person accepts constructive criticism.

Interest in Selling

A question that allows a candidate to express his or her openness to soliciting donations for a charity will assist an interviewer in understanding the applicant's desire to sell products and services for the hotel.

These questions may not always guarantee that the front office manager will choose wisely, but this effort will produce a more effective track record of screening for hospitality.

Developing an Orientation Program

The person who is hired to work in the front office is in a unique position. In no other department of the hotel is each employee expected to know the operations, personnel, and layout of the facilities in every other department. The front office employee is constantly bombarded with questions from guests and other employees concerning when a certain banquet or reception is being held, where key supervisors are, or how to find the lounge or pool area. The **orientation process** introduces new hires to the organization and work environment and is vital in providing employees with background information about the property. This program will help new hires to become aware of the activities, procedures, people, and layout of the hotel. This is a critical first step in training new employees.

Of the utmost importance is ensuring that orientation is thorough and well thought out. An employee who is given a brief introduction to the people who work the same shift, a quick tour of the location of the guest rooms, and information concerning the time clock can hardly be expected to be competent. By the time orientation is complete, new employees should be able to answer guests' questions competently. If they don't have answers at their fingertips, they should know how to find the answers quickly. For example, if someone asks for the general manager by name and the new front desk clerk responds, "Who is that?" an inefficient and unprofessional image of the organization is conveyed. The new employee should know who that person is and how to reach him or her. Moreover, orientation should prepare all new hires to provide correct and complete information to guests, the general public, or other employees.

Orientation programs for front office employees differ from one establishment to another. However, the following general outline can be used to develop a program for any establishment. This outline incorporates factors common to all properties, such as economic position of the establishment in the community, overview of the hotel, the employee handbook, the policy and procedure manual, and an introduction to the front office environment.

Economic Position of the Property in the Community

A new employee will benefit from knowing how a hotel fits into the economic scheme of the community and the region. He or she may be very impressed to learn, for example, that a particular hotel is responsible for 10 percent of the employment in the area. Information concerning the value of the tax dollars generated by employees, significance of the tourism market, number of conventions and subsequent guests who rely on the services of the operation, significant growth accomplishments, and other economic contributions will not only reassure new employees that they have chosen the right employer but also instill a sense of pride in the organization. These and other economic indicators will help the new hire think of the employer as a well-respected member of the business community. Larger organizations can prepare a slide or multimedia presentation to demonstrate their commitment to the business area.

Overview of the Lodging Establishment

An overview of the lodging establishment will include the number of rooms (accompanied by a detailed printed handout concerning the layout of the rooms), a list of services offered in the establishment, an organization chart of the people in the various departments, and of course, a tour of the property.

The guest rooms are a very important part of the day-to-day activity of the front office staff. The sooner the employee is aware of the location and contents of the rooms, the quicker he or she will feel comfortable with the job. Floor plans for each floor and a printed summary of the typical contents of the rooms will serve as handy references that the new person can review at a later time. For instance, if the odd-numbered floors have three suites and the even-numbered floors have study areas for businesspersons, including this information in the printed material will assist in the training process.

The services offered by the hotel (restaurants, banquet facilities, room services, lounges, pool, athletics room, and gift shops) should be identified during the orientation program so that the new employee can assist and direct guests. Hours of operation for each department listed will help the new employee learn more about the systematic operation of the hotel.

The people listed on the organization chart should be pointed out to the new hires. These people and their responsibilities should be explained. This background information will assist in decision making and communication of information to various department heads. It will also give the new hire a sense of belonging to the group.

The overview of the lodging establishment is not complete without a tour of the property. This tour should include the guest rooms and guest room areas, major departments, service areas such as restaurants, banquet rooms, gift shops, and recreational facilities. This tour can be informal yet specific in content. It will allow the new employee a chance to see the establishment as a place of work and a place of recreation for the guest. These tours also help the employee understand the front office's relationship to the entire establishment.

Employee Handbook

The **employee handbook** provides general guidelines concerning employee conduct and is a valuable resource for new hires. In this publication, hotel managers describe many topics related to personnel issues, including:

- Pay categories
- Evaluation procedures
- Vacation time
- Sick leave
- Holidays
- Paydays
- Use of controlled substances
- Social interaction with guests
- Resolving disputes with guests and other employees
- Insurance benefits
- Uniform requirements

Sometimes people being interviewed for positions at an establishment or new hires do not ask questions about these policies because they feel the employer may think them greedy, lazy, or overconcerned with a certain issue. On the contrary, these questions form the basis for a good employment contract. Employers should make the effort to discuss and explain their personnel policies.

Policy and Procedure Manual

The **policy and procedure manual** provides an outline of how the specific duties of each job are to be performed (this is also known as standard operating procedures [SOPs]). This is another specific set of guidelines that is valuable for employee training. The policy and procedure manual addresses such concepts as the following:

- Operation of the PMS and other equipment in the front office
- Reservations
- Registrations
- Posting
- Written and verbal communications with guests and other employees of the hotel
- Checkouts
- Preparation of the night audit
- Safety and security measures

The front office manager who takes the time to develop these guidelines will have prepared a very useful supervisory tool. Providing materials in writing to supplement the verbal training session allows new employees to review the skills they must master and retain more of what they are taught.

Introduction to the Front Office Staff

The final segment of the orientation process is an introduction to the front office itself. This introduction will prepare new hires for the training program that will follow. It familiarizes them with co-workers, equipment they will be using, personnel procedures, and interdepartmental relations.

New employees should be introduced to the current staff of front desk clerks, bellhops, telephone operators, reservation clerks, night auditors, supervisors, and others. A little planning on the front office manager's part is required to ensure that the new employee meets the entire staff in the first few days. Saying a few words about the role of each employee during the introductions will not only make new hires feel more comfortable with their co-workers but also make each current staff member feel like a special part of the team. The current staff will also appreciate meeting the new addition to the staff. Very often, this procedure is overlooked, and new employees feel awkward for days or weeks.

The various pieces of equipment in the front office should be described and shown to the new employee. Brief remarks about each piece of equipment will serve as a reference point when needed skills are explained in further detail during the training program. This part of the orientation program can be slowed down somewhat to allow the new hire to become familiar with the equipment. The operator of the call-accounting system may have the new person pull up a chair to see how calls are handled. The new employee may be encouraged to observe how registrations and checkouts are handled by using the PMS. The front office manager should assure the new employee that specific training will follow. This is a time for familiarization only.

The new employee should be shown how to check in for a shift on the PMS or the time clock. The location and timing of the posted schedule of shift coverage should also be indicated.

Interdepartmental cooperation must be stressed during the introduction to the front office. This is an ideal time to establish the importance of harmony among the housekeeping, maintenance, marketing and sales, food and beverage, and front office departments. The front office must take the lead in establishing good communications with the various departments. Since the front office is the initial contact for the guest, obtaining status reports, maintaining communications, and knowing the functions being hosted each day are the responsibilities of the front office staff. Overlooking trivial misunderstandings with other departments takes colossal effort on some days, but the front office must keep the communication lines open. The guest will benefit from and appreciate the efforts of a well-informed front office.

Administering the Orientation Program

Administering the orientation program requires planning by the front office manager. The front office is a hectic place, and there is much for the new employee to learn. Concern for the guests and the services and information they require must be a priority. A standard **orientation checklist** should be prepared, which summarizes all items that must be covered during orientation, such as that shown in Figure 12-1. This will ensure that the new employee has been properly introduced to the front office. This checklist should be initialed by both the new employee and the orientation supervisor after the program is complete, to verify that all policies have been covered. This ensures that no one can claim to be ignorant because there is written evidence that the material was covered in the orientation program.

The orientation program should be delivered by a member of the supervisory staff or a trained senior staff member in the front office. This person must have the ability to convey the attitude of the organization as well as the tasks of the employees. Whoever handles the orientation should not be on duty at the same time: it is impossible to explain so much about the property to a new employee while performing other tasks as well.

The orientation program helps the employer-employee relationship begin on the right foot. It introduces the workplace, guidelines and procedures, co-workers, and management staff to the new hire. The orientation program also introduces new employees to their work environment and encourages them to be a part of it.

Developing a Training Program

Training is an important management function and is required to develop and ensure quality performance.[1] In the hospitality industry, some hotel organizations take training seriously; others talk about it extensively but have no real program in place. Those that have developed, instituted, and continued to update their training programs consider them great assets in human resources management. They give the management team an opportunity to develop qualified employees who can perform jobs according to prede-

Figure 12-1. *An orientation checklist is a useful tool that assists in providing a comprehensive orientation.*

___ Economic position in community
___ Community geography
___ Printed floor plan of hotel
___ Visits to guest rooms
___ Hours for guest services
___ Organization chart
___ Explanation of key management personnel
___ Interdepartmental relations
___ Visits to:
  • Food and beverage areas
  • Housekeeping
  • Maintenance
  • Marketing and sales
  • Controller
  • Human resources department
  • Gift Shop
  • Pool and athletics areas
___ Sample restaurant menus
___ Employee handbook:
  • Dress code
  • Hygiene
  • Benefits
  • Pay rate
  • Paydays
  • Evaluation procedures
  • Vacation policy
  • Sick leave
  • Holiday policy
  • Drug and alcohol policy
  • Social interaction with guests
  • Schedules
  • Grievances
___ Policy and procedure manual
___ Co-workers in front office
___ Equipment in front office
___ Time clock
___ Fire and safety procedures
___ Training program

_____   _____
(Orientation Supervisor/Date)   *(Employee/Date)*

termined standards. A good training program ensures that errors will be reduced because the procedures have been explained and demonstrated.

Planning and developing a training program for front office employees includes identifying the tasks performed by the front office staff, preparing step-by-step procedures for each task, determining who will train employees, administering the training program, and reviewing the steps in the training process.

In your new role as front office manager, you remember reading about the importance of an orientation program to new hires, and you also remember the lack of an orientation at your first front desk job. You want to organize a thorough orientation program and present it to the general manager. How would you proceed?

Identification of Tasks and Job Management Skills

The tasks performed by each employee are usually identified through the job description. The job description is based on the job analysis (discussed in Chapter 2), which lists, in chronological order, the daily tasks performed by the employee. For example, the front desk clerk performs the following tasks on the day shift:

6:00 A.M. Enters start time with PMS.

6:05 Talks with night auditor about activities on the 11:00 P.M. to 7:00 A.M. shift; checks the front desk message book for current operational notes.

6:10 Obtains **cash bank,** a specific amount of paper money and coins issued to a cashier to be used for making change, from controller; counts and verifies contents.

6:30 Reviews daily report concerning occupancy rate and daily room rate.

6:35 Obtains function sheet (list of activities and special events, receptions, and the like) for the day.

6:37 Obtains housekeeper's report for the previous day.

6:40 Calls housekeeping and maintenance departments to determine the communications list (a log of unusual occurrences or special messages that the front office personnel should know about) from the previous shift(s).

6:45 Calls restaurant to learn specials for lunch and dinner.

6:50 Reviews expected checkouts and reservations for the day.

6:55 Checks out guests until 9:30 A.M.

All of the tasks identified in the job analysis must then be broken down further into specific skills to build a sound training program. This may seem like a very laborious procedure. It is! But the first step is always the most cumbersome. Using the job analysis for each of the jobs in the front office ensures that all tasks required to deliver hospitality to the guest are included in the training program.

Preparing Step-by-Step Procedures

Step-by-step procedures for each task help the trainee understand how to perform tasks correctly. This procedure also helps the trainer prepare and deliver training sessions more efficiently.

If a hotel front office has a PMS, the operator of the computer terminal must learn to enter data or commands sequentially. **Documentation,** written instructions on how to operate computer software, accompanies all property management systems. Documentation can be used as a basis for developing the step-by-step training procedure for using the PMS, and it can serve as a model for preparing step-by-step procedure for other tasks.

A step-by-step procedure to complete a guest checkout on the PMS might include the following:

1. Inquire about the guest's accommodations.

2. Enter the guest's room number.

3. Inquire about late charges.

4. Confirm method of payment.

5. Print a hard copy of the folio.

6. Allow the guest to review the folio.

7. Accept cash or credit card or bill-to-account.

8. Enter amount of payment.

9. Enter method of payment.

10. Enter department code.

11. Check for zero balance.

12. Give the guest a copy of the folio.

13. Inquire if additional reservations are needed.

14. Make farewell comments.

Each of these procedures can be further subdivided as necessary. For example, as part of step 6, the new desk clerk could be trained to point out major sections of the folio and charges incurred by the guest so that the guest is aware of all the charges that make up the total. The guest can then ask questions about any of the charges at this time, rather than after the bill is produced, thus eliminating extra work for the controller's department.

Management Concepts

In addition to task performance, other, less tangible skills need to be included in a training program for front office employees. Stress management, time management, and organizational skills are some of the areas that need to be discussed. Although these skills are often covered in seminar formats, they cannot be considered in isolation. These skills are better understood when integrated into the training program as a whole, so they can be applied to task performance. For example, the employee being trained to check out a guest should be made aware that this process may occur under stressful conditions: he or she could be in a situation in which there are long lines, many guests questioning charges, and pressure from other guests to keep the line moving. Remaining calm under these circumstances does come with experience, but the tenets of stress management will help even the new employee handle difficult situations. Self-control and concern for the guest's welfare are paramount.

Mastering time management is another important skill that enables employees to perform particular tasks at required times. For example, various departments depend on front office employees to relay messages to guests and other departments on a regular basis; otherwise, a great deal of confusion results for all concerned. Organizational skills help employees deal with their workloads systematically rather than jumping from one task to another without completing any of them. Completing paperwork on a regular basis, rather than allowing it to mount into an intimidating pile, is one example of how time management and organizational skills can improve performance.

Steps in the Training Process

The recommended steps in the training process include preparation, delivery, trial and error, and follow-up.

Preparation: "Get Ready"

The trainer must plan the details of the training session. The first step is to prepare behavioral objectives for trainees. These objectives will identify what trainees should know when the session is over and will allow the trainees to achieve expected changes in behavior. They will assist trainees in building their knowledge base as they develop skills. Behavioral objectives should define what the trainee should be able to do, how effectively he or she should do it, and when the task should be complete. For example, a behavioral objective for a training session on guest check-in might be: "The trainee will be able to perform the guest check-in procedure for a guest with a prior reservation on the PMS with 100 percent accuracy in five minutes." This focuses the trainer on the task of training a desk clerk in completing a check-in for a guest with a reservation, not a check-in for a guest without a reservation. The trainee must also have already mastered the step-by-step procedure for operating the registration module on the PMS. The goal of 100 percent accuracy in five minutes may be unrealistic to achieve during the actual training session because practice is required. The desk clerk will have to practice to achieve the speed.

In addition to preparing behavioral objectives for each training session, the trainer must know how to present the new skill to the trainee, relate the skill to other parts of the employee's job, review the presentation area and scheduling for the session, and supply ancillary materials, such as audiovisual presentation equipment and printed matter.

Presenting a skill requires the trainer to demonstrate the step-by-step procedure with the needs of the trainee in mind. This is not the time to show off how quickly the trainer can check in a guest. The trainer must be patient and consider the task from a beginner's point of view. First, the trainer must explain what the trainee is expected to learn. Next, he or she must repeat key instructions, particularly when demonstrating complicated equipment. The trainee must also be informed about where he or she can find assistance if help is needed (in printed instructions, with the user-friendly "help" program on the terminal, or from another employee). Trainers should always explain slowly and check that the trainee understands all explanations as he or she goes along.

Explaining how the skill being presented relates to other parts of the employee's job improves learning, enabling the trainee to understand how a particular task fits into the job as a whole. Trainees remember more when they understand why a task is important. Such explanations also teach new employees the importance of performing individual skills correctly; this, in turn, forms a basis for a whole series of jobs.

The trainer should also keep in mind what is best presented to trainees in various areas of the front office or hotel and at specific times of the day. Will the area be free of distractions and available for training? Is the time to present this skill better scheduled for the midmorning, early afternoon, or late evening? Training a new employee to use the PMS at the height of the morning rush almost guarantees failure. Of course, new employees will have to work under distracting and disorderly conditions, but during training, they need to be in a distraction-free, orderly area so that they can concentrate on mastering skills.

The trainer should also be sure the materials needed to deliver the session are in order. Have DVDs, CDs, and videotapes been ordered and received? Have they been previewed? Does the VCR work? Has the room been scheduled for the satellite or **PictureTel** reception, the use of telephone lines to send and receive video and audio impressions? Have **telephone initiation and reception agreements,** contracts between senders and receivers of PictureTel concerning specifications of the telephone call and who pays for the call, been set? Have the coordinates been set for the satellite dish reception? Has the printed material required for training and follow-up been duplicated? Are enough copies available? These preparations are all essential to providing a professional presentation. They allow in-depth training to take place without interruption and provide the trainee with a means for review after the session is over.

Delivery: "Show Me"

When demonstrating skills, the trainer must consider the presentation from the trainee's point of view. For example, present the skill with the trainee to your right or left so that the trainee can observe as it is presented. The trainee who cannot see the skill being presented will have a much harder time understanding and retaining the skill. If the trainee is left-handed, special presentation planning is required. Perhaps standing in front of the left-handed person for the presentation will allow him or her to reverse some of the items mentally. If the trainer is aware that the trainee is left-handed (in a right-handed operation), training time and employee errors will decrease.

The trainer must speak clearly and distinctly. Mumbling or talking too quickly will only confuse the trainee. The trainer must consider not only what he or she says but also how it is stated. If the trainer's tone of voice implies that the trainee is incompetent, he or she will alienate the trainee. Instead, the trainer should encourage the trainee's efforts, offer praise when a skill is mastered, and always be patient.

Every industry has its own jargon. Trainees should learn the jargon during training. For example, *house count, reg card, no-show, sleeper, full house, late arrival* are all terms used in the industry. Even if the trainee has had previous experience at another lodging property, it is still necessary to review these terms, to be sure that the trainee understands each term as it is used at the establishment where he or she will be working. For example, at a former job, the term *late arrivals* may have referred to guests who arrive after 9:00 P.M.; at the current establishment, however, *late arrival* may refer to anyone arriving after 4:00 P.M.

The presentation should be broken down into logical, sequential steps. The step-by-step procedure that was previously prepared will allow the front office manager to present the material in an orderly fashion. Trainees will understand such straightforward instructions as "Press this key on the keyboard to activate the registration menu" more easily than they will understand "Here is the registration menu . . . Oh, wait a minute. Let's go back to the reservation menu to see something . . ." Printed material that outlines the procedure will help the trainee to learn the skill with practice.

The trainer is encouraged to think out loud, explaining every step and its importance as the skill is demonstrated. The trainee can then logically follow the demonstration. If there are questions, the trainee will feel more comfortable asking them. This communication process also encourages the trainer, who can observe whether the trainee is picking up on the skill. The more the trainee is involved in the process, the more likely learning will occur.

After training is complete, a front office manager should watch how the employee performs on the job. If skills are performed correctly, it is a good indication that the training has been successful. Conversely, if the employee is confused or makes mistakes, it is possible that a trainer wasn't stopping to make sure that the trainee was following along. As with anything else, being a good trainer comes with experience.

METHODS OF PRESENTATION

The methods a trainer selects to train an employee will depend on the particular topic being presented. Clerical and computer skills are usually taught by demonstration and on-the-job training. Maintaining customer relations is usually handled with role-playing, videotaping and subsequent analysis of role-playing, or viewing and analysis of commercially prepared videos or cable network programs.

Skill Demonstration

In **skill demonstration**, the trainer demonstrates specific tasks required to complete a job. The trainer will perform a skill in a sequential manner and provide the trainee with an opportunity to practice, with the benefit of the trainer's being there to offer constructive feedback.

On-the-Job Training

On-the-job training is a process in which the employee observes and practices a task while performing his or her job. This method has been a mainstay of training in the hospitality industry. The planning and development of a training program and the organization of training sessions must be incorporated into on-the-job training if they are to be successful. This method trains the new employee to perform tasks on an "as-needed" basis: the employee learns a skill only when he or she has to use it on the job. With this method, however, the demands of the business come first, and training takes a backseat. A consequence of failing to follow through is that the employee is never taught the correct procedures for performing a task. When this occurs, it means that the ground on which a good training program is founded—planning, development, organization, delivery, and follow-up procedures—has been undermined. The consequence is an employee who does not have all the skills necessary to do the most efficient job.

Role-Playing

Role-playing gives the trainee an opportunity to practice a customer service situation by acting out the role before actually being required to do the job. The front office staff must often act as a sounding board for complaints and as a problem solver, even when the problem had nothing to do with the front office. Experience has taught us that, sooner or later, every front desk clerk will have a customer with a guaranteed reservation when there are no vacancies, a customer who has been given a key to a room that has not been cleaned, or a customer who must wait a long time to gain admittance to a guest room. The options available to handle such situations are very often not communicated to new employees. Only by trial and error do they learn to find other accommodations at another hotel when the hotel is overbooked, to offer a sincere apology and provide another room to the guest who has been sent to a dirty room, or to suggest a snack in the dining room or provide directions to the patio lounge to a guest who must wait an hour to get into a room. Role-playing allows the new employee to confront these situations before they actually occur. The goal is that when such situations really do occur, the employee will be able to act professionally and offer service with a smile.

If the hotel has the equipment to videotape employees, trainees can be taped during role-playing sessions. The tape can then be reviewed with the employee to provide feedback on his or her performance. The trainer can analyze the employee's eye contact, clarity of diction, talking speed, poise, manner of dress, and posture. This method is very valuable in preparing new employees to handle the stress of a busy front desk or an irate telephone caller.

Commercial Videos

Several commercially prepared videotapes are offered by the Educational Institute of the American Hotel & Lodging Association to front office managers to use in training front office employees. These tapes show customer service situations, enabling the new employee to see how other front office employees handle customer relations. The trainer should preview the tapes and prepare a list of discussion questions to be sure the employee understands the purpose of the tape and can apply on the job what he or she has seen.

Distance Learning

New inroads have been made in **distance learning,** providing educational and training opportunities anywhere, anytime, and at any place, through **Hospitality Television (HTV),** a commercial hospitality educational organization based in Louisville, Kentucky, that provides satellite broadcasts to hotels, restaurants, and food service facilities. HTV offers training segments on such topics as team building, marketing strategies, customer service, and sales building in food and beverage areas that allow hospitality managers to train their employees while on the job. This training has similar applications for front office operations. For instance, a manager can choose a particular training session and have several different shifts of employees watch it at various times throughout that week. Later on, the manager can use this information as a basis for training sessions.

Trial and Error: "Let Me Do It"

At this stage of the training process, the new employee demonstrates the skill to the trainer, who observes the initial attempt and offers constructive criticism of his or her performance. Here, the behavioral objective is useful, as the trainer can use it to determine whether the employee is performing the skill according to desired standards.

The trainee should be encouraged to perform the procedure as often as necessary to master it and meet the objective. The trainer may offer tips on how much practice other employees needed to learn this particular skill. Also, by encouraging trainees, saying things like, "Many employees must practice this five or six times before they catch on and come up to speed" will let the trainee know that instant mastery of the skill is not expected. The trainer should specify how long the trial-and-error period will last. Additional training may be required.

The step-by-step training procedure will be very helpful to the trainee in performing the skill. The parts of the skill demonstration that were confusing or fuzzy will be clarified through individual effort.

Follow-up: "Check My Progress"

The trainer must follow up with trainees after the program has been completed. This is a necessary final element in a sound training program. The trainer may develop a

Figure 12-2. *The tickler file helps the front office manager to check up on employee training status.*

Training File	Employee Name: _____
Session:	Orientation Program
Date:	12/1
Comments:	Employee very enthusiastic; possible interest in reservationist position
Follow-up:	12/5 Show rooms again.
	12/6 Meet night auditor.
Trainer:	JB
Session:	Guest Check-in
Date:	12/6
Comments:	Rated 80%, 1st attempt on 12/6
	Rated 85%, 4th attempt on 12/9
Follow-up:	12/15 Check to see if flow has picked up.
Trainer:	JB

training tickler file, a database that keeps track of training sessions and alerts trainers to important upcoming dates for each new employee, listing the name of the training session, date of the session, comments, and date for follow-up. Figure 12-2 demonstrates how this management tool can be used. This type of information can be processed in a separate database program on the PMS or maintained in an index card file.

The follow-up completes the training session because it provides the feedback the trainee needs to meet the behavioral objective. It also assures management that the skills necessary to deliver hospitality have been planned, demonstrated, practiced, and mastered.

Administering a Training Program

Planning the training program includes making provisions for administering it. Many details must be coordinated. Accurate but flexible schedules for offering training sessions must be set and maintained. Progress charts on employee training should be produced and displayed. Content preparation and duplication of training materials must be completed in a timely fashion.

You have been asked by the front office manager of a local hotel to offer some tips on training new employees at the front desk. What guidelines would you offer?

The responsibility of administering the training program rests with the front office manager. If this responsibility is delegated to an assistant in the front office or human resources department, details of administration need to be discussed with that person.

Effective training for front office positions is not easy to apply in the hospitality industry. The constant flow of people at the front desk, registrations and special events, telephone calls, emergencies, vendor calls, and other demands require the front office manager to be able to balance the needs of the moment with those of the future. However, if quality hospitality services and products are to be available, training procedures for new employees must be well planned and developed.

Cross-training

Even the most basic training programs must make provisions for developing employee skills that are useful to the organization. The unpredictable nature of business volume and employee availability in the hotel industry calls for a staff that is very versatile. **Cross-training,** which means training employees for performing multiple tasks and jobs, is key. A front office staff member who is able to perform multiple jobs has rescued many a front office manager during a crisis. The front office manager who discovers that one front desk clerk and one telephone operator are unexpectedly absent on the same day can attest to the value of cross-training. If a bellhop knows how to operate the PMS and the reservationist has been trained to use the switchboard, the day can be saved. Cross-training will get a front office manager out of many tight situations only if he or she has planned for it. Through training and maintaining accurate records that indicate which employees can handle other job responsibilities, cross-training can be vital in the hotel business. If cross-training is to be provided, this should be built into a job description and pay rate. However, before planning for cross-training, all managers must be aware that some labor unions prohibit the practice of assigning noncontractual duties, and in this case, cross-training would not be viable.

Developing a Trainer

Careful consideration should be given to selecting the individual who will train new employees. This person should have a professional attitude and provide trainees with positive attitudes and enthusiasm for their positions. The selected person should be in management or be a senior staff employee. The trainer must also be very well versed in all procedures pertaining to the employee's job and familiar with training methods.

Knowledge of performing tasks comes with practice after formal training. In a training session, there is no substitute for experience. The trainee will inevitably have specific questions about particular tasks, and the trainer must be able to answer them accurately and completely. Such answers are not always found in policy manuals and training handbooks—they are often learned only through hands-on experience.

The ability to teach is very important. The trainer must be able to plan the session in a logical, incremental fashion. It is also critical that the trainer possess good communication skills. The training session may include demonstrations, discussions, and workshops. The trainer should also be familiar with all front office equipment and know how to prepare printed instructions and how to operate audiovisual equipment. He or she should be familiar with the basic steps of the training process (discussed earlier in this chapter). Finally, trainers should try to empathize with the new employee, perhaps by recalling how inadequate they felt when they were new on the job. Patience is important, as is careful explanation. Trainers who give hurried explanations discourage questions and, as a result, end up with trainees who feel unprepared to do their jobs.

The trainer must also have a professional and positive personal view that supports the organization's goals of providing high-quality services and products, maximizing profits, and controlling costs. A professional attitude is evident in the way an employee handles his or her job responsibilities: explaining a foul-up in a room reservation, helping a guest locate another department in the hotel, participating in programs to increase room rates, and controlling operating expenses. The desk clerk whose responses to these duties are "This company always overbooks at this time of the year"; "Follow the signs on the wall to find the restaurant"; "I wouldn't help this place get higher room rates"; and "Take an extra 15 minutes on your break—this place can afford it" does not exhibit a professional attitude.

Experienced managers are well aware of the skilled senior employee who has mastered the skills involved in a job but holds a negative attitude toward the company or the management that represents the company. It is best not to enlist the assistance of such employees in training new hires. Managers are responsible for molding attitudes, teaching skills, and passing knowledge on to their employees. Exposing new employees to an unprofessional, negative attitude during training undermines the purpose of the training sessions. The trainer should represent the company and demonstrate good employer-employee relations.

Training for Empowerment

Empowerment, which was discussed in Chapter 11, needs to be applied to training employees. Empowerment, the act of delegating authority and responsibility concerning specific tasks to frontline employees, is an essential element in operating an efficient front

ront office employees must become aware of the importance of greeting international visitors, who have additional needs, such as information on currency, local geography, or local time. They may be unfamiliar with smoking regulations, operation of dining facilities, or observance of local customs. Planning a training program for greeting international visitors will include trainee role-playing and employee sharing of prior experiences concerning these topics. Sensitization of employees to the needs of international guests will go a long way in ensuring hospitality.

office. As part of the training program, a front office manager has to specify when an employee can credit a guest's folio within a certain dollar amount without the intervention of the front office manager. The trainer has to discuss this empowerment concept so that the employee knows when the dollar amount and the guest's satisfaction are in harmony. Yes, there are times when the front desk clerk may have to stretch the dollar amount because of extenuating circumstances. However, a daily review of credits that allows an opportunity for employee explanation will make empowerment work for the guest, the employee, and the front office.

According to Lawrence E. Sternberg, "contemporary management thinking is that the greatest gains in efficiency, productivity, and guest satisfaction are generated by making improvements in the system. Those improvements are most likely to occur when employees are empowered to recommend and implement changes on their own."[2]

Americans with Disabilities Act

The **Americans with Disabilities Act (ADA)** is a U.S. law enacted in 1990 that protects people with disabilities from being discriminated against when seeking accommodations and employment. There are two parts to this act: accommodations for the physically challenged and employment practices concerning hiring of the physically challenged. Because the rhetoric of the law is still being reviewed in the U.S. courts, it is important to review employment practices and implications. Not only is it important to adhere to the principles of the law, but the opportunity to employ an individual based solely on his or her talents is rewarding.

The ADA states that employers must make "reasonable accommodations" to the known disabilities of the person unless the employer demonstrates that this would constitute an "undue hardship." Section 1211 states that making "reasonable accommodations" includes making existing facilities used by employees readily accessible to people with disabilities and considering accommodations such as job

The front office manager has a difficult time in deciding which employee to hire. Mark and Tse have similar qualifications. Mark has two years' experience as a front desk clerk, but he was recently in an auto accident, which left him with a paralyzed right leg and in a wheelchair. Tse has two years' experience as a salesperson with an electronics firm and expressed interest in learning all he can in the hotel business. How would you proceed?

restructuring, part-time or modified work schedules, reassignment, and provision of readers or interpreters.[3]

Front office managers who have not worked with physically challenged individuals have to focus on the abilities of the job applicant. Well-written job descriptions should outline the specific tasks required to perform a job. These tasks provide the background to evaluate all job candidates. If there is a certain required task that is impossible for the physically challenged applicant to perform, then the front office manager should consult with the general manager on rearranging the work environment so the applicant can succeed. For example, if an applicant in a wheelchair applies for a job as a front desk clerk, initial reactions may be "It just won't work"; "There's no room for the wheelchair"; or "Too much movement is required between pieces of equipment." The front office manager should analyze how the physical work environment could be adjusted to meet the needs of this employee. Could pieces of equipment be clustered to provide easy access for an employee in a wheelchair? Could counter height be adjusted via a front desk that allows for vertical raising and lowering? All of this has to be evaluated in terms of associated financial costs. But these financial costs also have to be evaluated against the costs of recruiting employees and paying for incentive programs, the expense of new trainee mistakes, and the like.

Training a physically challenged employee is no different than training any other new employee, in most cases. All the same methods are still required. While the trainer may have to rethink the four steps involved in training, it will provide an opportunity for looking at a familiar situation and perhaps rethinking a routine process from another perspective.

The Marriott Foundation for People with Disabilities has made an exemplary effort in providing guidelines for working with handicapped persons and has developed a list of "Fears vs. Realities about Employing People with Disabilities."

The Marriott Foundation developed the list after interviewing employers and co-workers of young people with disabilities who participate in the Foundation's "Bridges . . . from school to work" program. "Bridges . . . from school to work" fosters the employment of young people with disabilities by facilitating paid internships for students with disabilities who are in their final year of high school.

Since the program's creation in 1989, Bridges has placed more than 5,000 (as of 2001) students in paid internships with over 1,300 employers (as of 2001). Eighty-seven percent of the students completing the program have received offers of continued employment. "Finding meaningful employment can be hard enough for young people, not to mention young people with disabilities," said Richard E. Marriott, chairman of the Marriott Foundation. "By working with school districts and employers, the Foundation's Bridges program is helping these young people and their employers break through the 'fear' barrier and think in terms of 'ability' versus 'disability,' "[4]

The seven "Fears vs. Realities about Employing People with Disabilities" are as follows:

1. Fear—People with disabilities need expensive accommodations.
   Reality—Often, no accommodation is needed. When necessary, most accommodations cost very little or nothing at all.

2. Fear—I'll have to do more work.
   Reality—Not true, especially when the abilities and skills of the individual are matched with the needs of the job. More effective matching up front will make disabilities largely irrelevant.

3. Fear—I'll have to supervise more.
   Reality—Most employees with disabilities do their jobs as well as, or better than, other employees in similar jobs, and often seem more motivated and dependable.

4. Fear—Turnover and absenteeism will be high.
   Reality—Studies show that employees with disabilities rate average to above average on attendance.

5. Fear—People with disabilities may not be able to do the job.
   Reality—Because people with disabilities often have to work harder to get the job they want and, therefore, appreciate what having a job means, they typically perform up to and beyond expectations. The key is effectively matching skills to job needs, focusing on ability.

6. Fear—People with disabilities need preferential treatment.
   Reality—People with disabilities neither require [n]or want to be treated any differently than employees without disabilities. What people with disabilities do need is an equal opportunity.

7. Fear—Will people with disabilities fit in?
   Reality—As part of a diverse workforce, employees with disabilities often bring unique life experiences which can be a shot in the arm for the entire workplace. Their perspectives on, and approach to their jobs can be contagious, creating a positive ripple effect.[5]

Solution to Opening Dilemma

Although an advertising agency may be part of the answer to this hotel's image problem, the real problem lies with the people who have been delivering hospitality. Determining the qualities required to provide hospitality in a hotel and screening job candidates for those qualities are essential in order to present an image that reflects the enthusiasm and professionalism of individuals who truly want to deliver hospitality.

Chapter Recap

If front office managers want to ensure that their employees deliver hospitality, they must begin by hiring people with character traits that they feel are necessary to handle front office responsibilities on a daily basis. This chapter began with a review of those character traits—extrovertedness, maturity, patience, positive attitude toward constructive criticism, and an ability to sell. Finding these qualities in job candidates can be accomplished by developing interview questions based on these traits. An orientation program is necessary to begin the process of training hospitality employees. An orientation checklist that tracks completion of the explanation of such matters as the economic position of the property in the community; an overview of the hotel's physical layout, services, and co-workers; and a tour of the property can be helpful. The orientation should also include a review of the employee handbook and policy and procedure manual. The new employee's introduction to the front office staff and general management staff would complete the orientation. Administering an orientation program provides a check on the continual planning and delivery of this personnel function.

Training practices were also discussed. The front office manager would start by identifying tasks and job management skills that are required to perform an entry-level front office job. Preparing step-by-step procedures is necessary to assist the trainer in developing a training session. The four-step training process—get ready, show me, let me do it, and check my progress—assists the trainer in working through the details of the training session. A discussion of methods of presentation included skill demonstrations, on-the-job training, role-playing, videotaping of role-playing, commercially prepared video training films, and cable training television such as Hospitality Television. Administration of the training program is an essential element to allow the continual delivery of quality hospitality.

Cross-training of employees assists the front office manager in handling the daily formation of a front office team. Employees who are cross-trained in various tasks and jobs allow the front office manager to deliver service as required.

Developing a trainer is an important part of training for hospitality. The selection of a trainer should be based on this person's knowledge of the tasks and jobs, ability to teach, and possession of a professional attitude that represents the hotel.

Empowerment was discussed as an essential element in the training process that will let hospitality flourish.

A discussion of the Americans with Disabilities Act provided the background, concepts, and applications of this important U.S. legislation. It stressed the value of providing the opportunity for physically challenged candidates to be offered employment and the benefits of hiring these candidates.

End of Chapter Questions

1. How does assessing personnel needs lead to a more efficiently managed front office?

2. How would you prepare to interview a front office job candidate? Develop a list of questions to use in interviewing an applicant for the position of front desk clerk.

3. If you are currently employed in the hospitality industry, describe the orientation you received. What would you have added to the program if you were the manager?

4. If you are currently employed in the hospitality industry, describe the training you received. How does it compare with what was recommended in this chapter?

5. Prepare a mock training session on how to check a guest out of a hotel room. Where would you begin? Incorporate the four-step training method into your training session. Have a separate group evaluate your success in delivering the training session.

6. How do you feel about the concept of using cable television as a resource for training?

7. How important is cross-training to operating a front desk?

8. If you were asked to choose a trainer, what qualities would you specify? Why are these qualities vital to the success of a training session?

9. What does empowerment mean to you? Have you ever experienced empowerment on the job? How did you feel? How did the customer feel?

10. If you had the opportunity to hire a physically chalenged job applicant as a cashier, what would you consider as a realistic assessment of the situation?

CASE STUDY 1201

Ana Chavarria, front office manager of The Times Hotel, is in the process of organizing an orientation program for the new front office staff. As part of the orientation program, she will introduce the front office equipment and the associated paperwork. Further training on each piece of equipment will be scheduled at a later time.

She begins by listing and describing the functions of all the equipment. She also spells out how each piece of equipment relates to the overall function of the front office. Since most of her front office staff are relatively new (turnover is very high), she decides she must deliver the orientation program herself.

Paolo and Brian have been hired at The Times Hotel as desk clerks. Paolo will start training on Monday at 7:00 A.M., and Brian will start on Monday at 3:00 P.M.

On Monday, a full house is going to check out by 11:15 A.M., and another full house will check in at 2:00 P.M. Ana greets Paolo at 6:45 A.M., only to find that the PMS is malfunctioning and a switchboard operator has called in sick. After attending to the crises at hand, she receives a request for 20 additional rooms for today that the marketing and sales office just received a request to fill. By 1:30 P.M., Paolo, who has helped out where he could, still has received no orientation. Ana feels that all is not lost—yet. Brian will be in at 2:45 P.M. She will keep Paolo on for another hour and deliver the orientation program to both new hires at once.

Brian shows up at 2:45 P.M. ready to go to work. Ana takes both Paolo and Brian to the coffee shop and begins a brief orientation to The Times Hotel. Returning to the front office half an hour later, she finds a long line of people waiting to check in. She tells Paolo, "Check out on the time clock; I will catch up with you tomorrow," and "Brian, go to work with the switchboard operator until we get this mess straightened out."

At 5:00 P.M., things have calmed down, and Brian is eager to learn his way around the front desk. In her desperation, Ana writes up a quick checklist and tells Brian to go to Kris, the switchboard operator, and Hoang, the front desk clerk, and have them explain how to operate the switchboard and the PMS registration module.

How does Ms. Chavarria's view of the orientation program compare to that presented in this chapter? What has she omitted from her orientation program? How realistic is her scheduling of this orientation program? Is it possible to have a senior employee conduct the orientation program? Under what circumstances? Do you think Ms. Chavarria's turnover rate has anything to do with her approach to orientation?

CASE STUDY 1202

Ana Chavarria, front office manager of The Times Hotel, is participating on a team in her professional organization—Regional Hotel Administrators (RHA)—to develop a procedure to screen candidates for front office employment that other front office managers will be able to use. A few of the team members feel this procedure will probably end up being tossed out by the general membership because interviewing has so many variables.

Ana disagrees and says that if team members look at common characteristics of their successes and failures in hiring, they may be on the road to producing something really useful. Teresa Valquez, the representative from the RHA Southern Chapter, feels this might work, but she still thinks it is an overwhelming task. Steve Harp, the representative from the RHA Western Chapter, says, "We have to do something. Our regional unemployment rate is so low that we have a hard time finding employees, so our decisions have to be good ones." It seems there is sufficient energy in the team to begin planning to produce such a document. The group has elected Ana as team leader, and she begins with a brainstorming session.

Play the roles of five team members (all front office managers) who have the goal of identifying desirable qualities in employees that reflect the ability to deliver hospitality and determining how to use that information in a screening interview.

Notes

1. The content of this section relies on ideas found in *Supervision in the Hospitality Industry*, 2d ed., Chapter 5, "Developing Job Expectations" (New York: John Wiley & Sons, 1992), by Jack Miller, Mary Porter, and Karen Eich Drummond.

2. Lawrence E. Sternberg, "Empowerment: Trust vs. Control," *Cornell Hotel and Restaurant Administration Quarterly* 33, no. 1 (February 1992): 72.

3. J. Deutsch, "Welcoming Those with Disabilities," *New York Times*, February 3, 1991, quoted in John M. Ivancevich, *Human Resource Management*, 6th ed. (Chicago: Richard D. Irwin, Inc., 1995), 75.

4. Marriott Foundation, " 'Fear of the Unknown' Invisible Barrier to Employment, says Marriott Foundation for People with Disabilities," Washington, D.C., September 30, 1997; edited July 23, 2001. Copyright Marriott Foundation for People with Disabilities.

5. Ibid.

Key Words

Americans with Disabilities Act (ADA)
cash bank
cross-training
distance learning
documentation
employee handbook
Hospitality Television (HTV)
on-the-job training
orientation checklist

orientation process
PictureTel
policy and procedure manual
role-playing
skill demonstration
telephone initiation and reception agreements
training tickler file

CHAPTER 13

Promoting In-House Sales

OPENING DILEMMA

The food and beverage manager has spent several thousand dollars on a marketing study to determine the dining needs of in-house guests. The chef has rewritten each menu to reflect those needs. However, the bell staff and front desk clerks continue to recommend the MidTown Deli around the corner as "a nice place to get something good to eat anytime of the day."

CHAPTER FOCUS POINTS

- Role of the front office in a hotel's marketing program
- Planning a point-of-sale front office

As the hospitality industry grows more sophisticated, with concern for delivering quality services, maximizing potential sales in all profit centers of the hotel is important. Additional sales to current guests—in the form of future reservations, in-house dining, room service, lounge and entertainment patronage, gift shop purchases, and the like—will assist in producing a favorable profit-and-loss statement. The front office plays a key role in promoting these sales, and the front office manager must develop and implement a plan to optimize the sales opportunities available to the front office staff. This plan includes focusing on areas for promotion, developing objectives and procedures, incentive programs, training programs for personnel, budgets, tracking systems for employee feedback, and profitability.

The Role of the Front Office in Marketing and Sales

The front office is often seen as an information source and a request center for guests and hotel employees. Front office staff may need to field questions such as: "Has the front

Figure 13-1. *Displays such as this one alert guests to in-house entertainment. (Photo courtesy of Lincoln Plaza Hotel & Conference Center, Reading, Pennsylvania.)*

office manager produced the room sales forecast yet?"; "Is there a block of rooms available for June 3–7?"; "To which rooms is this seminar group assigned?"; "Is there someone on duty who can greet and provide information for the tourist group that is arriving this afternoon?"; "Has the daily event board been set up in the lobby?"; or "Has the daily message been set on the great sign?" These are typical questions asked of the front office by other departments in the hotel. These tasks are a necessary part of any hotel's operations. However, today more than ever, hotel management demands more of the front office.

In an article published in *Canadian Hotel and Restaurant,* Avinash Narula reports:

> As market conditions have changed, the nature and importance of the functions performed by the front office have also changed from being an order-taking department to an order-generating or sales department. If one looks at the balance sheet of any hotel, it will become obvious that the major portion of the profits, on average 60 percent, come from room sales.[1]

This change in the nature of the front office's role, from a passive order taker to an active order generator, challenges the front office manager to review the front office staff's established routine. The front office manager needs to figure out the best way to direct the energies of the staff to support the efforts of the marketing and sales department.

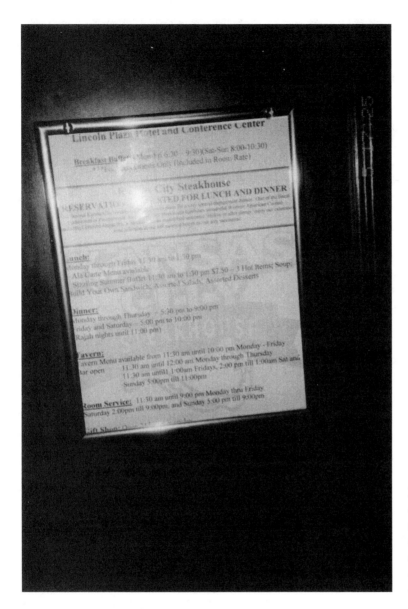

Figure 13-2. *Advertising other areas of the hotel at the front desk is an opportunity for marketing and sales to encourage profitability. (Photo courtesy of Lincoln Plaza Hotel & Conference Center, Reading, Pennsylvania.)*

The front office manager must first consider the attitudes of the front office staff. These employees have been trained and rewarded for accurate performance of clerical tasks, playing a passive role in the sales of services. How easy will it be to transform them into active salespeople, persuading guests to purchase additional reservations, services in the dining room and lounge, or products in the gift shop? At the outset, most front office managers would say this is a tall order. Established, routine habits are comfortable and

Lee Johnson is director of corporate sales at Pier 5 Hotel and Brookshire Suites at Baltimore, Maryland's Inner Harbor. After he graduated from Penn State Berks's associate degree program in Hotel, Restaurant, & Institutional Management, he worked in Reading, Pennsylvania, as a senior sales manager at the Sheraton Berkshire Hotel and as director of sales and marketing at the Riveredge.

Mr. Johnson relates the two primary ways in which he relies on the front office to do his job—communicating the needs of a group and operational issues. First, his office prepares a group résumé of an incoming group that outlines the details of paying the bill, approvals of persons allowed to bill to master accounts, and descriptions of concierge service for the front office staff as well as other details of the nature and needs of the group. His department also prepares a banquet event order that summarizes the details of a banquet, such as location, time, and menu. Second, there is a daily "coaches meeting" held early in the day with various department heads to discuss check-in and checkout patterns, storage requirements, and comment-card review.

His department also relies on the front desk staff to screen phone calls and channel them to the right person. This saves valuable time for the sales staff so they can spend their time "selling" instead of "screening." Because the front desk is on the frontline of hospitality, Mr. Johnson relies on the front desk to deliver on promises that were made in sales negotiations. He also depends on the front desk staff to load accurate details of a group registration into the computer.

Mr. Johnson encourages students of hospitality management to keep their career options open and to investigate the many opportunities both in the front and the back of the house.

---

less stressful. However, the front office manager is a member of the management team and will need to interact with members of the team as well as the employees as a plan is developed.

Planning a Point-of-Sale Front Office

To plan for a **point-of-sale front office,** a front office staff must promote other profit centers of the hotel. This planning includes setting objectives, brainstorming areas for promotion, evaluating alternatives, drawing up budgets, and developing an evaluation tool for feedback. Without a plan, a point-of-sale front office will have little chance of being successful. This plan should be developed in consultation with hotel management, department managers, and frontline employees from various departments. Team members are selected to assist in ensuring that a workable, profitable plan is developed.

Some of the goals Narula provides for the front office as it adopts a sales department attitude include the following:

- Sell rooms to guests who have not made prior reservations.
- **Upsell** [encourage a customer to consider buying a higher-priced product or

service than originally anticipated] to guests who have made prior reservations.

- Maintain the inventory of the product, i.e., the rooms.
- Convey information to guests about other products available for sale at the property, for example, food and beverages. The objective of the front office is to sell all available facilities at the hotel to the guests. Front office staff is probably the most important means of letting the guest know what services are available.
- Ensure that maximum revenue is generated from the sale of rooms by striking a balance between overbooking and a full house.
- Obtain guest feedback.[2]

If we take these goals as well as Narula's other goal of increasing communication between the front office and marketing and sales, then the planning can begin. Valuable information about the guest, essential for formulating an effective marketing strategy, can be conveyed by the front office staff. Changing market conditions require that such information be used by the marketing and sales division.[3] Based on this suggestion, we can infer that the marketing and sales department needs the vital feedback regarding customer satisfaction with the availability of hotel products and services.

Set Objectives

The ultimate goal of a sales-oriented front office is an increase in revenue from room sales, food and beverage sales, and sales in other hotel departments. A front office manager who wants to develop a plan for a point-of-sale front office must set realistic objectives. What is it that he or she wants to accomplish? Should restaurant sales be increased by 10 percent, lounge sales be increased by 15 percent, gift shop sales be increased by 20 percent, or business center sales be increased by 25 percent? Developing these objectives is carried out in consultation with the general manager and other department managers. The end result of these consultations may be one realistic objective that states: "Increase business center sales by 15 percent." This may be the objective for the next several months. A new objective would then be planned for future months.

Brainstorm Areas for Promotion

When developing a program to increase front office sales activity, the front office manager, in conjunction with other department directors and employees, should identify as specifically as possible the hotel products and services to be promoted. A typical outline of promotional areas would be as follows:

I. Front office
   A. Reservations
      1. Upselling when reservation is placed
      2. Additional reservations during registration and checkout

B. Rooms
1. Upgrading of reservation during registration
2. Promotional packages
3. Office rentals
4. Movie library rental
5. Computer games for children
C. Secretarial services
1. Photocopies
2. Dictation
3. Typing
4. Fax transmission
5. Laptop computer rental
6. In-room videocassette recorder rental
D. Personal services
1. Baby-sitting
2. Shopping
3. Bell staff assistance with luggage and equipment
4. Concierge
   a. Theater/music/art tickets
   b. General tourist information
   c. Tours of the area
   d. Airline reservations
   e. Emergency services
   f. Information on local transportation

II. Food and beverage department
A. Restaurants
1. Special menu items of the day
2. Signature menu items
3. Special pricing combinations for diners
4. Reservations
5. Gift certificates
B. Room service
1. Meals
2. Early-bird breakfast service
3. Party-service
4. Snacks
5. Beverages/alcohol
C. Banquet service
D. Lounge
1. Specials of the day
2. Special theme of the day
3. Featured entertainer
4. Promotional package

III. Gift shop
    A. Emergency items
        1. Clothing
        2. Toiletries
    B. Souvenirs
    C. Promotional sales in progress

IV. Health facilities
    A. Swimming pool
        1. Availability to guests
        2. Memberships/gift certificates
    B. Jogging paths and times of organized daily group runs
    C. Health club
        1. Availability to guests
        2. Memberships/gift certificates

Evaluate Alternatives

Planning teams have to determine which concepts produced in a brainstorming session warrant further consideration. This task is not always easy, but if the team refers to stated goals and objectives, then the job is much simpler. In this case, the overall purpose of the program would be to maximize sales by the front office staff of front office, food and beverage department, gift shop, and health facilities products and services. The team must decide which area or areas would be most profitable.

Devise Incentive Programs

During the brainstorming part of planning for a point-of-sale front office, the team should also consider supporting concepts that will play an important part in the success of a sales program—incentives. The point-of-sale plan should include an **incentive program,** which entails understanding employees' motivational concerns and developing opportunities for employees to achieve their goals. This will encourage cooperation among the frontline employees who will implement the point-of-sale plan.

The front office manager is responsible for determining how each employee is motivated. Many motivational strategies require a financial commitment by management. These costs must be included as a budget line item. When the owner can see additional sales being created as a result of these programs, the idea of sharing some of the profit is more acceptable.

Motivation, understanding employee needs and desires and developing a framework for meeting them, is an essential part of developing a point-of-sale front office. The question becomes, How does a front office manager discover what employees want? A number of theorists have explored this area; the theories of Douglas McGregor, Abraham Maslow, Elton Mayo, and Frederick Herzberg provide insight into what motivates employees to behave in desired ways (see Table 13-1). Once a front office manager knows what em-

Table 13-1. *Theories of Motivation*

McGregor	Theory X	Human beings have an inherent dislike of work.
	Theory Y	Work is as natural as play or rest.
Maslow	Satisfying individual needs	Used a triangle to indicate various levels of human needs; the most basic needs of food, clothing, and shelter must be met before higher-level needs such as self-actualization.
Mayo	Recognition of individuality in employees	Supervisors who recognize each employee as being special will achieve greater results than supervisors who treat employees as a group.
Herzberg	Hygiene factors	The only factors that lead to positive job attitudes are achievement, recognition for achievement, responsibility, interesting work, personal growth, and advancement.

ployees want, he or she must develop a means of meeting these needs in return for the desired behavior. The front office manager must work with the general manager and human resources department to develop effective programs that meet the employees' needs. In this process, effective programs are defined by the employee.

The objective of the sales incentive program for front office employees is to encourage the front office to promote products and services in various areas of the hotel, including the front office, the food and beverage department, the gift shop, and the health facilities. Each promotional area may be considered, or the front office manager might choose only a few areas, perhaps those that generate the most revenue, as incentive targets. A few examples follow:

1. *Upgrading a reservation during registration:* If a desk clerk can sell a room package costing $95 to a guest who has a reservation for a $75 room, a percentage of that $20 increase in sales will be awarded to the desk clerk.

2. *Selling a meal in the hotel's restaurant:* If a desk clerk successfully encourages a guest to patronize the hotel's restaurant, a percentage of the guest's check will be rebated to the desk clerk. At the restaurant, when the guest presents the VIP Guest Card signed by the desk clerk to the waiter or waitress and receives VIP service, the desk clerk receives the rebate.

3. *Selling room service:* If a desk clerk succeeds in convincing a guest to use room service, a percentage of the guest check is rebated to the clerk. The guest presents a VIP Guest Card signed by the desk clerk to the room service person, which proves that the sale was the result of that clerk's efforts.

Theories of Motivation

Douglas McGregor

Douglas McGregor theorized that management views employees in one of two ways. These theories are referred to as Theory X and Theory Y. Theory X states that the average human being has an inherent dislike of work and will avoid it if he or she can.[4] Theory Y states that the expenditure of physical and mental effort in work is as natural as play or rest.[5]

These two views of how human beings approach their jobs are vastly different. Theory X states that the supervisor must constantly expend direct effort to force the employee to do the job. Theory Y states that the employee brings to the job innate skills and talents that the supervisor can develop through an effective administrative and communication network. Supervisors who give serious thought to these two views will discover that sometimes they feel that one employee works best under Theory X, another employee works best under Theory Y, and yet another will require a combination of Theory X and Theory Y. This is exactly the intent of McGregor's efforts. He wants the supervisor to look at each employee as an individual who responds to a particular type of supervision.

Abraham Maslow

Abraham Maslow theorized that an individual's needs can be categorized by levels of importance, with the most basic need being the most important. The hierarchy of needs he identified was:

Fifth level: self-actualization, self-realization, and self-accomplishment
Fourth level: self-esteem and the esteem of others
Third level: love, affection, and belonging
Second level: safety (security and freedom from fear, anxiety, and chaos)
First level: physiological (food, clothing, and shelter)[6]

Maslow further theorized that individuals will strive to meet the first level of needs before even considering the second, and so on up the ladder. The physiological needs of food, clothing, and shelter must be provided for (by the paycheck) before the employee can be concerned with safety, stability, and security. The need for love cannot be a concern until the individual has satisfied his or her physiological and safety needs.

The front office manager can use Maslow's theories to identify the needs of individual employees and design programs that are appropriate. If an employee's wages do not cover his rent, he will want this physiological need for shelter met and will find a tuition-assistance program meaningless.

Through formal and informal communications, the employer should learn which needs are of utmost importance to each employee. Every employee has reached a different level in the hierarchy of needs, and it is important that supervisors recognize this. The front office manager should consider what levels of need each employee has met before attempting to provide for the next level of needs.

Elton Mayo

Experiments conducted at the Hawthorne plant of the Western Electric Company in Chicago, Illinois, from 1927 to 1932 led Elton Mayo to conclude that supervisors who recognize each employee as being special will achieve greater results than supervisors who treat employees as a group.[7] The employee who is recognized for special talents and skills will find this recognition an incentive to continue to do a good job. The front desk clerk who is recognized for being able to sell additional services in the hotel may find this rewarding; it may fit into her career progression plan. This recognition may motivate the employee to duplicate the task in other areas and at other times.

Frederick Herzberg

Frederick Herzberg contends that factors such as "supervision, interpersonal relations, physical working conditions, salary, company policies and administrative practices, benefits, and job security are actually dissatisfiers or hygiene factors. When these factors deteriorate to a level below that which the employee considers acceptable, then job dissatisfaction ensues. The factors that lead to positive job attitudes do so because they satisfy the individual's need for self-actualization in his work."[8]

According to Herzberg, minimum hygiene factors must be set to prevent a nonproductive environment. He believes that organizations that provide less than these are creating an atmosphere for dissatisfied employees. However, a truly productive organization requires improvement in the motivation factors: achievement, recognition for achievement, responsibility, interesting work, personal growth, and advancement. Herzberg questions whether, if a hotel provides five vacation days a year, that will be a motivational factor for a front desk clerk, if all other hotels in the area also offer five vacation days to their front desk clerks.[9]

Applying Motivation Theories

Applying these motivation theories is a managerial challenge for the front office manager. It offers the opportunity to review the needs of the employees to establish some framework for day-to-day contact and incentive programs.

The front office manager who reviews these motivational principles will learn that each member of his or her staff requires a different style of motivation. For example, Maslow's hierarchy of needs provides a way to determine motivational techniques based on level of need. The employee who works to be with people, the employee who is moonlighting to earn additional income for a family, and the employee who is working toward becoming a supervisor of the department will each require different motivational strategies. Someone who works to maintain social relationships is not concerned with an additional 50 cents per hour. This person might be more motivated by knowing that he or she can work the holiday shift. The person who is moonlighting would not be motivated by health insurance benefits if his or her primary job provides that benefit. An additional 50 cents per hour will motivate this person, as will the assurance of a specified number of scheduled work hours. The person working toward a supervisory position is not motivated by a better work schedule; it is the chance to be trained in all the various jobs in the front office or the opportunity to sit in on a general staff meeting that will motivate this employee.

Mayo's work on recognizing the efforts of the individual gives the front office manager the opportunity to explore the connections among communication, satisfaction, and cost savings. A few words of encouragement about continuing to do a good job, an expression of personal concern about the employee's family or close friends, or recognition of an outstanding performance will make the employee feel special, even in a large hotel.

Herzberg offers the supervisor a different approach to motivation. He claims that the chance for self-actualization—personal growth and fulfillment—improves performance. While the employee needs an adequate salary, job security, benefits, and the like, these are expected to be present in the job. Anything less than what is expected will cause dissatisfaction. Applying this theory requires the supervisor to analyze both the "hygiene factors" of a job and the opportunities for self-actualization. What is the hotel providing that should be appreciated but is not? Why doesn't the company picnic or holiday party get the group together? The answers to these questions are at the crux of employee motivation.

Training Programs for a Point-of-Sale Front Office

Another supportive concept to consider during the brainstorming part of planning is the training required to allow the successful delivery of sales techniques. It is not safe to assume that all front office personnel are born salespeople; indeed, it is probably safer to assume that no one is a born salesperson. The fear of rejection or of intruding on others when pitching a sale is far too real for many people. The front office manager must reduce the negative perception about sales by training and encouraging the staff. Otherwise, the program is doomed to failure. The objective of training is to develop and teach employees methods to use to promote various profit centers of the hotel.

The job of selling is more attractive if employees believe they are presenting opportunities to the guest. Front desk personnel who believe their suggestions are intended primarily to improve the guest's visit will feel more comfortable with the idea of selling. Confidence in selling will develop if the point-of-sale program is introduced gradually, promotion by promotion, giving employees a chance to try out various techniques. Incentive programs will strengthen employees' commitment.

Figure 13-3. *Planning the videotaping of a training session will assist in developing a unique aid. (Photo courtesy of Radisson Hotels.)*

An often overlooked but very effective practice is to allow front office employees to experience the services and products they sell. Familiarity with and appreciation for the chef's specials, the luxury of an upgraded room, the equipment in the health club, the new merchandise in the gift shop, and the personal assistance provided by the concierge enable the employee to promote these areas knowledgeably and enthusiastically.

Training concepts for each of the areas listed in the promotion target outline must be detailed. It is not sufficient simply to tell a front desk clerk to sell a higher-priced room to a guest with a reservation during registration. Employees should receive suggestions on what to say and when to say it: timing is an important part of the sales opportunity.

Using the video techniques discussed in Chapter 12, such as videotaping role-playing episodes of the desk clerks promoting hotel products and services within the hotel to the guest, is an extremely effective training procedure. These episodes do not have to be elaborate. They only need to highlight simple approaches to presenting opportunities that enhance the guest experience.

The front office manager who wants to use video as a training option needs to do a little homework first. Preparation for video training requires some thought as to just which skills and behaviors need teaching or reinforcement. Discussions with the directors of other hotel departments (marketing and sales, food and beverage) will provide a basis for promotional concepts. The front office manager will want to take an objective look

A few of the senior desk clerks have expressed distaste for having to promote future reservations at checkout. What do you think is the basis for their view? How would you handle the situation?

at the salesmanship skills of the front office staff. How outgoing are they? How adept are they at recognizing the needs and wants of the guests?

The front office manager must then decide which specific promotional areas will be highlighted in the video. At the outset, the front office manager may want to choose only one or two areas. With these promotional areas in mind, the front office manager should write a script for the role-playing episode. It should include the specific behaviors or skills that the employee is expected to master.

Producing the video will involve scheduling a time that is conducive to shooting a video. Employee work shifts will have to be adjusted accordingly. Time for rehearsal will also have to be planned. The planning will also need to take into consideration budgetary issues regarding the rental or purchase of a video camera and related equipment.

Budgeting for a Point-of-Sale Front Office

The front office manager will incur costs in operating a point-of-sale front office, including expenses involved in implementing incentive programs, producing training materials, and spending time to plan. These costs, while not meant to be overwhelming, should be anticipated. If all appropriate steps are taken, the income from increased sales should far outweigh the additional costs. This projection of sales and related expenses is very useful when deciding which marketing ideas to explore.

Feedback

Feedback on the evaluation of the success of the front office staff in promoting other areas of the hotel is an important consideration in preparing a point-of-sale front office program. How will the front office manager know if the staff is using the sales techniques in which they were trained? How does the front office manager determine how the staff feels about this program after the novelty wears off? How does the guest feel about being presented with all these alternatives? How financially successful is the program? Front office managers will not be able to tell exactly how effective this promotional strategy is, but they must make an effort to obtain as much feedback from staff and guests as possible.

This information will be very valuable in planning future promotional ideas, incentive programs, and training programs. The objective for this part of the plan could be stated as "to develop feedback systems concerning employee performance, employee attitude, guest perception, and profitability."

Guest Test

The standard **guest test** is one in which an outside person (known as the **plant**) is hired by the hotel to experience hotel services and report the findings to management. This test will enable the front office manager to evaluate the sales performance of the front desk clerk. If an unknown plant presents herself with a reservation and is greeted with "Yes, we have a reservation; please sign in," the front office manager knows that the front desk clerk is disregarding the sales procedure. The front office manager should discuss with the employee why the procedure was not followed. Perhaps the goals of the employee have shifted from a larger paycheck to a more reasonable work schedule. Or maybe he or she forgot there was a choice of incentives for the job. Perhaps too many guests were responding negatively to the promotion, and the clerk gave up trying. This information may indicate that unwanted goods or services are being targeted for promotion.

When the management of the hotel prepares the written information on the guest comment cards, questions concerning alternative promotion targets should be listed. Choices offered by hotel staff, such as upgrading reservations or information received about restaurants, gift shops, additional reservations, or other areas of the hotel, may be included. This information provides feedback as to whether the suggestions were made and how they were received. There is always the chance that guests may perceive an offer as pushy.

Financial Results

Another method for evaluating the program is reckoning the actual financial results. Were the anticipated profits outlined in the budget achieved? Use of a VIP Guest Card indicates to the restaurant manager that the guest was referred by the front desk clerk. Similar types of controls will enable management to pinpoint the origins of room reservations, gift shop purchases, and other sales. A recordkeeping system must be established to reflect the amount of money awarded to front office employees as incentives to increase sales in targeted areas. The details of this recordkeeping system must be worked out with the various department directors and the controller.

Planning a Point-of-Sale Front Office—An Example

A typical planning session for preparing a point-of-sale plan might be as follows: The front office manager has scheduled an informal meeting with the director of marketing and sales, the director of food and beverage, and a few frontline employees from each of the respective areas. Prior to the meeting, she has asked each of these members of the planning team to think of a few promotions they would like to stress in the next quarter. The food and beverage director begins the discussion by mentioning the following promotions that will run in the dining room:

1. Eat Wisely in January: Choice of entrée from the Eat Wisely lunch or dinner menu includes a free pass to the hotel health club.

2. Valentine Special in February: Dinner for two with choice of appetizer, dessert, or house wine at no charge.

3. Luncheon Special in March: Soup and salad bar free with entrée.

The director of marketing and sales wants to increase room sales during this quarter and suggests the following:

1. Increase convention bookings with I've Been There referrals.

2. Develop Weekend in the City packages.

After discussing the various promotions, all team members agree that the Eat Wisely menu and the I've Been There promotions should be the targets of front desk sales efforts. Incentives such as cash awards to front office employees for participation in Eat Wisely and I've Been There will be used. The team agrees that an in-house video should be developed to assist in training employees.

The front office manager has scheduled a time to shoot the training video, selected and scheduled a few senior employees to be the actors, arranged for rental of a video camera and related equipment, and received approval for the projected costs. After several days of writing and editing, the following script is ready:

Desk clerk: Good morning! Welcome to The Times Hotel. Did you have a pleasant trip to our city?

Guest: The airport was pretty busy, and getting a cab was unreal. Is it always this busy out here?

Desk clerk: At this time of year, there are usually several conventions in town. The city schedules extra public transportation, but sometimes delegates who arrive early get caught in the crunch. Do you have a reservation?

Guest: Yes, I'm Thomas Renton, with the Investment Group Conference. My reservation is for a room to be shared with Michael Dodson.

Desk clerk: Yes, Mr. Renton, I have a reservation for you, with departure scheduled for Friday, January 28. Mr. Dodson will be joining you tomorrow. All charges will be billed to Lawson Brothers Investment Firm. I have your room ready for you. Please sign the registration card.

Guest: Thank you. That certainly didn't take long. After that wait for a cab at the airport, I do appreciate this service.

Desk clerk: We appreciate your deciding to stay at The Times Hotel. Sir, I see from your reservation that you are on the board of directors of the Investment Group Conference. Our marketing and sales department is pleased to provide you with this special weekend pass, good for room and meals on another weekend. Perhaps you will be able to return to see how our new convention hall is progressing. It's scheduled to open this summer. The general manager told us that it will hold up to 10,000 delegates.

Guest: That sounds great. I'll have some free time later this month to use that weekend pass.

A budget for this plan will include the following revenue and expense categories. When the hard facts of projected revenues and related expenses are visualized, planning takes on a realistic dimension. Projected budgets that show how a small cash outlay can produce significant revenue are effective in convincing owners and senior management that a point-of-sale front office program is a realistic and potentially profitable concept.

TIMES HOTEL
Sales Budget—Front Office

Anticipated Increase in Sales

10 lunches @ $8 = $80/day × 365	$ 29,200
15 dinners @ $25 = $375/day × 365	136,875
5 room service @ $20 = $100/day × 365	36,500
5 room reservations @ $90 = $450/day × 365	164,250
5 gift shop referrals @ $20 = $100/day × 365	36,500
TOTAL	$403,325

Anticipated Increase in Costs

Incentives (cash awards for lunches, dinners, room service, room reservations, gift shop referrals)	$ 15,000
Management planning time	2,000
Employee overtime for producing three videos	3,000
Photocopies	300
Rental of video equipment	500
Hardware accessories	50
Purchase of VCR and monitor	500
Miscellaneous	500
Subtotal	$ 21,850

Related cost of goods sold:

$$
\text{Food} \begin{bmatrix} \text{Lunches} & 29,200 \times .35 = \$10,220 \\ \text{Dinners} & 136,875 \times .35 = 47,906 \\ \text{Room service} & 36,500 \times .35 = 12,775 \\ & \overline{\$70,901} \end{bmatrix} \qquad \$\ 70,901
$$

Room prep [5 × 365 = 1,825 × $15 = $27,375] $ 27,375

Merchandise   10,950

$109,226

TOTAL [$21,850 + $109,226 = $131,076] $131,076

ANTICIPATED PROFIT [$403,325 − $131,076 = $272,249] $272,249

The data that the team has gathered in deciding to use the two promotional concepts are useful in deciding whether these ideas will produce a profit for the efforts involved. The incentives, training, and budgets developed will support the operational efforts of the plan. Feedback mechanisms will include the standard guest test, comment cards, and monitoring of the source of sales for both promotions.

Solution to Opening Dilemma

Recommending restaurants outside of the hotel is a common occurrence in many hotels. The reason for this is that front office employees have not "bought in" to the hotel's profitability goal. It is management's responsibility to include frontline employees in developing a point-of-sale front office. In this situation, promoting the hotel's restaurant facility would become the focus of the point-of-sale. Frontline employees also should have the opportunity to decide which promotional programs will be most beneficial to the hotel and to each employee.

Chapter Recap

Front office management includes helping to promote the overall profitability of a hotel. Developing a point-of-sale front office involves developing a plan of action, which includes setting goals and objectives, brainstorming areas for promotion, evaluating alternatives, discussing supportive areas for consideration such as incentive programs and training programs, projecting anticipated revenues and related expenses in a budget, and preparing feedback mechanisms. This simple framework for planning will allow front office managers the opportunity to gain a larger perspective on the issue rather than pushing forward with desperate efforts to produce sales.

A team of managers from various departments who select a few promotional strategies and explain them to the front office staff will generate additional income. The front office manager is responsible for developing a plan for a point-of-sale front office that will provide the basis for a successful and continuous program. This plan must include goods and services to be promoted, objectives and procedures, incentive programs, training programs, budgets, and tracking systems for employee performance, guest response, and profitability. Students beginning a career in the hotel industry will find that promoting in-house sales is high on the front office manager's agenda for success.

End of Chapter Questions

1. Why is the front office often considered an extension of the marketing and sales department?

2. Is it possible to direct the energies of the front office staff to support the efforts of the marketing and sales department? Explain.

3. If you are employed at the front desk of a hotel, do you feel you are an extension of the marketing and sales department? Explain.

4. What is a point-of-sale front office?

5. How would you begin to develop a point-of-sale front office?

6. What are the major goals and objectives of a point-of-sale front office program?

7. Discuss the areas for maximizing sales opportunities outlined in the text.

8. How important are incentive programs to the operation of a point-of-sale front office? Give examples.

9. How would you go about developing a video program for training front office employees in sales techniques?

10. With a classmate, do a mock training session, using the video script in the text. Several students should observe your performance. Ask them to react to what they learned. Do you feel this is what you wanted to convey to train an employee in a point-of-sale front office? Explain your answer.

11. Why is budgeting so important to the success of this program?

12. How do well-constructed feedback systems help the point-of-sale front office program? What should they cover? What do they tell management?

13. If you are employed at a hotel front office and the hotel has a Web site, discuss feedback options on the Web site.

CASE STUDY 1301

The message at the staff meeting of The Times Hotel was loud and clear: increase sales! Ana Chavarria, front office manager, and other members of the management staff meet informally late that evening to brainstorm ideas for increasing sales for the hotel. Eric Jones, food and beverage manager, has brought along a copy of a recent hospitality publication that includes an article on increasing promotional efforts within the hotel as well as increasing marketing efforts outside the hotel. This concept gives Ana an idea: maybe the front office employees, as well as other employees in the hotel, have some ideas about promoting sales. Eric dismisses that thought, stating that management is the only group paid or trained to think. Frank Goss, director of marketing and sales, wants Ana to explain her idea further.

She feels the front office is a focal point for information for all guests. Maybe having her employees act as "internal sales agents" can increase sales in the hotel. She has a good rapport with her employees and feels they will give it a try. She is willing to put in the effort required to develop a plan.

How should Ana Chavarria proceed to develop an "internal sales agents" plan?

CASE STUDY 1302

Cynthia Restin, night auditor at The Times Hotel, has been discussing the decreased sales in the restaurant with Lorraine DeSantes, director of marketing and sales. Ms. DeSantes recently developed a plan whereby the front office staff would start promoting restaurant sales. This plan was well thought out and even included an incentive plan in which all front desk clerks (several of whom are college students) would receive dental care.

Lorraine approaches Ana Chavarria, front office manager, and asks her, "What's the problem with your staff? Why aren't they pushing restaurant sales like we planned?" Ana asks Lorraine what plan she is referring to. Lorraine reminds her of the plan to increase sales in the restaurant with the assistance of her front desk clerks. Ana says she vaguely remembers her talking about this at a staff meeting, but there wasn't any follow-up.

What parts of Lorraine DeSantes's plan were missing? How would you revise her plan for reimplementation?

Notes

1. Avinash Narula, "Boosting Sales through the Front Office," *Canadian Hotel and Restaurant* (February 1987): 37.

2. Ibid., 38.

3. Ibid.

4. Douglas McGregor, *The Human Side of Enterprise* (New York: McGraw-Hill, 1960), 33–34.

5. Ibid., 47–48.

6. Abraham H. Maslow, *Motivation and Personality,* 3d ed. (New York: Harper & Row, 1987), 15–22.

7. Elton Mayo, *The Human Problems of an Industrial Civilization* (New York: Viking, 1960).

8. Frederick Herzberg, B. Mausner, and B. B. Snyderman, *The Motivation to Work,* 2d ed. (New York: Wiley, 1967), 113–114.

9. Frederick Herzberg, personal communication with the author.

Key Words

guest test

incentive program

motivation

plant

point-of-sale front office

upsell

Security

OPENING DILEMMA

The general manager has been considering establishing an in-house security department. Security at the hotel has been outsourced in the past five years with minimal concern. However, with the recent media emphasis on the safety of both guests and employees, the general manager thinks it is time to prepare a plan of action to investigate the possibility of an in-house security department.

The act of delivering hospitality is thought to occur naturally. However, throughout this text, delivering hospitality has been discussed as a planned concept, complete with research on guests' needs, policy and program development, establishment and delivery of training programs, and follow-up information systems. Hospitality also includes providing a safe environment for guests, which requires a well-organized department to oversee and implement safety programs. The security department of a hotel is vital to delivering hospitality to guests. This department is responsible for establishing the details of the following systems:

- Guest and employee safety
- Room key security
- Fire safety systems
- Bomb threat action
- Emergency evacuation plans

- Employee safety training plans
- Emergency communication plans

These operational procedures are never really appreciated until a crime occurs or a disaster strikes a hotel. They are assumed to be in place but somehow seem to take second place to accommodating guests' more immediate needs and meeting the financial objectives of the organization.

National, state, and local safety codes and ordinances require the hotelier to provide a safe environment for guests. This chapter discusses safety awareness as it relates to the front office manager's job and how the front office helps to provide this essential service to guests.

Importance of a Security Department

The front office is a hotel's communication center; it is the vital link between the hotel management and the guest. When a guest calls for assistance because of fire, illness, theft, or any other emergency, it is usually the front office that must respond. The staff on duty at the front office cannot leave and resolve the emergency because they must continue to provide communication services and process financial transactions. The security department staff must react with speed and efficiency to serve the guest.

The security department is often regarded as a passive department, reacting only when called on. In reality, it is a very active department, setting policies, organizing programs, and delivering training programs to promote guest and employee safety. The director of security is a trained professional who must ensure that a busy hotel filled with guests, employees, and equipment stays safe. One of the department's goals is to prevent emergencies through planning. Another goal, however, is to train all hotel employees to respond to emergencies.

The importance of security to a hotel is emphasized in the following *Hotel Security Report* article by Patrick M. Murphy, CPP, director of loss prevention services at Marriott International, Inc., Washington, D.C., who reports on Marriott International's adoption of Crime Prevention through Environmental Design (CPTED) in its chain of 1,900 owned and managed properties worldwide:

> CPTED is part of a total security package. It can include anything and everything from the presence of security or loss prevention officers at a property to plans for protecting the interior, lobby, and guestrooms; exterior and parking area; and the surrounding neighborhood. Its goal is to keep the criminals from breaking into any area of the property; it accomplishes this by subtly making the environment uncomfortable for them.

The hotel priority areas in CPTED include the following.

- Building entrances—When reviewing a property we look to see that all entrances are inviting, brightly lit with no obstructing shrubbery. At night, side entrances should be restricted by use of card readers so that non-registered guests must pass through the lobby and past the main check-in desk.
- Hotel lobbies—They should be designed to be visually open, with minimal blind spots for front desk employees. Lobbies also should be designed so that persons walking through the front door must pass the front desk to reach the guestroom corridors or elevators.
- Guestrooms—These [electronic locking systems] create an environment where keys are automatically changed when a new guest checks in; locks also can be interrogated to determine the last person to enter the room.
- Guest amenities—Marriott designs its new properties with glass doors and walls to allow for maximum witness potential when providing swimming pools, exercise rooms, vending areas, and laundry facilities. Adding house phones in these areas makes it possible for guests to call for help if they feel uncomfortable or threatened by anyone.
- Exterior of the property—CPTED principles call for bright lighting at walkways and entrances. Traffic should be directed to the front of the hotel property to make would-be criminals as visible as possible. Entrances to the hotel grounds should be limited. Landscaping, such as hedges and shrubbery, can also create aesthetically pleasing barriers to promote the desired traffic and pedestrian flow.
- Parking—The preferred lighting is metal halide. High-pressure sodium should be avoided because it casts a harsh yellow light. The optimal parking lot or garage has one entrance and exit with well-marked routes of travel for both cars and pedestrians. Garages need to be as open as possible, encouraging clear lines of sight. Elevators and stairwells that lead from the garage into the hotel should terminate at the lobby level, where a transfer of elevators or a different set of stairs should be required to reach guestroom floors. Other CPTED features in the garage should include CCTV (closed-circuit television) cameras, installation of emergency call boxes, and painting the walls white to increase the luminosity of light fixtures while creating an atmosphere that is appealing to the eye.[1]

In today's **litigious society,** an environment in which consumers sue providers of products and services for not delivering those products and services according to expected operating standards, it is important to maintain a well-organized security department. The cost of a human life lost because of negligence or the financial loss due to a fire far outweighs the expense incurred in operating a security department.

The following case illustrates the expense that can result from security breaches:

Perhaps the most significant [of high-visibility hotel crimes] was the 1974 rape of singer/actress Connie Francis in a Westbury, N.Y. hotel, which resulted in a much-publicized trial culminating in a multimillion-dollar verdict against the hotel. The case is still considered the industry's "wake-up call" in terms of legal liability.[2]

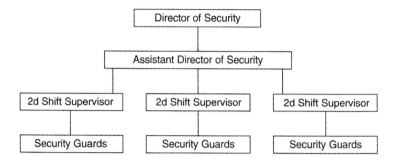

Figure 14-1. *Organization chart for a security department.*

Organization of a Security Department

The security department of a hotel is organized like any other department. At the head of the department is the director of security, who is responsible for maintaining a safe environment for guests and employees. The security director needs personnel, technology, and a budget to operate a 24-hour control system for the hotel. Depending on the size of the hotel, there may be an assistant director of security, who would act in the absence of the director and assist in the administrative and supervisory functions of the department. The director of security reports to and works with the general manager and interacts with each department director. Each of the shifts (7 A.M. to 3 P.M., 3 P.M. to 11 P.M., and 11 P.M. to 7 A.M.) is staffed with shift supervisors and security guards who are responsible for patrolling the grounds to watch the activities of the guests and employees and check on safety and security equipment. The number of people required to staff this department depends on the size of the hotel. Figure 14-1 is an organization chart of a security department for a large hotel.

Job Analysis of the Director of Security

The job analysis of a director of security outlines the administrative and supervisory tasks of this member of the management team. Active planning to ensure quick and effective reactions to problems and emergencies is the basis for successful job performance. A typical job analysis might be as follows:

8:00 A.M. Reports to the hotel.

8:05 Discusses the activities of the previous night with the parking garage attendant.

8:15 Discusses the activities of the previous night with the security shift supervisor or security guard on duty.

8:30 A.M.   Obtains notes concerning the activities of the previous night from the night auditor. Obtains the daily function sheet, which lists the events of the day.

8:40   Checks the audit report of fire and safety equipment located at the front desk.

8:45   Discusses the status of heating, ventilating, and air-conditioning equipment with the director of maintenance.

9:00   Meets with the security shift supervisor or security guards for the first shift to communicate activities and duties of the day.

9:30   Meets with the executive chef to be updated on special functions of the day and incidental activities in that department.

10:00   Meets with the housekeeper to discuss incidental activities in that department.

10:30   Returns to the office to review the daily security shift reports.

10:45   Updates the general manager on the status of security within the hotel and incidental departmental activities of importance.

11:00   Discusses the activities of the day with the restaurant manager.

11:30   Returns to the office to prepare the weekly schedule.

11:45   Responds to a call from the front office that a guest is stranded in the elevator. Assists maintenance in keeping order.

12:45 P.M.   Meets with the director of marketing and sales to determine the security needs for an upcoming high school prom and insurance executives convention.

1:00   Returns to the office to work on the budget for the next fiscal year.

1:30   Lunches with the city fire marshal to discuss plans for renovating the sprinkler system in the new wing.

2:15   Meets with the front office manager to discuss the fire emergency and bomb threat action plan for front office personnel.

2:45   Meets with the security shift supervisors for the first and second shifts to discuss operational procedures.

3:15   Conducts a fire emergency training program for fourth- and fifth-floor housekeeping personnel.

4:15   Returns to the office to revise the fire emergency and bomb threat action plan for front office personnel.

5:00 P.M.	Meets with the general manager to discuss the status of fire safety training in all departments.
5:30	Responds to a call from the front office that a guest has fallen on hotel property. Assists the guest with first aid and arranges for transportation to a medical facility. Completes an accident report. Assists the family of the guest in making arrangements for an extended stay.
6:00	Confers with maintenance personnel on the operational status of fire safety equipment.
6:15	Prepares a "to do" list for the next day.
6:30	Checks with the banquet captain on the status of guests at scheduled banquets.
6:45	Checks with the lounge manager on the status of guests.
6:55	Checks with the front office manager on the status of guest check-in.
7:00	Checks with the garage attendant for an update on activities.
7:05	Checks with the shift security supervisor for an update on patrol activities.
7:10	Departs for the day.

This job analysis shows the security director to be very involved with managing details concerning the whereabouts of people and showing a proactive concern for their safety. There is constant interaction with various department directors, employees, government officials, guests, and operational equipment. All of these job tasks describe a very responsible position in the hotel. The following comment on hotel guest safety outlines the objective of a hotel's obligations to guests:

The hotel is not the insurer of guest safety but it must exercise the care of a reasonable and prudent operator in protecting the guest. This duty extends to an innkeeper's obligation to protect guests from

- negligent or deliberate acts of hotel employees
- acts of other guests
- acts by nonguests committed on the premises.

FRONTLINE REALITIES

 A guest calls down to the front desk indicating that her son has not returned from the vending machine area. He has been gone for 25 minutes. How should the desk clerk respond? What systems need to be in place for prompt, efficient actions?

John Juliano is director of safety and security at the Royal Sonesta Hotel, Cambridge, Massachusetts. After earning a bachelor's degree in criminal justice, he worked in private security and then went on to work in hotels for the past 17 years.

Mr. Juliano feels a safe, secure environment is very important to travelers. He has been told by guests that they feel as if they are at home when they stay at the Royal Sonesta Hotel; they want to feel as safe there as they do in their own house.

He is responsible for the day-to-day operations of the security department, including scheduling and management. He investigates incidents (theft, damaged property, etc.) and acts as a liaison with the hotel's safety committee. He is involved with employee training (CPR, airborne antigens, etc.); disseminates information on state, federal, and OSHA requirements to supervisors; and helps to implement new safety procedures.

Mr. Juliano says that his job requires more in the way of management than operations. He develops protective/preventative measures to keep the hotel from experiencing security problems and liability lawsuits. He needs to be knowledgeable about local ordinances as well as state laws and OSHA regulations. Mr. Juliano's department is as involved with guest relations as the front desk, guest services, or the concierge. He has a very good relationship with the front office manager. He provides the front office manager with informational guidelines. By following these guidelines, the front office manager and staff come to develop an understanding of what to do in certain situations. While Mr. Juliano does not interact with the front office manager on a daily basis, the front office manager will call him about situations that occur and ask for his feedback. Mostly, he deals directly with guests or with a hotel employee when something goes wrong.

Failure to conform to the reasonableness standard in these three areas provides a liability risk for the hotel.[3]

The responsibilities outlined in the job description for the director of security may be assigned to other workers in some hotels due to budgetary reasons. The general manager in a limited-service property, for example, may assign the **crisis management** role of maintaining control of an emergency situation to the manager on duty. The administrative role may be shared with the assistant manager, reservations manager, and/or housekeeper.

In-House Security Departments versus Contracted Security Services

General managers of hotels must determine if operating an in-house security department is cost-effective. Operating a well-organized security department must be the primary concern when considering the hiring of an outside security firm. As the job analysis for the director of security indicated, there is more to the position than patrolling the halls and grounds of the hotel. **Foot patrol**—walking the halls, corridors, and outside property of a hotel to detect breaches of guest and employee safety—is an important feature of security, but it is a preventive measure, not an active means of organizing security. However, in some situations, a general manager will be forced, for economic reasons, to consider the purchase of an outside service. Administrative and planning procedures for operating a security department are delegated to other department heads. The cost consideration must be weighed against planning and coordinating a safe environment for the guest and employee.

The hourly rate charged by the security service for **escort service,** having a uniformed security guard escort a hotel employee to a financial institution to make bank deposits; for performing regular hall patrol; and for maintaining surveillance of the parking garage may seem very attractive compared to the annual salaries and administrative overhead incurred by operating an in-house security department 24 hours a day. But more than cost must be considered. Who will work with the other department directors to establish fire safety and security procedures? Who will plan and deliver fire safety and security training sessions? Who will monitor fire safety devices? Who will work with city officials in interpreting fire and safety codes? Who will update management on the latest technology to ensure a safe environment? These and other questions will have to be answered if owners and management are committed to the concept of security.

If an outside security service is hired, the role of maintaining security is parceled out to the various department directors. The director of maintenance will operate the fire safety and security equipment, maintain operating records of fire safety equipment and elevators, and react to hazardous situations. The general manager will, if time permits, establish a safety committee that reacts to government guidelines and potential hazards. Each department director will, if time permits, establish security guidelines based on previous personal experiences. Under such circumstances, safety and security become low priorities. The lack of coordination almost guarantees disaster when an emergency strikes.

In an article concerning hotel security, a director of security reports the following:

"Creating the biggest security problems in the past several years are liability, risk management and loss control," according to Mark Beaudry, director of security at the Westin Boston. "Crime prevention education and training have moved to the forefront in order to prevent lawsuits when possible, especially when administrative work from litigation can take up almost one-third of a security director's time. Directors of security have been assigned new duties such as risk management. They must be the liaison with the police in defending the hotel and also must know civil and criminal laws," said Beaudry.[4]

Meeting the challenges of providing security for guests and employees requires a full-time approach. Part-time efforts to control crises in a hotel may be shortsighted. The following story shows the consequences of not providing adequate security.

Figure 14-2. *The security department in a hotel works closely with the front office manager. (Photo courtesy of Pinkerton Security and Investigation Services.)*

The verdict against Hilton Hotels Corp. in the Tailhook case could have far-reaching implications concerning hotel liabilities in providing security for guests, according to hospitality legal experts. In this case, former Navy Lt. Paula Coughlin sued Hilton for failing to provide adequate security during the Tailhook Association convention at the Las Vegas Hilton in 1991. Jurors awarded Coughlin $1.7 million in compensatory damages and $5 million in punitive damages. Hilton claimed that three security guards were adequate for the 5,000 people at the event.[5]

Room Key Security

One of the responsibilities of the director of security is to establish and maintain a **room key control system,** an administrative procedure that authorizes certain personnel and registered guests to have access to keys. One court found that "as a general proposition, a guest has an expectation of privacy in his or her room and a hotel has an affirmative duty not to allow unregistered guests, unauthorized employees, and third parties to gain access to a guest's room."[6]

Although issuing and filing keys are duties of front office employees, there is more to room key control. Room locks and keys are one of the single most effective ways to ensure guest safety. According to an article in *Hotel & Motel Management*:

> To minimize your risk and the potential for costly lawsuits, it is wise to invest in electronic-locking systems. . . . And franchise hotel chains are responding to that call in droves. Most refer to such franchise-hotel chain mandates as the "three-year window," where operators must implement improved locking systems or risk losing their flags.
>
> According to Ray Ellis, a former operations consultant to the American Hotel & Motel Association, January 1, 1997, is the hallmark date for Sheraton, Hilton Hotels, and Holiday Inn to implement electronic-locking systems. He added that Quality Inns, Hotels & Suites, Days Inns of America, Super 8 Motels and Howard Johnson Franchise Systems are planning similar mandates for their properties.[7]

Usually one of two different lock systems is used—the hard-key system or the electronic key system. **Hard-key systems** consist of the traditional large key that fits into a keyhole in a lock; preset tumblers inside the lock are turned by the designated key. The **electronic key system** is composed of:

> battery-powered or, less frequently, hardwired locks, a host computer and terminals, keypuncher, and special entry cards which are used as keys. The host computer generates the combinations for the locks, cancels the old ones and keeps track of master keying systems. The front desk staff uses at least one computer terminal to register the guest and an accompanying keypuncher to produce the card. An electronic locking system allows the hotel to issue a "fresh" key to each guest. When the guest inserts his or her key into the door, the lock's intelligent microchip scans the combination punched on the key and accepts it as the new, valid combination for the door, registering all previous combinations unacceptable.[8]

Another version of the electronic key is the **smart card,** an electronic device with a computer chip that allows a hotel guest or an employee access to a designated area, tracking, and debit-card capabilities for the guest. Bruce Adams reports the following update on smart cards:

> One of those enhancements is that keeping track of room access by hotel management has never been easier. Employees have smartcards that grant them access to different levels of security. The cards track what level of key was used, who was there, and creates an audit trail that is easy to manage.
>
> Beyond state-of-the-art locking and tracking capability, the smartcards serve as guest identification cards, which include the guest's name and dates of stay at Por-

tofino Bay Hotel at Universal Studios theme park. "Their card functions as an ID card, which gives them special privileges at the theme park," [said Michael] Sansbury [regional vice president for Loews Hotels]. "Some of those benefits include front-of-line privileges at rides and events, early admission to the park and priority seating in restaurants. The smart cards also serve as charge cards at the hotel and park." "The smartcard is linked to the guest account in the hotel," Sansbury said. "The credit limit in the hotel is transmitted to the smartcard. Merchants at any shop or restaurant at Universal Studios can swipe the smartcard the same way they swipe a credit card. It works the same way as a credit card," [reports Sansbury]. "If they lose their smartcard, it is very easy to invalidate," Sansbury said.[9]

The hard-key system is less expensive at the time of initial purchase. However, over the long run, the purchase of additional keys and the cost of rekeying locks need to be considered. Also, reissuing the same keys to guest after guest presents a security problem. Often, the guest fails to return the key at the time of checkout. If a careless guest discards a room key or a criminal steals a key, guest safety is jeopardized. If regular maintenance and rekeying lock tumblers are not part of the preventive maintenance plan (and budget), guest security is compromised.

The electronic key system and smart card can be used for guest rooms as well as other areas of the hotel; they are an investment in guest security and safety. As each new guest registers, a fresh plastic key is produced. The new combination for the guest room lock will respond only to the new guest room key. This procedure almost guarantees guest safety. The initial investment in this type of system has to be evaluated against overall maintenance and replacement costs of a hard-key system and increased guest security.

Electronic key access is one of many alternatives from which facility managers can choose. The system includes an electronically coded key and door controllers that can be easily programmed to recognize one or more codes. Since the electronic keys are assigned codes from one of several billion possible combinations, they are virtually impossible to duplicate.

High-end electronic access control systems can be equipped with numerous . . . features . . . [such as] recording who entered an area and at what time . . . [and] link this information with a central computer allowing facility managers to provide reports on the activities of thousands of users through thousands of doors. These reports are extremely helpful during the investigation phase of a crime incident. Access control systems also can be equipped with a panic alert that allows the individual to send a distress signal in the event they are being coerced to open the door.[10]

While the hard-key system is the traditional method that hotels have been using for many years, the cumbersome and costly maintenance of that system indicates that it should be replaced with advanced technology. It will be a slow process but will greatly improve guest, employee, and inventory safety. The economies of scale will make the electronic key system an affordable necessity.

Fire Safety

Hearing someone shout "Fire!" will panic anyone who is unprepared to deal with this dangerous situation. Well-orchestrated safety procedures that are well managed at the onset of a fire can have lifesaving implications for guests and employees. The front office manager and the director of security must develop effective fire safety and evacuation plans, as well as training programs for employees, to ensure their effectiveness.

Fire Code General Requirements

Fire safety plans begin with the fire safety codes of the municipality where the hotel is located. These codes will stipulate construction materials, interior design fabrics, entrance and exit requirements, space limitations, smoke alarm installation and maintenance, sprinkler system installation and maintenance, fire drill testing, fire alarm operation and maintenance, and the like. These extensive codes were developed to ensure guest safety. They may require extra financial investment, but they are intended to protect the guest and the occupants of the building.

Guest Expectations

Hotel guests expect, either consciously or unconsciously, to find a safe environment during their visit. Some guests may ask for a room on the lower levels or inquire if the rooms have smoke alarms. However, most guests are concerned about other matters and will not ask about fire safety procedures. When the guest settles into a guest room, he or she may give a passing glance at the fire evacuation procedure posted behind the door. Some guests may even count the number of doors to the nearest exit. Is this enough? Will human lives be in jeopardy because guests' other, more pressing concerns have caused them to place their safety in the hands of the management and employees of the hotel?

Fire Safety Plan

The front office manager who wants to take active measures to ensure guest safety must develop a simple fire safety plan, communicate it to employees and guests, and train employees and guests to handle a stressful situation. This will include the following commonsense concepts:

1. Equip all guest rooms and public areas with smoke detectors that are tied in to a central communications area.

Table 14-1. *Maintenance Records for Smoke Detector Tests*

401	12/1	OK	JB inspector	1/10	OK	JB inspector
402	12/1	OK	JB inspector	1/10	OK	JB inspector
403	12/1	bat. repl.	JB inspector	1/10	OK	JB inspector
404	12/2	OK	JB inspector	1/10	OK	JB inspector
405	12/2	OK	JB inspector	1/10	OK	JB inspector
406	12/2	OK	JB inspector	1/10	OK	JB inspector
407	12/2	OK	JB inspector	1/10	OK	JB inspector
408	12/2	OK	JB inspector	1/13	OK	JB inspector
409	12/2	OK	JB inspector	1/13	OK	JB inspector
410	12/2	OK	JB inspector	1/13	OK	JB inspector
411	12/2	OK	JB inspector	1/13	OK	JB inspector
412	12/2	OK	JB inspector	1/13	OK	JB inspector
413	12/3	bat. repl.	JB inspector	1/15	OK	JB inspector
414	12/3	bat. repl.	JB inspector	1/15	OK	JB inspector
415	12/3	OK	JB inspector	1/15	OK	JB inspector

JB = inspector's initials
bat. repl. = batteries replaced

2. Regularly test and maintain smoke detectors; keep up-to-date records of the tests, as shown in Table 14-1.

3. Install, maintain, and test fire alarms as required by local fire code regulations; again, keep up-to-date records of the tests, as shown in Table 14-2.

4. Constantly monitor smoke detectors and fire alarm systems (preferably at the front desk).

5. Prepare and post floor plans showing fire exit locations by area—public areas, work areas, and guest-room areas (see Figures 14-3 and 14-4).

6. Provide instructions for employees and guests on where the nearest fire extinguishers and fire alarms are located, as well as procedures for building evacuation and fire safety guidelines (Figure 14-5).

7. Develop a fire action communication procedure for front office personnel.

Table 14-2. *Maintenance Records for Fire Alarm Tests*

Location	Date	Status	
Floor 1, station A	4/10	OK	JB inspector
Floor 1, station B	4/10	OK	JB inspector
Floor 2, station A	4/10	OK	JB inspector
Floor 2, station B	4/10	OK	JB inspector
Floor 3, station A	4/10	OK	JB inspector
Floor 3, station B	4/10	OK	JB inspector
Floor 4, station A	4/10	OK	JB inspector
Floor 4, station B	4/10	OK	JB inspector
Floor 5, station A	4/10	no sound; repaired 4/10	JB inspector
Floor 5, station B	4/10	no sound; repaired 4/10	JB inspector
Floor 6, station A	4/10	OK	JB inspector
Floor 6, station B	4/10	OK	JB inspector
Kitchen	4/10	OK	JB inspector
Bakery	4/10	OK	JB inspector
Banquet A	4/10	OK	JB inspector
Banquet B	4/10	OK	JB inspector
Lounge	4/10	OK	JB inspector
Lobby	4/10	OK	JB inspector
Laundry	4/10	OK	JB inspector
Gift shop	4/10	OK	JB inspector

Employee Training in Fire Safety

Providing training programs for employees on the locations of the fire exits, fire extinguishers, and fire alarms and on methods of building evacuation will greatly increase the chances that all occupants will escape the building safely when necessary. After new and current employees have been taught the locations of fire exits, extinguishers, and alarms throughout the building, supervisors can spot-check the effectiveness of the training with random questions such as: "Where is the nearest fire exit when you are cleaning room 707? Where is the nearest fire extinguisher when you are in the bakery? Where is the nearest fire alarm when you are in the laundry?" These simple questions, repeated often enough, impress employees with the importance of fire safety.

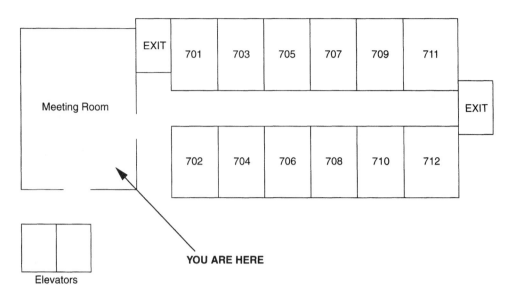

Figure 14-3. *Well-marked exits from public areas are very important.*

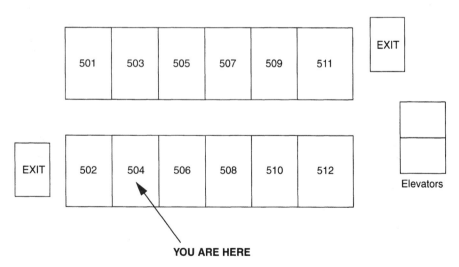

Figure 14-4. *Signs such as this one are mounted on the backs of doors to guest rooms to provide fire safety information for guests.*

Figure 14-5. *Hotel fire safety procedures should be displayed in guest rooms.*

1. When you check into any hotel or motel, ask for a copy of the fire procedures plan. If they do not have one, ask why.

2. Check to see if there is a smoke detector in your room. If there isn't any, ask for a room that has one.

3. Familiarize yourself with the locations of the fire exits and count the number of doors from your room to the nearest fire exit. (If the corridor is smoky, you may not be able to see the exit, but you can feel your way along the floor.)

4. Get into the habit of keeping your key in the same place every time you stay at a motel or hotel so that you'll always know exactly where it is. Then, if you have to leave your room, be sure to take your key with you. (If you cannot reach the exit, you may have to return to your room because of fire or smoke in the hallway.)

5. If you wake up and find your room is beginning to fill with smoke, grab your key, roll off the bed, and head for the door on your hands and knees. You'll want to save your eyes and lungs as long as possible, and the air five or six feet up may be filled with odorless carbon monoxide.

6. Before leaving your room, feel the door with the palm of your hand. If it is hot, or even warm, do not open it! If it is not warm, slowly open it a crack, with the palm of your hand still on the door (in case you have to slam it shut), and peek into the hallway to see what's happening.

7. If the coast is clear, crawl into the hallway, feeling your way along the exit side of the wall. It's easy to get lost or disoriented in smoke. Count the doors as you go.

8. Do not use an elevator as a fire exit. Smoke, heat, and fire may put it out of operation.

9. When you reach the exit, walk down the stairs to the first floor. (Exit doors are locked on the stairwell side, so you cannot enter any other floor.)

10. If you encounter smoke in the stairwell on the way down, the smoke may be "stacking" on the floors under it, and the stairwell would be impassable. Do not try to run through it. Turn around and go up to the roof.

11. When you reach the roof, open the door and leave it open so the stairwell can vent itself. Find the windward side of the building so you won't be caught up in the smoke. Then, have a seat and wait for the firefighters to find you.

12. If you cannot get out of your room safely, fill the bathtub or sink with water. Soak towels and stuff them under the door and between the cracks to keep the smoke out. With your ice bucket, bail water onto the door to keep it cool. If the walls are hot, bail water on them too. Wet your mattress and put it up against the door. Keep everything wet.

13. If smoke does begin to seep into your room, open the window. (Keep the window closed if there is no smoke. There may be smoke outside.) If you see fire through the window, pull the drapes down so that they will not catch fire. Also, wet a handkerchief or washcloth and breathe through it.

14. DO NOT JUMP unless you are certain of injury if you stay in your room *one minute longer*. Most people hurt themselves jumping, even from the second floor; from the third floor, quite severely. If you're higher than the third floor, chances are you will not survive the fall. You would be better off fighting the fire in your room.

Source: National Safety Council. Courtesy of Knights Inn. Cardinal Industries, Inc., Reynoldsburg. OH © 1989 Cardinal Lodging Group, Inc., management company for Knights Inns and Arborgate Inns.

Local fire departments or the director of security can train employees to use fire extinguishers. These informal training sessions should include operational procedures and information on applying the appropriate type of fire extinguisher. The time to start reading directions is not during the fire. These training sessions will give employees confidence in their ability to handle an emergency.

Guest Instruction in Fire Safety

Often, instructing guests on fire safety is overlooked. They are at the hotel for a relaxing, enjoyable visit. But fire can strike at any time, even during relaxing, enjoyable visits. Inform each guest that all rooms are equipped with smoke detectors, that the nearest fire exit from any room is, at the most, four doors to the right of the room, that a fire extinguisher is located next to the elevator on each floor, and that a fire can be reported by dialing "0" for the hotel operator. Guests will appreciate that the hotel cares about their well-being and that the hotel has taken every precaution to ensure that the equipment is available and in working order. Management may want to encourage guests to read the fire evacuation guidelines posted on the door of the guest room by offering enticing promotions. For example, on registering, the guest is informed of a special coupon attached to the fire evacuation plan located on the door. This coupon may be redeemed for a two-for-one breakfast special, a free cover charge in the lounge, a free morning newspaper, a discount in the gift shop, or some other incentive.

Accommodations for guests who are physically challenged should also be a concern for hotel managers. **Visual alarm systems,** flashing lights that indicate a fire or other emergency in a hotel room, should be installed to alert hearing-impaired guests. A report of the locations of physically challenged guests should be easy to retrieve in case of an emergency.

Fire Action Communication Procedure

The front office employees will have to take the lead in controlling the panic that may arise when a fire strikes. The fire communications training program developed by the front office manager must be taught to all front office personnel. If the fire strikes during the middle of the day, more than one person will probably be available to assist in maintaining control of the situation. But if the disaster occurs at 10:30 P.M., there may be only one person on duty to orchestrate communications.

The communications procedure begins when a guest or an employee calls the switchboard to report a fire. Unfortunately, in many cases, some time has already been wasted in attempts to extinguish the fire. Seconds are important in reporting the fire to the local fire company. At some properties, the fire company is immediately notified via the interface of the hotel's fire alarm with the municipal or private monitoring station. But front office personnel should never assume that the fire company has been notified and should immediately call the fire station to report the fire. The call may duplicate an earlier report, but it is better to have two notifications than none.

A guest calls the front desk and reports that an iron has overheated and set the bedspread on fire. What action should the front desk clerk initiate? What previous fire safety planning would ensure prompt, efficient action?

After the fire has been reported, security and management should be alerted. Guest and employee evacuation procedures must be initiated and organized. Prior established procedures stipulating who should be informed and in what manner, as well as who is to assist the guests and employees in evacuating, will result in an efficient evacuation. The front desk clerk will have to produce a list of occupied guest rooms immediately. The rooms located on the floor where the fire is reported and the rooms located on the floors immediately above and below the fire room will be of vital importance to firefighters and volunteers who assist in the evacuation.

On arrival, firefighters will immediately report to the front desk. They will want to know where the fire is located and what guest rooms are occupied. Duplicate copies of the list of rooms occupied and any special notes on whether the occupants are children or physically challenged will aid in the rescue efforts.

Front office personnel must remain calm throughout the ordeal. The switchboard will be active, with calls from inside and outside the hotel. Requests for information from the fire emergency crew and first-aid and rescue squad will be mixed with phone calls from the media and persons related to hotel guests. Switchboard operators should keep phone calls brief so the phone lines are open.

Security should not be forgotten during crises. Some people will take advantage of the confusion to loot and pilfer. Cash drawers and other documents should be secured.

Each hotel must develop its own communications procedure for a fire. Each plan will vary, based on the strengths of the employees in the front office. Training the staff with fire drills will aid all employees in handling the emergency; everyone must be part of the drill, no matter how calmly they may react to ordinary crises. Holding fire drills on each of the various shifts gives employees practice and is worth the effort.

The following stories highlight the importance of being prepared to react in an emergency situation:

[James T. Davidson, executive director, Training Services, Educational Institute] was working as a front desk clerk in Bermuda during the arson riots in 1976. Rioters set fire to the top floor of the hotel. [The hotel's] communications tower was on the roof and [it] lost communications within moments, even though [the hotel's management] thought [that it] had a fool-proof system. Several people were killed, including some guests who tried to use the elevator—it took them straight to the blaze. There was an emergency plan for evacuating guests, but no real plan for getting them a safe distance away from the burning building.

Years later, [he] was general manager of a property on the Seychelles Islands during two attempted coups d'etat. A total curfew was imposed during both coup attempts, but the second was worse because it happened during the middle of the night when [the] staff was limited. For six days, [the hotel] made do with a staff of 13 for 300 guests and lived off the food that was at the hotel. The 13 staff members worked in just about every department at one time or another. [They] enlisted guests to help keep the hotel running, and most were glad to pitch in.

Each incident taught [him] the importance of planning and communications, and how essential it is to have regular emergency procedure drills.[11]

Emergency Communication

There are times when guests and employees must evacuate a building in a nonemergency situation. Although it is imperative that the building be emptied, evacuation is not as urgent as it is during a fire. Examples of such situations include a bomb threat, a fire in an adjacent building, a gas leak, or an electrical power outage. When these situations occur, an emergency communication system must be in place to ensure an efficient evacuation.

The director of security, in conjunction with the front office manager and civil authorities, should develop a plan for all departments. The role of the front office is essential in directing communications with guests and employees. The front office staff is responsible for alerting employees and guests that an emergency situation exists. The emergency communication plan should establish a **communications hierarchy,** which is a listing of the order in which management personnel may be called on to take charge; emphasize cooperation between the hotel and civil authorities; and provide training.

The 1993 bombing of the World Trade Center provides a cautionary lesson in preparedness:

When disaster strikes, inadequate or incomplete preparation becomes painfully evident—and costly. These hard lessons became clear in the immediate aftermath of the February 26, 1993 bombing of New York's World Trade Center, when the staff of the adjacent Vista Hotel reacted heroically to a very daunting situation. Loss of the facility's main telephone switch made it impossible to communicate with management and arrange emergency recovery services. Cellular phones could have fetched thousands of dollars apiece that day. Drawings illustrating how the hotel was built were not easily accessible, creating confusion among the rescue teams.[12]

Here is another incident of a more urgent emergency nature:

A natural gas explosion tore through the property's [Embassy Suites Outdoor World at Dallas/Ft. Worth International Airport] swimming pool maintenance room at 6:25 P.M., August 6, 2000, just four days after the hotel's opening, forcing guests to flee the property. Rapid response by the hotel's staff, led by GM Bill Bretches, as well as police, firefighters and paramedics, helped clear the property swiftly and minimize injuries. Two hundred fifteen of the hotel's 329 guest suites were occupied at the time of the explosion, with many of the guests in the property's atrium for the evening reception.

Guests were brought to the hotel's parking lot, where they were given water and clothing provided by Bass Pro Shops Outdoor World, a part of the hotel complex. Staff accounted for guests by matching names with the registration list. All guests accompanied by Embassy Suites staff, were relocated within 90 minutes to nearby hotels.[13]

The following discussion of planning for effective emergency communication outlines the most important features of such a plan.

Developing the Emergency Communication Plan

The emergency communication plan is developed in cooperation with the director of security, the front office manager, and local civil authorities. These individuals are responsible for developing a plan that will be used in the event of an impending life-threatening emergency and will also include considerations for training staff and employees.

EMERGENCY COMMUNICATIONS MANAGER ON DUTY

The job description of each management position will include a task entitled "emergency communications manager on duty." This duty requires the person to act as the liaison between the hotel and the civil authorities. Each member of the management staff will receive adequate training in the responsibilities of the job.

The role of emergency communications manager on duty is assumed in the following order:

General manager

Assistant general manager

Director of security

Director of maintenance

Food and beverage manager

Banquet manager

Restaurant manager

Director of marketing and sales

Controller

Housekeeper

Front office manager

Front desk clerk on duty

Night auditor

RESPONSIBILITIES OF THE FRONT OFFICE

On receipt of a call informing the hotel that the guests and employees are in danger, these procedures are to be followed (Figure 14-6):

Figure 14-6. *The switchboard operator plays a pivotal role in an emergency communication plan. (Photo courtesy of Northern Telecom.)*

1. Remain calm. Write down the name, phone number, affiliation, and location of the person making the call.

2. Immediately alert the emergency communications manager on duty to the impending danger. If main telephone service to the hotel has been inactivated, use a cellular phone.

3. Inform the front desk clerk of the impending danger. Produce a room list of all registered guests in the hotel. Produce a list of all social functions that are in progress.

4. Alert the emergency communications leaders on duty in each hotel department. These people will report to the front office immediately. An emergency action meeting will be held with the emergency communications manager on duty. The lists of registered guests and social functions in progress will assist in the evacuation.

5. The emergency communications manager on duty will advise you which authorities should be alerted.

   - Police department: 000–0000
   - Fire department: 000–0000
   - Bomb squad: 000–0000
   - Electric company: 000–0000
   - Gas company: 000–0000
   - Water company: 000–0000
   - Rescue squad: 000–0000
   - Red Cross: 000–0000
   - Owner of hotel: 000–0000
   - General manager: 000–0000

6. Respond to phone inquiries as directed by the emergency communications manager on duty.

7. Remain at the front office to manage emergency communications until directed to evacuate by the emergency communications manager on duty.

RESPONSIBILITIES OF OTHER HOTEL DEPARTMENTS

Delegating the task of emergency communications leader on duty to other responsible members of a department requires the following considerations:

- Each department director will develop a hierarchy of positions to assume the responsibility of emergency communications leader.
- Each emergency communications leader on duty will receive adequate training in the responsibilities of this job duty.
- Upon receiving information indicating that the hotel guests and employees are in immediate danger, immediately relay the information to the front office—dial "0."

John Juliano, the director of safety and security at the Royal Sonesta Hotel in Cambridge, Massachusetts, mentioned his participation in the Security Directors' Network, which consists of a group of hotels that gather and share information on security issues. For instance, if an incident occurs at the Royal Sonesta Hotel involving a nonpaying guest, he fills out a report and faxes it to the director of security at the Boston Marriott Copley Place, who then faxes the information to 30–35 other hotels in the greater Boston area. This is especially helpful when a person goes from hotel to hotel causing problems. For example, several years ago in Boston, a man went to several hotels and set off fire alarms (he actually set a fire at one hotel); when the unsuspecting and panicked guests ran from their rooms, he would enter and steal the guests' possessions. The network was helpful in tracking his actions. However, nine of ten times when he receives a request for information about a specific person, Mr. Juliano will have no information to supply.

- All emergency communications leaders on duty are to report to the front office for an emergency communications meeting. Directions will be given for assisting guests and employees to evacuate.
- Employees on duty will take direction from the emergency communications leaders on duty on assisting guests and employees in evacuating the hotel.

TRAINING

The emergency communications managers on duty should receive ten or more hours of training in leading a crisis situation. This training must be documented, with two hours of refresher training every year.

Current employees will receive two hours of training in emergency evacuation procedures. New employees will receive training in emergency evacuation at the time of orientation. Refresher training, two hours every year, is required of all employees.

Employee Safety Programs

The hospitality industry is rife with opportunities for employee accidents. Behind the scenes are many people crowded into small work areas, busy preparing food and beverages and performing other services for the guests. The employees who are most in danger include those whose equipment is in need of repair or who work in areas that are too small or who depend on other employees who are not attentive to the job at hand. The front of the house also provides opportunities for accidents. Employees and guests must use public areas that may be overcrowded or worn from continual use. The following information on hotel law provides insight into an innkeeper's responsibility:

The innkeeper must periodically inspect the facility to discover hidden or latent defects and then to remove or repair those defects. During the time prior to repair the innkeeper has a duty to warn the guests about the existence and location of the dangers.[14]

How does hotel management begin to develop guidelines for employee safety?

Employee Safety Committee

The best way to begin is to establish a **safety committee,** a group of frontline employees and supervisors who discuss safety issues concerning guests and employees. Frontline employees know the details of day-to-day hazards. They deal with the faulty equipment, traverse the crowded banquet rooms, work next to one another in a poorly laid-out kitchen, process soiled laundry, push carts through busy public corridors, and hear guest complaints during checkout. Moreover, these people make up part of the group that employee safety procedures are supposed to protect. Why not give them an opportunity to make their environment better? Although some employees do not want this responsibility, other employees will welcome this opportunity. With positive results, there may be a few more volunteers the next time. Management is a necessary part of the committee, not only because it is used to carrying out long-range plans but because it supplies the clout and support needed to implement the procedures.

COMPOSITION AND ACTIVITIES OF THE SAFETY COMMITTEE

The safety committee should include representatives from all departments in the hotel. If this is not possible, then co-committees for each shift might be an option. Management should convey the importance of the safety committee. Every comment received from the members is worthwhile and should be noted in the minutes of the meeting (Figure 14-7). Checklists with assignments for fact-finding tours, to be reported on at the next meeting, should be distributed to begin the process. The meetings should not be mere formalities, quickly conducted with little thought about their content. At each meeting, the minutes of the previous meeting should be read, and progress made in accomplishing goals should be reported. Members will want to see that the tiles in the laundry room, the leak in the stack steamer, and the worn rug in the lobby have been repaired or replaced as suggested.

Department Supervisors Responsibility

Each department director must encourage a safety-conscious attitude. Management members can set an example by following safety procedures themselves when operating equipment and by scheduling adequate staff during busy time periods and following up on requests for repairs. If employees know that you place safety first, they will also adopt that attitude.

Figure 14-7. *Minutes from a safety meeting keep participants on track.*

Hotel Safety Committee Minutes 5/19

Members present:

A. Johnson, Housekeeping	T. Hopewell, Food and Beverage Manager
S. Thomas, Housekeeping	J. Harper, Banquets
L. Retter, Food Production	T. Senton, Restaurant
K. Wotson, Food Production	M. Povik, Lounge
M. Benssinger, Front Desk	A. Smith, Maintenance
V. Howe, Front Desk	J. Hanley, Maintenance
F. Black, Gift Shop	D. Frank, Parking Garage
B. Lacey, Director of Security	A. Gricki, Accounting

1. The minutes from the 4/12 meeting were read. M. Benssinger noted that the minutes stated that Johnson Rug Inc. was in the process of repairing the rug in the lobby. This was not the case at all. No one to her knowledge has repaired the seams on the rug. The minutes were corrected.

2. B. Lacey gave an update regarding the progress on suggestions for improving safety, compiled at the 3/01 meeting.
   - The safety valves on the steam pressure equipment in the kitchen have all been replaced.
   - The electrical cords on the vacuum cleaners on the 11th and 15th floors have been repaired.
   - Five of the kitchen employees have been enrolled in a sanitation correspondence course. T. Hopewell is monitoring their progress.
   - The basement has been cleaned up, and excess trash has been removed. Old furniture that was stored near the heating plant has been removed and will be sold at an auction.
   - A new trash removal service has been selected. Regular trash removal will occur daily, instead of three times a week.
   - The lights in the east stairwell have been replaced. Maintenance has initiated a new preventive maintenance program for replacement of lights in stairwells and the garage.
   - Three employees have volunteered to enroll in a substance abuse program. Their enrollment is anonymous to management and other employees.

3. M. Povik reported that the beer coolers are not maintaining the proper temperature. Several requests for service from the Gentry Refrigeration Service have been ignored. The director of maintenance will be informed of this situation.

4. A. Gricki reported that her efforts to reach Johnson Rug Inc. to repair the rug have not been successful. The situation is dangerous. One guest almost tripped in the lobby yesterday. The director of housekeeping will be informed of this situation.

5. A. Johnson would like support from the committee to request the purchase of two training films on the correct procedure for heavy lifting and the proper use of chemicals. The committee agreed to write a memo to the general manager in support of this motion.

6. Members of the committee will meet at convenient times to do an informal safety survey of the maintenance department, housekeeping department, and kitchen. These surveys will provide feedback for department directors. All surveys are to be returned by June 1.

7. Meeting was adjourned at 4:42 P.M. Next meeting will be held June 10.

After slipping on some debris while assisting a guest with his luggage, a front office employee shrugs off the injury, saying, "I needed a few days off anyway." Discuss the danger inherent in this type of employee attitude.

Safety Training Programs

Specific safety training programs should be developed by each department director. The directors will review their departments to determine where safety training is needed. Security, equipment operation, sanitation, chemical use, transport of materials, and movement of equipment are areas to examine in compiling a program. The orientation program is the best opportunity for providing employees with safety training. Films, handouts, and booklets produced specifically to teach the safe way to perform a task will help to reinforce on-the-job training and practice.

Regularly scheduled training sessions with notations of progress for use in the annual employee review are a necessity; otherwise, the employee gets the impression that management is showing that same old film again just to meet the insurance company's requirements. Safety training sessions should be scheduled when the employee is able to concentrate on the session and is not distracted by other duties. This may mean that sessions must be scheduled before or after a shift, with additional pay. If management wants to enhance safety with training programs, then this has to become a budget item. Planning for safety takes time and financial investment.

Solution to Opening Dilemma

The plan of action to investigate the possibility of establishing an in-house security department could address the following topics:

- How are communications with public safety officials regarding safety issues handled?
- How are fire safety and emergency communication plans developed?
- Who is responsible for establishing and maintaining an employee safety training committee?
- Who is responsible for maintaining the integrity of the key system in the hotel?
- Who is responsible for the safe delivery of cash deposits?
- How are smoke detector and fire alarm tests conducted and records maintained?
- Who conducts fire and emergency evacuation training and drills?

- How can all members of the hotel staff adopt an attitude to be cautious of potential terrorist activities?

Chapter Recap

The expense of the security department is a vital expenditure. This chapter examined security as it relates both to the front office and to the overall objective of the hotel in providing a safe environment for guests and employees. The organization and operation of a security department, along with the job analysis of the director of security, were all outlined to demonstrate the many facets of this department. The decision about whether to use an in-house security department or to contract outside security services should be based on ensuring the safety and security of hotel guests rather than on costs.

Both the front office and the security department are involved in room key security, which is easier to guarantee with the new electronic key and smart card systems than it is with hard-key systems. Building evacuation requires that established procedures be in place and that both employees and guests receive instruction on how to react during a fire. An employee safety program should involve both staff and management and include a safety committee that addresses safety concerns on a regular basis and a training program for all employees. Emergency communications procedures should be developed, with a plan that involves management, employees, and civil authorities.

End of Chapter Questions

1. How does the security department interact with the front office? Give examples.

2. Visit a hotel that has an in-house security department. How is this department structured? How many employees are needed to provide 24-hour coverage? What are the typical job duties of employees in this department?

3. Visit a hotel that has contracted with a private security agency for security services. What services does this agency provide? How satisfied is management with the level and range of services provided?

4. Compare your answers to questions 2 and 3.

5. Contrast the level of security in a hotel that uses a hard-key system with that in a hotel that uses an electronic key or smart card system.

6. Discuss the features of a hard-key system.

7. Discuss the features of an electronic key system.

8. Discuss the features of a smart card system.

9. How can a hotel take a proactive stance on fire safety?

10. Why are testing and maintenance of smoke detectors and fire alarms so important?

11. Consider the fire safety procedures provided in guest rooms. How detailed do you think they should be? How can hotels encourage guests to read them?

12. Why is it important for management to include employees when developing safety programs?

13. Review the minutes of the safety committee meeting in Figure 14-7. What issues do you feel are top priorities? Which are low priorities?

14. What value do you see in preparing an emergency communications system to be used in a hotel?

15. Review the emergency communication plan presented in this chapter. What are the important features of the plan?

CASE STUDY 1401

Ana Chavarria, front office manager of The Times Hotel, has scheduled an appointment with the director of security, Ed Silver. Mr. Silver has just learned that a nearby hotel, Remington Veranda, recently received a bomb threat that required the evacuation of all guests and employees. The situation caused a great deal of confusion and panic. Several employees were screaming, "Bomb! Bomb! Run for your life!" while other employees and guests were absolutely stunned and couldn't move. Although the bomb threat was of no substance, five guests and three employees had to be treated in the emergency room for shock and broken limbs caused by the crush to evacuate the building.

After reviewing the files in the security department, Ed Silver feels that he and Ana should develop an emergency communication procedure to be sure that the situation that occurred at Remington Veranda will not be repeated at The Times Hotel. Ana agrees; her prior experience at a hotel on the East Coast makes her realize the importance of such a plan.

Give Ana and Ed some suggestions for developing an emergency communication plan.

CASE STUDY 1402

Cynthia Restin, night auditor of The Times Hotel, waited to see Ana Chavarria, front office manager, after her shift was over. She related a few incidents to Ana that occurred during her evening shift. She said she received a call from a guest in room 470 who said that he had received a threatening call from someone at 1:45 A.M. Cynthia discussed the incident with the guest and said she would alert the security guard on duty. At 2:05 A.M., Cynthia called the guest to see if he was OK.

He thanked her for her concern and said he was ready to retire for the evening.

At 2:35 A.M., a guest in 521 called Cynthia at the front desk reporting some loud noise coming from the room located below him. Cynthia alerted the security guard on duty and asked him to go to room 421 to investigate the situation. The security guard found the door ajar and the room vacant. There was no sign of violence, and the guest's belongings were removed; otherwise, everything looked like a normal self-checkout.

At 3:29 A.M., Cynthia noticed a green sports car circling the portico of the hotel. The driver stopped the car once and drove off after 15 seconds. Cynthia again alerted the security guard on duty.

Ana asked Cynthia to stay a few more minutes and prepare a report of the three incidents for the file. She said she would be talking with Ed Silver, The Times Hotel's director of security, later on and she wanted to discuss the events with him. These incidents seem to have been increasing over the past several weeks, and Ana feels there could be some problem.

The discussion with Ed Silver was brief. He said he feels that these incidents are no cause for alarm but that a training program for front desk personnel on safety and security procedures should be initiated. Ana indicated that similar situations have occurred in other hotels where she worked and were the beginning of large problems for those hotels. Ana said she wanted the local police department involved and agreed that a training program on safety and security procedures is critical.

What do you think of Ana's suggestion of involving the police? What major topics would you include in a training program on safety and security procedures for front office personnel?

Notes

1. Patrick M. Murphy, "How Marriott Employs CPTED in Its Properties' Total Security Package," *Hotel Security Report* 19, no. 2 (Port Washington, N.Y.: Rusting Publications, January 2001): 1–2.

2. Timothy N. Troy, "Keys to Security," *Hotel & Motel Management* 209, no. 20 (November 21, 1994): 17.

3. Mahmood Khan, Michael Olsen, and Turgut Var, *VNR's Encyclopedia of Hospitality and Tourism.* (New York: Van Nostrand Reinhold, 1993), 585.

4. Shannon McMullen, "Loss Control, Risk Management Major Factors Affecting Hotel Security," *Hotel Business* 4, no. 3 (February 7–20, 1995): 8, 10.

5. Toni Giovanetti, "Looking at the Law," *Hotel Business* 3, no. 23 (December 7–20, 1994): 1.

6. *Campbell v. Womack,* 35 So. 2d 96 La. App. (1977), quoted in Khan, Olsen, and Var, *Encyclopedia of Hospitality and Tourism, 586.*

7. Troy, "Keys to Security," 17.

8. "Securing Guest Safety," *Lodging Hospitality* 42, no. 1 (January 1986): 66.

9. *Hotel & Motel Management,* vol. 215, no. 12 (July 3, 2000), p. 62, "A Few Hotels Are Reaping Benefits from Smartcards," by Bruce Adams.

10. Richard B. Cooper, "Secure Facilities Depend on Functional Design," *Hotel & Motel Management* 210, no. 9 (May 22, 1995): 23. Copyright *Hotels* magazine, a division of Reed USA.

11. James T. Davidson, "Are You Ready for an Emergency?" *Hotels* 28, no. 10 (October 1994): 20.

12. Michael Meyer, "Girding for Disaster," *Lodging Hospitality* 50, no. 7 (July 1994): 42.

13. Stefani C. O'Connor, "Embassy Suiks Hotel in Dallas Exhibits Exemplary Crisis Management Skills," *Hotel Business* (August 16, 2000), www.hotelbusiness.com.

14. Khan, Olsen, and Var, *Encyclopedia of Hospitality and Tourism,* 585.

Key Words

communications hierarchy	litigious society
crisis management	room key control system
electronic key system	safety committee
escort service	smart card
foot patrol	visual alarm systems
hard-key system	

Glossary

access time: the amount of time required for a processor to retrieve information from the hard drive; recorded in milliseconds

accounts payable: financial obligations the hotel owes to private and government-related agencies and vendors

accounts receivable: amounts of money owed to the hotel by guests

aging of accounts: indication of the stage of the payment cycle—such as 10 days old, 30 days overdue, 60 days overdue

all-suites: a level of service provided by a hotel for a guest who will desire a more at-home atmosphere

amenities: personal toiletry items such as shampoo, toothpaste, mouthwash, and electrical equipment

American Hotel & Lodging Association: a professional association of hotel owners, managers, and related occupations

American plan: a room rate that includes meals, usually breakfast and the evening meal, as well as room rental in the room rate

Americans with Disabilities Act (ADA): a U.S. law enacted in 1990 that protects people with disabilities from being discriminated against when seeking accommodations and employment

assets: items that have monetary value

assistant general manager: a person in the hotel who executes plans developed by the corporate owners, general manager, and other members of the management staff

athletics director: the person responsible for supervising physical exercise facilities for guests

atrium concept: a design in which guest rooms overlook the lobby from the first floor to the roof

average daily rate (ADR): a measure of the hotel staff's ability to sell available room rates; the method to compute the ADR is:

$$\frac{\text{room revenue}}{\text{number of rooms sold}}$$

back office: the accounting office of a hotel

back office accounts payable: amounts of money that have been prepaid on behalf of the guest for future consumption of a good or service (sometimes referred to as back office cash accounts)

balance sheet: an official financial listing of assets, liabilities, and owner's equity

bank cards: credit cards issued by banks, examples of which include Visa, MasterCard, and JCB

banquet manager: a person who is responsible for fulfilling the details of service for a banquet or special event

banquet sheet: a listing of the details of an event at which food and beverages are served

bell captain: the supervisor of the bell staff

bell staff: people who lift and tote baggage, familiarize guests with their new surroundings, run errands, deliver supplies, provide guests with information on in-house marketing efforts and local attractions, and act as the hospitality link between the lodging establishment and the guest

bill-to-account: an extension of credit to a guest by an individual hotel, which requires the guest or the guest's employer to establish a line of credit and to adhere to a regular payment schedule

blackout: total loss of electricity

blocking on the horizon: reserving guest rooms in the distant future

blocking procedure: process of reserving a room on a specific day

bottom up: a sales method that involves presenting the least expensive rate first

brownouts: partial loss of electricity

bus association network: an organization of bus tour owners and operators who offer transportation and travel information to groups

business affiliations: chain or independent ownership of hotels

business services and communications center: guest services that include copying, computers, fax, etc.

call accounting: a computerized system that allows for automatic tracking and posting of outgoing guest room calls

cancellation code: a sequential series of alphanumeric combinations that provide the guest with a reference for a cancellation of a guaranteed reservation

cash bank: a specific amount of paper money and coins issued to a cashier to be used for making change

cashier: a person who processes guest checkouts and guest legal tender and makes change for guests

cashier's report: a daily cash control report that lists cashier activity of cash and credit cards and machine totals by cashier shift

chain: a group of hotels that follow standard operating procedures such as marketing, reservations, quality of service, food and beverage operations, housekeeping, and accounting

chain affiliations: hotels that purchase operational and marketing services from a corporation

city ledger accounts: a collection of accounts receivable of nonregistered guests who use the services of the hotel

collective bargaining unit: a labor union

commercial cards: credit cards issued by corporations, an example of which is Diners Club

commercial hotels: hotels that provide short-term accommodations for traveling guests

commercial rates: room rates for businesspeople who represent a company but do not necessarily have less bargaining power because of their infrequent or sporadic pattern of travel

communications hierarchy: a listing of the order in which management personnel may be called on to take charge in an emergency situation

company-owned property: a hotel that is owned and operated by a chain organization

complimentary rate (comp): a rate for which there is no charge to the guest

computer supplies: paper, forms, ribbons, ink cartridges, and floppy disks needed to operate the system

concierge: a person who provides an endless array of information on entertainment, sports, amusements, transportation, tours, church services, and baby-sitting in a particular city or town

conference call: a conversation in which three or more persons are linked by telephone

confirmed reservations: prospective guests who have a reservation for accommodations that is honored until a specified time

continental breakfast: juice, fruit, sweet roll, and/or cereal

controller: the internal accountant for the hotel

convention guests: guests who attend a large convention and receive a special room rate

corporate client: a hotel guest who represents a business or is a guest of that business and provides the hotel with an opportunity to establish a regular flow of business during sales periods that would normally be flat

corporate guests: frequent guests who are employed by a company and receive a special room rate

corporate rates: room rates offered to corporate clients staying in the hotel

CPS (characters per second): measure of the speed with which individual characters are printed

credit: a decrease in an asset or an increase in a liability, or an amount of money the hotel owes the guest

credit balance: amounts of money a hotel owes guests in future services

credit-card imprinter: makes an imprint of the credit card the guest will use as the method of payment

credit-card validator: a computer terminal linked to a credit-card data bank that holds information concerning the customer's current balance and security status

crisis management: maintaining control of an emergency situation

cross-training: training employees for performing multiple tasks and jobs

cumulative total feature: an electronic feature of a PMS that adds all posted room rate amounts previously entered into one grand total

current guests: guests who are registered in the hotel

cursor: a flashing point on a monitor that indicates where data can be entered on a computer screen

cycle of service: the progression of a guest's request for products and services through a hotel's departments

daily announcement board: an inside listing of the daily activities of the hotel (time, group, and room assignment)

daily blocking: assigning guests to their particular rooms on a daily basis

daily flash report: a PMS listing of departmental totals by day, period to date, and year to date, which helps the manager to determine the financial success of the previous day and the current status in achieving other financial goals

daily function sheet: a listing of the planned events in the hotel

daily sales report: a financial activity report produced by a department in a hotel that reflects daily sales activities with accompanying cash register tapes or point-of-sale audit tapes

database interfaces: the sharing of information among computers

data sorts: report options in a PMS that indicate groupings of information

debit: an increase in an asset or a decrease in a liability

debit balance: an amount of money the guest owes the hotel

debit cards: embossed plastic cards with a magnetic strip on the reverse side that authorize direct transfer of funds from a customer's bank account to the commercial organization's bank account for purchase of goods and services

demographic data: size, density, distribution, vital statistics of a population, broken down into, for example, age, sex, marital status, and occupation categories

departmental accounts: income- and expense-generating areas of the hotel, such as restaurants, gift shop, and banquets

desk clerk: the person who verifies guest reservations, registers guests, assigns rooms, distributes keys, communicates with the housekeeping staff, answers telephones, gives information about and directions to local attractions, accepts cash and gives change, and acts as liaison between the lodging establishment and the guest as well as the community

direct-mail letters: letters sent directly to individuals in a targeted market group in a marketing effort

director of marketing and sales: the person who analyzes available markets, suggests products and services to meet the needs of those markets, and sells these products and services at a profit

director of security: the person who works with department directors to develop procedures that help ensure employee honesty and guest safety

discount rate: a percentage of the total sale that is charged by the credit card agency to the commercial enterprise for the convenience of accepting credit cards

discretionary income: the money remaining from wages after paying for necessities such as food, clothing, and shelter

disk drive: a place in the computer where data is stored or read; hard or floppy—3½-inch versus 5¼-inch

distance learning: learning that takes place via satellite broadcasts, PictureTel, or on-line computer interaction

documentation: printed or on-screen (monitor) instructions for operating hardware or software that accompany a specific PMS

dot-matrix: a printer that produces small dots printed with an inked ribbon on paper

double occupancy percentage: a measure of a hotel's staff ability to attract more than one guest to a room; the method to compute double occupancy percentage is:

$$\frac{\text{number of guests} - \text{number of rooms sold}}{\text{number of rooms sold}} \times 100$$

draft-style: a good type of dot-matrix print

ecotourists: tourists who plan vacations to understand the culture and environment of a particular area

electronic key: a plastic key with electronic codes embedded on a magnetic strip

electronic key system: a system composed of battery-powered or, less frequently, hard-wired locks; a host computer and terminals; a keypuncher; and special entry cards that are used as keys

elevator operator: a person who manually operates the mechanical controls of the elevator

E-mail: a communication system that uses an electronic network to send messages via computers

employee handbook: publication that provides general guidelines concerning employee conduct

empowerment: management's act of delegating certain authority and responsibility to frontline employees

ergonomics: the study of how people relate psychologically and physiologically to machines

escort service: having a uniformed security guard escort a hotel employee to a financial institution

euro: the accepted currency for some European states: Belgium, Germany, Spain, France, Ireland, Italy, Luxembourg, the Netherlands, Austria, Portugal, Finland, and Greece

European plan: a rate that quotes room charges only

executive housekeeper: a person who is responsible for the upkeep of the guest rooms and public areas of the lodging property as well as control of guest room inventory items

express checkout: means by which the guest uses computer technology in a guest room or a computer in the hotel lobby to check out

extended stay: a level of service that attracts long-term guests by providing light food service and amenities that include fully equipped kitchenette, spacious bedrooms, and living areas for relaxation and work

FAM (familiarization) tours: complimentary visits sponsored by the lodging property that host representatives of travel organizations, bus associations, social and nonprofit organizations, and local corporate traffic managers

family rates: room rates offered to encourage visits by families with children

fax machine: equipment for facsimile reproduction via telephone lines

fire safety display terminal: a device that ensures a constant surveillance of sprinkler systems and smoke detectors

float: the delay in payment from an account after using a credit card or personal check

floor inspector: a person who supervises the housekeeping function on a floor of a hotel

floor limit: a dollar amount set by the credit-card agency that allows for a maximum amount of guest charges

flow analysis processes: the preparation of a schematic drawing of the operations included in a particular function

flowchart: an analysis of the delivery of a particular product or service

folio: a guest's record of charges and payments

folio well: a device that holds the individual guest folios and city ledger folios

food and beverage director: a person who is responsible for the efficient operation of the kitchen, dining rooms, banquet service, room service, and lounge

foot patrol: walking the halls, corridors, and outside property of a hotel to detect breaches of guest and employee safety

forecasting: projecting room sales for a specific period

franchisee: a hotel owner who has access to a national reservation system and receives the benefits of the corporation's management expertise, financial backing, national advertising, and group purchasing

frontline employees: employees who deliver service to guests as front desk clerks, cashiers, switchboard operators, bellhops, concierge, and housekeeping employees

front office: the communication, accounting, and service center of the hotel

front office manager: the person responsible for leading the front office staff in delivering hospitality

full house: 100 percent hotel occupancy; a hotel that has all its guest rooms occupied

full service: a level of service provided by a hotel with a wide range of conveniences for the guest

function sheet: listing of the daily events in a hotel, such as meetings, etc.

general ledger: a collection of accounts that the controller uses to organize the financial activities of the hotel

general manager: the person in charge of directing and leading the hotel staff in meeting its financial, environmental, and community responsibilities

gigabyte: 1,024 megabytes of formatted capacity

group planner: the person responsible for securing guest room accommodations, food and beverage programs, transportation reservations, meeting facilities, registration procedures, tours, and information on sightseeing, while maintaining a budget for group travelers

group rates: room rates offered to large groups of people visiting the hotel for a common reason

group travelers: persons who are traveling on business or for pleasure in an organized fashion

guaranteed reservations: prospective guests who have made a contract with the hotel for a guest room

guest folio: a form imprinted with the hotel's logo and a control number and allowing space for room number, guest identification, date in and date out, and room rate in the upper left-hand corner; it allows for guest charges to be imprinted with a PMS and is filed in room-number sequence

guest histories: details concerning the guests' visits, such as zip code, frequency of visits, corporate affiliation, or special needs

guest test: evaluation procedure in which an outside person is hired by the hotel to experience hotel services and report the findings to management

half-day rate: a room rate based on length of guest stay in a room

hard key: a metal device used to trip tumblers in a mechanical lock

hard-key system: a security device consisting of the traditional hard key that fits into a keyhole in a lock; preset tumblers inside the lock are turned by the designated key

hardware: computer equipment used to process software, such as central processing units, keyboards, monitors, and printers

hospitality: the generous and cordial provision of services to a guest

Hospitality Television (HTV): a commercial hospitality educational organization based in Louisville, Kentucky, that provides satellite broadcasts to hotels, restaurants, and food service facilities

hotel broker: a person who sells hotel room prize packages to corporations, sweepstakes promoters, game shows, and other sponsors

hotel representative: a member of the marketing and sales department of the hotel who actively seeks out group activities planners

house count: the number of persons registered in a hotel on a specific night

housekeeper's room report: a daily report that lists the occupancy status of each room according to the housekeeping department

housekeeping room status: terminology that indicates availability of a guest room such as AVAILABLE, CLEAN, or READY (room is ready to be occupied), OCCUPIED (guest or guests are already occupying a room), DIRTY or STAYOVER (guest will not be checking out of a room on the current day), ON CHANGE (guest has checked out of the room, but the housekeeping staff has not released the room for occupancy), and OUT-OF-ORDER (the room is not available for occupancy because of a mechanical malfunction)

house limit: a dollar amount set by the hotel that allows for a maximum amount of guest charges

Hubbart formula: a method used to compute room rates that considers such factors as operating expenses, desired return on investment, and income from various departments in the hotel

human resources manager: the person responsible for administering federal, state, and local employment laws as well as advertising, screening, interviewing, selecting, orienting, training, and evaluating employees

incentive program: an organized effort by management to understand employees' motivational concerns and develop opportunities for employees to achieve both their goals and the goals of the hotel

independent hotel: a hotel that is not associated with a franchise

in-house laundry: a hotel-operated department that launders linens, uniforms, bedspreads, etc.

ink-jet: a printer that produces small dots printed with liquid ink on paper

inquiries/reports: a feature of the PMS that enables management to maintain a current view of operations and finances

in-room guest checkout: a feature of the property management system that allows the guest to use a guest room television to check out of a hotel

in-service education: courses that update a professional's educational background for use in current practice

interdepartmental communication: communication between departments

interfacing: the ability of computers to communicate electronically and share data

interhotel property referrals: a system in which one member-property recommends another member-property to a guest

Internet: a network of computer systems that share information over high-speed electronic connections

intersell cards: credit cards issued by a hotel corporation, similar to private label cards

intradepartmental communication: communication inside a department

I/O ports (input/output devices): keyboards, monitors, modems, mouse, joystick, light pen, printers, and track balls

job analysis: a detailed listing of the tasks performed in a job, which provides the basis for a sound job description

job description: a listing of required duties to be performed by an employee in a particular job

keyboard: a standard or Dvorak-type typewriter-style keypad that allows the operator to enter or retrieve data

key clerk: a person who issues keys to registered guests and other hotel personnel and sorts incoming mail for registered guests and management staff

key drawer: a drawer located underneath the counter of the front desk that holds room keys in slots in numerical order

key fob: a decorative and descriptive plastic or metal tag attached to a hard key

keypad: a numeric collection of typewriter keys and function keys that allows the operator to enter numbers or perform math functions in a computer

laser: a printer that produces photo images on paper

late charges: guest charges that might not be included on the guest folio because of a delay in posting by other departments

letter-quality: a better type of dot-matrix print

liabilities: financial or other contractual obligations or debts

limited service: a level of service provided by a hotel with guest room accommodations and limited food service and meeting space

litigious society: an environment in which consumers sue providers of products and services for not delivering those products and services according to expected operating standards

main menu: on-screen list of all the available individual programs (modules) that are included in the software system

maintenance manager: a staff member in a limited-service property who maintains the heating and air-conditioning plant, produces guest room keys, assists housekeeping attendants as required, and assists with guest safety and security

management contract property: a hotel that is operated by a consulting company that provides operational and marketing expertise and a professional staff

manager's report: a listing of occupancy statistics from the previous day, such as occupancy percentage, yield percentage, average daily rate, RevPAR, and number of guests

market segments: identifiable groups of customers with similar needs for products and services

marquee: the curbside message board, which includes the logo of the hotel and space for a message

mass marketing: advertising products and services through mass communications such as television, radio, and the Internet

master credit card account: an accounts receivable that tracks bank, commercial, private label, and intersell credit cards such as Visa, MasterCard, and JCB

megabyte: 1,024 kilobytes of formatted capacity

megahertz(mHz): one million cycles per second; indicates computer speed

message book: a loose-leaf binder in which the front desk staff on various shifts can record important messages

military and educational rates: room rates established for military personnel and educators

modem: computer hardware that allows for transfer of data through telephone lines, data expressed in baud—information transfer—rates

modified American plan: a room rate that offers one meal with the price of a room rental

moments of truth: every time the hotel guest comes in contact with some aspect of the hotel, he or she judges its hospitality

money wire: an electronic message that authorizes money from one person to be issued to another person

monitor: a television screen with color or monochrome capacity to view input and output data, control column width and line length of display, adjust height of character display, and allow visual control

moonlighter: a person who holds a full-time job at one organization and a part-time job at another organization

motivation: investigating employee needs and desires and developing a framework for meeting them

Murphy bed: a bed that is hinged at the base of the headboard and swings up into the wall for storage, an example being the SICO brand wallbed

needs analysis: assessment of the flow of information and services of a specific property to determine if proposed new equipment can improve the flow

night audit: the control process whereby the financial activity of guests' accounts is maintained and balanced on a daily basis

night auditor: a person who balances the daily financial transactions of guests who have used hotel services, acts as a desk clerk for the night shift, and communicates with the controller

no-show factor: percentage of guests with confirmed or guaranteed reservations who do not show up

occupancy management formula: calculation that considers confirmed reservations, guaranteed reservations, no-show factors of these two types of reservations, predicted stayovers, predicted understays, and predicted walk-ins to determine the number of additional room reservations needed to achieve 100 percent occupancy

occupancy percentage: the number of rooms sold divided by the number of rooms available

on-line: operational and connected to the main computer system

on-the-job training: a training process in which the employee observes and practices a task while performing his or her job

operational effectiveness: the ability of a manager to control costs and meet profit goals

operational reports: operational data on critical financial aspects of hotel operations

optimal occupancy: achieving 100 percent occupancy with room sales that will yield the highest room rate

optimal room rate: a room rate that approaches the rack rate

organization charts: schematic drawings that list management positions in an organization

orientation checklist: a summary of all items that must be covered during orientation

orientation process: the introduction of new hires to the organization and work environment, in order to provide background information about the property

outsourcing: provision of service to the hotel—for example, a central reservation system—by an agency outside of the hotel

outstanding balance report: a listing of guests' folio balances

overbooking: accepting reservations for more rooms than are available by forecasting the number of no-show reservations, stayovers, understays, and walk-ins, with the goal of attaining 100 percent occupancy

package rate: room rates that include goods and services in addition to rental of a room

paid in advance (PIA): guests who paid cash at check-in

paid-outs: amounts of monies paid out of the cashier's drawer on behalf of a guest or an employee of the hotel

paid-out slips: prenumbered forms that authorize cash disbursement from the front desk clerk's bank for products on behalf of a guest or an employee of the hotel

parking garage manager: the person responsible for supervising garage attendants and maintaining security of guests and cars in the parking garage

payback period: the period of time required for the hotel to recoup purchase price, installation charges, financing fees, and so forth through cost savings and increased guest satisfaction; assists in deciding whether to install computers

Peddler's Club: a marketing program meant to encourage repeat business by frequent business guests

percent occupancy: the number of rooms sold divided by the number of rooms available multiplied by 100

percent yield: the number of rooms sold at average daily rate versus number of rooms available at rack rate multiplied by 100

physical plant engineer: the person who oversees a team of electricians; plumbers; heating, ventilating, and air-conditioning contractors; and general repair people to provide behind-the-scenes services to the guests and employees of the lodging property

PictureTel: the use of telephone lines to send and receive video and audio impressions

plant: an outside person who is hired by a hotel to experience hotel services and report the findings to management

pleasure travelers: people who travel alone or with others on their own for visits to points of interest, to relatives, or for other personal reasons

point-of-sale: an outlet in the hotel that generates income, such as a restaurant, gift shop, spa, or garage

point-of-sale front office: a front office whose staff promotes other profit centers of the hotel

point-of-sale terminals: computerized cash registers that interface with a property management system

policy and procedure manual: publication that provides an outline of how the specific duties of each job are to be performed

postal code: *See* zip or postal code

posting: the process of debiting and crediting charges and payments to a guest folio

potential gross income: the amount of sales a hotel might obtain at a given level of occupancy, average daily rate, and anticipated yield

ppm (pages per minute): printing speed capability

predicted house count: an estimate of the number of guests expected to register based on previous occupancy activities

printer: computer hardware in dot-matrix, ink-jet, or laser models that produces hard copies of output data in letter quality or draft style in various print fonts, with printing speed being expressed in CPS (characters per second), number of characters per line, and pages per minute and paper insertion being tractor-fed, single-sheet, or continuous-form

prior approved credit: use of a credit card to establish creditworthiness

private label cards: credit cards issued by a retail organization, such as a department store or gasoline company

processor speed: how fast a CPU (central processing unit) makes calculations per second; expressed in MHz (the abbreviation for "megahertz")

profit-and-loss statement: a listing of revenues and expenses for a certain time period

property management system (PMS): a generic term used to describe applications of computer hardware and software used to manage a hotel by networking reservation and registration databases, point-of-sale systems, accounting systems, and other office software

psychographic data: emotional and motivational forces that affect a service or product for potential markets

rack rate: the highest room rate category offered by a hotel

real estate investment trust (REIT): a form of financing an investment in real estate through a mutual fund

recreation director: the person who is in charge of developing and organization recreational activities for guests

referral member: a hotel owner or developer who has access to the national reservation system

referral property: a hotel operating as an independent that wishes to be associated with a certain chain; uses national reservation system

referral reservation service: a service offered by a management company of a chain of hotels to franchisee members

registration card: a form on which the guest indicates name, home or billing address, home or billing phone number, vehicle information, date of departure, and method of payment

reservation code: a sequential series of alphanumeric combinations that provide the guest with a reference for a guaranteed reservation

reservation referral system: a worldwide organization that processes requests for room reservations at a particular member-hotel

reservations manager: the person who takes and confirms incoming requests for rooms, noting special requests for service; provides guest with requested information; maintains an accurate room inventory; and communicates with marketing and sales

reservation status: terminology used to indicate the availability of a guest room to be rented on a particular night, i.e., OPEN (room is available for renting), CONFIRMED (room has been reserved until 4:00 P.M. or 6:00 P.M.) GUARANTEED (room has been reserved until guest arrives), and REPAIR (room is not available for guest rental)

residential hotels: hotels that provide long-term accommodations for guests

revenue account: part of owner's equity

revenue per available room (RevPAR): the amount of dollars each hotel room produces for the overall financial success of the hotel, determined by dividing room revenues received for a specific day by the number of rooms available in the hotel for that day

revenue potential: the room revenue that could be received if all the rooms were sold at the rack rate

revenue realized: the actual amount of room revenue earned (number of rooms sold $\times$ actual rate)

role-playing: acting out a role before actually being required to do the job.

room attendants: employees who clean and maintain guest rooms and public areas

room blocking: reserving rooms for guests who are holding reservations

room key control system: an administrative procedure that authorizes certain personnel and registered guests to have access to keys

room revenues: the amount of room sales received

room sales figure: the total of posted daily guest room charges

room sales projections: a weekly report prepared and distributed by the front office manager that indicates the number of departures, arrivals, walk-ins, stayovers, and no-shows

rooms forecast: the projection of room sales for a specific period

room status: information on availability of entry to a guest room—reservation (open, confirmed, guaranteed, or repair) or housekeeping (ready, on change, or out-of-order)

rule-of-thumb method for determining room rates: guideline stipulating that the room rate should be $1 for every $1,000 of construction costs (this figure is from the 1960s; the current figure is $2 for every $1,000 of construction costs)

safety committee: a group of frontline employees and supervisors who discuss safety issues concerning guests and employees

sales associate: a person who books the guest's requirements for banquets and other special events

sales indicators: number of guests and revenue generated

self-check-in process: a procedure that requires the guest to insert a credit card having a magnetic stripe containing personal and financial data into a self-check-in terminal and answer a few simple questions concerning the guest stay

service management program: a management program that highlights a company's focus on meeting customers' needs and allows a hotel to achieve its financial goals

service strategy statement: a formal recognition by management that the hotel will strive to deliver the products and services desired by the guest in a professional manner

shift leader: the person responsible for directing the efforts of a particular work shift

single-sheet: a type of printer that uses single-sheet paper

skill demonstration: demonstration of specific tasks required to complete a job

sleeper: a room that is thought to be occupied but is in fact vacant

smart card: an electronic device with a computer chip that allows a guest or an employee access to a designated area, tracking, and debit-card capabilities for the hotel guest

software: computer-designed applications that process data such as guest information and aid in financial transactions and report generation

statement of cash flows: a projection of income from various income-generating areas of the hotel

stayovers: currently registered guests who wish to extend their stay beyond the time for which they made reservations

surcharge rates: telephone rates for adding service charges for out-of-state long-distance telephone service

tax cumulative total feature: an electronic feature of a PMS that adds all posted room tax amounts previously entered into one grand total

telephone initiation and reception agreements: contracts between senders and receivers of PictureTel concerning specifications of the telephone call and who pays for the call

telephone operator: the person who handles incoming and outgoing calls, locates registered guests and management staff, deals with emergency communication, and assists the desk clerk and cashier when necessary

tickler files: files used to prompt notice that certain events will be occurring

top down: a sales method that involves presenting the most expensive rate first

total quality management (TQM: a management technique that encourages managers to look at processes used to produce products and services with a critical eye

total restaurant sales figure: total of all sales incurred at restaurants or food outlets in the hotel

touch screen: a type of computer monitor screen that allows the operator to input data by touch

tractor-fed: a type of printer that uses a continuous roll of paper

traffic managers: persons who direct hotel guests to available elevators in the lobby

training tickler file: a database that keeps track of training sessions and alerts trainers to important upcoming dates

transfer slip: a form used to transfer an amount of money from one account to another while creating a paper trail

travel directories: organized listings of hotel reservation access methods and hotel geographic and specific accommodations information

traveler's checks: prepaid checks that have been issued by a bank or other financial organization

trial balance: a first run on a set of debits to determine their accuracy against a corresponding set of credits

true integration: the sharing of a reservation database by a hotel's central reservation system and property management system

understays: guests who arrive on time but decide to leave before their predicted date of departure

upsell: to encourage a customer to consider buying a higher-priced product or service than originally anticipated

visual alarm systems: flashing lights that indicate a fire or other emergency in a hotel room

walking a guest with a reservation: offering accommodations at another hotel to a guest who has a reservation when your hotel is overbooked

walk-in guests: guests who request a room rental without having made a reservation

working supervisor: a person who participates in the actual work performed while supervising

yield: the percentage of income that could be secured if 100 percent of available rooms are sold at their full rack rate

yield management: a process of planning to achieve maximum room rates and most profitable guests (guests who will spend money at the hotel's food and beverage outlets, gift shops, etc.), which encourages front office managers, general managers, and marketing and sales directors to target sales periods and develop sales programs that will maximize profit for the hotel

yield percentage: the effectiveness of a hotel at selling its rooms at the highest rate available to the most profitable guest

zip drive: a computer accessory that holds data; a 100-megabyte Zip drive holds an equivalent of 70 floppy disks

zip or postal code: an individual local postal designation assigned by a country

Index